Object-Oriented Design with ABAP

A Practical Approach

James E. McDonough

Apress®

Object-Oriented Design with ABAP: A Practical Approach

James E. McDonough
Pennington, New Jersey, USA

ISBN-13 (pbk): 978-1-4842-2837-1   ISBN-13 (electronic): 978-1-4842-2838-8
DOI 10.1007/978-1-4842-2838-8

Library of Congress Control Number: 2017943501

Cover image designed by Kjpargeter - Freepik.com

Managing Director: Welmoed Spahr
Editorial Director: Todd Green
Acquisitions Editor: Susan McDermott
Development Editor: Laura Berendson
Technical Reviewer: Paul Hardy
Coordinating Editor: Rita Fernando
Copy Editor: Mary Behr
Compositor: SPi Global
Indexer: SPi Global

Distributed to the book trade worldwide by Springer Science+Business Media New York, 233 Spring Street, 6th Floor, New York, NY 10013. Phone 1-800-SPRINGER, fax (201) 348-4505, e-mail orders-ny@springer-sbm.com, or visit www.springeronline.com. Apress Media, LLC is a California LLC and the sole member (owner) is Springer Science + Business Media Finance Inc (SSBM Finance Inc). SSBM Finance Inc is a **Delaware** corporation.

For information on translations, please e-mail rights@apress.com, or visit http://www.apress.com/rights-permissions.

Apress titles may be purchased in bulk for academic, corporate, or promotional use. eBook versions and licenses are also available for most titles. For more information, reference our Print and eBook Bulk Sales web page at http://www.apress.com/bulk-sales.

Any source code or other supplementary material referenced by the author in this book is available to readers on GitHub via the book's product page, located at www.apress.com/9781484228371. For more detailed information, please visit http://www.apress.com/source-code.

Printed on acid-free paper

To my wife, Lorraine, who, at a time in my life when
I needed a career change, suggested
I consider the field of computer programming.

Contents at a Glance

v

Contents

About the Author

James E. McDonough received a degree in music education from Trenton State College. After teaching music for only two years in the New Jersey public school system, he changed careers. He's spent the past 35 years as a computer programmer while also maintaining an active presence as a freelance jazz bassist between New York and Philadelphia. Having switched from mainframe programming to ABAP 20 years ago, he now works as a contract ABAP programmer designing and writing ABAP programs on a daily basis. An advocate of using the object-oriented programming features available with ABAP, he has been teaching private ABAP education courses over the past few years, where his background in education enables him to present and explain complicated concepts in a way that makes sense to beginners.

About the Technical Reviewer

Paul Hardy joined Heidelberg Cement in the UK in 1990. For the first seven years, he worked as an accountant. In 1997, a global SAP rollout came along; he jumped on board and has never looked back. He has worked on country-specific SAP implementations in the United Kingdom, Germany, Israel, and Australia.

After starting off as a business analyst configuring the good old IMG, Paul swiftly moved on to the wonderful world of ABAP programming. After the initial run of data conversion programs, ALV reports, interactive DYNPRO screens, and (urrggh) SAPscript forms, he yearned for something more and since then has been eagerly investigating each new technology as it comes out, which culminated in him writing the SAP Press book *ABAP To The Future*.

Paul became an SAP mentor in March 2017 and can regularly be found blogging away on the SCN site. He wrote a series of blogs comparing the merits of object-orientated vs. procedural programming.

He often presents at SAP conferences in Australia (Mastering SAP Technology and the SAP Australian User Group annual conference) and at SAP TECHED Las Vegas. If you ever happen to be at one of these conferences, Paul invites you to have a drink with him at the networking event in the evening and to ask him the most difficult questions you can think of, preferably about SAP.

Acknowledgments

I could not have done this project without the help of others.

I extend my gratitude to Brian Brennan, who introduced me to the book *Head First Design Patterns*, which started me on the road to discovery of the power of object-oriented programming and eventually led to my decision to create the Object-Oriented Chalk Talks curriculum, lecture series, and accompanying exercises.

Thanks go to those of my colleagues on a project in southern New Jersey who dedicated their time and effort to attend the Object-Oriented Chalk Talks and perform the accompanying exercises, providing me with a laboratory setting in which I could receive the kind of feedback enabling me to refine the content in this book.

I am very grateful to Paul Hardy for agreeing to undertake the task of reviewing the content of the book and for doing such a magnificent job at it, offering many suggestions for improvement.

Susan McDermott, Rita Fernando, and Laura Berendson, my editors at Apress Media, LLC, were of enormous help in guiding me through the publication process and resolving the technical glitches we encountered along the way.

Finally, it would have been much more difficult to complete this project without the love and understanding I received from my family for tolerating my absences during those long hours on weekends and holidays while I was secluded in deep thought about how to organize and present this content.

Introduction

Although many books have been published on the subject of object-oriented design, this book caters specifically to programmers familiar primarily with ABAP, a language with an origin in procedural design, but after years of evolution, now accommodates both the procedural and object-oriented design paradigms. A significant aspect of this book is its accompaniment by a set of exercise programs, each one of which reinforces an object-oriented design concept presented in the book.

For Whom This Book Is Applicable

This book is applicable to virtually all experienced ABAP programmers in one way or another. It is subdivided into three parts, each part applicable to a specific level of familiarity and comfort by the reader with the content it presents.

The first part of the book is intended for ABAP programmers already skilled with the procedural aspects of writing code but who either know nothing about object-oriented programming or simply want to become more comfortable with the object-oriented paradigm. The basic principles of object-oriented programming and design are covered here.

The second and third parts of the book are intended for ABAP programmers already familiar with the basic principles of object-oriented programming but not yet familiar or comfortable with design patterns. The second part of the book presents an introduction to Unified Modeling Language and the third part of the book introduces many of the various design patterns typically associated with object-oriented design.

Those ABAP programmers already familiar with both the object-oriented basic principles as well as Unified Modeling Language and design patterns may find this book covers some design patterns that are altogether new to them or described and illustrated in a context applicable to ABAP programming.

How This Book Should Be Used

ABAP programmers unfamiliar with object-oriented programming should read the book sequentially from the beginning. Indeed, the book is organized primarily for the benefit of such programmers, with each subsequent chapter referring to concepts covered in previous chapters.

ABAP programmers already familiar with object-oriented concepts may skip the first part of the book and start with the second part, to become more familiar with the Unified Modeling Language and design patterns.

ABAP programmers already familiar with design patterns may find it most helpful simply to use this book as a reference.

Regardless of the level of comfort with object-oriented design, this book is modeled on the "learn by doing" premise. Accordingly, Appendix B contains information about retrieving the functional and technical requirements documentation for the accompanying comprehensive set of executable ABAP exercise programs, with each exercise program illustrating some new concept introduced in the book, from the most basic principles of object-oriented programming to the most advanced design patterns. This provides for a multitude of options for using the book and *doing* the corresponding exercise programs, among them:

- Writing each new exercise program based solely on the information provided by the requirements documentation and the diagrams accompanying the collection of executable example ABAP exercise program

- Writing each new exercise program after looking at how the new concepts were implemented in the corresponding executable example ABAP exercise program

- Dispensing entirely with writing any code and simply relying on the corresponding executable example ABAP exercise programs to illustrate the implementation

Refer to Appendix B for instructions for retrieving the accompanying collection of executable example ABAP exercise programs and their corresponding diagrams.

Why This Book Was Written

In March, 2013 I began presenting a series of weekly one-hour lunch-and-learn lectures on object-oriented programming concepts. These "Object-Oriented Chalk Talks," as I called them, were attended by my colleagues, all ABAP programmers and all highly skilled in the procedural style of coding, but, having learned their programming skills when ABAP was still a procedural language, they mostly were uncomfortable with the new object-oriented aspects recently introduced to the ABAP language. I pitched the class as one where I would cover general object-oriented concepts in a lecture format, mostly using nothing more than a white board, but that the class was specifically not about ABAP objects.[1] My goal was to introduce to my colleagues the *reasons why* there is an object-oriented paradigm for writing programs, and not merely to show *how* these concepts could be coded in ABAP, the syntax of which all of them already knew from having attended extensive training on that subject a few months earlier. I stated up front that students probably would be making a commitment of about 26 weeks (half a year) before we would complete all the material to be covered. Although the lectures were to focus on concepts and not a specific language, all the exercises accompanying the lectures were written in ABAP. The idea behind this arrangement was that students would attend the lecture, learn the concepts, and then go perform the associated exercises on their own before the next lecture.

This first class began with about 16 students, fewer than the 20 students I considered to be the maximum number of students per class considering the facilities at our disposal. Many others had heard about the Object-Oriented Chalk Talks and expressed interest in attending. I soon announced another section would begin in July of 2013, to which the response was so overwhelming that I needed to schedule two other concurrent sections of the Object-Oriented Chalk Talks to accommodate the unexpectedly high number of students wanting to attend. With still others expressing interest in the class, I started a fourth section in September of 2013, and other sections soon followed.

---

[1] *ABAP Objects* is the main title of two books by Horst Keller and Sacha Krüger (*ABAP Objects: An Introduction to Programming SAP Applications*, Addison Wesley, 2003) and its successor, *ABAP Objects: ABAP Programming in SAP NetWeaver*, 2nd edition, Galileo Press, 2007). Many developers now refer to *ABAP Objects* to mean the object-oriented aspects of the ABAP language.

From the feedback I received, the classes proved to be wildly popular and interesting to my colleagues. Considering that so many of my fellow ABAP programmers were finding so much value in the Object-Oriented Chalk Talks, I reasoned there probably are thousands of other ABAP programmers who find themselves in the same situation: being very capable programmers with the procedural aspects of ABAP but having difficulty making the leap to the object-oriented paradigm. I wrote this book to share the material covered in the Object-Oriented Chalk Talks with other programmers beyond my reach in a classroom format.

Credentials of the Author

My formal training in the data processing industry consists of one year at a community college learning mainframe languages (IBM assembler, COBOL, and PL/I) and, nearly 15 years later, a six-week seminar on ABAP programming. Compared with some of my colleagues over the years, I have very little formal training in computer programming. Indeed, I have absolutely no formal training in the concepts of object-oriented programming; everything I know on that subject I learned on my own. So, what makes me think I am qualified to teach anyone else about these concepts?

Prior to getting into the data processing industry over 30 years ago, I earned a college degree in Music Education and taught instrumental music for two years in two different public school districts in the state of New Jersey. During my college years I made an effort to learn and gain some modicum of proficiency with all of the band and orchestra instruments. My perception then was that I could be a better music educator by understanding more about the struggles students endure when they endeavor to learn to play a musical instrument. How, I thought, could I presume to teach a 7th grader how to play the trombone if I were not able to play it myself?

This philosophy on education served me well those two years I taught in the public schools, and I have continued with this approach ever since. Accordingly, although my credentials in data processing may not be as impressive as those of some of my colleagues, my background as an educator enables me to perceive the problems students are likely to encounter when learning any new skill. So I have learned all I could, on my own, about object-oriented programming, and over the past few years have been able to use this programming style with most of my ABAP development efforts. I believe that now, having gained a certain level of proficiency in this subject, I am ready to impart what I know to others who also wish to become familiar with this fascinating field of object-oriented programming.

Internationalization Considerations

I have made an attempt to consider the various backgrounds of potential readers, and consequently to avoid phrases and references that could be expected to be understood only by programmers who are familiar with daily life in the United States. However, having been exposed only to US culture all my life, the tone of the book exhibits a corresponding slant. This is particularly evident when describing examples where weights and measures are involved, since often the reader will be subjected to the U.S. Customary System of measurement, a system used by virtually no other nations of the world, instead of the much more logical International System of Units (a.k.a. the metric system) used virtually everywhere else. I trust this will not present too formidable a challenge to readers primarily steeped in other cultures.

PART I

Understanding the Concepts of Object-Oriented Design

CHAPTER 1

■ ■ ■

Preparing to Take the First Step

Object-oriented design offers many new concepts for us to explore, so we will want to be certain we've taken the necessary precautions to insure a successful expedition into this new realm. Accordingly, let's take a moment to prepare ourselves for the adventure we are about to undertake, to pause and give consideration to both the journey itself and the expectations we have about what we will encounter along the way.

Road Map to Object-Oriented Design

A road map is a useful metaphor to illustrate the path we will take from our familiar surroundings of procedural programming to the unfamiliar new territory known as object-oriented design. The road map shows the way. We know we will need to travel the road between these two locations, eventually reaching our destination, but that each step along the way is dependent upon having taken the previous steps. That is, we move continuously in one general direction from our point of origin to our destination, covering each mile as we encounter it, not beginning to cover the tenth mile until after we already have passed through the ninth mile to get there. Accordingly, we become familiar with those parts of the road closest to our point of origin before those parts farther along. As with most such journeys, we may find that the terrain associated with the first few steps is very similar to our starting location, but the terrain changes as we continue moving. This similarity of terrain between adjacent steps enables us to adapt gradually to the changes awaiting us along the road.

So, before we start on our journey to object-oriented design, let's give some consideration toward preparing for a successful trip.

1. Where are we now?

2. Where are we going?

3. Why are we going there?

4. How are we going to get there?

Where We Are Now

If you are like many other programmers using SAP, you gained your experience with ABAP before SAP introduced object-oriented features into the ABAP language, or if these features had been introduced, your organization was not using a release where they were available to you. Some of you are former (perhaps even current) COBOL programmers. Regardless of how you found your way to ABAP, chances are you have been using only the "procedural" style of programming and have been very successful at it for years. SAP now refers to this as the "classical" ABAP programming style.

© James E. McDonough 2017

J. E. McDonough, *Object-Oriented Design with ABAP*, DOI 10.1007/978-1-4842-2838-8_1

With classical ABAP programming, we may have learned many bad habits, ones that are no longer tolerated with the object-oriented language features. However, because SAP has maintained backward compatibility with the ABAP compiler, there has never been a requirement for ABAP programmers to begin using the object-oriented paradigm. As a consequence, we have been happily sticking with the classical ABAP programming style for years now, shunning the newfangled object-oriented features because 1) it would take some time and effort to learn them and 2) once we began using these features, the compiler would flag our use of those bad habits we had honed so carefully over the years.

SAP now provides a fork in the road regarding ABAP programming style. There are two different sets of ABAP language features available, one facilitating the classic procedural style we have been using for years, and another facilitating the object-oriented paradigm. Although they are mostly compatible, there are some restrictions. We could continue using classical ABAP and perhaps be successful with it for quite a while into the future. Conversely, we could bite the bullet and learn what we can about the object-oriented features and begin to use those.

One thing to consider when pondering this choice is that each new release of SAP contains more and more vendor ABAP code that makes use of the object-oriented features. Prior to using ABAP, we might have worked with an Enterprise Resource Planning (ERP) package where seldom, if ever, would we see vendor source code, regardless of the original language. But as ABAP programmers, it is commonplace to browse the source code of ABAP components supplied by SAP with the standard ERP release. The more this standard SAP code is written using the object-oriented style, the more reason we have to learn and understand it.

However, becoming familiar with the syntax associated with the implementation of object-oriented features into the ABAP language is only one of the hurdles we must overcome. An even larger hurdle is understanding the fundamental concepts of object-oriented programming.

So here is where we find ourselves: capable classical ABAP developers, knowing very little about the new object-oriented ABAP statements and knowing even less about how to use those statements effectively. It should come as no surprise that many ABAP programmers contemplating this challenge will choose to continue on with their classical style and avoid the object-oriented features so long as the ABAP compiler enables them to do so. However, other ABAP programmers, who appreciate the significance of these new changes, who have become enlightened to the benefits of object-oriented programming, and who want to leverage these new capabilities, will undertake to embrace this new paradigm and use it to their full advantage.

Where We Are Going

Object-oriented programming languages have been in existence since the 1960s when Ole-Johan Dahl and Kristen Nygaard of the Norwegian Computing Center introduced the language named Simula I and its successor, Simula 67.[1] Since then, object-oriented concepts have provided the foundation for such languages as Smalltalk, C++, and Java. Other languages initially based on the procedural model have been extended to provide some object-oriented capabilities. ABAP falls into this latter category.

In our quest to reach this district known as object-oriented design, we are headed for a place that was founded over half a century ago and has since grown into a thriving metropolis within the data processing landscape, so it is hardly new. However, it is new to us. This is a place where we can use these object-oriented programming techniques in our ABAP programming efforts as freely and comfortably as the procedural style of coding ABAP has provided since its inception.

---

[1]http://campus.hesge.ch/daehne/2004-2005/langages/simula.htm

Why We Are Going There

Statistics show that the initial development effort of writing a computer program consumes only a small fraction of the total time spent during its life cycle, and that most of the time we devote to programming is in pursuit of maintenance efforts – change.[2] A significant reason offered by many experts for using the object-oriented programming paradigm is that it is much better than procedural programming at facilitating maintenance efforts. According to Scott Ambler, reusability is one of the great promises of object-oriented technology.[3] Simplifying program maintenance is a central theme with object-oriented design and one that is interwoven throughout this book. Also, as noted, each new release of SAP contains more and more object-oriented code, and it is in our best interest to become familiar with this new paradigm so we can more easily understand how the system works, where and how we might place enhancements into the standard SAP code, and how we might begin to make effective use of the vast SAP-supplied global class repository. Although we could continue to ignore this new way of writing code for some time and still experience successes in our programming efforts, we do so at our peril.

How We Are Going to Get There

We are going to start where we are most comfortable and familiar, and then move slowly and methodically until we have mastered the fundamentals of object-oriented programming. This means we will start from the familiar surroundings in our home town of Procedureton and travel along the path of least resistance to our destination of Objectropolis.

Along the way from Procedureton to Objectropolis we will pass through the following districts:

- Encapsulation

- Abstraction

- Inheritance

- Polymorphism

- Interfaces

Each district will present its own unique landscape distinguishing it from the other districts. Although we will use this book primarily to provide the directions for navigating the new terrain, we will also take the opportunity to pause in each district long enough to become more familiar with the new concepts we will encounter by performing exercises designed to strengthen our grasp of the nuances and idiosyncrasies each district has to offer. In the same way that merely reading a book about swimming could not sufficiently prepare us for the experience of actually jumping into the water for the first time, merely reading this book without performing the accompanying exercises would leave us less than sufficiently prepared for the experience of actually using what we will be learning.

The first district we will encounter along the road to Objectropolis is Encapsulation, where the residents excel at organizing components in a way that reduces repetition and conceals those details we don't need to see. This is first because we already have some familiarity with this concept from procedural programming.

Farther down the road we will move through Abstraction, where the residents have mastered the art of describing the aspects of an entity and assigning a level of detail to components. They are also experts at *instantiation*, a technique used to make copies of things but where each copy has it own unique attribute values. We also will see how Abstraction and Encapsulation are related to each other.

---

[2]Software maintenance costs can be 75% of software total ownership costs ... http://galorath.com/wp-content/uploads/2014/08/software_total_ownership_costs-development_is_only_job_one.pdf
[3]www.drdobbs.com/a-realistic-look-at-object-oriented-reus/184415594

After Abstraction we will cross into Inheritance, a place where members of the same family tree exhibit similar attributes and behaviors. In some cases, the parents in this district perform many tasks on behalf of their children; in other cases, the children are offered guidance for how to perform tasks themselves; and in still other cases, the children decide they know better than their parents how to perform some tasks and insist on doing things their own way.

Beyond Inheritance lies Polymorphism, where the residents exhibit multiple personalities, behaving differently from one moment to the next depending on how they are type-cast.

Finally, we will traverse through Interfaces, where the residents excel at developing standardized processes for communicating and exchanging information.

Upon passing through all these districts and reaching the end of the road, we will have arrived in Objectropolis, where we will stick our toe into the vast sea known as Unified Modeling Language (UML) from which we will learn some map-making skills, enabling us to orient ourselves as we continue to travel further into the inner sanctum of object-oriented design.

Eventually, we will leave the constraints inherent in the roads we had thus traveled and venture out beyond the stars, exploring the galaxy known as Design Patterns,[4] the center of which is an inferno providing the nuclear fusion for blending the concepts of Encapsulation, Abstraction, Inheritance, Polymorphism, and Interfaces into robust solutions to our programming challenges. So, buckle up as we embark on a celestial journey throughout the universe known as Object-Oriented Design.

Overcoming Psychological Barriers

I recall first hearing the term "object-oriented programming" in 1988 while I was working at Applied Data Research (ADR)[5] writing programs for mainframe computers predominately using proprietary languages. Some of the languages I used were invented by ADR and others by IBM, but I was writing code primarily in the primitive IBM 370-assembler language. I paid no attention to object-oriented concepts at that time. Years later I began hearing experts in the industry proclaiming that programmers who were familiar with procedural languages, by which many of them meant COBOL, had difficulty becoming familiar with and using object-oriented languages. The following statement from an article written by Michael Kölling of Monash University summarizes this claim:

> Learning to program in an object-oriented style seems to be very difficult after being used to a procedural style.[6]

I was one of these programmers already used to a procedural style, so naturally I assumed that I would encounter difficulty if ever I were to pursue learning an object-oriented language.

I learned the ABAP language in 1997 while it still was only a procedural language. Ten years later, undaunted by the Kölling claim, I took it upon myself to learn the object-oriented aspects of ABAP after already having spent years working in environments where the language included the object paradigm. Unlike some other languages, ABAP has evolved and now is considered amongst those languages that had their start as procedural languages, but have been extended with some object-oriented features. Having become comfortable with object-oriented concepts, I can now reflect on the Kölling statement above and attest that the difficulty lies not in the new programming style but in the fact that programming techniques

---

[4]"Roads? ... Where we're going, we don't need *roads*."; Dr. Emmett Brown in the 1985 movie *Back to the Future*. This is a fitting metaphor to illustrate the comparison between understanding the fundamentals of object-oriented design encountered along the road from Procedureton to Objectropolis and understanding the advanced level of power to which these fundamentals can be raised when incorporated into design patterns.

[5]Later that same year ADR was acquired by Computer Associates.

[6]Kölling, M., "The Problem of Teaching Object-Oriented Programming, Part 1: Languages," *Journal of Object-Oriented Programming*, 11(8): 8-15, 1999.

of any kind, procedural or otherwise, eventually become second nature, subconscious and automatic, and the programming techniques of any new and unfamiliar language and programming paradigm likewise will need to become second nature, subconscious and automatic.

Flip Turns

As a college undergraduate I was a member of the swimming team and specialized in the backstroke. For me, the primary event at a swim meet was the 200-yard backstroke, which required the swimmer to swim eight laps of a 25-yard pool. This entailed touching the wall of the pool and turning after seven of those eight laps. The most efficient way to make the turn is to use a technique known to swimmers as a flip-turn, whereupon, for the backstroke event, in touching the wall with the hand, the swimmer uses the leverage of the hand on the wall to flip backward, in a crouching position until upside down, twisting in mid-flip, throwing both feet against the wall, and then pushing off the wall in the other direction as quickly as possible. I finally mastered this early in my first year on the team.

During that first year I had reached a plateau with my event times. The coach took me aside and explained that he thought he could help. The conversation went something like this:

> "Jim, I think I know why your times are not improving. During your approach for a turn, you always reach for the wall with your right hand. Are you aware of that?"

> "Yes," I replied, "I always touch the wall with my right hand. It is the only way I am able to perform a flip turn."

> "You are losing precious time in those instances where your stroke cadence would not put your right hand on the wall when you arrive there, forcing you either to take a quick short stroke or to delay taking a stroke at all. You need to learn to perform a flip turn left-handed so you can turn with whichever hand is about to touch the wall. This will improve your times."

I worked on this for several weeks. At first it felt uncomfortable because of my proclivity to twist to the right upon touching the wall. I had to do this slowly so I could unlearn the automatic reflex to twist right and to get the feel of making the twist dependent on whichever hand was touching the wall.

Eventually I was able to perform the flip turn with either hand. My times began to improve noticeably because I was no longer handicapping myself to insure touching the wall right-handed. Indeed, much to my surprise, by the end of that first season I found that performing the turns left-handed had become my preference.

As with flip turns in swimming, we want to have the ability to *flip comfortably between the styles for both procedural code and object-oriented code* depending on the circumstances in which we find ourselves.

Baseball Bats

Most of us have played or watched a game of baseball, or at least are familiar with some athletic event where a long stick is held with both hands, such as cricket, ice and field hockey, lacrosse, golf, and pole vault. Most baseball players have a preference for holding the bat with the thumb of one hand touching or close to the pinky of other hand, a preference also applicable when holding the stick in those other sports mentioned. When held this way, whichever direction the bat is pointing in reference to the player holding both arms extended straight forward indicates whether the player is left-handed or right-handed. Once baseball players develop some skill with the game, they are most competitive when holding the bat their favored way, but can barely function when holding it opposite-handed. A few players are skillful when holding the bat either way; in baseball they are known as switch-hitters, able to "swing both ways," and are prized by their teams since they can stand in the batters box on whichever side of home plate gives them the most advantage at that point in the game, such as batting left-handed against a pitcher who is strongest against right-handed batters.

With baseball, swinging a bat left-handed is neither more difficult nor less difficult than doing so right-handed, but we will find one way to be more difficult than the other only after our preferred way of swinging the bat becomes subconscious and we no longer need to think about it. As with baseball bats, we want to *develop our programing skills to be able to "code both ways,"* so that we are equally comfortable whether it is procedural or object-oriented code pitched at us.

Keyboards

Consider for a moment the keyboard you use to write code, which perhaps is the familiar QWERTY keyboard, so named because these are the first six letters of the first row of letters on the keyboard. Probably you have such facility with the keyboard by now that you do not even think where letters are located; typing has become second nature to you. The location of the letters on the QWERTY keyboard has an historical significance dating back to the time when typewriters were mechanical machines. These first generation typewriters had metal arms called type bars aligned in a semicircle within the machine, with each arm connected to one of the keys of the keyboard. At the other end of the metal arm was the "type," the print character that would strike a ribbon and leave the ink impression on the page. Typing characters in rapid succession would result in the type bar for one character retreating from the page and the type bar for another character advancing to strike the page. Some combinations of characters would cause adjacent type bars to move, with the respective type bars hitting each other as one was retreating and the other advancing, often causing jams that needed to be fixed manually. After some study, the characters were placed on the keys to avoid the most common combinations of characters from being adjacent type bars, and QWERTY was the result.

Now that typewriters have become relics of a past era, with their mechanical type bars having been replaced by electronics, there is no longer a need for the QWERTY keyboard. The constraint that caused this key arrangement to be invented in the first place no longer exists. Yet today we still use the QWERTY keyboard due to its use having become automatic for so many typists over the decades. Upon first seeing a QWERTY keyboard, many school children inquire why the letters are not arranged in the familiar alphabet series with which they recently have become familiar, and even some adults new to typing wonder why this keyboard is arranged the way it is as they struggle to master it. If we were to ask adults who have acquired some skill with the QWERTY keyboard to consider now using a keyboard where the letters are arranged in the alphabet series, we probably would find them resistant to the idea.[7] Here again, people respond this way because it becomes difficult to learn *anything* that deviates from what already has become established as second nature. Similarly, we want to *hone our facility with object-oriented programming concepts to the point where it becomes second nature to us* to the same degree as our facility with procedural programming concepts.

Programming from the Subconscious

The point here illustrated by flip turns, baseball bats, and QWERTY keyboards is that some aspects of our lives become automatic and subconscious, and this includes writing programs. We simply need to absorb the new programming paradigm into our subconscious, so that we can make the automatic response dependent on the programming paradigm in which we find ourselves writing code. It is not so much a case of difficulty with a new style as it is with what we are capable and incapable of doing subconsciously and automatically.

---

[7]One of my Object-Oriented Chalk Talks classes was attended by a woman who had immigrated to the United States from the former Soviet Union. When I raised this topic about switching from the familiar QWERTY keyboard, she related her story of already being familiar with a Cyrillic keyboard, and upon arriving in the US being confronted with the challenge of having to *switch to* QWERTY.

Getting Back on the Horse

Many readers may have already tried learning object-oriented programming on their own once before, abandoning the effort prior to completion when it became evident the task was more challenging than anticipated. This often leads to the perception that learning the concepts of object-oriented programming on one's own is an insurmountable obstacle.

After starting and abandoning an endeavour at the first sign of a problem, one usually is advised to "get back on the horse," a phrase meaning that one's confidence in overcoming a challenge should not be allowed to be defeated by the first fall, but simply to try again, perhaps using a different approach. Accordingly, this book provides a different approach for those who may be seeking one.

Ready to Take the First Step

Despite any previous attempts we might have made in trying to learn object-oriented programming and design, we have now prepared ourselves mentally and psychologically to meet the challenges we might encounter during the journey upon which we are about to embark. By now we should no longer subscribe to the notion that object-oriented design is so difficult that it cannot easily be understood by those who are familiar primarily with procedural design, a notion that only serves to shackle our efforts to absorb object-oriented concepts into our subconscious such that they become as familiar as procedural concepts. Although we may stumble at times along the way, we now possess the confidence not to let such minor setbacks impede steady progress toward our goal of reaching Objectropolis and beyond.

CHAPTER 2

■ ■ ■

The Elements of Object-Oriented Programming

In this chapter, we will cover the basic elements of object-oriented programming and how they differ from the elements found in procedural programming. The associated concepts are applicable to virtually all object-oriented languages, so we will not see anything specific to ABAP in this chapter. Some new vocabulary will be introduced to describe the corresponding concepts and some suggestions will be presented for how to approach the task of extracting design information from the paragraphs found in associated requirements documentation.

So, how, exactly, is object-oriented programming different from procedural programming? Whereas the focus with procedural programming is on the processes to be applied to data, the focus with object-oriented programming is on the data upon which those processes are applied. The architecture of a procedural programming environment lends itself to components containing steps in a process, whereas the architecture of an object-oriented programming environment lends itself to components containing real-world representations of entities that can contribute to a process. While procedural programming is achieved through writing components such as programs and utility functions, object-oriented programming is achieved through writing components known as classes. Indeed, the *class* is a fundamental concept of object-oriented design. Whereas procedural programs are composed of main routines, subroutines, and the data fields on which they operate, object-oriented classes are composed of *attributes* and the *behaviors* defined for those attributes. Attributes are the data fields of a class (constants, variables, etc.), while the behaviors, also known as *methods*, are the actions applicable upon those attributes. Methods may be defined with a parameter interface, also known as a *signature*, by which information can be exchanged between the method and its caller. Both the attributes and the behaviors of a class are known collectively as its *members*. Although there are other aspects involved with object-oriented programming, classes, attributes, and behaviors constitute the basic elements of this programming paradigm.

Because it can have multiple attributes and various behaviors associated with those attributes, a class is known as a *complex data object*. Compare this with a simple data object, which represents a value primarily through a data type and a length, with occasional additional information. For example, a material number might be defined as 18 (its length) left-justified characters (its data type), while a sale price might be defined as 13 (its length) right-justified digits (its data type) where 3 of those digits constitute decimal positions (its additional information). In contrast, a class might be defined as a *sales order item*, and, amongst others, it may contain the two attributes (material number and sale price) just described, as well as behaviors to get and set the value of the material attribute and to calculate its sale price. Indeed, a complex data object is not restricted to containing only simple data objects as attributes; it may have other complex data objects as its own attributes. An example of this might be a class defined as *sales order*, which might contain an attribute defining an internal table of its associated sales order items, each of which, as just described, defined as a class containing the material and sale price of each item.

© James E. McDonough 2017
J. E. McDonough, *Object-Oriented Design with ABAP*, DOI 10.1007/978-1-4842-2838-8_2

Just as a program may have multiple data fields defined to hold the values of material numbers (simple data objects), so too can it have multiple data fields defined as classes (complex data objects), although the correct way to describe this is to say that the data fields are *references to class objects*. Populating a field defined as a material number is a simple matter of moving a value into the field. Populating a field defined as a class reference is a bit different: in this case we *create* a class *object*.[1] Creating an object of a class is performed by the program at execution time and is known as creating an *instance* of the class, a process also described by the term *object instantiation*. For example, a beer *class* describes the aspects of beer, whereas a beer *instance* represents a specific glass of beer. We cannot drink the aspects of beer, but we can drink a glass of beer, and this is the reason why the beer has to be instantiated – that is, poured.[2]

So, in just the first few steps along the road from Procedureton to Objectropolis we have already learned some important new words in the vocabulary of object-oriented programming:

Class	The definition of a complex data object composed mainly of data fields and actions applicable to those data fields
Attribute	The term used to describe a data field defined for a class
Behavior	The term used to describe an action applicable to an attribute
Method	Another name for behavior
Signature	The term used to describe the parameter interface facilitating the exchange of information between a method and its caller
Member	The term used to refer generically to any component of a class
Object	A term used to describe the result of creating a class entity during program execution
Instance	Another name for an object
Instantiation	The term used to describe creation of an instance of a class

A Simple Approach to Object-Oriented Design

Often in object-oriented design it is helpful to conceive of these elements using words associated with sentence construction and grammar:

- Classes are described using *nouns*.

- Attributes are described using *adjectives*.

- Behaviors are described using *verbs*.

Let's see how this works using an example: we can define a class called *car* and attributes for it describing such things as relative age, appearance, aerodynamic quality, and color. Accordingly, we can define within our program two data fields which are references to objects of class *car*, and then, through object instantiation, place into them references to the instances of this class and describe each one using its corresponding adjectives:

1. The old, dirty, boxy, blue car.

2. The new, clean, sleek, red car.

---

[1]We shall see that we can also move values from one class reference field to another, but creating an object into one of those class reference fields is what enables moving a value into another class reference field.
[2]A brilliant metaphor contributed by Paul Hardy.

Here we see that *car*, the description of the class, is a noun, and the values for its attributes *relative age* (old; new), *appearance* (dirty; clean), *aerodynamic quality* (boxy; sleek), and *color* (blue; red) are all adjectives. Furthermore, we can define behaviors for the *car* class enabling us to set and get these attributes: *set_color, get_color, set_relative_age, get_relative_age*, etc. For behaviors, the first word represents the verb associated with each behavior, in this case, *set* and *get*.[3]

Taking this example to the next step, let's define a program, using the pseudocode shown in Listing 2-1, which contains two fields to hold the references to the two car objects and show how the program interacts with those objects.

Listing 2-1. Pseudocode for a Program Referencing Two Car Objects

```
relative_age          type string
appearance            type string
aerodynamic_quality   type string
color                 type string
car_01                type class of car
car_02                type class of car

create new instance of car object into car_01
invoke behavior set_relative_age      of car_01 with "old"
invoke behavior set_appearance        of car_01 with "dirty"
invoke behavior set_aerodynamic_quality of car_01 with "boxy"
invoke behavior set_color             of car_01 with "blue"

create new instance of car object into car_02
invoke behavior set_relative_age      of car_02 with "new"
invoke behavior set_appearance        of car_02 with "clean"
invoke behavior set_aerodynamic_quality of car_02 with "sleek"
invoke behavior set_color             of car_02 with "red"

(more processing occurs here ...)

invoke behavior get_relative_age      of car_01 into relative_age
invoke behavior get_appearance        of car_01 into appearance
invoke behavior get_aerodynamic_quality of car_01 into aerodynamic_quality
invoke behavior get_color             of car_01 into color
display "car 01:", relative_age, appearance, aerodynamic_quality, color

invoke behavior get_relative_age      of car_02 into relative_age
invoke behavior get_appearance        of car_02 into appearance
invoke behavior get_aerodynamic_quality of car_02 into aerodynamic_quality
invoke behavior get_color             of car_02 into color
display "car 02:", relative_age, appearance, aerodynamic_quality, color
```

---

[3]*Set* and *get* probably are the two most common verbs you will see associated with methods of classes, and for good reason: set behaviors enable external callers to apply changes to the attributes of class objects, while get behaviors enable external callers to retrieve the values of those attributes. Methods enabling changing and retrieving attribute values are known as *accessor* methods. Using *setter* and *getter* methods provides a distinct advantage over accessing the attributes directly, as we will see later.

13

Indeed, much of object-oriented design can be gleaned from simple sentences. Here is a famous sentence:

The quick brown fox jumps over the lazy dog.[4]

Simply by identifying the nouns, verbs, and adjectives in this sentence leads us to a rough object-oriented design. The nouns are *fox* and *dog*. This means we will have two classes: a fox class and a dog class. The verb is *jumps* and it describes a behavior of the fox. Accordingly, our fox class will have a behavior (method) called jump. The adjectives describing the fox are *quick* and *brown,* so we might define two attributes for the fox class: one called *alacrity* which can hold the value "quick," and another called *color* which can hold the value "brown." Similarly, the adjective *lazy* describes the dog and is comparable to the adjective *quick* describing the fox, so we might define one attribute for the dog class, also called alacrity, which can hold the value "lazy."[5]

Upon completing this simple exercise of identifying sentence words, we find we have the beginning of an object-oriented design, as shown in Table 2-1.

Table 2-1. *The Beginning of an Object-Oriented Design*

Class	fox	dog
Attributes	alacrity color	alacrity
Behaviors	jump	

At this point, we can take the liberty of adding two behaviors to the fox class, set_color and set_alacrity, and one behavior to the dog class, set_alacrity, to enable us to change the values of their corresponding attributes.

Let's provide some pseudo-code to fulfill the intent of the original statement from which we extracted these classes, attributes, and behaviors. The syntax of the pseudocode shown in Listing 2-2 follows the "object.action" model for classes. That is, to invoke a behavior of a class we first specify the class separated from its behavior by a dot; any parameters that follow are enclosed in parenthesis.

Listing 2-2. Pseudocode to Fulfill the Intent of the Original Statement

```
create object fox
fox.set_color("brown")
fox.set_alacrity("quick")

create object dog
dog.set_alacrity("lazy")

fox.jump(dog)
```

The signatures for the behaviors (to set the color of the fox, to set the alacrity of the fox and dog, and for the fox to jump) implied in the statements above exemplify a technique using what are known as *positional parameters.* With positional parameters, the corresponding method accepts the values in the sequence specified on the statement into the method signature parameters in the order they appear. In the example above, we see only single values being passed to each method in its signature. Let's change this a bit by

---

[4]This is an example of a *pangram*, a statement which contains every letter of the English language.
[5]We might also consider that since both fox and dog have an attribute for alacrity, it might be appropriate that both also have an attribute for color; however, this famous sentence does not provide any information about the color of the dog.

defining the signature for the set_color method to accept a color specified using the RGB[6] color model, where three integer parameters denote the light intensity values to be used for the colors red, green, and blue. We would change our example statement above for setting the color of the fox to the following statement:

```
fox.set_color(165,42,42)[7]
```

Some object-oriented environments support positional parameters in method signatures while others provide support for a technique that uses what are known as *keyword parameters,* where each value is associated with a keyword, as illustrated in the following modified example of the statement to invoke the method to set the color of the fox:

```
fox.set_color(red=165,green=42,blue=42)
```

Here, each parameter is associated with a keyword identifying its corresponding value, such as the keyword "red" associating the RGB setting for red with the value 165. Keyword parameters provide programmers the advantage of being able to specify multiple parameters in any order, since it is its keyword, not its sequence, that associates a value with a method signature parameter.

Indeed, this concept of positional and keyword format for parameters is not unique to object-oriented environments, each format having existed in procedural languages for decades.

Rarely do we ever encounter foxes and dogs in our programming efforts, so let's take this to the next level and inspect a sentence with more applicability to data processing:

> A hazardous-material sales order must be assigned a placard value prior to transmitting as an outbound XML document through the exchange portal.

Here, again, to get a rough object-oriented design, we simply identify the nouns, verbs, and adjectives in the sentence. Through identifying the nouns we define three classes: *sales order, XML document, exchange portal.*[8] Through identifying the adjectives, we assign 1) to the sales order an attribute we'll call *material type*, which indicates whether or not it is for a *hazardous material*, 2) to the XML document an attribute we'll call *direction*, which indicates whether it is inbound or *outbound*, and 3) to the exchange portal no attributes at all. Through identifying the verbs we assign *transmit* as a behavior for an XML document and *assign placard* as a behavior for a sales order. The result is shown in Table 2-2.

Table 2-2. *Result of Extracting Information from the Statement with More Applicability to Data processing*

Classes	sales order	XML document	exchange portal
Attributes	material type	direction	
Behaviors	assign placard	transmit	

Actual object-oriented design is not nearly so neat and simple as depicted here, but this illustrates how you might parse the sentences representing requirements outlined in a design document to arrive at a general set of object-oriented classes as a starting point to satisfy the design requirements.

---

[6]RGB is the acronym for each of the additive primary colors (red, green, blue) used to set the colors of light for, among other things, pixels on computer monitors. See www.rapidtables.com/web/color/RGB_Color.htm.

[7]This RGB color setting (red at 165, green at 42, and blue at 42) represents the color brown.

[8]A case can be made that "sales" is an adjective for "order", and that "XML" similarly qualifies "document." Here we will regard "sales order" as a distinct entity (a noun) and likewise "XML document" and "exchange portal" as distinct entities.

Pillars of Object-Oriented Design

There are many different object-oriented languages and software development environments in popular use today, each with its own unique characteristics. In general, there are four aspects of object-oriented design, regarded by many experts as *principles* shared by virtually all of these languages and environments:

- Encapsulation
- Abstraction
- Inheritance
- Polymorphism

These can be regarded as the pillars of object-oriented design, each contributing its relevant concepts in support of the overall architecture of an object-oriented system. As illustrated in Figure 2-1, object-oriented design rests upon these four pillars. Remove one of the pillars and the architecture becomes out of balance, no longer capable of fully supporting an object-oriented environment.

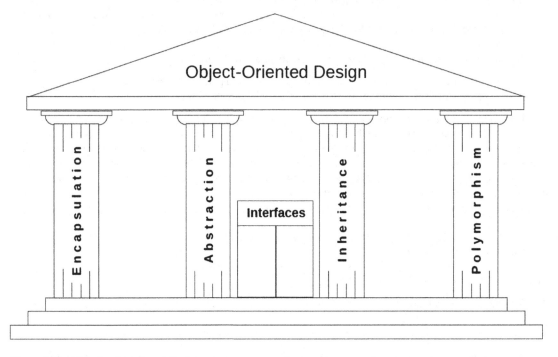

Figure 2-1. *Object-oriented architecture*

A fifth aspect of object-oriented design, Interfaces, is found in some but not all such environments. Its purpose is to provide external access to object members through established communication and data exchange formats, so it is illustrated in our colonnade graphic in Figure 2-1 as a doorway.

Summary

In this chapter, we learned how object-oriented programming primarily differs from procedural programming, specifically that procedural design focuses on the process to be performed whereas the focus with object-oriented design is on managing the data used. We also learned how to begin the process of identifying the various classes we might need for a software design by extracting information from the sentences we find in the corresponding requirements. Some new vocabulary words applicable to object-oriented design were presented:

- Class
- Attribute
- Behavior
- Method
- Signature
- Member
- Object
- Instance
- Instantiation

In addition, we learned that there are certain principles shared by virtually all object-oriented environments:

- Encapsulation
- Abstraction
- Inheritance
- Polymorphism

We saw how all of these terms contribute to supporting the architecture of object-oriented design and learned that interfaces, while also a principle of object-oriented design, is not applicable to all object-oriented environments.

Exercise Preparation

Refer to Chapters 1 and 2 of the functional and technical requirements documentation (see Appendix B) describing the accompanying ABAP exercise programs. Take a break from reading the book at this point to become familiar with the concepts behind the exercises and to prepare your ABAP training environment for writing, changing, and executing the corresponding exercise programs.

CHAPTER 3

Encapsulation

We start our journey to Objectropolis from the perspective of Encapsulation, largely because this is the object-oriented design concept with which most procedural programmers already are familiar. The word *encapsulate* means "to encase in or as if in a capsule."[1] Procedural programmers have been doing this for years via subroutines and locally-defined variables.

To illustrate this concept, let's establish a familiar frame of reference for encapsulation. Suppose we write a procedural program like any one of thousands you might find in your own programming environment. It might be constructed similar to the outline shown in Listing 3-1.

Listing 3-1. Representative Procedural Program

```
program bnx0037
global_variable_1
global_variable_2
global_variable_3
   o
   o
   o
global_variable_n
main_routine
   do subroutine_a
   do subroutine_b
subroutine_a
   local_variable_1
   local_variable_2
   statement 1
   statement 2
subroutine_b
   local_variable_3
   statement 3
   statement 4
```

With this example we see a program containing a set of global variables, a main driving routine, and two subroutines. The two subroutines illustrate encapsulation of code, procedures to be performed from some other point in the program, in this case from the main routine. These subroutines also illustrate

---

[1]*American Heritage Dictionary of the English Language*, 4th edition, Houghton Mifflin Company, 2000, p. 588.

encapsulation of data fields, where each subroutine has its own local variables. For this program, the subroutines are visible and available only within the program unit bnx0037 and are not visible beyond the constraints of this program unit[2].

The global variables also are visible and available from anywhere within he program unit bnx0037, but are not accessible beyond this program unit. Similarly, access to local variables defined within a subroutine are visible and available from anywhere with the subroutine[3], but are restricted to the scope of the subroutine, and are not visible beyond the constraints of the subroutine in which the local variable is defined.

Separation of Concerns

Encapsulation is a technique used to facilitate modularizing code in pursuit of the design principle known as *separation of concerns*. This concept, credited as first being presented by Edsger W. Dijkstra in a 1974 paper he wrote titled "On the Role of Scientific Thought"[4], addresses the maintenance benefits to be gained by arranging software components into modules such that the processing performed by a single module is limited to a specific concern and does not cross the distinct boundaries separating areas of processing. This often is illustrated using the Model-View-Controller design pattern, which segregates the programming logic for the application (model), presentation (view), and manipulation (controller) of information into separate components.

Visibility

Encapsulation is often associated with the concept of *information hiding*[5], whereby elements and implementations defined in software components can be segregated from each other and from outside entities under the expectation that subsequent changes would not require a proliferation of modifications across many components. The degree to which information within a class can be hidden is facilitated in many object-oriented languages through the assignment of a *visibility* level to that information.

The term *visibility* describes a fundamental concept associated with the object-oriented principle of encapsulation. Each member of each class has a visibility level, controlled by the programmer, similar to the global and local visibility just described in the procedural program example. The visibility of a member is a designation of how that member is visible to other entities. With object-oriented programming, visibility is described using neither global nor local, but using other words that denote gradations between most visible and least visible.

To illustrate this, we'll use the tapered shape diagram shown in Figure 3-1, which illustrates maximum visibility at the widest part and minimum visibility at the narrowest part, and places the visibility descriptors in their natural sequence from least visibility to most visibility.

---

[2]In some programming languages, notably ABAP, such subroutines *are* accessible from outside the program unit, but also require the name of the program as a qualifier for access to them, as in

```
perform subroutine_b in program bnx0037 ...
```

This is now considered an obsolete ABAP programming technique and is discouraged for any new development efforts.
[3]In some languages, the placement of the definition for a local variable has an effect on its availability within the subroutine, making it available only beyond the point at which it is defined. This generally is the case with ABAP, although some dynamic techniques enable access to fields defined subsequently.
[4]See www.cs.utexas.edu/users/EWD/transcriptions/EWD04xx/EWD447.html.
[5]See www.defit.org/information-hiding/.

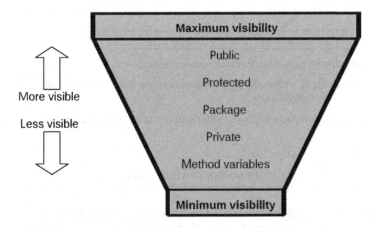

Figure 3-1. *Visibility gradations*

The bottom of the taper depicts the most restrictive visibility to class members. This lowest level of visibility is reserved for *method variables*, which are the functional equivalent of local variables in procedural programming.[6] Technically, these method variables are not themselves members of classes, but are variables defined within methods that are members of classes.

The next widest level of visibility is called *private*. It describes the visibility level of members whose visibility is restricted to this class only, and might be considered the functional equivalent to the visibility of both subroutines and global variables in procedural programming.

The next widest level is called *package*[7]. It describes the visibility level of members whose visibility is restricted to this class and any other components within the same package. This visibility level has no equivalent in procedural programming. In Java, this is known as *package-private* visibility.

The next widest level is called *protected*. It describes the visibility level of members whose visibility is restricted to this class, any other components within the same package and any classes inheriting[8] from this class. This visibility level has also no equivalent in procedural programming.

The next widest level is called *public*. It describes the visibility level of members whose visibility is not restricted at all; that is, a member with public visibility is visible to any other component within the programming environment. This visibility level is similar in nature to the way ABAP reports are available to any other component through the SUBMIT statement, as well as to the way ABAP function modules are available to any other component through the CALL FUNCTION statement, to the way global class and interface definitions in ABAP are available to any other component simply by referring to the global class or interface, and to the way domains, data elements, tables, etc. defined in the ABAP DataDictionary are available to virtually any other objects defined within the ABAP repository.

Visibility levels also are known as *access modifiers*. Table 3-1 summarizes the visibility settings for class members.

---

[6]Here we are using the term *variable* to refer to these entities; however, this also would include constants, type definitions, and any other variation of defining or assisting in defining a data field.

[7]This visibility level is not available in all object-oriented environments. Java provides support for this visibility level. It was not available to ABAP with the first release containing object-oriented support, but evidence that it is becoming available can be found at https://help.sap.com/saphelp_nwpi71/helpdata/en/45/c2b44f23b352f5e10000000a1553f7/content.htm.

[8]This will be explained in more detail in the section on Inheritance.

Table 3-1. *Visibility Levels*

Visibility level	Accessibility
Public	Accessible to any other entity within the same environment.
Protected	Accessible within this class, within any other entities assigned the same package, and within any inheritors of this class.
Package	Accessible within this class and within any other entities assigned the same package.
Private	Accessible within this class only.
Method variable	A variable is accessible only within the method in which it is defined.

Figure 3-2 shows the same information using a different format[9], where the rows of the visibility level column show increasingly wider levels of visibility from bottom to top, and where the columns to the right of the visibility level column show increasingly greater levels of access from right to left. Notice how the "Yes" and "No" accessibility values fall evenly distributed on both sides of the diagonal line.

Visibility level	Accessible by other members of same class?	Accessible by other members of same package?	Accessible by members of a subclass?	Accessible by any other entity?
Public	Yes	Yes	Yes	Yes
Protected	Yes	Yes	Yes	No
Package	Yes	Yes	No	No
Private	Yes	No	No	No
Method variable	No	No	No	No

Figure 3-2. *Visibility levels with indications of access to same class, same package, subclass, and other entities*

Let's explore this concept through an example. Suppose we have groves of oak trees in various settings around town, offering the benefits of shade in summer and spectacular changes of color in autumn. We will define a visibility level to each grove of oak trees based upon the particular setting in which we find it.

First we will consider a grove of oak trees we find in the public park in the center of town. This grove of oak trees is a member of the park, and being a public park, the grove is accessible to all residents of the town as well as to all non-residents of the town. The benefits offered by this grove are available to everyone who strolls through the park. Accordingly, we assign the grove of oak trees *public* visibility.

Next we will consider a grove of oak trees we find in a wildlife sanctuary located on the outskirts of town. This grove of oak trees is a member of the wildlife sanctuary, and being a protected place, the grove is not accessible to all town residents and non-residents. While there are many ways these folks can become associated with the wildlife sanctuary, the benefits offered by this grove of oak trees are available only to those who have a reason for strolling through this protected wilderness. Accordingly, we assign the grove of oak trees *protected* visibility, meaning only those folks with a specific type of association to the wildlife sanctuary, and their friends,[10] have access to the grove of oak trees.

---

[9]The format is borrowed from the chart available at `http://docs.oracle.com/javase/tutorial/java/javaOO/accesscontrol.html`.
[10]Friendship is a concept related to encapsulation and will be covered later in this chapter.

Next we will consider a grove of oak trees we find in a common area of a gated community also located on the outskirts of town. This grove of oak trees is a member of the common area of the gated community. The maintenance for this grove of oak trees comes from the homeowners association fees paid by the residents who live in the gated community. The homeowners association fees are part of the package of regulations accepted by all residents of the gated community for the privilege of living within its walls. The grove is accessible only to the residents of the gated community. Accordingly, we assign the grove of oak trees *package* visibility, meaning only those folks who have accepted the same package of regulations for being residents of the gated community and their friends have access to the grove of oak trees.

Next we will consider a grove of oak trees we find in the backyard of a house located near the center of town. This grove of oak trees is a member of the property on which the house sits, and since it is located on private property, the grove is accessible only to the residents of this house. Accordingly, we assign the grove of oak trees *private* visibility, meaning only the residents of the house on this property and their friends have access to the grove of oak trees.

Finally we will consider a grove of oak trees appearing in a picture hanging on the wall of the den we find in that same house near the center of town. This grove of oak trees is a member of only one room of the house. Residents of the house have access to this grove of oak trees only when they enter the den, and it immediately becomes unavailable to them when they leave the den. Accordingly, we assign the grove of oak trees *method variable* visibility, meaning only those residents engaged in the behavior of using the den have access to the grove of oak trees.

Regarding visibility, the conventional wisdom within the object-oriented community is to define these variables, attributes, and methods with the most restrictive visibility possible while still enabling access to them as necessary. This means

- Variables should be defined as local method variables unless there is a compelling reason for them to be defined as attributes of the class.

- Class members should be assigned private visibility unless there is a compelling reason for the visibility to be set to a wider visibility level.

My advice with new object-oriented development is to define all variables as method variables and all methods with private visibility, and then to widen the visibility level as necessary, but then only to the extent of the least visibility that will still accommodate the required access.

Why Visibility Matters

My experience with existing procedural programs has been to find a proliferation of global variables that have no reason to be defined with global visibility. This occurs for a variety of reasons:

- The author developed a bad habit of defining all variables with global visibility rather than giving any thought towards which of them should be defined locally.

- The author recognized there were multiple subroutines that required using the same set of local variables, and so defined them once globally rather than locally for each subroutine.

- The author might have been enticed by the presence of program segments, generated manually or automatically, the primary purpose of which is to contain global components of programs.[11]

- Some aspects of the programming language or environment work only when interacting with variables defined globally.[12]

---

[11]In ABAP, the so-called TOP include of function groups is a good example of this type of program segment.
[12]In ABAP, the interaction with screen definitions is based implicitly upon defining global variables in the program with the same names as those defined for the screens.

- A precedent had been set by the original author, who defined variables unnecessarily with a global visibility, and this style was perpetuated by subsequent maintenance programmers to retain stylistic consistency.

Regardless of the reason why, the indiscriminate use of global variables is one of the biggest impediments to subsequent maintenance efforts. Too often it requires the maintenance programmer to perform an exhaustive search through the program for each global variable to determine whether or not it is safe to use or change its value at some critical point in the code. Frequently it is expediency in writing the first release of a program that lures developers into taking shortcuts with the design, trading ease of initial design for subsequent ease of maintenance. Since it is likely that much more time will be spent in the maintenance of a program than in its initial design, such cavalier inattention to variable visibility eventually causes problems, and usually it is only during subsequent maintenance efforts where the consequences become evident.

Visibility assigned at the most restrictive level to permit the necessary processing becomes a benefit during maintenance efforts by reducing the time it takes the developer to identify the necessary changes required as well as enabling the refactoring of code to be performed without any concern for rendering other components syntactically invalid. This is why visibility matters. Accordingly, developers who take the time to apply the appropriate visibility levels to program variables during design enable subsequent maintenance programmers to reap the benefit of shorter maintenance efforts.

With most of my object-oriented endeavors, I have found that attributes usually have a more restrictive visibility assigned to them than behaviors. Indeed, I usually tell my students that if they follow the advice offered by object-oriented scholars they will probably arrive at a class design that incorporates "public behaviors and private attributes." This arrangement stems from the necessity to offer external entities access to the values of the attributes of a class but not to the attributes themselves. Accordingly, many times there will be definitions for methods known as *getter* and *setter* methods, behaviors that offer public access by external entities to values of attributes of a class that are defined with a visibility level other than public. External entities use *getter* methods to make a request to *get* the value of an attribute of the class, and *setter* methods to make a request to *set* the value of an attribute of the class. In both cases, the class is in complete control over whether the value of the attribute will be allowed to be retrieved by the getter method or altered by the setter method.

Realm

In some object-oriented environments, members of classes belong to one of two different realms:

- Those members that *are* associated with a specific instance of a class
- Those members that *are not* associated with a specific instance of a class

Virtually every object-oriented environment supports the definition within a class of members that are associated with a specific instance of the class. Those that also offer support for class members not associated with a specific instance of the class include C++, C#, Visual Basic, Smalltalk, Java, and, of course, ABAP. In most of these languages, those members not associated with a specific instance of a class are known as *static* members.[13] Accordingly, we can refer to which one of these two realms a member is associated by the following terms:

- Instance member
- Static member

---

[13]In Smalltalk, these are known as *class* variables and methods. In Visual Basic, these are known as *shared* members because the term *static* has a wholly different meaning in this language.

In many object-oriented languages, including C++, C#, Java, and ABAP, a static member is marked so by including a qualifier with the definition of the member indicating it is a static member, with the absence of a such a qualifier indicating it is an instance member. Indeed, in the languages C++, C#, and Java, the qualifier used with a member definition to denote that it is a static member is the word *static*.[14]

Whereas instance members are bound with a specific instance of the class, static members are available and accessible to all instances of the same class. Indeed, static members of a class are available during execution even when there have been *no instantiations of the class,* meaning that these members are available immediately once a program containing the class definition begins to execute. It is not necessary to create any instances of the class to use its static members. The same rules of visibility apply equally to static members and instance members.

An instance attribute will exist once for each instance of the class with which it is associated. In contrast, a static attribute of a class exists only once for the entire execution of the program and is shared across all instances of its class. Instance methods have access to both the instance members and static members of its class. In contrast, static methods have access only to the static members of its class. Instance members exist only upon instantiation of the class, and only for as long as the instance remains active. In contrast, static members exist during the entire execution of the program, irrespective of the presence or absence of instances of its class.

The following example expands upon our fox and dog classes from the preceding chapter. Here we have included some new members for the dog class, shown highlighted in Table 3-2:

- A new instance attribute called registration_number

- A new instance behavior called set_registration_number, which will use the value it receives to set the new instance attribute registration_number

- A new static attribute called last_used_registration_number

- A new static behavior called get_next_registration_number, which will add 1 to the last_used_registration_number and return the new value

Table 3-2. *Attributes and Behaviors for the Fox and Dog Classes*

Class	Fox	Dog
Attributes	alacrity color	alacrity **registration_number** **static last_used_registration_number**
Behaviors	jump	**set_registration_number** **static get_next_registration_number**

Notice that all members of the fox and dog classes that are not explicitly described as static are, by default, instance members. This includes all of the attributes and behaviors of the fox, the alacrity and registration_number attributes of the dog, and the set_registration_number behavior of the dog. The dog class also has a static attribute called last_used_registration_number and a static behavior called get_next_registration_number. Notice also that the dog class now has a combination of both instance and static members.

Now, each time we create a new instance of class dog, we can assign it a registration number unique from all other dog instances simply by invoking the static method get_next_registration_number of the dog class to get the next value and then calling the instance method set_registration_number to apply it to our dog instance attribute registration_number. This works because the static attribute last_used_registration_number is available to all dog instances. Upon creating the first dog instance and invoking the static behavior

---

[14]As we shall see, the prefix "class-" is used to denote a static member in ABAP.

get_next_registration_number, the static attribute last_used_registration_number would be incremented and the new value returned to us, which we would place into the instance attribute registration_number of our new dog instance via the set_registration_number behavior. Then when we create a second dog instance, we would go through the same series of actions but we would get a different registration number. This is because the static members are shared amongst all instances of the dog class, and retrieving a registration number for our second dog instance uses the same static attribute that had been used to register our first dog instance. Accordingly, if we were to continue using this sequence we would get a unique registration number with each new instantiation of a dog class, as each new dog instance leaves behind its registration number in the static attribute last_used_registration_number for the next dog instance to see.

This concept of instance members versus static members may be difficult to grasp, so let's use a metaphor that illustrates it more clearly. Suppose we learn that our management has made arrangements for us to attend one of the annual technology conventions in Las Vegas, Nevada this year. Upon arriving at our hotel we find that we have a reservation for one of the hotel guest rooms, each of which is virtually identical to each of the other guest rooms. Accordingly, our reservation permits us to occupy one instance of a guest room. Others who are attending the same technology convention also are staying at the same hotel, but each person has a unique hotel reservation, permitting each person to occupy some other instance of a guest room. Our room has a unique room number on the door and we have been issued a card key for entrance to the room.

This is the only instance of *hotel room* to which we have sole access; it is our specific instance. Upon entering the room, we can turn on one of its many lights, tune the television to our favorite channel, and adjust the climate controls of our guest room without these changes having any effect upon the lights, television, or climate of any other guest room in the same hotel. Indeed, the other guests could be making similar changes to lights, television, and climate in their guest rooms, but their changes do not affect our guest room. We could sit in one of the chairs in our guest room, and then even proceed to rearrange the furniture in our room, with no effect upon the furniture in any of the other guest rooms. In this case, the lights, television, climate controls, and furniture constitute instance attributes of the hotel room, accessible only to the guest occupying the room, and the actions turn_on_guest_room_light, tune_guest_room_television, adjust_guest_room_climate_controls, and rearrange_guest_room_furniture constitute instance methods applicable to these instance attributes.

Later, we decide to leave our guest room and visit the hotel lobby, a room in the hotel shared by all of the hotel guests. The lobby also has lights, a television, climate controls, and furniture, things that are not associated with a specific hotel guest but are available to all hotel guests, and constitute static members of hotel room. Now if we find an empty chair in the lobby and sit in it, the chair cannot be used by any of the other hotel guests until we unseat ourselves from it. Similarly, if we were to reset the lobby lights, change the channel on the lobby television, alter the lobby climate controls, and rearrange the lobby furniture, these changes would immediately affect every hotel guest who also is visiting the lobby. In addition, when one of the other hotel guests makes changes to these things while we are in the lobby, these changes immediately affect us. In this case, the lights, television, climate controls, and furniture constitute static members of hotel room, shared by and accessible to all hotel guests, and the actions turn_on_lobby_light, tune_lobby_television, adjust_lobby_climate_controls, and rearrange_lobby_furniture constitute static methods applicable to these static attributes. As guests of the hotel, we have access to the instance members of our own guest room as well as those static members located in the hotel lobby.

Furthermore, we could depart our own hotel and walk down the street to the next hotel, where none of its guests have yet arrived and registered. Accordingly, it has no instances of guest room occupants. Despite no instances of guests, and even though we have no intention of registering as a guest at this hotel, we still are able to walk into its lobby and sit in a seat, which now cannot be used by anyone else visiting the lobby of this hotel. Indeed, there is nothing to stop us from resetting the lobby lights, changing the channel on the lobby television, altering the lobby climate controls, and rearranging the lobby furniture,[15] all of which would have an immediate effect upon every other person also visiting the lobby. In this case, the lights, television,

---

[15]Except, perhaps, hotel security guards, who might not tolerate our adventures in lobby redecorating.

climate controls, and furniture still constitute static members of this hotel room, but now we see that even though they are shared by and accessible to all hotel guests, they also are available to those who are not guests of the hotel, even at a time when the hotel does not yet have any guest room occupants. Because we are not guests of this hotel, we have access only to the static members of the hotel room, and not to any instance members of a guest hotel room.

In summary, an instance attribute exists once per instance of the class, and each one is unique and separate from the instance attributes of other instantiations of the class, whereas static attributes exist once per program execution, are available to all instances of the class, and are available to external entities even when there are no corresponding instances of the class. Instance methods have access to both the instance attributes and static attributes of its class, whereas static methods have access only to the static attributes of its class.

The Encapsulation Unit

Encapsulation unit is a term referring to the boundaries of encapsulation exhibited by an entity. In object-oriented design, encapsulation units exist at two different levels.

At one level, the entire class definition serves as the encapsulation unit. It can be regarded as a container with a lid, as shown in Figure 3-3. The walls of the container define the boundaries of the encapsulation unit. External access to the class members is available only through the public interface, which is represented by the neck of the container and its open lid. Only those attributes and behaviors that have public visibility are accessible through the public interface. Class members having any other visibility are not publicly accessible, but they are contained within the class encapsulation unit and are accessible to the other members within the same class.

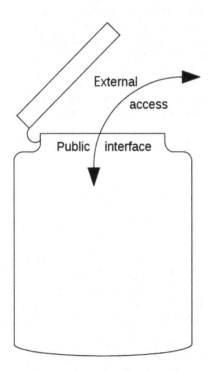

Figure 3-3. Encapsulation unit

A new class-level encapsulation unit is established when a class is instantiated. This encapsulation unit remains in effect for the life of the class instance.

At another level, each method of the class is itself an encapsulation unit, allowing for the definition of local variables that are not available outside the method. A new method-level encapsulation unit is established with each invocation of a method, and is destroyed upon exiting the method. Any local variables defined within the method are set with their initial or default values upon entering the method.[16] This means that the values of these local variables from a previous invocation *are not retained* for any subsequent invocations.[17]

Instance Encapsulation Units

We can define a class such that every one of its members belongs to the instance realm; that is, none of its members are marked as static. This constitutes an *instance class*. It is necessary to create instances of an instance class in order to access its members. Instance classes are used in those cases where we need multiple instances of the class to facilitate the necessary processing, when each instance would contain the same set of attributes but when each instance has different values assigned to those attributes. For example, we might define a class *sales order item* for which we might expect there to be multiple instances of its objects to handle the processing for a single sales order, and we would expect that no two instances of sales order item would have identical attribute values.[18]

Static Encapsulation Units

We can define a class such that every one of its members belongs to the static realm; that is, each member is marked as static. This constitutes a *static class*. It is not necessary to create any instances of a static class in order to access its members. Indeed, while it may be technically possible to create an instance of a static class, it would have no instance members that could be accessed. On the other hand, because a static class is not instantiated, there can be only one copy of its members available for access. This means that a static class should be used only in those cases where we need only one entity of the class to facilitate the necessary processing. For instance, we would expect to have multiple instances of the sales order item class, noted above, to handle the processing for a single sales order. Meanwhile, we might define a class called screen manager for which we certainly would not want multiple instances; a single screen manager is all we would need to manage the presentation of information to the user, and having more than one screen manager would present a conflict.

---

[16]The concept that subroutine variables are initialized with every invocation is not unique to object-oriented languages. This also applies to local variables defined between form and endform in classical ABAP.

[17]This even applies to recursive invocations of methods, where the values of local variables in an outer level of method invocation are not available to each subsequent inner level unless these values explicitly have been passed between these levels via the method signature.

[18]Although it is not mandatory that each instance of a sales order item, or for that matter a pair of instances for any type of class, contain a unique combination of attribute values, it stands to reason that if any two of them had the same values, they could simply be consolidated into a single instance, which could indicate the aggregate quantity of the two instead of having separate identical instances.

Some object-oriented scholars dismiss the idea of static classes as a technique that falls short of the necessary requirements to be truly considered object-oriented, discouraging their use and pointing out that there is no concept of *object* associated with a static class[19]. Indeed, in object-oriented environments, supporting multi-threading static classes is not considered "thread safe."[20] While it is true that static classes will not be able to take full advantage of all the principles of object-oriented programming (for instance, polymorphism is not possible within static classes), they do offer a stepping stone for procedural programmers to become more comfortable with programming in object-oriented environments. Of note, in ABAP environments, static classes are very similar to simple function groups.[21] Since function groups are an area of ABAP familiar to most procedural programmers, perhaps it would be helpful to compare the two to see how they are similar and how they differ:

- Both static classes and function groups encapsulate their components.

- Neither static classes nor function groups need to be instantiated to be used.

- The function modules of a function group are equivalent to the public methods of a static class.

- The data definitions usually defined in the TOP include of a function group are equivalent to the private attributes defined for a static class.

- The subroutines defined within function groups are equivalent to the private behaviors defined for a static class.

Static classes offer some other advantages not available to function groups:

- A static class can define public attributes, such as constants, field formats, and structures to be used with parameters of public method signatures

  For example, a class alarm_clock can define a public type alarm_setting, defined as type single character, along with public constants alarm_on and alarm_off as type alarm_clock.alarm_setting, having values X and space, respectively, and public method set_alarm whose signature contains parameter alarm defined as type alarm_clock.alarm_setting. An external entity using class alarm_clock can now define its own field using the public type alarm_clock.alarm_setting, and then move the public constant alarm_clock.alarm_on into this field before using it with the alarm parameter on a call to the set_alarm method. In this way, the caller can refer to the class in terms the class provides.

- The ABAP compiler enforces a stricter compliance with syntax for static classes than it can for function groups

Accordingly, a static class can be defined as a substitute for a simple function group, offering all the same features and capabilities available to simple function groups, and more.

---

[19]The design pattern known as Singleton, covered in a subsequent chapter, is a better alternative to a static class, offering a way to define a class for which we expect one and only one instance to be available.

[20]See https://msdn.microsoft.com/en-us/library/a8544e2s.aspx.

[21]By simple function groups, I mean those that do not have function modules defined with the extra clauses for special operation, such as "destination," "starting new task," "in background task," and "in update task," as well as those that are written to facilitate special features such as BAPI and IDOC processing.

Hybrid Encapsulation Units

We can define a class such that some of its members belong to the instance realm while other members belong to the static realm. This constitutes a *hybrid class*. It is not necessary to create any instances of a hybrid class in order to access its static members; however, its instance members become accessible only upon creating an instance of a hybrid class. This is a common scenario in object-oriented design.

A good example of how this can be used effectively is to take the example of the sales order item class we have been using so far and embellish it. To turn this otherwise instance class into a hybrid class, we need to include some static members. We could include a static attribute to represent the next available sales order item number as well as a static behavior to get the next sales order item number, which when invoked will increment the static attribute holding the next available sales order item number and then send this value back to the caller. Since the new attribute and new method are both static, they both are available to all instances of sales order item, with the value of the attribute holding the next sales order item number being shared across all instances of sales order item. Upon creating each new instance of a sales order item, this static method can be invoked to insure that the item number assigned to the new instance is unique amongst the set of all instances of sales order items being created.

Constructors and Destructors

A special type of method, known as a *constructor*, can be defined for a class to specify the activities to be undertaken during the creation of the class encapsulation unit, such as initializing the values of attributes. Another special type of method, known as a *destructor*, also can be defined for a class to specify the activities to be undertaken during the destruction of the class encapsulation unit, such as releasing those resources an object might have acquired.

A class encapsulation unit can be created regardless of whether or not the class has a constructor method defined for it, and similarly can be destroyed regardless of whether or not there is a destructor method defined for it. These constructor and destructor methods are defined by the programmer to instruct the runtime environment what to do *in addition* to creating and destroying the class encapsulation unit.

Although they are known as methods, constructors and destructors are not regarded as members of the class since they can be used only to create and destroy the class encapsulation unit and are not otherwise available during the lifetime of the class. Furthermore, constructors and destructors are defined such that each one applies either to the static realm or to the instance realm.

Instance Constructors and Destructors

Instance constructors are invoked automatically by the runtime environment when a new object is being created. The instance constructor facilitates setting the new object to an initial state, and will be executed once and only once for an object. Because new instances of objects are requested explicitly, an instance constructor can include a method signature, the parameters of which are available for use during the process of creating the instance. Instance constructors have access to both static and instance members of the class.

Instance destructors are invoked automatically by the runtime environment when an existing object is to be destroyed. The instance destructor facilitates any cleanup activities required during object destruction.

Whereas virtually every object-oriented environment supports instance constructors, only some provide support for instance destructors. Object-oriented environments providing support for the concept of Resource Acquisition Is Initialization (RAII),[22] such as C++, necessarily provide support for instance destructors.[23] In contrast, object-oriented environments providing support for what is known as automatic garbage collection[24] employ the dispose pattern[25] for resource cleanup, and some of these environments, such as Java and ABAP, provide no support for the explicit definition of instance destructors.[26]

Static Constructors and Destructors

Static constructors are invoked automatically by the runtime environment when a class is first accessed, which may be due to an external reference to a static member of the class or to the creation of the first instance of the class. The static constructor facilitates setting the static attributes of the class to an initial state, and will execute once and only once for the class. When the static constructor is triggered due to the creation of the first instance of the class,[27] it will run to completion before creation of the first instance begins. This means that the static constructor for a class will always start and finish prior to the start of the instance constructor when creating the first instance of that class. Because there is no specific statement that will cause a static constructor to be invoked, a static constructor cannot include a method signature. Static constructors have access to the static members of the class, but cannot access instance members.

Static destructors are invoked automatically by the runtime environment when the static members of a class are to be destroyed. The static destructor facilitates any cleanup activities required during class destruction.

Only some object-oriented environments provide support for static constructors. C# and ABAP are two that do. Neither C++ nor Java supports this concept, although Java does support what are known as static initialization blocks.

Meanwhile, it is rare to find any object-oriented environment supporting static destructors. C++, C#, Java, and ABAP do not offer support for this.[28]

Friendship

Some object-oriented languages, among them C++ and ABAP, offer the capability for a class to enable other specific classes to have unrestricted access to its members. This effectively renders all members of the class publicly visible to those other classes. This capability is known as *friendship.*[29] A class offers friendship to other classes by specifying the names of those classes that it considers its friends.

Friendship only can be offered; it is not reciprocated. That is, a class offering friendship to another class does not itself suddenly become a friend of that other class; the other class also needs to offer its own explicit friendship.

---

[22]See `http://en.cppreference.com/w/cpp/language/raii`.
[23]See `http://en.cppreference.com/w/cpp/language/destructor`.
[24]See `http://basen.oru.se/kurser/koi/2008-2009-p1/texter/gc/index.html`.
[25]See `https://msdn.microsoft.com/en-us/library/b1yfkh5e(v=vs.110).aspx`.
[26]Some languages running in environments with garbage collection provide a clean-up method, such as Java's *finalize,* which is invoked during the garbage collection phase, but it is indeterminate exactly when the corresponding object will be garbage collected. Meanwhile, destructors are invoked immediately as the object is being destroyed. The difference typically stems from the capability in the language explicitly to delete an object. Objects in C++ can be explicitly deleted, so a destructor method is applicable. Objects in Java and ABAP are not explicitly deleted.
[27]A static constructor can be triggered well before the creation of the first instance of the class, but if not, then it is certainly triggered upon creation of the first instance of the class.
[28]One language that does support static destructors is D, in which the static destructor for a class is invoked upon thread termination. See `http://dlang.org/class.html#StaticDestructor`.
[29]See Friend classes at `www.cplusplus.com/doc/tutorial/inheritance/`.

Since a friend class has what amounts to public visibility to all of the members of the class offering the friendship, it has the undesirable effect of *breaking encapsulation*, because the class no longer is in complete control over its own members. Other classes can change the values of non-public attributes of the class offering the friendship as well as invoke its non-public methods.

Also, with friendship in effect, it is now more difficult to perform subsequent maintenance and refactoring on the class offering the friendship because now it requires more careful consideration when making changes to protected and private members. For instance, we may change the definition of a private attribute and change all of the references to it within the class and think we have completed the task, but now we may have rendered a friend class syntactically incorrect for those statements that access the private attribute in statements that relied on a specific type of definition. This also applies to the signature of private methods, which also could render friend classes invoking those methods syntactically incorrect for a variety of reasons, such as the wrong type used with a parameter, or is now missing a parameter that has not been marked optional.

Some in the object-oriented community repudiate the use of friendship while others advise using friendship with caution.

Considerations for Using Encapsulation Effectively

So, how do we go about deciding what to include in an encapsulation unit? Here are some guidelines:

- **Encapsulate repetition.**

   This is a technique also used in procedural programming: write the code once and call it from multiple locations as necessary. This can be applied at the method encapsulation unit level, where a method of a class is invoked by other methods of the same class. It also can be applied at the class encapsulation unit level, where one class will provide the repetitive activities to be performed at the request of other classes.

- **Encapsulate complexity.**

   This is another technique used in procedural programming: write particularly long and complex algorithms or processing sequences in their own subroutines.[30] As with repetition, this also can be applied at the method encapsulation unit level, where a method of a class is invoked by another method of the same class, as well as at the class encapsulation unit level, where one class will provide the complex processing to be made available to other classes.

- **Encapsulate what is likely to vary.**

   When it is known the code contains processes likely to change in the future, separate these processes into their own encapsulation units. By *vary* we do not mean applying changes to code for the purpose of fixing bugs, but changes to code because the user is asking for new features and capabilities. For instance, a pizza parlor might have software to handle online customer orders. The boilerplate code handling such things as estimating time to deliver the order, collecting payment, and printing receipts probably is unlikely to change often, but the various menu entries, toppings available, item prices, and promotional campaigns are likely to change to keep up with customer demands.

---

[30]I've lost count of the number of times I have encountered ABAP subroutines containing hundreds of lines of code where the execution of two or three long and complex algorithms are made mutually exclusive based on some simple logical condition. Instead of moving the algorithms to their own subroutines, the authors chose to leave them embedded in the conditional logic found in the subroutine. In cases like these, the conditional logic becomes lost amongst the hundreds of lines of algorithms.

- **Encapsulation units should have only a single responsibility.**

   Restricting encapsulation units to only a single responsibility is to comply with what is known as the *Single Responsibility Principle,*[31] a term coined by Robert C. Martin, who regards a *responsibility* as a *reason to make a modification.* This can be applied at the method encapsulation unit level, where, for instance, a class handling printed output will have one method to facilitate setting print parameters and another method to facilitate issuing the request for printing. If a single method were to facilitate both of these requirements, then a change to the way the method accommodates print parameters and a change to the way a request is made for printing would constitute two different reasons for changing the same method. This can also be applied at the class encapsulation unit level, where, for instance, there is one class to facilitate printing content and another class to facilitate displaying content, despite that both classes handle output of content.

ABAP Language Support for Encapsulation

The object-oriented extensions to the ABAP language accommodate encapsulation in the following ways:

- By supporting the concept of a class with attributes and behaviors (methods)
- By providing a way to assign a visibility level to class members
- By facilitating the definition and use of method variables
- By supporting both instance and static members for classes
- By supporting instance classes, static classes, and hybrid classes
- By supporting both instance and static constructors for classes
- By enabling a class to offer friendship to other classes

Unlike most other object-oriented languages, the syntax for defining a class in ABAP separates its definition from its implementation. The definition component must precede the implementation component. This is achieved through these complementary class constructs:

```
class class_name definition [options].
  o
  o
  o
endclass.
class class_name implementation.
  o
  o
  o
endclass.
```

Attributes and method signatures are specified within *visibility sections* appearing in the definition component. Each visibility section begins with the section name and ends with the definition of the next visibility section name or with the endclass scope terminator. Those members defined within a visibility section are assigned that corresponding visibility.

---

[31]See http://butunclebob.com/ArticleS.UncleBob.PrinciplesOfOod.

Listing 3-2 shows an example of the ABAP syntax for a class describing a car.

Listing 3-2. ABAP Code for the Car Class

```
class car definition.
  public section.
    methods      : get_year exporting year type string
                 , set_year importing year type string
                 .
  private section.
    data         : model_year      type string
                 .
endclass.
class car implementation.
  method get_year.
    year                           = model_year.
  endmethod.
  method set_year.
    model_year                     = year.
  endmethod.
endclass.
```

Here we see both a public and a private visibility section in the definition component. The public section defines two methods and their signatures: get_year and set_year. The private section defines one attribute: model_year. The implementation component contains the implementation for each of the two public methods defined in the definition component.

In this example, the only statements with which an experienced procedural ABAP programmer would be expected to be familiar are the data statement defining the attribute model_year and the assignment statements in the implementations for each of the methods. Everything else is new with object-oriented ABAP.

New, perhaps, but not entirely unfamiliar. The method-endmethod construct appearing in the implementation component is functionally identical to the subroutines defined in procedural ABAP using the form-endform construct. They differ only in syntax; the procedural form-endform construct accommodates a signature on the form statement itself, whereas the object-oriented method-endmethod construct has its signature provided by its counterpart *methods* statement in the class definition component. Indeed, the concepts associated with defining and using local variables apply equally to both procedural subroutines and object-oriented methods.

The example in Listing 3-2 shows a class where all of its members belong to the instance realm. Accordingly, we would need to create an instance of this class in order to access these members. This is done via the *create object* statement:

```
report.
  o
  o
  o
    data         : rental_car      type ref to car.
  o
  o
  o
    create object rental_car.
```

Here we have defined a data field, rental_car, which defines an object reference variable to an object whose type is class car. Upon encountering the create object statement, an object of class car is created, somewhere in storage, by the runtime environment, and a reference to this storage is placed into the object reference variable rental_car. Once the object is created, it is through the object reference variable that we can access the object:

```
call method rental_car->set_year
  exporting year = '2014'.
```

The call method statement initiates access to a method of a class object through the object reference variable. In the preceding example statement, rental_car is the reference variable providing access to the car object, set_year is the name of a public method defined for the car object, and year is a parameter specified in the signature for the public method set_year. The -> symbol separating the name of the object reference variable from the name of the method is known as the *object component selector* and is used to access instance members of an object. There are variations on the statement to invoke methods of objects which are not covered here.[32]

An alternative to defining the car class, as shown in Listing 3-2, is to define the class such that all of its members belong to the static realm. In ABAP, the qualifier *class-*, prefixed to the data and methods statements in the definition component of the class, as shown highlighted in the Listing 3-3, consigns these members to the static realm.

Listing 3-3. Static Definition for the Car Class

```
class car definition.
  public section.
    class-methods: get_year exporting year type string
                 , set_year importing year type string
                 .
  private section.
    class-data  : model_year    type string
                 .
endclass.
class car implementation.
  method get_year.
    year                       = model_year.
  endmethod.
  method set_year.
    model_year                 = year.
  endmethod.
endclass.
```

Accordingly, the definition component of a class accommodates assigning both member visibility and member realm. Note that this now relegates the car class as a static encapsulation unit, one for which multiple instances are not possible and for which the create object statement is not applicable. A class defined this way, a static class, is one that is immediately available for use in a program (it does not require instantiation) and its behaviors also can be accessed by a call method statement, but the syntax of the call method statement differs in two significant aspects:

- Members of the class are accessed simply via the name of the class instead of through an object reference variable.

---

[32]Refer to Horst Keller and Sascha Krüger, *ABAP Objects: ABAP Programming in SAP Netweaver*, 2nd edition, Galileo Press, 2007.

- In place of the object component selector, a *class component selector* (=>) is used to access the static members of the class.

Here is the same call method statement we saw before, altered accordingly for accessing a member of a static class, with differences highlighted:

```
call method car=>set_year
  exporting year = '2014'.
```

It is easy for us to see that the example in Listing 3-3 defines a static class; every one of its members is relegated to the static realm, with its single attribute defined using class-data and each of its two behaviors defined using class-methods. If we were to have even one member defined to the instance realm, then the class could no longer be considered a static class. Once a class has a significant number of members defined for it, determining whether or not it is a static class becomes more difficult through the process of checking whether or not there is at least one instance member. Imagine a class with over 100 attributes and more than that many methods[33]. It would be easy to miss a single instance member buried among such a large class definition, and a few years later, when we find ourselves maintaining this class, we long ago would have forgotten whether or not we had defined it as a static class. A way to determine this instantly is to apply some optional qualifiers on the class definition statement:

```
class class_name definition abstract final.
```

Here we see the additional qualifiers called abstract and final. Abstract indicates that the class cannot be instantiated. Final indicates that the class cannot have any subclasses[34]. Together they insure that there can be no instantiations of the class. Applying these two qualifiers to a class intended to function as a static class is an easy way both to guarantee as well as to document that the class is indeed a static class. It also alleviates the programmer from the tedious and potentially inaccurate process of visually applying a full body scan of the class definition only to arrive at the same conclusion.

The ABAP language provides for both instance and static constructors, as shown highlighted in Listing 3-4 of the car class, which has both instance and static members.

Listing 3-4. Car Class with Both Static and Instance Members

```
class car definition.
  public section.
    class-methods: class_constructor
                 , get_next_serial_number
                             exporting next_serial_number type i
                 .
    methods      : constructor
                 , get_year exporting year type string
                 , set_year importing year type string
                 .
  private section.
    class-data   : last_used_serial_number
                                   type i
                 .
    data         : serial_number  type i
                 , model_year     type string
                 .
```

---

[33]Although such a class can exist, it represents a class that should be divided into multiple smaller classes.
[34]I will cover subclasses later in the book.

```
endclass.
class car implementation.
  method class_constructor.
    last_used_serial_number      = 1000.
  endmethod.
  method constructor.
    call method get_next_serial_number
      importing
        next_serial_number       = serial_number.
  endmethod.
  method get_next_serial_number.
    add 01 to last_used_serial_number.
    serial_number                = last_used_serial_number.
  endmethod.
  method get_year.
    year                         = model_year.
  endmethod.
  method set_year.
    model_year                   = year.
  endmethod.
endclass.
```

As illustrated in Listing 3-4, in addition to being defined to contain only instance members or only static members, a class can also be defined as a hybrid, containing a mix of both static and instance members.

Local method variables are defined within the bounding method and endmethod scope terminators, similar to how they would be defined between the procedural form and endform scope terminators:

```
method validate_registration.
  data        : is_registered  type abap_bool.
    o
    o
    o
  if licence_plate is not initial.
    is_registered = abap_true.
  endif.
    o
    o
    o
endmethod.
```

When specified for a class, ABAP requires the programmer to use the names constructor and class_constructor for the instance and static constructors, respectively. The static constructor appears on a class-methods statement in the public visibility section and must have no signature. The instance constructor appears on a methods statement in an appropriate visibility section[35] and may have a signature.

In the example, the presence of a static constructor will cause the corresponding method implementation to be invoked when the class is first accessed. As shown in Listing 3-4, the method class_constructor will set the static attribute last_used_serial_number to the value 1000. This simply initializes this field to a starting value before any instances of the class are created. The static constructor should be used for such setup tasks associated with its static attributes.

---

[35]There was a time when ABAP required the instance constructor to be defined only in the public visibility section. This no longer is the case. Refer to the ABAP language documentation for more detail.

Meanwhile, the presence of an instance constructor will cause the corresponding method implementation to be invoked each time a new instance of the class is created. As shown in Listing 3-4, the constructor method will invoke method get_next_serial_number of class car to receive the serial number for the new car instance. Notice here that method get_next_serial_number is defined as a static method, and it references the static attribute last_used_serial_number. After incrementing the value of this static attribute, method get_next_serial_number returns the updated value to the caller via the method signature. Accordingly, because static attributes are shared across all instances of a class, each newly instantiated car object will get a unique serial number since the value used for the previous car instance will be left behind to be incremented for the next one.

Since ABAP provides no explicit support for destructors, the way to destroy an object that no longer is required, and as a consequence release the storage it occupies, is simply to clear the value in the corresponding object reference variable. The ABAP runtime environment automatically keeps track of all the active references to an object, and when it detects that an object no longer has any active references, it marks the object for *garbage collection*, a storage optimization feature of the runtime environment.

Finally, the ABAP language provides for a class to offer friendship to other classes by naming them on the class definition statement in a friends clause:

```
class car definition [global | local] friends <friend1 [friend2 ...] >.
```

Encapsulation Units in ABAP

Since the concept of the encapsulation unit is not new to ABAP, perhaps it would be helpful to distinguish between those encapsulation units typically associated with procedural (classic) ABAP and those that are new with object-oriented ABAP.

Table 3-3 shows on the left those encapsulation units available to procedural programming and on the right those new with object-oriented programming, along with the ABAP statements to access the encapsulation unit.

Table 3-3. Comparison of Procedural and Object-Oriented Encapsulation Units

Procedural (classic) encapsulation units	Object-oriented encapsulation units
Report/program (SUBMIT)	Class
Subroutines within report (PERFORM) Function group (CALL FUNCTION) Transaction/dialog (CALL TRANSACTION)	Method (CALL METHOD)
Screens (CALL SCREEN)	(No direct screen processing capability)[36]

It should be noted that most of the encapsulation units associated with procedural ABAP are available for use by the encapsulation units associated with object-oriented ABAP, and vice versa. That is, a method of a class may contain a PERFORM (local class only) or CALL FUNCTION statement to a procedural encapsulation unit, and a classic ABAP subroutine or function module may contain a CALL METHOD statement to an object-oriented encapsulation unit.

---

[36]Screen processing within object-oriented ABAP is provided through WebDynpro and its successors or through the use of function groups that encapsulate screen definitions and their processing.

Managing Class Encapsulation Units in the ABAP Repository

The ABAP source code repository facilitates retaining objects containing the ABAP code describing classes using two different designations. One designation makes the described class available to all other objects contained within the ABAP source code repository; the other designation limits the availability of the described class exclusively to the compilation unit with which it is used. The ABAP developer chooses which designation to use based on whether the class has the potential to be used in multiple settings. Accordingly, each class definition will be designated either a *global* class or a *local* class.

A global class is created and maintained via the Class Builder (transaction SE24). Once defined and activated, the class becomes available for use by any other object in the ABAP repository. Using the Class Builder to build a class is analogous to using the Function Builder (transaction SE37) to build a function of a function group. Both the Class Builder and Function Builder guide the developer to define the class or function module using a form-based approach, through which the developer is presented a set of tabs enabling the assignment of some aspect of the class or function module. The Class Builder also has the option of a source code-based approach, enabling the developer to create and maintain the entire class definition on a single editor screen, and provides the capability to toggle between the form-based and source code-based approaches as desired.

A local class is created and maintained via one of the standard ABAP source code editors (e.g., SE38, SE80). Local classes can coexist in an object with other non-class code. A typical scenario is one where local classes are embedded in a classic procedural report program, either in the same object as the procedural code or in an INCLUDE object that is included along with the other components to compose a complete compilation unit. Once defined and activated, the local class becomes available to all other components in the same compilation unit. That is, when included with a report, the local class can be used by all the procedural components defined in the report, but it is unavailable to entities defined outside the boundaries of the report. Indeed, local classes may be defined within function groups and global classes, and when they are, their availability is restricted to the components within the function group or global class compilation unit. A common use of local classes is to define classes to facilitate ABAP unit testing, the automated unit testing feature provided as part of the ABAP workbench, since the ABAP unit feature is initiated only through the methods of local classes.

Whether using the global class source code-based editor or one of the standard ABAP editors to define a local class, in both cases the definition portion of the class must physically precede its implementation portion. When multiple local classes are defined in a single component, it is common for these two complementary portions of the class to be adjacent to each other. There are situations, however, where the definition and implementation portions defining a single class will be separated from each other by the definition portions of one or more other local classes. This usually becomes necessary when there is an interdependency between multiple local classes, and is a consequence of the ABAP compiler being a single-pass compiler[37]. For instance, a local physician class holds a reference to a local patient class, and the local patient class holds a reference to the local physician class; the local classes are mutually dependent. In cases such as this, it is necessary for the definition portion of both local classes to precede the implementation portion of either class.[38] This anomaly does not apply to global classes since only a single global class may be contained within a global class compilation unit.

Orienting Ourselves After Having Traversed Encapsulation

So, we have traveled some distance along the path from Procedureton to Objectropolis, and now, having completed our traversal through the object-oriented district known as Encapsulation, we are familiar with its principles and can now speak the language spoken by the residents in this district. Since this is such a new

---

[37]See www.uobabylon.edu.iq/eprints/publication_10_847_344.pdf.

[38]We will see an example of where this becomes necessary in the chapter on the State design pattern (Chapter 22).

place for us, it would be helpful to orient ourselves and determine where we are in relation to some other place with which we are more familiar. Accordingly, let's determine how far away we are from a place we know so well in ABAP procedural programming: Function Groups. We have learned that static classes have many similarities with function groups, but we also know that classes offer other capabilities beyond just static classes.

Refer to the chart in Appendix A, illustrating the comparison between function groups and classes on how each one facilitates the capabilities of the principles of object-oriented programming. The first 10 rows show how these two programming formats support the principles of Encapsulation. Although function groups, a place more familiar to us than classes, do not support all of these principles, there is enough common ground for us to conclude we are not that far away from the district where we would find function groups to be prominent; the terrain is similar, but we find geographical features in the object-oriented landscape of encapsulation that we do not find in function groups.

Summary

In this chapter, we became more familiar with the object-oriented concept of Encapsulation, and that it facilitates adherence to the design principle known as Separation of Concerns. We now know about visibility, how it is applied to components of classes using words representing a scale of gradations from least to most visibility, and why this is such an important concept to understand. We also learned that members of classes can exist in one of two realms:

- Static realm

- Instance realm

We also learned about encapsulation units and that classes can be defined as purely static encapsulation units, as purely instance encapsulation units, or as a hybrid combination of both static and instance encapsulation units. The concepts of constructors and destructors were introduced, which also have an aspect of applying either to the static realm or the instance realm. We learned about friendship, a concept applicable only to some object-oriented environments, and that using it breaks encapsulation. We also learned some considerations for using the principle of encapsulation effectively:

- Encapsulate repetition.

- Encapsulate complexity.

- Encapsulate what is likely to vary.

- Encapsulation units should have only a single responsibility.

Encapsulation Exercises

Refer to Chapter 3 of the functional and technical requirements documentation (see Appendix B) for the accompanying ABAP exercise programs associated with this chapter. Take a break from reading the book at this point to reinforce what you have read by changing and executing the corresponding exercise programs. The exercise programs associated with this chapter are those in the 101 series: ZOOT101A through ZOOT101E.

CHAPTER 4

■ ■ ■

Abstraction

The next stop on our journey to Objectropolis takes us from Encapsulation to a place called Abstraction. The word abstract means

> "Considered apart from concrete existence ... thought of or stated without reference to a specific instance."[1]

It is at this point where we depart familiar procedural territory.

Some definitions for abstraction in object-oriented programming describe it as the representation of real-world entities.

> "The objects in an object-oriented system are often intended to correspond directly to entities in the 'real world.'"[2]

This certainly is an important aspect of abstraction, but, as we shall see, it is not the only aspect. Erich Gamma and his colleagues offer the following advisory:

> "[O]bject-oriented designs often end up with classes that have no counterparts in the real world. ... Strict modeling of the real world leads to a system that reflects today's realities but not necessarily tomorrow's. The abstractions that emerge during design are key to making a design flexible."[3]

Abstract Art

One good way to envision abstraction is to consider how a cartoon image conveys information about an entity.

If I were to try to describe a car to you, I might draw a cartoon picture of a car, applying to it only those details relevant to the discussion. The cartoon would be an abstraction of a car. It would not represent any particular car, but merely serve as a generalization for any car simply to facilitate the discussion I wanted to have about cars. The discussion might be about car windshields. If at some point in the discussion I were to tell everyone to go outside into the parking lot to find a car with the type of windshield I was discussing, it is unlikely that everyone would gravitate to the same car. This is because my cartoon image of the car would not exhibit enough detail for everyone to identify the same car; it is simply an abstraction for any car possessing the level of detail I provided for it.

---

[1] *American Heritage Dictionary of the English Language*, 4th edition, Houghton Mifflin Company, 2000, p. 8.
[2] www.prenhall.com/divisions/esm/app/kafura/secure/chapter1/html/1.2_abstraction.htm
[3] Erich Gamma, Richard Helm, Ralph Johnson, and John Vlissides, *Design Patterns: Elements of Reusable Object-Oriented Software*, Addison-Wesley, 1994, p. 11.

Another way to envision abstraction is to consider how authors of romance novels develop their characters. A typical trio of characters is hero, villain, and damsel in distress. Each of these characters is developed as the novel progresses, but the author provides only enough information about them to support the story, and we use our imagination to fill in the missing details. Accordingly, each reader of the novel creates their own unique images of each character, perhaps drawing upon similarities with themselves or people they know, enjoying the novel even though each character is an abstraction for a person and not intended to represent any particular person.

Representing Real-World Entities

Car, bank account, and *weather forecast* are three examples of real-world entities. We can represent these entities in an object-oriented program by defining each one as a class: a *car* class, a *bank account* class, and a *weather forecast* class. These classes represent abstractions for their real-world counterparts.

Each of these classes can include definitions for its attributes. The *car* class can include attributes for make, model, year, serial number, average miles per gallon, speed, direction, remaining fuel quantity, etc. The *bank account* class can include attributes for account number, type of account, current balance, minimum balance, interest rate, overdraft penalty, etc. The *weather forecast* can include attributes for expected high temperature for today; expected overnight low temperature; chance of precipitation for today, tomorrow, the next day; etc.

Each of these classes can also include definitions for behaviors that act upon its attributes. The car class can include behaviors for start, stop, turn and accelerate, each having an effect upon the attributes retaining information about fuel consumption, movement, and direction of travel. Likewise, the bank account class can include behaviors for deposit, withdraw, and calculate interest, each having an effect upon the attributes retaining information about current balance and overdraft penalty. Similarly, the weather forecast class can include behaviors for both updating and disclosing its own attribute values for tracking the weather.

So, how is this different from the procedural programming style with which we are so familiar?

While procedural programs are primarily designed to address a specific processing requirement, classes are primarily designed to manage information. The car class manages information about a car, but has no capacity to manage any other type of information, such as how many other cars have ever been owned by the driver, information that, while it might be important to us, has nothing to do with the car class.

Let's see this through an example. A manufacturer of replacement vehicle mufflers needs to track the quantity and location of finished goods in transit between its manufacturing plant in Cleveland, Ohio and its three regional warehouses in Linden, New Jersey; Kansas City, Missouri; and Hayward, California, each of which receive their inventory of mufflers via shipping containers moving by both rail and truck. A report is required to show the various shipping containers in use, indicating the container id, which of them are being loaded, which are being unloaded, and for those in transit, which are on trucks and the name of the trucking company, which are on rail cars and the name of the railroad company, where each one is located, the warehouse to receive the shipping container, and its estimated time of arrival. The format of the report is similar to the output shown in Table 4-1.

Table 4-1. *Example Output for Report*

Container id	Destination warehouse	Current location	Status	Carrier	ETA
HGF107588	Linden, NJ	Linden, NJ	Unloading		
YKZ503401	Linden, NJ	Altoona, PA	On rail car	Norfolk Southern	Tomorrow
BNX969443	Linden, NJ	Newark, NJ	On truck	RNX Logistics	Today
BNX969447	Kansas City, MO	Indianapolis, IN	On rail car	BNSF	Tomorrow
BNX963850	Kansas City, MO	Kansas City, MO	Unloading		
YKZ500067	Kansas City, MO	Kansas City, MO	On truck	Harris Transport	Today
HGF109905	Hayward, CA	Salt Lake City, UT	On rail car	BNSF	Two days
YKZ501991	Hayward, CA	Chicago, IL	On rail car	BNSF	Four days
HGF103556	Hayward, CA	Oakland, CA	On truck	Western Express	Today
HGF102002	Hayward, CA	Cleveland, OH	Loading		Five days

When writing this program using the procedural style we might define a global variable as a table to keep track of all the information required for shipping containers as well as other variables to record information about the three warehouses, the trucking companies, the railroad companies, and the manufacturing plant. It may be composed of various subroutines for resolving the information about each shipping container and presenting this information in a report. Such a program is designed like many other procedural programs: it focuses on the processing requirement.

When writing this program using the object-oriented style we might define classes for shipping container, warehouse, manufacturing plant, truck, trucking company, rail car, railroad company, and report. Each of these classes is an abstraction of its real-world counterpart and has its respective attributes and behaviors. The report class produces the report while the shipping container class keeps track of information about a single shipping container. Each class retains information relevant to the abstraction it represents *and no other information*. Such a program is designed like many other object-oriented programs; it focuses on data and how the data is organized and managed.

Comparing the two programming styles illustrated above, we see that the procedural program contains information about every contributing entity all combined into one single program. There is no discernible separation between a shipping container and the truck that might be carrying it, since information for both is retained in the same global table. By contrast, the object-oriented program manages the information by segregating it into distinct classes, where each class manages only the information relevant to it. The shipping container retains the container id and its quantity, but knows nothing about the truck or rail car transporting it.

Class Cohesion

The degree to which members defined for a class are relevant to each other is a measure of the *cohesion* of a class.[4] A class containing only those members relevant to its corresponding abstraction reflects high cohesion among its members, while a class containing members that have little relevancy to one another reflects low cohesion. Classes should be defined in a way that offers high cohesion among its members.

---

[4]See www.aivosto.com/project/help/pm-oo-cohesion.html.

In the previous example for the manufacturer of replacement vehicle mufflers, a variety of classes were proposed to facilitate the object-oriented programming style. The class proposed to represent an abstraction for a shipping container offers high cohesion when its attributes and behaviors all relate to each other. For example, its attributes might be container id, color, height, width, depth, storage capacity, tare weight, maximum gross weight, net weight, quantity of loaded items, and current security tag number; and its behaviors might include, load, unload, get_gross_weight, and apply_security_tag. All of them offer the class high cohesion since they all relate to a shipping container. If we were to include for this class an attribute to hold the name of the trucking company moving the container, we would cause the class to offer lower cohesion since this attribute has little to do with a shipping container, but instead is relevant only when a truck is transporting it. It would represent an example of an attribute that would not be applicable when the shipping container is being transported by train. Worse, to include in the shipping container class an attribute to represent the number of employees working for the manufacturer of mufflers the previous year would further diminish the cohesiveness of the class since this information is completely irrelevant to shipping containers.

Reusable Components

The report on shipping containers in use illustrated in Table 4-1 might cause us to consider whether its construction using the object-oriented programming model is worth the effort. An argument could be made that we might be able to complete it faster using the procedural programming model. This is a good point to ponder, but we should consider that rarely do we ever encounter business organizations where only one type of report provides sufficient information about business entities such as shipping containers. Instead, we are likely to find ourselves given requirements later to write a report on those shipping containers that are out of circulation due to having sustained damage or in the process of being repaired and refurbished, on the current age and expected lifespan of active shipping containers, and a host of other reports related to shipping containers.

With this in mind, it makes sense to use the object-oriented programming model so that the shipping container class we define for the in-use report can also be reused with these other reports. Not only that, but during the maintenance of each report it becomes easier to identify the discrete component having responsibility for managing the information we seek to convey in the report. Eventually we will have compiled a comprehensive library of reusable components, each component representing a ready-to-use abstraction for an entity that needs to participate in the next new report program that becomes necessary.

Establishing a Level of Abstraction

An abstraction level provides aspects for both detail and scope of an entity and is a measure of the precision we choose to assign it. This provides us with the ability to manage the complexity of an entity through a more practical perspective, allowing us to ignore details that may not be relevant to the way in which we need to use the entity. We see more detail at lower levels of abstraction and fewer details at higher levels. Similarly, we are afforded wider scope at higher levels of abstraction and narrower scope at lower levels. The two aspects of detail and scope have an inverse relationship with each other; as one increases, the other decreases.

For example, we might find ourselves standing on a patio adjoining the back of a house. The patio is composed of common red bricks measuring about 20cm long x 10cm wide x 5cm deep and they arranged in a herringbone pattern, such as presented in Figure 4-1.

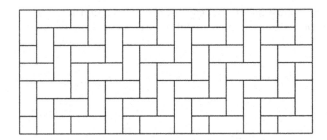

Figure 4-1. *Herringbone pattern*

When we are standing on the patio, our eyes are about five feet above it. At this level of abstraction, when we look down at the patio, we can see distinct red bricks in a herringbone pattern. If we were to raise our abstraction level to 50 feet above the patio, we now might see red blocks arranged in a herringbone pattern; however, we can no longer identify that they are bricks. Raise the abstraction level to 500 feet and we might see that the patio is red, but we can no longer tell there is a herringbone pattern. At 5,000 feet, we can no longer tell that the patio is red. At 50,000 feet, we can no longer see the patio.

Similarly, at the five-foot abstraction level, our scope is limited to only the portion of the patio on which we are standing. At the 50-foot abstraction level, our scope widens and we can see the entire patio, the roof of the adjoining house, and some of the yard surrounding it. At 500 feet, our scope widens still more and we also can see some of the neighbors' houses and their patios. At 5,000 feet, we can see the entire town. At 50,000 feet, we can see the entire county.

Table 4-2 organizes these different vertical perceptions of patios, enabling us to compare the corresponding scope and level of detail as we change our level of abstraction.

Table 4-2. *Relationship between Scope and Level of Detail*

Altitude (in feet)	Scope	Level of Detail
50,000	We can see the entire county.	We cannot discern any patios.
5,000	We can see the entire town.	We can discern patios but cannot resolve their color, pattern, or material.
500	We can see a few houses in the neighborhood.	We can discern patios and their color but cannot resolve their pattern or material.
50	We can see this entire patio, the roof of the adjoining house, and some of its yard.	We can discern the entire patio color and pattern but cannot resolve its material.
5	We can see a portion of this patio.	We can discern for a section of the patio its color, pattern, and material.

Let's put this into terms of classes and their members. Suppose we have three classes representing three different abstraction levels:

1. Enclosed shape

2. Enclosed shape with at least one angle

3. Rectangle

We have arranged these classes in Figure 4-2 to illustrate the vertical nature of the relationship between these classes, with each class providing less scope and more detail as we descend from the top of the chart to the bottom.

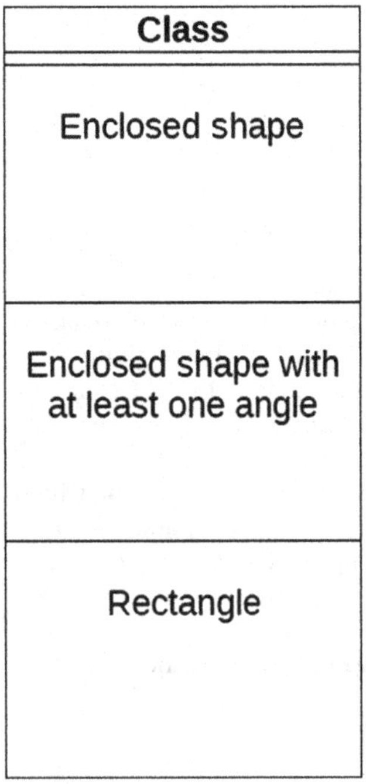

Class
Enclosed shape
Enclosed shape with at least one angle
Rectangle

Figure 4-2. *Classes arranged where scope is greatest at top and level of detail is greatest at bottom*

Now we will ask three people selected at random (Boris, Natasha, and Sherman) to provide two-dimensional drawings for each class, instructing them to "use your imagination" but stay within the constraints as described by the name of the class. As shown in Figure 4-3, none of these people provided the same drawing, but all their drawings conform to the criteria described by the name of each class.

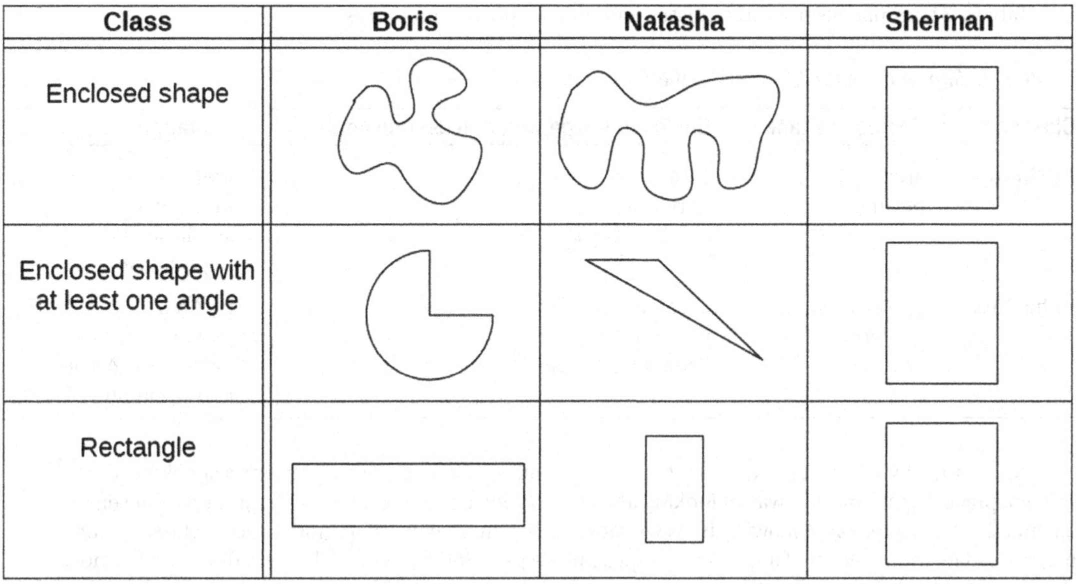

Class	Boris	Natasha	Sherman
Enclosed shape			
Enclosed shape with at least one angle			
Rectangle			

Figure 4-3. *Drawings provided by Boris, Natasha, and Sherman*

Let's define some members for these classes.

Area and perimeter are two attributes we should be able to apply to any two-dimensional enclosed shape, so for the *Enclosed shape* class we'll define these two attributes and two corresponding methods, getArea and getPerimeter.

The *Enclosed shape with at least one angle* class can accommodate all of the members defined for *Enclosed shape*, but this class is at a lower level of abstraction, providing more detail and less scope. Its scope is limited to those drawings with at least one angle, and so cannot accommodate the drawings for the *Enclosed shape* class provided by Boris and Natasha. However, because its level of abstraction includes the detail "at least one angle," we can define for it additional members to reflect this level of detail. Let's define for it an attribute called smallest angle and a corresponding method getSmallestAngle.

Similarly, the *Rectangle* class can accommodate all of the members defined both for *Enclosed shape* and for *Enclosed shape with at least one angle*. Since it has a lower level of abstraction than *Enclosed shape with at least one angle*, let's capitalize on this and provide it with an attribute called hypotenuse and a corresponding method named getHypotenuse. Here we specify for *Rectangle* more detail, but we also know that its scope does not permit it to accommodate any of the drawings for the *Enclosed shape* or *Enclosed shape with at least one angle* classes provided by both Boris and Natasha.

Sherman provided the same drawing for all three classes; however, we need to recognize that even though a rectangle was provided for the *Enclosed shape* class, this class has neither a hypotenuse attribute nor a getHypotenuse method. The *Enclosed shape* class can determine only the area and the perimeter of a rectangle since this is the extent of information its level of abstraction allows it to see for the drawing it holds.

Table 4-3 summarizes our three classes and their respective members.

Table 4-3. *Summary of the Members of the Three Classes*

Classes	Enclosed shape	Enclosed shape with at least one angle	Rectangle
Attributes	area perimeter	area perimeter smallest angle	area perimeter smallest angle hypotenuse
Behaviors	getArea getPerimeter	getArea getPerimeter getSmallestAngle	getArea getPerimeter getSmallestAngle getHypotenuse

Notice that, by virtue of its additional members, each successive class represents a specialization of the one preceding it. Another way of looking at this is to consider that each preceding class represents a generalization of the one following it. As we move from a more general to more specific class, we can accommodate a smaller set of applicable shapes but we gain detail about each one (additional members of the class). Similarly, as we move from a more specific to more general class, we can accommodate a larger set of applicable shapes but we lose detail about each one (fewer members of the class). The set of shapes that can be considered a *Rectangle* is a subset of the larger set of shapes that can be considered an *Enclosed shape with at least one angle*. Likewise, the set of shapes that can be considered an *Enclosed shape with at least one angle* is a subset of the larger set of shapes that can be considered an *Enclosed shape*.

We can correlate this set of classes and their respective members with the perspectives illustrated by the patio metaphor noted above. Let's imagine the *Rectangle* class offers us a perspective on shapes from 50 feet away, the *Enclosed shape with at least one angle* offers a perspective from 500 feet, and *Enclosed shape* offers a perspective from 5,000 feet. At 50 feet, we can see via *Rectangle* that a shape has an area, perimeter, smallest angle, and hypotenuse. At 500 feet, we can see via *Enclosed shape with at least one angle* that a shape has an area, perimeter, and smallest angle, but we can no longer see whether it has a hypotenuse; this perspective offers us fewer details. However, the shapes we can see are now no longer limited to rectangles; it offers us a wider scope of applicable shapes. Similarly, at 5,000 feet, we can see via *Enclosed shape* that a shape has an area and a perimeter, but we can no longer see whether it has either a smallest angle or a hypotenuse, offering us even fewer details. However, the shapes we can see are now no longer limited to those with at least one angle, offering us a wider scope of shapes.

Suppose we find ourselves with the requirement to create a report that shows the area and perimeter of a set of shapes. Which of the classes shown in Table 4-3 should we choose to facilitate this? The most appropriate class would be the *Enclosed shape*. It provides the necessary level of detail to reflect the area and perimeter of any shape we might encounter. Whereas one of the shapes our report program may encounter could be a rectangle, and there is a *Rectangle* class among the choices above, the report does not need to use any attribute or behavior applicable specifically to rectangles. The smallest angle and hypotenuse attributes offered by the *Rectangle* class represent details beyond those required for a report showing simple area and perimeters of shapes. Accordingly, our report does not need to know that it is working with a rectangle to produce the information required; the *Enclosed shape* class is a sufficient level of abstraction to handle any rectangle shapes that would participate in the report.

Multiple Instantiations

Once we have established its level of abstraction, we now have a class that can act as a proxy for its real-world counterpart, offering only the level of detail applicable to the entity it represents. We also have a pattern for an entity from which multiple instances of the entity may be created. There is a word used to describe each instance of an abstraction: *object*.

This is the very foundation for the term "object-oriented" in describing both the language and the design concepts associated with object-oriented programming.

Classes define these entities. Objects are their instantiation. In this context, object means the same thing as instance of a class. In a single program there is virtually no limit to the number of objects that can be instantiated for a class. Once an object is instantiated, it becomes a concrete representation of the abstraction, because although objects of the same class all have the same attributes and behaviors according to the class definition, each object has its own unique attribute values.

While abstraction represents a conceptualization for some entity, a concretion denotes a tangible instance. Table 4-4 gives some other examples of the relationship between abstraction and concretion.

Table 4-4. *Examples of the Relationship Between Abstraction and Concretion*

Abstraction	Concretion
General	Specific
Potential	Actual
Conceptual	Tangible
Product mold	Product
Cookie cutter	Cookie
Car	My first car
Book	This copy of this book
Building	Carnegie Hall
Road	Pennsylvania Turnpike
River	Rhine
Mountain range	Andes
Continent	Antarctica
Planet	Jupiter
Star	Rigel
Galaxy	Andromeda

Relationship Between Abstraction and Encapsulation

The principles of abstraction and encapsulation have a complementary relationship. A class is an abstraction of an entity and the class encapsulates the attributes and behaviors relevant to the corresponding level of abstraction represented by the class.

Steve McConnell, author of *Code Complete*, offers an interesting perspective on this. After summarizing the concept of abstraction with the following paragraph:

> Abstraction is the ability to engage with a concept while safely ignoring some of its details – handling different details at different levels. ... If you refer to an object as a "house" rather than a combination of glass, wood and nails, you're making an abstraction. If you refer to a collection of houses as a "town," you're making another abstraction.[5]

he describes the relationship between abstraction and encapsulation with this exquisite passage:

> Encapsulation picks up where abstraction leaves off. Abstraction says "You're allowed to look at an object at a high level of detail." Encapsulation says, "Furthermore, you aren't allowed to look at an object at any other level of detail."[6]

driving the concept home with this explanation:

> Encapsulation says that, not only are you allowed to take a simpler view of a complex concept, you are *not* allowed to look at any of the details of the complex concept. What you see is what you get – it's all you get![7]

where the simple view of a complex concept is represented by an abstraction.

ABAP Language Support for Abstraction

The object-oriented extensions to the ABAP language accommodate abstraction in the following ways:

- By providing the ability to define representations for real-world entities
- By providing the capability to establish a clear level of abstraction
- By supporting the concept of creating multiple instances of a class

The same statements we saw for encapsulation also enable us to accommodate abstraction, with the construct block

```
class class_name definition [options].
  o
  o
  o
endclass.
```

providing the ability to define representations for real-world entities and establishing clear levels of abstraction through judicious selection of a class name, and also facilitating effective class cohesion by establishing the boundaries for containing the members to be included in the class.

Among the options available on the class definition are the qualifiers *abstract* and *final*. A class may have either or both of these qualifiers, and, as discussed in the section on encapsulation, when both are present it indicates a static class. As described in that section on encapsulation, the qualifier *abstract* insures that the class cannot be instantiated. It is the absence of the *abstract* qualifier that enables instances of the class to be created.

---

[5]Steve McConnell, *Code Complete*, 2nd edition, Microsoft Press, 2004, p. 89.
[6]Ibid, p. 90.
[7]Ibid, p. 91.

Another of the class definition qualifiers, the *create* qualifier, controls the creation of instances of the class. The *create* qualifier is followed by a word ascribing an instantiability level to the class and restricts the relationship an entity must have with the class for it to be able to create an instance of the class. The syntax is

```
... create [public | protected | private] ...
```

where *create private* means that only the class itself may create instances of the class; *create protected* means that only the class itself and any inheriting subclasses may create instances of the class; and *create public* means that any entity may create instances of the class. When not explicitly indicated on a class definition statement, *create public* is the default.

Notice the similarities between the words used to assign visibility levels for class members discussed in the section on encapsulation and the instantiability level available with the create qualifier of the class definition statement noted above, where object creation levels also indicate gradations from most visible to least visible. The visibility of the members of a class and the instantiability level assigned to the class are completely independent of each other. However, the same implications class friendship has upon visibility levels of class members also apply to the ability of a class to be instantiated by a friend class; specifically, the instantiability level of a class also is elevated to *create public* for its friends regardless of the actual create level assigned on its class definition statement.

In addition, the ability to create multiple instances of a class is facilitated by the use of the same class name on multiple reference variables and then creating instances of the same class into each one of these, as illustrated in this example:

```
report.
  o
  o
  o
    data        : rental_car     type ref to car
                , classic_show_car
                                  type ref to car
                , limousine       type ref to car
                , hearse          type ref to car
                .
  o
  o
  o
    create object: rental_car
                , classic_show_car
                , limousine
                , hearse
                .
```

Orienting Ourselves After Having Traversed Abstraction

So, we have made more progress on our journey from Procedureton to Objectropolis, and now, having completed our traversal through the object-oriented district known as Abstraction, we are familiar with its principles and can now converse in the dialect characteristic of the local population. The landscape in Abstraction may have some similarity with that of our home town of Procedureton, but it also offers some new exotic features. Even so, we have become familiar with the peculiarities commonplace in this district and feel confident we can orient ourselves to maneuver effectively over the terrain of Abstraction.

Refer again to the chart in Appendix A, illustrating the comparison between function groups and classes of how each one facilitates the capabilities of the principles of object-oriented programming. Rows 11 through 14 show how these two programming formats support the principles of abstraction. We can see that function groups offer some support for this principle.

Summary

In this chapter, we became more familiar with the object-oriented concept of abstraction. We learned that classes are used to represent abstractions for real-world entities and reinforced the idea that a significant difference between procedural and object-oriented design is their primary focus on processes and data, respectively. We were introduced to the concept of class cohesion, a measure of the relevance a member of a class has to all its other members. We also are familiar with two aspects associated with abstraction:

- Level of abstraction
- Multiple instantiations

We also are aware of the relationship between the principles of encapsulation and abstraction.

Abstraction Exercises

Refer to Chapter 4 of the functional and technical requirements documentation (see Appendix B) for the accompanying ABAP exercise programs associated with this chapter. Take a break from reading the book at this point to reinforce what you have read by changing and executing the corresponding exercise programs. The exercise programs associated with this chapter are those in the 102 series: ZOOT102A through ZOOT102C.

CHAPTER 5

■ ■ ■

Inheritance

The next stop on our journey to Objectropolis takes us from Abstraction to a place called Inheritance.

Let's return to Table 4-3 (from the previous chapter) to describe the relationship between the abstraction levels for Enclosed shape, Enclosed shape with at least one angle, and Rectangle, shown again here in Table 5-1.

Table 5-1. *Summary of the Members of the Three Classes*

Classes	Enclosed shape	Enclosed shape with at least one angle	Rectangle
Attributes	area perimeter	area perimeter smallest angle	area perimeter smallest angle hypotenuse
Behaviors	getArea getPerimeter	getArea getPerimeter getSmallestAngle	getArea getPerimeter getSmallestAngle getHypotenuse

All three classes have a behavior for getArea. This means that each of these classes has its own implementation for a getArea method.

Upon further consideration, we might realize that not only does Rectangle represent a specialization of Enclosed shape with at least one angle, but in fact Rectangle *is a* Enclosed shape with at least one angle, and, likewise, Enclosed shape with at least one angle *is an* Enclosed shape. Indeed, we might conclude that the implementation we provided for the getArea method of Enclosed shape would work just as well for both Rectangle and Enclosed shape with at least one angle since Rectangle *is a* Enclosed shape and Enclosed shape with at least one angle also *is a* Enclosed shape.

Accordingly, instead of writing a unique implementation for the getArea methods of Rectangle and Enclosed shape with at least one angle, we can simply copy the implementation we wrote for the getArea method of Enclosed shape over to the getArea methods of these other classes. In fact, anytime we have this kind of "is a" relationship between two classes, we should be able to copy the implementation of the method from the more general class to the more specific class. Furthermore, this also applies to attributes, so we could copy our area and perimeter attribute definitions for Enclosed shape and paste them unchanged as the area and perimeter attribute definitions for both of the other classes.

Wow, just look how much work we are able to save ourselves! Rather than writing code from scratch, we can simply copy code from the more general class definitions into those classes with the more specific definitions wherever we find this "is a" relationship. It may be difficult for some of us to contain our euphoria upon realizing this reduction in our workload upon discovering Abstraction and that its aspect of levels of abstraction offers this "is a" concept.

© James E. McDonough 2017
J. E. McDonough, *Object-Oriented Design with ABAP*, DOI 10.1007/978-1-4842-2838-8_5

Indeed, the designers of object-oriented principles also noticed this relationship and decided to implement a technique that eliminates even the need to copy the implementation code between classes related via "is a." Instead of requiring programmers to replicate code, a language technique has been devised for programmers to simply indicate that an "is a" relationship exists between classes and let the language environment make the code defined in the more general class implicitly available to the more specific class. This capability, a fundamental principle of object-oriented programming, is known as *inheritance.*

Inheritance is what enables a class to have members that are not defined within the class itself. Instead, a class indicates those other classes from which it inherits members. This allows a class to reuse functionality defined in other classes and gives rise to the concept of a *class hierarchy.*[1]

Class Hierarchy

The ability for classes to inherit some of its members from another class begets a hierarchy of classes where each class indicates the other classes from which it inherits. So, let's rework the collection of shape classes into an inheritance hierarchy, as shown Figure 5-1.

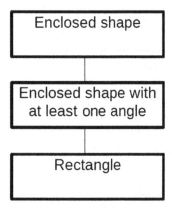

Figure 5-1. *Shape classes illustrated as an inheritance hierarchy*

In this diagram, the classes still are arranged to reflect the vertical nature of their respective levels of abstraction, with each class providing less scope and more detail as we descend from the top of the diagram to the bottom, but now the connecting line between two classes denotes that the lower class inherits from the upper class.[2] For this to occur, the lower class must indicate in its definition that it inherits from the upper class. We can now refer to Rectangle as a class inheriting from class Enclosed shape with at least one angle, and further can refer to class Enclosed shape with at least one angle as a class inheriting from class Enclosed shape.

The attributes area and perimeter, which previously had been defined for each of these classes, now can be defined only in the Enclosed shape class and their definitions inherited by both classes Enclosed shape with at least one angle and Rectangle. Similarly, the behaviors getArea and getPerimeter, which previously had also been defined for each of these classes, can now also be defined only in the Enclosed shape class and their definitions also inherited by both classes Enclosed shape with at least one angle and

---

[1]See www.ctp.bilkent.edu.tr/~russell/java/LectureNotes/10_Inheritance.htm.
[2]We will see a more formal method by which to establish this inheritance relationship in diagrams in the chapter covering the Unified Modeling Language.

Rectangle. In this hierarchy diagram, class Enclosed shape with at least one angle inherits directly from class Enclosed shape by virtue of the vertical line connecting the two blocks representing their classes, but class Rectangle inherits indirectly from class Enclosed shape because the blocks representing these two classes are separated from each other by the intervening block representing class Enclosed shape with at least one angle.

Whereas class Rectangle previously required implementing four behaviors – one each for getArea, getPerimeter, getSmallestAngle, and getHypotenuse – now we can dispense with implementations for any of those behaviors it can inherit from other classes. In this case, class Rectangle need only provide an implementation for getHypotenuse since that is the only behavior that it cannot inherit directly or indirectly from another class. Through inheritance, class Rectangle can now make use of the implementation of behavior getSmallestAngle provided by class Enclosed shape with at least one angle, and from the implementations of behaviors getArea and getPerimeter provided by class Enclosed shape.

Various word pairs are used to describe the relationship between a class that offers inheritance to other classes and a class that takes advantage of this offer of inheritance. Table 5-2 shows pairs of words where the upper word/phrase of a pair describes the class offering inheritance and the lower word/phrase describes the class that does the inheriting.

Table 5-2. *Combinations of Terms Used to Denote Inheritance*

base class	ancestor class	parent class	superclass
derived class	descendant class	child class	subclass

The pair of terms chosen to be used in design discussions is usually the one primarily associated with the particular object-oriented programming environment. Much of the literature describing C++ uses the terms *base class* and *derived class*. With ABAP, the preference seems to be for the pair of words *superclass* and *subclass*, perhaps owing to the fact that the Object Builder transaction used for defining global classes has a property tab with a slot to designate the name of the class from which this class inherits, and its title is Superclass.

Some object-oriented languages have a root base class, provided by the language itself, existing at the top of the class hierarchy from which all other classes implicitly inherit. Languages C#, Java, and ABAP all have a root base class called "object." The language Objective-C has a root base class called "NSObject." In other object-oriented languages, such as C++, there is no concept of a root base class.

Each child class is aware of its parent classes because it must indicate in its definition the names of those classes from which it inherits. Meanwhile, a parent class knows nothing about any child classes it may have. This is an important distinction because a parent class should never contain any definitions or implementations for its behaviors which presume the existence of a specific child class.

Paths of Inheritance

The relationships between classes in an inheritance hierarchy establish a path of the possible ways descendant classes can inherit from ancestor classes. There is essentially no limit to the number of levels an inheritance hierarchy can have. Each class at the bottom of an inheritance path acquires all the attributes and behaviors of all the ancestor classes in all the paths leading to it. Figure 5-2 shows the inheritance hierarchy of the collection of shape classes side by side with a set of classes defining student employee.

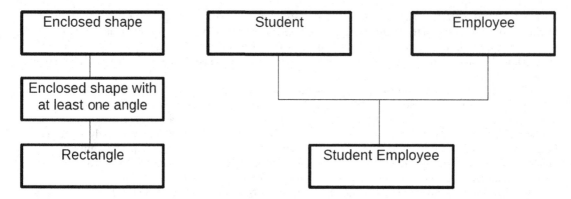

Figure 5-2. *At left is an inheritance hierarchy of the collection of shape classes; at right is an inheritance hierarchy for the set of classes defining student employee*

Once again, the hierarchy on the left shows that Rectangle "is a" Enclosed shape with at least one angle, which itself "is a" Enclosed shape, where the phrase "is a" denotes the clear inheritance path between the classes. The hierarchy on the right shows that StudentEmployee "is a" Student and also that StudentEmployee "is a" Employee.

Single Inheritance

In the case of class Rectangle, although it inherits from both Enclosed shape and Enclosed shape with at least one angle, its inheritance hierarchy is an example of *single inheritance*. Single inheritance is where each class has *one and only one* direct ancestor class. The relationship between class Rectangle and class Enclosed shape is indirect due to the intervening presence of class Enclosed shape with at least one angle in the inheritance path between them, but this still constitutes single inheritance due to the fact that all classes in the hierarchy have only one direct ancestor class.

Multiple Inheritance

In contrast, the inheritance hierarchy for class Student Employee is an example of *multiple inheritance*. Multiple inheritance occurs when a class has more than one direct ancestor class, as illustrated by class Student Employee having a direct ancestry path both to the Student class and to the Employee class.

Overriding Inherited Behaviors

As we have seen, a class inheriting from other classes will gain the functionality offered by the classes from which it inherits. Usually this is satisfactory, but occasionally we do not want to use the same implementation of a method offered by a parent class. Object-oriented languages enable us to ignore an inherited behavior and substitute a different implementation. This is known as *overriding* the behavior offered by the parent class. With method override, we indicate our intent to substitute the implemented behavior of an inherited method with a different behavior, but we are still bound to use the same signature for the method as it is defined in the parent class.

Method overriding is applicable only to *instance* methods. Whereas static methods can be inherited from a parent class, the class inheriting these methods cannot override their implementations.[3]

To illustrate an example of method overriding, suppose we have determined that the implementation for the getArea behavior implemented by the Enclosed shape class is very complicated due to the necessity to handle virtually any type of shape, and further that we have discovered that execution of this method takes its toll on computing resources as it calculates the answer. This very same implementation of getArea also is performed for class Rectangle since our class hierarchy indicates that Rectangle inherits indirectly from Enclosed shape.

Meanwhile, we know that the calculation for the area of a rectangle is simply the product of its height and width. Certainly this is much simpler than the complicated implementation for getArea we inherit from Enclosed shape. We can reduce the utilization of computing resources and improve the response time if we substitute this inherited implementation with a simple "height multiplied by width" calculation. To do this, we indicate that class Rectangle overrides the getArea method it inherits from Enclosed shape, and then we provide Rectangle with our simpler substitution implementation for calculating its area. Then, at execution time, when the getArea method of the Rectangle class is invoked, it will be the implementation of the getArea method specific to Rectangle that will provide the answer. We do not – indeed, cannot – change the signature of the getArea in any way; we simply change how to calculate the answer.

The preceding example is one where the behavior of a method inherited from a parent class is completely ignored in favor of a behavior provided by the child class. There also is the possibility that the child class not only overrides the inherited behavior but also intends to make use of it. In this scenario, the overriding implementation invokes the inherited implementation. This technique is often used to provide an implementation for a method at a more specific abstraction level with processing that includes but goes beyond the implementation provided by the parent class.

Let's see this with an example. Suppose we define a new class Hollow Rectangle, which "is a" Rectangle with some inner shape area missing, as shown in Figure 5-3.

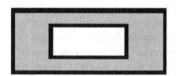

Figure 5-3. *Hollow rectangle*

We indicate that Hollow Rectangle inherits from Rectangle. Its area is the area of the outer rectangle minus the area of the inner shape, which in this case is also depicted as a rectangle. Hollow Rectangle inherits the getArea method from Rectangle, but cannot allow that method to provide the area value since it does not account for the inner missing shape. Instead, Hollow Rectangle overrides getArea and provides its own implementation for the getArea method. However, one of the things this method still needs to do is calculate the area of the outer rectangle. Here is where an overriding method would be able to invoke the implementation of this method supplied by its parent class. In this case, the getArea method of Hollow Rectangle would first calculate the area of the inner shape, then invoke the getArea method implementation provided by parent class Rectangle to get the area of the outer rectangle, and then simply subtract the inner area value from the outer area value.

[3]Although the Internet is full of discussion threads on the topic of whether or not static methods can be or should be able to be overridden, it seems that none of the more common object-oriented languages providing a static realm support this capability.

Object-oriented languages enable this capability by providing a way to explicitly invoke the method implementation defined in the parent class. In some languages, such as C++, the implementation in the child class invokes the same-named method in the parent class by qualifying the call to the method with the name of the parent class. Other languages provide a generic qualifier which serves as a reference to the parent class, such as "base" (C#) and "super" (both Java and ABAP).

Inheriting Unimplemented Behaviors

In some cases, a parent class will provide the name of a method and its signature but will not provide an implementation for the method. The intent here is that an inheriting child class will – in fact, must – provide the missing implementation. This is very similar to the case of overriding an inherited behavior, the difference here being that the parent class does not provide any implementation of the behavior to be overridden.

Indeed, methods defined in a parent class but lacking a corresponding implementation are known as *abstract methods*. Such methods must be marked abstract so the compiler will not require an accompanying implementation for them. Furthermore, a class that contains definitions for abstract methods must itself be defined as an *abstract class*. The significance of this designation at the class level is that abstract classes *cannot be instantiated*. The reason abstract classes cannot be instantiated is that they provide no implementation for any of their abstract methods.

Controlling Inheritance

In contrast to what most of us know about family genealogy, where parents choose to have children, with object-oriented inheritance hierarchies it is the child that gets to pick its parents. Accordingly, a child class indicates on its definition those classes from which it inherits. A class becomes a child class simply by naming one or more other classes as parents. This also implicitly designates the named classes as parent classes.

By marking it as a *final method,* a programmer can indicate that the method in a parent class may not be overridden by a substitute implementation in a child class. This means that any child classes must use the method as it is implemented in the parent class. This concept also applies to the class, which also can be marked as a *final class*. This means that the class cannot be used as a parent class; that is, no child classes are allowed from a class marked as final.[4]

Effects of Inheritance

The principle of inheritance casts a long shadow, causing effects upon some of the other aspects of object-oriented design we have covered already.

Effect of Inheritance upon Member Visibility

Inheritance offers classes the use of a new level of visibility that can be assigned to its members, which is more restrictive than public visibility but not as restrictive as private visibility. This level of visibility is known as *protected*. Members marked protected are visible only to the class in which the members are defined and to any child classes inheriting directly or indirectly from the class. In order for a child class to have visibility to a member it inherits from its parent class, the member must be defined *at least* with protected visibility. Those members defined in a parent class with private visibility are inaccessible to child classes.[5]

---

[4]As we will see later, the Singleton design pattern is an example of a class marked as final.
[5]Technically, a child class inherits everything from its parent class, but those members defined in the parent class with private visibility will not be visible to the child class.

As mentioned, it is commonplace for attributes of a class to have a level of visibility more restrictive than the behaviors of the class. This concept is also applicable to inheritance. A class might provide public getter and setter methods to external entities that have no visibility to the attributes of the class, an arrangement embodied by the phrase "public behaviors and private attributes." Private attributes of a parent class are not visible to a child class. It is *protected* visibility that makes inherited attributes visible to the child class at the same time keeping them invisible to external entities. This continues to conform with the idea of attributes having a level of visibility more restrictive than the behaviors of a class, but to accommodate the effect of inheritance we need to expand the visibility phrase to become "public behaviors and private *and protected* attributes."

Effect of Inheritance upon Constructor Methods

As explained previously, instance constructor methods are invoked automatically during the instantiation of an object and static constructor methods are invoked automatically upon the first encounter of a statement referencing the class. With inheritance, the constructor methods of each parent class in the ancestry path also participate. A class in the inheritance hierarchy that does not explicitly define an instance constructor method or a static constructor method implicitly will have these made available to it.

Figure 5-4 shows an example inheritance hierarchy with a maximum depth of five levels and containing classes exhibiting both single and multiple inheritance. At the lowest level we see three classes of dogs (beagle, chihuahua, and dachshund) all inheriting from class dog. Class dog, in turn, inherits both from class canine and from class domesticPet, and is the only class in this inheritance hierarchy to inherit from more than one other class. We will use this diagram to describe how the static and instance constructors of parent classes get invoked.

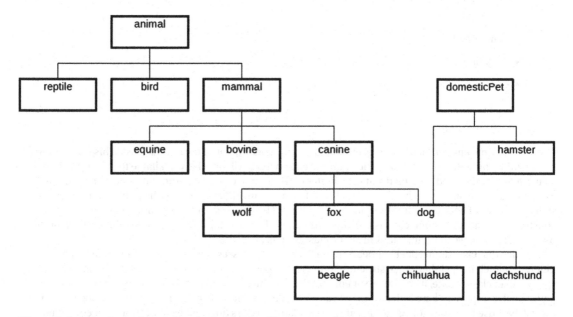

Figure 5-4. *Inheritance hierarchy where class dog illustrates multiple inheritance*

Effect of Inheritance upon Static Constructor Methods

As mentioned, a static constructor is used to initialize the static attributes of the class, does not have access to any of the instance members of its class and, because there is no specific statement that will cause a static constructor to be invoked, cannot include a method signature. Recall also that static constructors are invoked automatically by the runtime environment when a class is first accessed. Within a class inheritance hierarchy, the runtime environment insures that the static constructors of more specialized classes will be started only after all of the static constructors of more generalized classes in the hierarchy have finished.

To understand why it is necessary to delay static constructor execution until the static constructors of all superclasses have finished, let's suppose that every one of the classes we see in the inheritance hierarchy diagram in Figure 5-4 includes static attributes that span the spectrum of visibility: public, protected, package, and private. For those static attributes with public and protected (and perhaps package) visibility, the static constructor of a subclass will also have access to these attributes during its processing. These attributes will need to be initialized by their own static constructor before the static constructor of the subclass can use them effectively. Accordingly, the static constructors of a class inheritance hierarchy are executed in order from most generalized class to most specialized class for whichever classes have not yet been accessed once already. So, when a class is accessed for the first time, the runtime system will identify the names of the classes participating in the inheritance hierarchy, make a list of them, sort the list from most generalized to most specialized, and then run through the list, starting with the most generalized class, executing the corresponding static constructor, if one exists and has not yet been executed.

For example, let's say a program calls for the instantiation of a dachshund class, the class shown in the lower right of the inheritance hierarchy in Figure 5-4, and this is the first time any one of these classes has been accessed. The names of the classes participating in the inheritance hierarchy, from most general to most specific, are

- animal

- mammal

- canine

- domesticPet

- dog

- dachshund

The runtime environment will first execute the static constructor of the animal class. This is followed by executing the static constructor of the mammal class, which will now have available to it accurate initial values for the public and protected static attributes of the animal class. Then the static constructor of the canine class is executed, which will have available to it accurate initial values for the public and protected static attributes of both the animal and mammal classes. This process continues until finally the static constructor of the dachshund class is executed, which will have available to it accurate initial values for the public and protected static attributes of all the classes of its ancestry.

Notice that class domesticPet appears in the list between classes canine and dog, and represents a different branch in the inheritance structure from class dachshund. It is neither more general nor more specific than class canine, its predecessor entry in the list, since they do not share the same inheritance path. What is important here is that both the canine and the domesticPet classes precede the dog class in the list, because both are more generalized classes relative to class dog, and each of their respective static constructors must be executed prior to executing the static constructor of class dog.

For another example, let's say a program first calls for the instantiation of an equine class, and this is the first time any one of these classes has been accessed. The names of the classes participating in the inheritance hierarchy in Figure 5-4, from most general to most specific, are

- animal

- mammal

- equine

The runtime environment will execute the static constructors of the animal class, mammal class, and equine class, in that order. Subsequent processing in the same program calls for the instantiation of a fox class. Now the names of the classes participating in the inheritance hierarchy, from most general to most specific, are

- animal

- mammal

- canine

- fox

The runtime environment will execute the static constructors of the canine class and fox class, in that order. The static constructors for the animal and mammal classes will not be executed since they were already executed during the creation of the equine instance.

Effect of Inheritance upon Instance Constructor Methods

Remember that instance constructors are executed automatically by the runtime environment when a new object is being created, and because new instances of objects are requested explicitly, an instance constructor can include a method signature. Accordingly, the programmer causes an instance constructor to be executed by creating a new object.

In the previous section, it was explained how the runtime environment insures that, within a class inheritance hierarchy, the static constructors of more specialized classes will be *started* only after all of the static constructors of more generalized classes in the hierarchy have *finished*. In contrast, instance constructors of more specialized classes are started prior to the start of instance constructors of more generalized classes. In some object-oriented environments, the first action of the instance constructor must be to invoke the instance constructors of its superclasses. In other object-oriented environments, an instance constructor may perform some processing prior to invoking the instance constructors of its superclasses. C++ and Java fall into the former category where an instance constructor first must invoke its superclass instance constructors. ABAP falls into the latter category where an instance constructor may delay invoking the instance constructors of its superclasses. Regardless of which of these approaches is in effect, the same fundamental concept applying to static attributes also applies to instance attributes; specifically, a superclass needs to be able to initialize the public and protected instance attributes before a subclass can use them effectively. Indeed, an instance constructor *must* invoke the instance constructors of its superclasses at some point so that this initialization can occur.

For those environments in which an instance constructor may perform some processing prior to invoking the instance constructors of its superclasses, the programmer has control over the point at which the instance constructors of the superclasses get invoked. Until that point, the instance constructor may not make reference to any instance attributes or invoke any instance methods; its access is restricted to static attributes and static methods, parameters defined by the signature of the instance constructor, and any local variables that may have been defined within the instance constructor method. It is only upon return from invoking the superclass instance constructors when all instance attributes and methods become available to a constructor method.

Now, let's return to the famous sentence we saw in Chapter 2:

The quick brown fox jumps over the lazy dog.

To review, we determined that this sentence implies two classes, a fox class and a dog class, and further, as shown in Table 5-3 (a copy of Table 2-1 from Chapter 2), that the dog class has an attribute for alacrity, and that the fox class has attributes for alacrity and color as well as a behavior for jump.

Table 5-3. *The Beginning of an Object-Oriented Design*

Class	Fox	dog
Attributes	alacrity color	alacrity
Behaviors	jump	

Table 5-4 includes the fox class and dog class, and all of their respective parent classes based on our example class inheritance hierarchy diagram shown in Figure 5-4. Here the attributes and behaviors shown for the fox and dog classes in the preceding chart have been assigned to the most appropriate inheritance level, where the attribute for color has been renamed to furColor. Some instance attributes and behaviors that might be associated with each class also have been included.

Table 5-4. *Classes and Their Members for the Inheritance Hierarchy Described by Figure 5-4*

Class	Attributes	Behaviors
animal	height weight age alacrity	eat sleep speak
mammal		nurseOffspring
canine	furColor	run jump followScentTrail
domesticPet	petName ownerName lastVeterinarianVisit	getPetName setPetName visitVeterinarian
dog		chaseCat fetch
fox		raidChickenCoop

Further, suppose that we have decided to define an instance constructor for class animal that accommodates setting a value for its alacrity attribute, and we have decided to also define an instance constructor for class canine that accommodates setting a value for its furColor attribute, as shown in Table 5-5.

Table 5-5. *Indication of Classes Having Instance Constructors for Inheritance Hierarchy Described by Figure 5-4*

Class	Attributes	Behaviors	Instance constructor
animal	height weight age alacrity	eat sleep speak	yes
Mammal		nurseOffspring	no
Canine	furColor	run jump followScentTrail	yes
domesticPet	petName ownerName lastVeterinarianVisit	visitVeterinarian	no
Dog		chaseCat fetch	no
Fox		raidChickenCoop	no

Table 5-6 shows the complete fox and dog classes with all of the attributes and behaviors inherited from other classes as illustrated in Table 5-5.

Table 5-6. *Complete fox and dog Classes*

Class	fox	dog
Attributes	height weight age alacrity furColor	height weight age alacrity furColor petName ownerName lastVeterinarianVisit
Behaviors	eat sleep speak nurseOffspring run jump followScentTrail raidChickenCoop	eat sleep speak nurseOffspring run jump followScentTrail chaseCat fetch visitVeterinarian

In Chapter 2, we provided the following lines of pseudocode to fulfill the intent of the original statement:

```
create object fox
fox.set_color("brown")
fox.set_alacrity("quick")

create object dog
dog.set_alacrity("lazy")

fox.jump(dog)
```

This, of course, was before we understood about constructors. Now that we are familiar with the concept of constructors, we can use the following abbreviated pseudocode and get the same result:

```
create object fox("brown","quick")

create object dog(" "    ,"lazy")

fox.jump(dog)
```

Here we no longer have the statements explicitly setting the color and alacrity attributes after the instances of fox and dog have been created, but include this information with the request to instantiate these objects. This technique requires that we define constructor methods for both the fox and dog classes, which will set the instance attributes accordingly.

Consider that with this inheritance hierarchy, these attributes – alacrity and furColor (formerly simply called color) – are contributed by two different classes in the hierarchy: classes fox and dog both inherit the attribute furColor from class canine, but they inherit the attribute alacrity from class animal. Furthermore, recall that it was decided to define two instance constructors: one for class animal to facilitate setting a value for its alacrity attribute, and another for class canine to facilitate setting a value for its furColor attribute.

When an object is instantiated, it becomes an aggregation of its own attributes and methods and all of the attributes and methods it inherits from all classes in its inheritance hierarchy. In addition, all the instance constructors defined for each contributing class are executed to perform whatever actions are defined in those respective instance constructor methods. Those classes with no explicit instance constructor will have an implicit instance constructor that facilitates calling the instance constructor at the next highest level in the hierarchy, thus insuring that instance constructors defined throughout the inheritance hierarchy are executed.

In the case of the fox class, for the statement

```
create object fox("brown","quick")
```

the parameter values "brown" and "quick" are passed to the instance constructor methods accordingly. The instance constructor method for class canine would use "brown" to set the value of the furColor attribute it contributes to the new instance of fox, and the instance constructor method for class animal would use "quick" to set the value of the alacrity attribute it contributes.

Similarly, in the case of the dog class, for the statement

```
create object dog(" "    ,"lazy")
```

the parameter values " " and "quick" also are passed to the instance constructor methods. The instance constructor method for class canine would use a blank to set the value of the furColor attribute it contributes to the new instance of dog, and the instance constructor method for class animal would use "lazy" to set the value of the alacrity attribute it contributes.

We should recognize in this case that there are no instance constructor methods defined for classes fox, dog, or mammal, even though the instance constructors of their respective parent classes are executed.

This example vastly oversimplifies the interaction of instance constructors during instance creation. Each object-oriented environment has its own protocol for facilitating, during object instantiation, the call to the constructor method for each successive class in the inheritance hierarchy. There needs to be a way to pass up through the inheritance hierarchy only those values that apply to parent classes along the same line of ancestry, so that the respective instance constructor methods may perform their processing. To achieve this, each instance constructor invokes the instance constructor of its parent class.

Since the design calls for an instance constructor for class animal to set a value for attribute alacrity and an instance constructor for class canine to set a value for attribute furColor, let's use pseudocode to define a sequence of instance constructor methods that can facilitate making these settings when we create an instance of class fox:

> We indicated no instance constructor for class fox. In the absence of an instance constructor defined for a class, the runtime system will implicitly invoke the instance constructor for whatever next level in the class hierarchy provides one.
>
> The next level in the class hierarchy for which we have indicated the presence of an instance constructor is class canine, which would be defined to accept parameter values for furColor and alacrity. It would use the parameter value for furColor to set the corresponding attribute it contributes, but would in turn invoke the instance constructor of its parent class passing to it the parameter value for alacrity:

```
class canine constructor(furColor,alacrity)
   invoke superclass instance constructor(alacrity)
   set attribute furColor to parameter value furColor
```

> The next level in the class hierarchy is mammal, for which we indicated no instance constructor. Again, in the absence of an instance constructor defined for a class, the runtime system will implicitly invoke the instance constructor for whatever next level in the class hierarchy provides one.
>
> The next level in the class hierarchy for which we have indicated the presence of an instance constructor is class animal, which would be defined to accept a parameter value for alacrity, using it to set the corresponding attribute it contributes:

```
class animal constructor(alacrity)
   set attribute alacrity to parameter value alacrity
```

At the conclusion of this instance constructor invocation sequence, the instance constructor defined for each class within the ancestry hierarchy has had its chance to perform its processing. Afterward, the instance created (in this case, fox) now is in a state where it can be used.

Traversing the inheritance hierarchy of class fox shows an example of a *single inheritance* ancestry. Class fox has only one parent class (canine) which itself has only one parent class (mammal) which also has only one parent class (animal).

Class dog also follows this same ancestry path as fox, but dog also inherits from class domesticPet. This is an example of *multiple inheritance*; class dog has multiple parent classes. Consequently, when a dog instance is created, in addition to invoking the same instance constructors invoked for class fox, there is also the necessity to invoke the instance constructors of any classes in the ancestry path through domesticPet. Each object-oriented language supporting multiple inheritance has its own protocol for the sequence of invoking the instance constructors of these multiple inheritance paths. For example, in C++, the instance constructors of the multiple parent classes defined for a class are invoked in the same sequence as they appear on the definition of the class, and changing this sequence will change the order in which the instance constructors are invoked.

Effect of Inheritance upon Reference Variables

Reference variables enable a component to hold a pointer to an instance of a class. When a reference variable is defined in a program, it is associated with the type of class of which it is capable of holding a reference.[6] However, a fundamental concept in object-oriented programming is that a reference variable may hold not only a reference to the type of class with which it is associated but may hold a reference *to any type of child class inheriting directly or indirectly from its associated class*. In short, a reference variable can hold a pointer to any type of class instance as long as the instance "is a" type of class assigned to the reference.

Because of this, a reference variable has an additional quality to be considered beyond just the instance of a class to which it is pointing. This additional quality is known as the "reference variable type." There are two aspects of a reference variable type:

- Static type

- Dynamic type

Every reference variable has both of these two aspects of reference variable type. In some object-oriented languages, this concept of dynamic type is known as runtime type information (RTTI).

The *static type* refers to the type of class assigned with the definition of the reference variable. It is known as *static* because the programmer assigns a type of class to the reference variable and it will not change once the source code is compiled. Changing a static type to some other type of class requires a change to the source code.

The *dynamic type* refers to the type of class to which the reference variable is actually pointing during execution. It is known as *dynamic* because the type of class to which the reference variable is pointing may change from moment to moment during program execution. Changes to the dynamic type are a consequence of moving a pointer to an object into the reference variable.

When the type of class instance to which a reference variable is pointing at execution is the same as the one with which the reference variable is associated, then the static type and dynamic type of the reference variable are identical. When the type of class instance to which a reference variable is pointing at execution is a direct or indirect child class to the one with which the reference variable is associated, then the static type and dynamic type of the reference variable are different. Without inheritance, the static type and dynamic type of a reference variable would always be the same, and perhaps it would be unnecessary even to be aware of the concept of reference variable type. However, it is when inheritance is introduced that a dynamic type of a reference variable could be different from its static type.

---

[6]As we shall see later, a reference variable does not always need to be associated with a type of *class*, but for now we will keep it simple and limit the discussion to class references.

A fundamental concept in object-oriented programming is that a reference variable can offer access only to those members of an instance *that are defined by the class associated with its static type*. That is, the *static type* of a reference variable determines which instance members are accessible through the reference variable. Accordingly, we can define two reference variables to two different abstraction levels within the same class inheritance hierarchy, like

```
this_enclosed_shape     type enclosed_shape
this_rectangle          type rectangle
```

and then create an instance of a rectangle into the reference variable with the static type defined for class rectangle, like

```
create object this_rectangle
```

and then copy the pointer to this instantiated class to the other reference variable, like

```
this_enclosed_shape = this_rectangle
```

At this point we have two reference variables both pointing to the same instance. Whereas reference variable this_rectangle has both a static type and dynamic type of rectangle, reference variable this_enclosed_shape has a dynamic type of rectangle, but its static type is enclosed_shape. Despite that both are pointing to exactly the same instance of a rectangle, we can access the method get_hypotenuse only through the reference variable this_rectangle. Access to the members of the rectangle instance through reference variable this_enclosed_shape is limited to only those members made available by class enclosed_shape, since that is the static type of the reference variable.

Effect of Inheritance upon Subsequent Maintenance

When used intelligently, inheritance is an indispensable object-oriented principle used in the design of software. When used indiscriminately, inheritance can cause difficulties with software design and maintenance. Steve McConnell states this very succinctly:

> "Inheritance is one of object-oriented programming's most powerful tools. It can provide great benefits when used well, and it can do great damage when used naively."[7]

Of the four pillars of object-oriented programming, inheritance is arguably the one that needs to be approached with the most caution. It is tempting to define elaborate class inheritance hierarchies once programmers become aware of its power. This can lead to class relationships that in subsequent maintenance cycles become too difficult to comprehend or require significant development effort to manage effectively.

Having been introduced with the first generation of object-oriented languages, inheritance has since fallen out of favor with many object-oriented scholars who now recommend using a technique known as *composition*.[8] This is not to suggest that inheritance should not be used, but simply that it requires some discipline on the part of software designers in deciding where it is applicable. The conventional wisdom

---

[7]Steve McConnell, *Code Complete: A practical handbook of software construction*, 2nd edition, Microsoft Press, 2004, p. 92
[8]We will cover the technique of composition in more detail in the section on Design Patterns.

these days is that inheritance hierarchies should remain shallow.[9] I usually recommend to my students that three levels of inheritance are easily managed and that four levels still are acceptable, but once the hierarchy extends to five or more levels we are exposing ourselves and any subsequent maintenance programmers to potential difficulties managing and understanding the hierarchy.[10]

Meanwhile, inheritance enables writing entirely new classes that include members defined in other classes. This *reuse* of established components facilitates constructing new entities from those that already exist *without the need to change the existing entities*. Accordingly, a new class inheriting from an existing class can benefit not only from the code the parent class contributes but also from all the testing to which the parent class has already been subjected, minimizing the amount of work necessary to prepare a new subclass for use.

Effect of Inheritance upon Design

The extensive use of inheritance imposes certain constraints upon program design, including

Singleness	Inheritance is restricted to only a single superclass.
Static	Inheritance hierarchies are fixed during execution and cannot change other than by modifying code to rearrange the structure of the inheritance hierarchies.
Visibility	An entity having access to an object also has access to the members defined by its superclass.

Some object-oriented languages, among them Java and ABAP, have accommodated these design constraints as fundamental restrictions built into those languages. Neither language supports multiple inheritance, leaving singleness not so much a design choice as a design requirement. Both languages adhere to the static nature of inheritance hierarchies, but also provide support for using object composition as well. Both languages also facilitate subclass access to its superclass members by offering the *protected* access modifier for confining the visibility of some of its members only to its inheritors, avoiding the requirement for the superclass to otherwise make those members publicly visible.

Indeed, languages that lack support for multiple inheritance entirely eliminate the possibility of a classic design problem from ever creeping into software systems. Known as the *diamond problem*,[11] it occurs when a class inherits from two parent classes, where at least one of these classes overrides a method of the same class from which both inherit. It gets its name from the shape of the relationships between classes composing this type of hierarchy, as illustrated in Figure 5-5.

---

[9]Shallow inheritance hierarchies avoid what is known as the yo-yo problem.
[10]There are many tales of programmers having created deep inheritance structures that became unmanageable during subsequent maintenance cycles; this may account for why it has fallen out of favor among scholars.
[11]See "The diamond problem" section at www.geeksforgeeks.org/multiple-inheritance-in-c/.

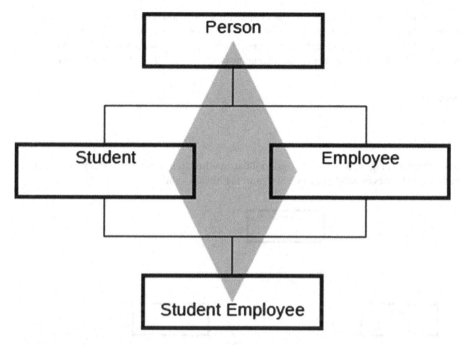

Figure 5-5. *Illustration of the diamond problem*

Here we see through the connecting lines that class Student Employee inherits both from class Student and from class Employee, and further that classes Student and Employee both inherit from class Person, and that this constitutes a diamond relationship as depicted by the gray background shape.

Suppose class Person provides both the definition and implementation for a public method called getInformation, and that class Employee overrides the implementation of this method. It now becomes indeterminate which implementation will be applicable to class Student Employee, since the original implementation provided by Person is available via its Student superclass but the overridden implementation is available via its Employee superclass. Accordingly, since they both enforce the singleness design constraint, neither Java nor ABAP succumbs to the infamous diamond problem.

Manipulating Values in Reference Variables

Since it is inheritance that introduces the possibility where the static type and dynamic type of a reference variable can be dissimilar, it is only fitting that we devote some attention to the exchange of values between object reference variables when inheritance is in effect.

Moving a value between reference variables where both source and target are defined the same way (identical static types) is a simple move where only the pointer value is copied from one to the other. After such a move, there will be (at least) two reference variables pointing to the same instance of a class.

By contrast, moving a value between reference variables where the source and target are not defined the same way (dissimilar static types) is valid only when the *dynamic* type of the source is compatible with the *static* type of the target. By compatible, we mean that the dynamic type of the source "is a" static type of the target. Such moves between object reference variables with dissimilar static types fall into one of the following three categories:

- It is never valid.

- It may be valid.

- It is always valid.

The class hierarchy shown in Figure 5-6 will be used to illustrate the circumstances under which such reference variable exchanges are never valid, may be valid, and are always valid.

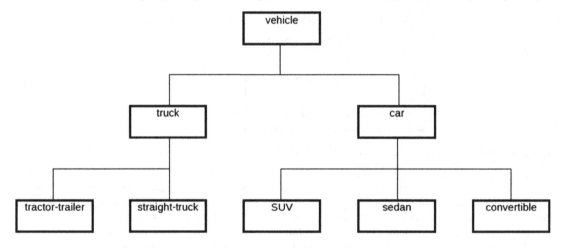

Figure 5-6. *Hierarchy used to illustrate the validity of reference variable exchange*

This class inheritance hierarchy shows a vehicle class with two child classes: truck and car. The truck class also has two child classes (tractor-trailer and straight-truck), while the car class has three child classes (SUV, sedan, and convertible).

A move between reference variables is *never* valid when the types of classes represented by the source and target reference variables *do not lie* in the same child-to-parent path in the class inheritance hierarchy. An example of this is when we have a reference variable to class car and we attempt to move it to a reference variable to class truck. Truck and car are not in the same child-to-parent path in the inheritance hierarchy. That is, we cannot start in the hierarchy at either of these classes and find the other one by moving only from a child class to its parent class. As such, a reference variable defined as type car (its static type) can never have a dynamic type that is compatible with a reference variable defined as type truck. Similar never-valid moves apply from SUV to sedan, from convertible to straight-truck, and from tractor-trailer to car for the same reason that we can never move between the two classes in the hierarchy using only a child-to-parent movement.

A move between reference variables is *always* valid when both of the following conditions are true:

- The types of classes represented by the source and target reference variables *do lie* in the same child-to-parent path in the class inheritance hierarchy.

- The target is the direct or indirect parent class of the source.

An example of this is when we have a reference variable to class car and we attempt to move this to a reference variable to class vehicle. Since vehicle is the direct parent class to car, the move is always valid. As such, a reference variable defined as type car (its static type) will always have a dynamic type that is compatible with a reference variable defined as type vehicle. Similar always-valid moves apply from sedan to car, from straight-truck to truck, and from convertible to vehicle for the same reason that we always can move from a source to a direct or indirect target using only a child-to-parent movement. A useful metaphor for keeping this straight is to understand that the move is always valid when the source "is a" target.

A move between reference variables *may be* valid when both of the following conditions are true:

- The types of classes represented by the source and target reference variables *do lie* in the same child-to-parent path in the class inheritance hierarchy.

- The source is the direct or indirect parent class of the target.

An example of this is when we have a reference variable to class car and we attempt to move this to a reference variable to class convertible. Since car is the direct parent class to convertible, the move may be valid, but it is valid only when the reference variable to class car holds a reference to an instance of class convertible. That is, the move is valid only when the *dynamic* type of the source is compatible with the *static* type of the target. Since the dynamic type of the source object reference variable cannot be known until execution, such moves require identifying the dynamic type of the source during execution to determine its compatibility with the target, and is the reason why the move *may be* valid.

Casting

When a move occurs between two reference variables with dissimilar static types, the corresponding instance to which the source variable is pointing is made available as though it were an instance of the static type of the target variable. This is known as *casting* the instance. No change takes place to the instance itself; what does change is the level of abstraction to the instance accessible through the target variable. This level of abstraction becomes either more general or more specific depending on whether the static type of the target reference variable is, directly or indirectly, a child class or parent class to the static type of the source reference variable.

This idea of casting is usually associated with a qualifier further describing the type of casting. Some programmers refer to casting by the terms *up casting* and *down casting*, which refer to the direction in the class inheritance hierarchy one traverses when moving between inheritance levels. Others refer to this as *widen casting* and *narrow casting*, which refers to a range or precision aspect associated with the different inheritance levels. Unfortunately, many explanations for the definition of these terms over the years by various object-oriented scholars have become so contradictory as to render these terms meaningless. Let's see why.

In the case of up and down casting, many have described the class inheritance hierarchy using the *tree* metaphor. With this metaphor, classes are described as having *branches* to child classes, and to move from any leaf of the tree in the direction where all branches converge is to move *down* the tree. Others have described the inheritance hierarchy as a corporate organization chart, with a president at the top and branches descending to vice presidents of marketing, manufacturing, sales, personnel, etc., with each of these having subsequent branches to other levels, eventually identifying everyone in the corporation. With this metaphor, classes also are described as having branches to child classes, but in this case moving in the direction where all branches converge is to move *up* the corporate ladder. Thus there are two opposing definitions for what is meant by up and down, generating confusion by those who use these terms.

Similarly, widen casting has been used by some to describe movement to a target class having more members than the source class, the target class offering a wider array of attributes and/or behaviors. The class with more members is the child class. Going the other direction constitutes narrow casting due to moving to a class with fewer members – to the parent class. Others use widen casting to describe movement to a target class accommodating a larger set of classes than that handled by the source class – to the parent class – and use narrow casting to describe movement to a target class accommodating only a subset of classes handled by the source – to the child class. Again, we have two opposing definitions for what is meant by widening and narrowing, continuing the confusion further.

I have chosen to abandon the terms up casting, down casting, widen casting, and narrow casting in favor of the following terms:

- *Generalizing cast*

- *Specializing cast*

One of the classes will be more specialized than the other, and it would be difficult to invert the meaning to the extent where a parent class could be considered more specialized than one of its child classes. Accordingly, moving an object pointer from a reference variable of class car to a reference variable of class vehicle constitutes a generalizing cast, since the receiving field defines a reference to a class more general than that of the source field. In contrast, moving an object pointer from a reference variable to class vehicle to a reference variable of class car constitutes a specializing cast, since the receiving field defines a reference to a class more specialized than that of the source field.

As noted in the previous section on manipulating values in reference variables, moving object pointer values between reference variables will work only when the *dynamic* type of the source variable is compatible with the *static* type of the target variable; that is, the source dynamic type "is a" target static type. Accordingly, a generalizing cast will always work because the dynamic type of the source variable always "is a" static type of the target variable. By contrast, a specializing cast may work and it may not work. When the source dynamic type "is a" target static type, then the casting move will work, but when the source dynamic type "is not a" target static type, then the casting move will fail. As such, we need to accommodate those attempts when a casting move assignment would not or does not work.

For specializing casts, each object-oriented language has its own ways of determining whether such a casting move assignment *will work* or *did work*. Java has the "instanceof" operator to test the dynamic type of the source variable against a known static type, so that it can avoid making the casting assignment when this test fails, and is an example of checking whether the casting assignment *will* work; that is, we check the assignment validity first before making the assignment. The languages C++ and ABAP provide what is known as a try-block, where the casting move assignment is embedded in a protected block of code that has *catch* clauses to intercept any exceptions *thrown* by the failure of the assignment. The applicable metaphor used here with try-blocks and catch clauses is a *ball*: when a casting move assignment fails, the try-block "throws" the ball (exception) and the catch clause "catches" the thrown ball (exception). Each catch clause identifies the type of exception(s) it is capable of intercepting. Try-blocks are not limited only to exception processing for casting move assignment failures; they are used to intercept other types of runtime failures, such as object creation failures, arithmetic failures, resource unavailable failures, etc. When used with casting, try-blocks and their catch clauses are examples of checking whether the casting move *did* work; that is, we *try* to make the assignment and then determine afterward whether it succeeded.

Metaphors for Understanding the Concept of Reference Variable Type

I have found that grasping the concept of *reference variable type* can be elusive to some programmers, due in part to describing its aspects using words like *static* and *dynamic*, words that have different meanings in other contexts of object-oriented programming. To solidify this concept, it may be helpful to use metaphors.

Postal Metaphor

The President of the United States lives in the White House. Mail addressed to the holder of this office requires something similar to the following:

> 1600 Pennsylvania Avenue NW
>
> Washington, D.C.

This would probably be enough for mail originating within the United States, but for parcels mailed from other countries, the following enhanced address might be required:

> 1600 Pennsylvania Avenue NW
>
> Washington, D.C.
>
> USA

Someday in the distant future it may be necessary to extend this address with other qualifiers, such as

> 1600 Pennsylvania Avenue NW
>
> Washington, D.C.
>
> USA
>
> North America
>
> Earth
>
> Solar System
>
> Gould Belt
>
> Orion Arm
>
> Milky Way
>
> The Universe[12]

Absurd, perhaps, but this illustrates a series of locations where each subsequent entry is more general than the one it follows.

---

[12]Preceding entries paraphrased from www.astronoo.com/en/gould-belt.html.

Recall the red brick patio analogy from the chapter on Abstraction, where the level of abstraction above the patio determined the detail we could see. Let's apply this same concept to intergalactic mail destined for the White House. First, let's sort the address qualifiers in order from most general to most specific:

> The Universe
>
> Milky Way
>
> Orion Arm
>
> Gould Belt
>
> Solar System
>
> Earth
>
> North America
>
> USA
>
> Washington, D.C.
>
> 1600 Pennsylvania Avenue NW

They are now arranged such that we can ascend from 1600 Pennsylvania Avenue NW to a higher abstraction level to see all of Washington, D.C., and from there still higher to see all of the United States, and so on, moving from a distance of 5 meters above a patio at 1600 Pennsylvania Avenue NW to 5 kilometers above, to 5 parsecs above, until finally measuring our distance above the patio in light years.

The parcel posts (mail service providers) handling postal traffic corresponding to these abstraction levels might have designations as shown in Table 5-7.

Table 5-7. *Address Qualifier and Corresponding Parcel Post*

Address qualifier	Parcel post
The Universe	Universe
Milky Way	Galaxy
Orion Arm	Galaxy sector
Gould Belt	Galaxy subsector
Solar System	Star system
Earth	Planet
North America	Continent
USA	Country
Washington, D.C.	City
1600 Pennsylvania Avenue NW	Neighborhood

In each case, the parcel post corresponds to a class capable of handling mail at that abstraction level. Each of these classes would have behaviors relevant to their abstraction levels, as indicated in Table 5-8.

Table 5-8. Address Qualifier, Corresponding Parcel Post, and Associated Behaviors

Address qualifier	Parcel post/Class	Behavior
The Universe	Universe	
Milky Way	Galaxy	Route parcel to other galaxy post of this universe. Route parcel to sector post of this galaxy.
Orion Arm	Galaxy sector	Route parcel to this galaxy post. Route parcel to other sector post of this galaxy. Route parcel to subsector post of this galaxy sector.
Gould Belt	Galaxy subsector	Route parcel to this galaxy sector post. Route parcel to other subsector post of this galaxy sector. Route parcel to star system post of this galaxy subsector.
Solar System	Star system	Route parcel to this galaxy subsector post. Route parcel to other star system post of this galaxy subsector. Route parcel to planet post of this star system.
Earth	Planet	Route parcel to this star system post. Route parcel to other planet post of this star system. Route parcel to continent post of this planet.
North America	Continent	Route parcel to this planet post. Route parcel to other continent post of this planet. Route parcel to country post of this continent.
USA	Country	Route parcel to this continent post. Route parcel to other country post of this continent. Route parcel to city post of this country.
Washington, D.C.	City	Route parcel to this country post. Route parcel to other city post of this country. Route parcel to neighborhood post of this city.
1600 Pennsylvania Avenue NW	Neighborhood	Route parcel to this city post. Route parcel to street address of this neighborhood.

The behaviors associated with each parcel post/class represent the postal capabilities available at that corresponding parcel post abstraction level. Where applicable, the behaviors accommodate moving a parcel up to the superordinate parcel post, laterally to a sibling parcel post, or down to a subordinate parcel post.

If we were to define a parcel post object reference variable associated with the class *planet*, its *static* type would be *planet* and the capabilities it could offer as services would be limited to these three:

- Route parcel to this star system post.

- Route parcel to other planet post of this star system.

- Route parcel to continent post of this planet.

Now, suppose a postal item intended for the President of the United States originated long ago in a galaxy far, far away. The intergalactic mail service facilitating postal traffic throughout The Universe would route this to the Milky Way parcel post. At this point the intragalactic mail service facilitating the Milky Way would take over and route this to the Orion Arm parcel post. It would pass through each successive, more-specific parcel post, including Earth, until it eventually reached the White House. The parcel post handling the northwest (NW) neighborhood of Washington, D.C. is at an abstraction level at which it has visibility to the detail of the roads in that neighborhood, including Pennsylvania Avenue. Meanwhile, roads (members of a neighbourhood) are at a level of detail beyond the perception of the parcel post handling Earth, which can recognize only its own star system, other planets in this star system, and continents on this planet. Similarly, continents (members of a planet) are at a level of detail beyond the perception of the parcel post handling Solar System, which can recognize only its own galaxy subsector, other star systems in this galaxy subsector, and stellar bodies orbiting the sun.

Although 1600 Pennsylvania Avenue exists as a detail in The Universe, it cannot be detected by the various parcel posts until we get to a level of abstraction close enough where this level of detail becomes visible.

Think of each parcel post as providing a virtual visor by which its mail carriers can see the detail of its own members. This visor offers visibility only to those members available through the *static* type of the parcel post. Despite handling a piece of mail with a more *dynamic* characteristic, it can provide visibility only at the level of detail the parcel post's *static* type visor permits. That is, although the parcel may indeed have a street address in Washington, D.C., a mail carrier working at the Earth parcel post cannot perceive a *city* level of detail, and so has no behavior for routing the mail directly to any city.

For a different perspective, let's suppose we have traveled the two and a half million light years from Earth to the Andromeda galaxy and have been able to establish an astronomical observatory on an earth-like planet, equipped with a telescope having the latest state-of-the-art technology available. Although we could aim the telescope toward the Milky Way galaxy, which we know has a Planet Earth with a President of the United States living in the White House at 1600 Pennsylvania Avenue NW, Washington, D.C., the magnifying power of our telescope would not enable us to perceive the Solar System, let alone Planet Earth, let alone Washington, D.C., even though we could be certain these would lie within our field of vision.

Cinematic Metaphor

Let's suppose we are involved with filming a movie titled *The Smith Family Goes To The County Fair*. The script writers have called for different *characters* to be portrayed in the various scenes, and each character plays a specific *role*. Some of the required characters and their respective roles are shown in Table 5-9.

Table 5-9. *Characters and Roles Associated with the Movie Being Filmed*

Character	Role
Edward Smith	Father of the Smith family
Margaret Smith	Mother of the Smith family
Jessica Smith	Teen daughter of the Smith family
Frederick Smith	Preteen son of the Smith family
Karen	Contestant in women's three-legged race
Susan	Contestant in women's three-legged race
William	Contestant in men's three-legged race
Brian	Contestant in men's three-legged race
Pat	Owner of vehicle on display at classic car show
Chris	Driver of vehicle in demolition derby
Shelly	Winner of pie-eating contest
Extras	Spectators at classic car show
Extras	Spectators at demolition derby
Extras	County Fair attendees

To fill these roles, we need *actors*, persons with the ability to portray a role in a movie.

Now that we have identified *character*, *role*, and *actor*, we can draw the analogy between film-making and object-oriented programming:

- A *character* in this movie is analogous to a *reference variable* in an object-oriented program.

- A *role* in this movie is analogous to the *static type* of a reference variable in an object-oriented program.

- An *actor* is analogous to the *dynamic type* of a reference variable in an object-oriented program.

This is illustrated in Table 5-10.

Table 5-10. *Relationship Between Features in Object-Oriented Programming and Features in Film Making*

Features in object-oriented programming	Analogous features in film-making
reference variable	character
reference variable static type	role
reference variable dynamic type	actor

The roles require both male and female actors as well as adult and youngster actors. Accordingly, gender and age become specific character traits required for some of the roles, and the roles have been listed in the order they require specific gender and/or age traits. The roles for the Smith family characters require both gender and age-specific traits. They are followed by roles for contestants in the women's and men's three-legged races, which require specific gender but not specific age. They are followed by roles for owners of cars in the classic car show and drivers participating in the demolition derby, which require adult age but not specific gender. They are followed by the role for the winner of the pie-eating contest as well as the roles for spectators and attendees, which require neither specific gender nor specific age, and are simply listed as Shelly (winner of the pie-eating contest) or Extras (unnamed characters filled by those who respond to a casting call to be extras in a movie).

Before we begin shooting, our casting director will assemble the names of actors and begin the task of assigning actors to roles. Accordingly, the casting director will identify which types of actors can be assigned to which roles based on the gender and age requirements of each role, as shown in Table 5-11.

Table 5-11. *Characters, Roles, and Actors Associated with the Movie Being Filmed*

Character	Role	Actor
Edward Smith	Father of the Smith family	Male adult
Margaret Smith	Mother of the Smith family	Female adult
Jessica Smith	Teen daughter of the Smith family	Female youngster
Frederick Smith	Preteen son of the Smith family	Male youngster
Karen	Contestant in women's three-legged race	Female
Susan	Contestant in women's three-legged race	Female
William	Contestant in men's three-legged race	Male
Brian	Contestant in men's three-legged race	Male
Pat	Owner of vehicle on display at classic car show	Adult
Chris	Driver of vehicle in demolition derby	Adult
Shelly	Winner of pie-eating contest	Any
Extras	Spectators at classic car show	Any
Extras	Spectators at demolition derby	Any
Extras	County Fair attendees	Any

The role (static type) *Father of the Smith family* calls for a male adult. The actor (dynamic type) assigned to play that role needs to be both male and adult. In this case, the requirement of the role (static type) and the traits of the assigned actor (dynamic type) are identical; both are *male adult*. This same concept applies to the role *Mother of the Smith family* (female adult), to *teen daughter of the Smith family* (female youngster), and to *preteen son of the Smith family* (male youngster), where the requirement for the role matches the traits of the assigned actor. For reference variables, this is similar to both its static type and dynamic type being identical.

The role of *Susan* calls for a female actor. It may be played by an adult or a youngster, so long as the actor is female. In this case, the actor will have more of a specialization than is required for the role (she will be adult or youngster), but certainly has the necessary trait called for by the role (female). As such, the role will call upon the gender of the actor but not upon the age of the actor. So, even though the role may be filled by a youngster actor, the role does not require the actor to act in any way specific to being a youngster. Accordingly, the actor has excess capacity that is not required for the role. For reference variables, this is similar to its static type being more general than its dynamic type.

Similarly, the role of *Chris* calls for an adult actor. It may be played by a male or female, so long as the actor is adult. Again in this case, the actor will have more of a specialization than is required for the role (actor will be male or female), but certainly has the necessary trait called for by the role (adult). As such, the role will call upon the age of the actor but not upon the gender of the actor. So, even though the role may be filled by a female actor, the role does not require the actor to act in any way specific to being female. Here again the actor has excess capacity that is not required for the role, and again is similar to a reference variable static type being more general than its dynamic type.

Likewise, the role of *Shelly* calls for any actor. It may be played by a male or female, adult or youngster. Again in this case, the actor will have more of a specialization than is required for the role (he or she will be adult or youngster), but certainly has the necessary trait called for by the role (any). As such, the role will call upon neither the age nor the gender of the actor. So, even though the role may be filled by a male youngster actor, the role does not require the actor to act in any way specific to being male or being a youngster. Here again the actor has excess capacity that is not required for the role, and again is similar to a reference variable static type being more general than its dynamic type.

In all of these cases, the role makes no assumption about the actor playing the part, and does not call upon the actor to behave in any way beyond the requirements of the role. Accordingly, only those behaviors offered by the role can be portrayed by the actor. For reference variables, this means that only those behaviors offered by its static type can be requested by the corresponding acting object occupying the reference variable, despite the acting object having behaviors beyond those associated with the static type.

Our casting director will also want to assign understudies to some of these characters.

In those cases where an actor is assigned to a role that requires more specialization than a role for which the actor is being considered for understudy, the casting director does not need to be the least bit cautious of possibly assigning an actor to a role they cannot fill; the understudy assignment is always applicable to a role requiring less behavior than the role already assigned. For example, the actor playing the role of Frederick Smith (preteen son of the Smith family) is assigned to a role in which gender and age already are requirements. Accordingly, this actor can be assigned as an understudy for any of the other roles that require only male (characters William and Brian) or that require neither gender nor age (character Shelly). Accordingly, the casting director could *cast* the actor playing the Frederick Smith character as the understudy to the William, Brian, or Shelly characters without having to consider whether such a casting is incompatible. This is analogous to a *generalizing* cast between reference variables; it is always valid.

In those cases where an actor is assigned to a role that requires less specialization than a role for which the actor is being considered for understudy, the casting director will need to exercise caution over possibly assigning an actor to a role they cannot fill; the understudy assignment may not be applicable to a role requiring more behavior than the role already assigned. For example, the actor playing the role of Shelly (winner of pie-eating contest) is assigned to a role in which gender and age are not requirements. Accordingly, this actor can be assigned as an understudy for the role of William (contestant in men's three-legged race) only if the actor playing Shelly is male, and can be assigned as an understudy for the role of Jessica Smith (teen daughter of the Smith family) only if the actor playing Shelly is both female and a youngster. Accordingly, the casting director could *cast* the actor playing the Shelly character as the understudy to the William or Jessica Smith characters only by first considering the attributes the actor possesses beyond the attributes required for their assigned role. When the actor playing the Shelly character is male, then he can be assigned to understudy the William character, and when a female youngster, can be assigned to understudy the Jessica Smith character. This is analogous to a *specializing* cast between reference variables; it may be valid, but it is only valid when the actor actually has the traits required for the role into which the actor would be cast.

ABAP Language Support for Inheritance

The object-oriented extensions to the ABAP language accommodate inheritance in the following ways:

- By providing a root base class - *object* - from which all other classes implicitly inherit
- By supporting the concept of single inheritance, where a class indicates its immediate parent class
- By providing class member visibility specifically intended to be accessed only by the parent class and any child classes inheriting from it
- By insuring that constructors at every abstraction level along the inheritance hierarchy are invoked in the proper sequence
- By providing the capability to override the method implementation provided by a parent class
- By providing an overriding method implementation the ability to invoke the implementation provided by the parent class
- By enabling both classes and methods to be defined as final
- By enabling both classes and methods to be defined as abstract
- By supporting both generalizing and specializing casting assignments

The indication of inheritance is placed on the definition statement for the class that does the inheriting:

```
class child_class definition inheriting from parent_class [options].
  o
  o
  o
endclass.
class child_class implementation.
  o
  o
  o
endclass.
```

When a class does not explicitly indicate a parent class from which it inherits, it implicitly inherits from class *object*.

A parent class can make members available to itself and any inheriting classes by defining these members in the protected visibility section of the parent class:

```
class parent_class definition.
  public section.
    o
    o
  protected section.
    [types ...]
    [constants ...]
    [[class-]data ...]
    [[class-]methods ...]
    o
    o
endclass.
```

The instance constructor of an inheriting class requires an explicit call to the constructor of its parent class. Until that point, the instance constructor can work with static members, parameters defined in the signature of the instance constructor, and any local variables defined within the instance constructor method, but has no access to instance members. It is only after the call to the constructor of its parent class that instance members become available:

```
  o
  o
  method constructor.
    o
    (at this point, only static members, parameters and local
     variables are available)
    o
    call method super->constructor [exporting ...].
    o
    (at this point, instance members are now avaiable)
    o
  endmethod.
```

A method implementation provided by a parent class can be overridden by the child class, optionally invoking the implementation of the parent class as part of its own processing:

```
class child_class definition inheriting from parent_class.
  public section.
    methods name_of_parent_class_public_method redefinition.
    o
    o
  protected section.
    methods name_of_parent_class_protected_method redefinition.
    o
    o
endclass.
class child_class implementation.
  method name_of_parent_class_public_method.
    o
```

```
    o
    [call method super->name_of_parent_class_public_method.]
    o
    o
  endmethod.
  method name_of_parent_class_protected_method.
    o
    o
    [call method super->name_of_parent_class_protected_method.]
    o
    o
  endmethod.
  o
  o
  o
endclass.
```

A class can indicate that it does not allow inheritors:

```
class childless_class definition final.
```

A parent class can indicate that it does not allow inheriting classes to redefine one or more of its methods:

```
class parent_class definition.
  public section.
    methods public_method final.
    o
    o
  protected section.
    methods protected_method final.
    o
    o
endclass.
```

A parent class can indicate that it cannot be instantiated:

```
class parent_class definition abstract.
```

A parent class can indicate that it does not provide an implementation for one or more of its methods, thus requiring the child class to provide an implementation:

```
class parent_class definition abstract.
  public section.
    methods public_method abstract.
    o
    o
  protected section.
    methods protected_method abstract.
    o
    o
endclass.
```

82

A casting assignment may be made from a reference variable of a more specialized class to a reference variable of a more generalized class just like any other type of assignment:

```
class generalized_class definition.
  o
  o
class specialized_class definition inheriting from generalized_class.
  o
  o
  data this_generalized_item type ref to generalized_class.
  data this_specialized_item type ref to specialized_class.
  o
  o
  this_generalized_item = this_specialized_item.
```

A casting assignment may be made from a reference variable of a more generalized class to a reference variable of a more specialized class by using the move-cast operator on the assignment statement and by embedding the assignment statement within a try-endtry block having a catch statement to intercept an exception of type cx_sy_move_cast_error:

```
class generalized_class definition.
  o
  o
class specialized_class definition inheriting from generalized_class.
  o
  o
  data this_generalized_item type ref to generalized_class.
  data this_specialized_item type ref to specialized_class.
  o
  o
  try.
    o
    o
    this_specialized_item ?= this_generalized_item.
    o
    o
  catch cx_sy_move_cast_error.
    o
    o
  endtry.
```

Orienting Ourselves After Having Traversed Inheritance

So, we have traveled yet further along the path from Procedureton to Objectropolis. Now, having completed our traversal through the object-oriented district known as Inheritance, we are familiar with its principles and can speak the language spoken by the residents in this district. Contrary to what we found with Abstraction, with Inheritance we have no recognizable guideposts or familiar terrain; everything here is new. This is a completely different landscape, having no counterpart in our home town of Procedureton. Nonetheless, we are now as familiar with this district as the residents who live here and we are capable of navigating our way around Inheritance as skilfully as those who were raised here.

Refer again to the chart in Appendix A, illustrating the comparison between function groups and classes of how each one facilitates the capabilities of the principles of object-oriented programming. Row 15 shows how these two programming formats support the principles of inheritance. We can see that function groups have no support for this principle; it is unique to classes.

Summary

In this chapter, we became more familiar with the object-oriented concept of Inheritance. We learned how classes can be arranged into a hierarchy where the definition of a class can be supplemented by content provided by a class from which it inherits, enabling us to reuse components previously defined when defining new components, and though child classes are aware of their parent classes, parent classes are unaware of any child classes they may have. We learned that although there are two types of inheritance (single and multiple) available to object-oriented environments, the ABAP language supports only single inheritance. We also learned how to override behavior implementations provided by a superclass, and that this is applicable only to instance behaviors. In addition, we are familiar with the concept of abstract methods, which require implementations supplied by subclasses, and how to indicate that a method of a class may not be overridden. Also covered were the effects inheritance has upon member visibility, constructor methods, maintenance, and some of the dangers of using inheritance indiscriminately.
A significant concept presented here is the distinction between the static type and the dynamic type aspects applicable to every reference variable, and how these aspects govern the movement of values between fields defined as instance references. Also covered was the concept of casting, with attention given to the distinction between generalizing casts and specializing casts and how to use them properly. Finally, we were presented with the postal and cinematic metaphors to help grasp the concepts associated with the static type and the dynamic type aspects of reference variables.

Inheritance Exercises

Refer to Chapter 5 of the functional and technical requirements documentation (see Appendix B) for the accompanying ABAP exercise programs associated with this chapter. Take a break from reading the book at this point to reinforce what you have read by changing and executing the corresponding exercise programs. The exercise programs associated with this chapter are those in the 103 series: ZOOT103A through ZOOT103D.

CHAPTER 6

Polymorphism

The next stop on our journey to Objectropolis takes us from Inheritance to a place called Polymorphism.

Long before the advent of object-oriented programming, the word *polymorphism* applied predominately to the fields of biology and chemistry. It means many (poly) shapes (morph) quality (ism). Applied to computer programming, it is

> "...the provision of a single interface to entities of different types."[1]

It enables us to elicit different behaviors from the same class method by controlling some aspect of the call to the method. Support for polymorphism in object-oriented languages is usually provided using one or both of the following alternatives:

- Static polymorphism

- Dynamic polymorphism

Whereas we have seen the word *dynamic* used in the context of *dynamic type*, as described in the chapter on inheritance, we have seen the word *static* used in many more contexts, primarily in opposition to the word instance, as with *static and instance members* as well as in opposition to the word *dynamic*, as with *static and dynamic type*, and now with *static and dynamic polymorphism*. Such overuse of a word runs the risk of causing confusion to those trying to learn the underlying concepts.[2]

Static Polymorphism

Static polymorphism is made available through a technique known as *method overloading*. With method overloading, a class contains multiple definitions for the same method name, but each of these definitions has a unique signature with a corresponding unique implementation. Each unique signature is different from those of the other methods of the same name either by the number of parameters or by the type of parameter.

Here is a simple example of pseudocode showing a text formatter class that has more than one definition for method advancePointer:

```
class textFormatter
  method advancePointer(a type integer, b type integer)
    return a + b
  method advancePointer(a type integer, b type integer, c type integer)
    return a + b + c
```

---

[1]https://docs.oracle.com/javase/tutorial/java/IandI/polymorphism.html
[2]Indeed, we already have seen the word *static* used as a qualifier to describe encapsulation units, constructors and destructors, classes and members of classes, realm, reference variable type, and design constraints.

© James E. McDonough 2017
J. E. McDonough, *Object-Oriented Design with ABAP*, DOI 10.1007/978-1-4842-2838-8_6

One of these advancePointer methods defines a signature accepting two integers; the other defines a signature accepting three integers. Accordingly, the advancePointer method is *overloaded* with two different signatures.

So how do we know which implementation will be executed when we invoke the advancePointer method? This is determined by the number of parameters supplied by the caller of the method, as illustrated in the following snippet of pseudocode:

```
o
o
spacesBetweenWords              type integer
positionOfThisWord             type integer
lengthOfThisWord               type integer
o
o
positionOfNextWord = advancePointer(positionOfThisWord
                                    lengthOfThisWord
                                    spacesBetweenWords)
o
o
positionOfComma    = advancePointer(positionOfThisWord
                                    lengthOfThisWord)
```

The calculation for positionOfNextWord invokes method advancePointer with three integer parameters, and so it will invoke the implementation of the advancePointer method accepting three integer parameters, whereas the calculation for positionOfComma, having provided only two integer parameters, will invoke the implementation of the advancePointer method accepting two integer parameters.

With static polymorphism, the programmer explicitly controls the method invocation by specifying matching parameters for an overloaded method. That is, the selection of overloaded method implementation to execute is made by providing on the method call whatever number and type of parameters match that variation of method signature. This means invocations of these overloaded methods are statically bound when the program is compiled, and will not change until the code is subsequently changed to alter this arrangement and recompiled. It is known as *static* polymorphism because the selected behavior cannot be changed during execution.

Many object-oriented languages support static polymorphism, among them C++, C#, and Java. ABAP does not support static polymorphism.[3]

Dynamic Polymorphism

Dynamic polymorphism is made available through a process known as *dynamic dispatch*. With dynamic dispatch, the implementation to be invoked when a method is called is determined during execution. This is achieved by accessing the implementation of the method offered by the actual instance through which the method call is being made; that is, it's made using the *dynamic type* of the corresponding object reference variable.

Dynamic polymorphism relies on *method overriding*, whereby a subclass provides its own implementation to override a method inherited from a parent class. Accordingly, it is not applicable to static methods for the simple reason that static method implementations cannot be overridden in subclasses.

---

[3]This is one of a few examples where the implementation of object-oriented capabilities in ABAP deviates from the Java model.

Dynamic polymorphism occurs when a call is made to a method of an instance addressed through an object reference variable for which its static type and dynamic type are different. Indeed, dynamic *dispatch* is used to facilitate invoking methods of instances even when the static and dynamic types of the object reference variable are the same, but dynamic *polymorphism* is at work only when they are different.

To illustrate how this works, let's use a class inheritance hierarchy describing a small collection of watercrafts, as shown in Figure 6-1. In this hierarchy, classes motorBoat and sailBoat both inherit from class boat.

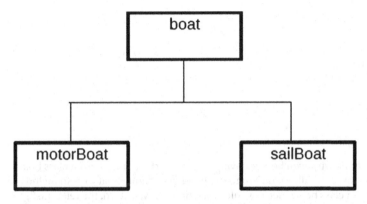

Figure 6-1. *Watercraft hierarchy*

Class boat is represented by the pseudocode shown in Listing 6-1.

Listing 6-1. Pseudocode for Class boat

```
abstract class boat
  public abstract method start
  public abstract method turnLeft
  public abstract method turnRight
  public abstract method stop
endclass
```

Class boat offers only four methods, all of which are abstract, meaning that the responsibility to provide an implementation for these methods is incumbent upon the inheriting subclasses; that is, each subclass needs to override these four methods. At first glance, we might consider the idea of inherited methods to exemplify the notion of reusing code, but we soon realize that the absence of implementations for these methods seems to nullify this advantage since we are required to provide our own implementations for every inherited method in every subclass inheriting from boat. Indeed, at this point we might be wondering why even bother having a boat class when it provides so little in the way of code reusability. This is a very good question, and if you find yourself pondering it at this moment, then perhaps the next few paragraphs will provide a convincing justification that this might actually be a good idea.

Class motorBoat is represented by the pseudocode shown in Listing 6-2.

Listing 6-2. Pseudocode for Class motorBoat

```
class motorBoat inherits from boat
  public method start
    engage propeller
  endmethod
  public method turnLeft
    rotate steering wheel counterclockwise
  endmethod
  public method turnRight
    rotate steering wheel clockwise
  endmethod
  public method stop
    disengage propeller
  endmethod
endclass
```

Perhaps by now you may be wondering why even bother having class motorBoat inherit from class boat. After all, it would seem at this point to make virtually no difference whether class motorBoat were to include or omit the indication that it inherits from class boat since it would work either way; indeed, the relationship seems frivolous and arbitrary, offering very little value to class motorBoat.

Class sailBoat is represented by the pseudocode shown in Listing 6-3.

Listing 6-3. Pseudocode for Class sailBoat

```
class sailBoat inherits from boat
  public method start
    raise sail
  endmethod
  public method turnLeft
    push tiller to right
  endmethod
  public method turnRight
    push tiller to left
  public endmethod
  method stop
    lower sail
  endmethod
endclass
```

Here again we see little reason for class sailBoat to inherit from class boat since class sailBoat gains very little from the inheritance, and represents yet another example of a frivolous and arbitrary relationship, offering very little value to class sailBoat.

Now let's use these classes in the pseudocode describing a marina, shown in Listing 6-4.

Listing 6-4. Pseudocode for Class marina

```
class marina
  public method launchMotorBoat
    thisMotorBoat                type class of motorBoat
    create new instance of motorBoat into thisMotorBoat
    call method maneuverMotorBoat(thisMotorBoat)
  endmethod
  public method launchSailBoat
    thisSailBoat                 type class of sailBoat
    create new instance of sailBoat into thisSailBoat
    call method maneuverSailBoat(thisSailBoat)
  endmethod
  private method maneuverMotorBoat(thisBoat type class of motorBoat)
    invoke behavior start     of thisBoat
    invoke behavior turnLeft  of thisBoat
    invoke behavior turnRight of thisBoat
    invoke behavior stop      of thisBoat
  endmethod
  private method maneuverSailBoat(thisBoat type class of sailBoat)
    invoke behavior start     of thisBoat
    invoke behavior turnLeft  of thisBoat
    invoke behavior turnRight of thisBoat
    invoke behavior stop      of thisBoat
  endmethod
endclass
```

This further reinforces our skepticism about the need for class boat, which now appears to be completely unnecessary as a parent class to motorBoat and sailBoat.

Notice in Listing 6-4 that for method launchMotorBoat, the static type of variable thisMotorBoat is motorBoat and its dynamic type is also motorBoat according to the next statement creating an instance of motorBoat into it. Furthermore, the next statement after that invokes method maneuverMotorBoat, which is defined with a signature, represented by the parenthetical phrase, accepting a single parameter thisBoat, defined as type class of motorBoat, denoting the static type of the parameter and requiring that the instance the caller sends must be one of class motorBoat or of some class inheriting from motorBoat. During execution, the static types and dynamic types are the same for all of them: motorBoat. Polymorphism does not apply when the static type and dynamic type are the same. This same concept also applies to method launchSailBoat and its call to method maneuverSailBoat, for which, during execution, the static types and dynamic types also are the same for all of them: in this case, sailBoat. Again, no polymorphism applies.

Meanwhile, since the same sequence of maneuvers is being performed for both the motorBoat and the sailBoat, let's consider whether or not we could consolidate some of this code. Upon closer inspection it is found that methods maneuverMotorBoat and maneuverSailBoat are identical except for the type of class each one accepts in its signature. Method maneuverMotorBoat accepts an instance of class motorBoat while maneuverSailBoat accepts an instance of class sailBoat.

Since, according to the inheritance diagram, motorBoat "is a" boat and sailBoat also "is a" boat, we can consolidate the methods maneuverMotorBoat and maneuverSailBoat into a single method called maneuverBoat defined with a signature accepting an instance of class boat, as shown in Listing 6-5, which describes the reworked marina pseudocode in which the changes required to consolidate the two methods into one are highlighted.

Listing 6-5. Pseudocode for Class marina Where Methods maneuverMotorBoat and maneuverSailBoat Have Been Consolidated into the Single Method maneuverBoat

```
class marina
  public method launchMotorBoat
    thisMotorBoat              type class of motorBoat
    create new instance of motorBoat into thisMotorBoat
    call method maneuverBoat(thisMotorBoat)
  endmethod
  public method launchSailBoat
    thisSailBoat               type class of sailBoat
    create new instance of sailBoat into thisSailBoat
    call method maneuverBoat(thisSailBoat)
  endmethod
  private method maneuverBoat(thisBoat type class of boat)
    invoke behavior start     of thisBoat
    invoke behavior turnLeft  of thisBoat
    invoke behavior turnRight of thisBoat
    invoke behavior stop      of thisBoat
  endmethod
endclass
```

Whereas the former maneuverMotorBoat and maneuverSailBoat methods had accepted instances of class motorBoat and sailBoat, respectively, method maneuverBoat accepts an instance of class boat, a more generalized level of abstraction than that required with the maneuverMotorBoat and maneuverSailBoat methods. Accordingly, method maneuverBoat can accept an instance of a motorBoat as well as a sailBoat, *but it treats each one simply as an instance of boat.*

In this reworked example in Listing 6-5, the static type of the parameter thisBoat, defined in the signature for method maneuverBoat, is now type boat. During execution, this method will be passed an instance of a motorBoat by the launchMotorBoat method, and will be passed an instance of a sailBoat by the launchSailBoat method. This means that in both cases the static type of this parameter, boat, and the dynamic type it receives, either motorBoat or sailboat, from one of the calling methods will not be the same. Accordingly, as maneuverBoat invokes the sequence of behaviors (start, turnLeft, turnRight, and stop) of the thisBoat parameter, the actual behavior will depend on whether it is working with an instance of a motorBoat or a sailBoat. For example, its call to the start method of the boat instance represented by the thisBoat parameter will result in engaging the propeller when maneuverBoat is working with an instance of motorBoat, but will result in raising the sail when working with an instance of sailBoat. This is because dynamic dispatch will locate and execute the method implementation associated with the dynamic type of the thisBoat parameter, and illustrates the very essence of polymorphism: different behaviors resulting from different executions of the same fragment of code.

Perhaps now we understand the value conferred upon classes motorBoat and sailBoat by inheriting from class boat. Instances of motorBoat and sailBoat can be regarded simply as instances of boat. When we first saw the definition of class boat in Listing 6-1 we were skeptical of its importance because it offered so little in the way of code reuse. We had similar reactions when we saw how little the boat class improved upon the motorBoat (Listing 6-2) and SailBoat (Listing 6-3) classes, each of which indicated inheriting from boat. We drew this conclusion based solely on the perceived notion that the value for creating a class is in its ability to contribute to *code reuse*. But now, with the benefits of polymorphism drawn into full focus for us, it becomes clear that there are other reasons for defining classes beyond just the advantages offered by code reusability. Indeed, the power of polymorphism lies in the ability to regard a class instance at an abstraction level more general than the level of abstraction at which it is defined.

To reflect upon how dynamic polymorphism applies to some of the other levels of abstraction we have already explored,

- A rectangle and an enclosed shape with at least one angle each can be regarded simply as an enclosed shape.

- A dog and a fox each can be regarded simply as a mammal.

- A mammal and a reptile each can be regarded simply as an animal.

- A convertible and a sedan each can be regarded simply as a car.

- A convertible and a truck each can be regarded simply as a vehicle.

- A male adult, female adult, male youngster, and female youngster all can be regarded simply as a winner of a pie-eating contest.

This ability to regard an instance of a class as though it were defined at a higher level of abstraction than it actually is defined represents a fundamental characteristic of object-oriented environments, presenting a new dimension to programming and offering a profound advancement in software design beyond the capabilities available to procedural environments.

Eliminating Conditional Logic

Compare the classes shown in the preceding listings with the equivalent procedural pseudosubroutines that might be required for maneuvering boats, shown in Listing 6-6.

Listing 6-6. Procedural Subroutine Code Equivalent to Classes

```
form start
  case boat_type
    when motor_boat
      engage propeller
    when sail_boat
      raise sail
  endcase
endform

form turn_left
  case boat_type
    when motor_boat
      rotate steering wheel counterclockwise
    when sail_boat
      push tiller to right
  endcase
endform

form turn_right
  case boat_type
    when motor_boat
      rotate steering wheel clockwise
    when sail_boat
      push tiller to left
  endcase
endform
```

```
form stop
  case boat_type
    when motor_boat
      disengage propeller
    when sail_boat
      lower sail
  endcase
endform
```

Each subroutine facilitates a boat maneuvering behavior, and every one of them contains conditional logic for determining the specific action to take based on the type of boat to be maneuvered. The equivalent classes required no conditional logic because each of the classes inheriting from class boat implicitly designated the type of boat to be maneuvered, rendering any checking of the type of boat to maneuver completely unnecessary![4] Accordingly, polymorphism facilitates what Horst Keller and Sascha Krüger refer to as *case-less programming*.[5]

Effect of Polymorphism upon Subsequent Maintenance

Frequently we find such procedural processes designed to rely on conditional programming scattered throughout different components, testing some condition for a specific value in order to determine the correct processing to apply at that point, and often this is implemented through a cascade condition, where a sequential series of tests determine which one of a multitude of possible options is the correct one. Such proliferation of conditional logic makes the task of maintenance that much harder when some new feature needs to be implemented.

For the scenario described above, let's consider for a moment the impact upon the code if we were given a maintenance task to introduce a new type of boat: a row boat. The procedural subroutines would all need to change to facilitate the new type of boat, as shown in Listing 6-7 where differences from Listing 6-6 are highlighted.

Listing 6-7. Procedural Subroutines to Facilitate a New Type of Boat, with Differences from Listing 6-6 Highlighted

```
form start
  case boat_type
    when motor_boat
      engage propeller
    when sail_boat
      raise sail
    when row_boat
      pull both oars
  endcase
endform
```

---

[4]One could argue that we could define these subroutines specific to the type of boat to be maneuvered, such as start_motor_boat and turn_sail_boat_right, but that only shifts to the caller the location of the conditional logic to make the determination of both the type of boat and its maneuver.

[5]Horst Keller and Sascha Krüger, *ABAP Objects: An Introduction to Programming SAP Applications*, Addison Wesley, 2002, p.294.

```
form turn_left
  case boat_type
    when motor_boat
      rotate steering wheel counterclockwise
    when sail_boat
      push tiller to right
    when row_boat
      pull right oar while dragging left oar
  endcase
endform

form turn_right
  case boat_type
    when motor_boat
      rotate steering wheel clockwise
    when sail_boat
      push tiller to left
    when row_boat
      pull left oar while dragging right oar
  endcase
endform

form stop
  case boat_type
    when motor_boat
      disengage propeller
    when sail_boat
      lower sail
    when row_boat
      push both oars
  endcase
endform
```

In each case we altered the subroutine handling a specific boat maneuvering action to include a new type of boat to maneuver. By contrast, the corresponding object-oriented change requires only the definition of a new class inheriting from class boat, as shown in Listing 6-8.

Listing 6-8. New Class to Handle New Type of Boat

```
class rowBoat inherits from boat
  public method start
    pull both oars
  endmethod
  public method turnLeft
    push right oar while dragging left oar
  endmethod
  public method turnRight
    push left oar while dragging right oar
  public endmethod
  method stop
    push both oars
  endmethod
endclass
```

Here the object-oriented version in Listing 6-8 required 14 lines of code, compared with the 8 lines added to the procedural subroutines shown in Listing 6-7. There are those who would point to this difference in new lines and proclaim the procedural programming paradigm superior to object-oriented due to the fewer lines of code required for this maintenance task. However, a closer look reveals other, perhaps more important, benefits with the object-oriented approach:

- Whereas the extra lines of procedural code were distributed across four different existing subroutines, all of the new code required with the object-oriented approach was contained within a single new class.

- Whereas the extra lines of procedural code all were conditional statements, none of the object-oriented code required any conditional statements.

Indeed, not only did the object-oriented approach have no conditional logic prior to the maintenance effort, as shown in Listings 6-2 and 6-3, neither was any required for the additional maintenance to implement the new feature as shown in Listing 6-8. Compare this with the procedural approach shown in Listing 6-7, which not only had conditional logic prior to the changes, but resulted in increasing the amount of conditional statements to facilitate the new feature. At some point in the future, the continued maintenance required with the procedural approach would spiral out of control and result in brittle software that is difficult to maintain. This example clearly illustrates the distinction between a procedural design, with its focus on managing the process, and an object-oriented design, with its focus on manging the data.

Using a more fitting example of code we are likely to find in the real world, suppose we are working at Seven Seas Forwarding Company, a corporation facilitating the movement of international cargo via ocean-going vessels. One of the programs of the software package supporting the everyday business activities at this corporation prints shipping paperwork to accompany the cargo to be shipped. Part of preparing this paperwork includes determining the following:

- The language spoken at the receiving port

- The cost to ship the cargo

- Any additional import tariffs imposed by the receiving port country

- The gross weight of the cargo

- Container placards

Listing 6-9 shows the pseudocode for a typical cascade condition for determining the language spoken at the receiving port.

Listing 6-9. Example of Cascade Condition for Determining Language

```
if receivingPort is "Melbourne" or "New Orleans" or ...
  paperworkLanguage = "English"
else
  if receivingPort is "Le Havre" or "Majunga" ...
    paperworkLanguage = "French"
  else
    if receivingPort is "Santos" or "Lisbon" ...
      paperworkLanguage = "Portuguese"
    else
      if receivingPort is ...
        o
        o
        o
execute printPaperwork(paperworkLanguage)
```

Listing 6-10 shows a cascade condition for determining the unit of measure in which to express the gross weight of the cargo.

Listing 6-10. Example of a Cascade Condition for Determining Applicable Unit of Measure

```
if receivingCountry is "United States" or "Liberia"
  grossWeightUnit = "pound"
else
  if receivingCountry is "Myanmar"
    grossWeightUnit = "peittha"
  else
    grossWeightUnit = "kilogram"

execute calculateGrossWeight(grossWeightUnit)
```

Most of us have encountered code exhibiting similar constructions, though often far more complicated than these simple examples, which also could be solved using simple configuration techniques. The problem with such cascading conditions, aside from their difficulty to easily discern as they get longer and longer, is that they are often scattered among different components, and when a change needs to be applied, such as including a receiving port where a new language is spoken or adding a receiving country where a different unit of measure is used, it often requires adjustments to be made in multiple locations. Worse, every one of these changed locations presumably had been working correctly until the new change was introduced, so it now would require retesting every one of these changed locations, triggering all formerly existing conditions along with all the new conditions.

We can avoid this maintenance headache if we create a class that can define the methods required, such as printPaperwork and calculateGrossWeight as shown in the pseudocode of Listings 6-9 and 6-10, but leave the implementation up to subclasses. This way we can instantiate a subclass written specifically to handle the destination port and eliminate all the conditional logic that would otherwise be required in scattered locations, as in the ABAP example shown in Listing 6-11.

Listing 6-11. ABAP Code for a Subclass Supplying Implementation for Abstract Methods

```
class destination_port definition.
  public section.
    o
    o
    methods     : print_paperwork abstract
                    importing
                      target_language
                        type language
                  , calculate_gross_weight abstract
                    importing
                      weight
                        type quantity
                      gross_weight_unit
                        type weight_unit
                    exporting
                      gross_weight
                        type quantity
                  .
endclass.
```

```
class destination_port_new_orleans definition
                               inheriting from destination_port.
  public section.
    o
    o
    methods      : print_paperwork redefinition
                 , calculate_gross_weight redefinition
                 .
  private section.
    constants    : gross_weight_unit
                              type mass_unit value 'pound'
                 , paperwork_language
                              type language  value 'English'
                 .
endclass.
    o
    o
```

Now we can create an instance of a destination_port_new_orleans into a reference variable of type destination_port, and invoke its methods, which will not require any conditional logic to determine the language spoken at the receiving port, cost to ship the cargo, any additional import tariffs imposed by the receiving port country, gross weight of the cargo, or container placards, because these conditions are implicit in the implementation of the class itself. The only time we need conditional logic is for determining which subclass of class destination_port to instantiate; once instantiated, we no longer need all of the scattered conditional logic otherwise required to determine the associated processing to apply. This means, among other things, we no longer need to change working logic scattered throughout the code just to include one additional receiving port, simplifying not only the task of finding these locations and applying the correct changes there but also avoiding the necessity for testing components that now don't need to change.

Accordingly, one of the most significant benefits of polymorphism is the way it eliminates the need for introducing more and more conditional programming during maintenance cycles, leaving the code in a state where it can withstand repeated maintenance cycles without requiring excessive effort to understand or change.

ABAP Language Support for Polymorphism

The object-oriented extensions to the ABAP language accommodate polymorphism in the following ways:

- By accommodating dynamic polymorphism (dynamic dispatch)
- By supporting abstract methods
- By providing for redefinition of inherited method implementations

There are no specific statements for facilitating polymorphism.[6] It occurs as a consequence of providing implementations for methods of a class that inherits these method definitions from a superclass,[7] and then references an instance of the class as though it were an instance of its superclass.

---

[6]We might consider the word *redefinition,* qualifying a methods statement of a subclass definition, as a word enabling polymorphic behavior; however, this qualifier may also be used in the absence of polymorphism.
[7]We shall see in a subsequent chapter that such method definitions can be provided in ways other than just through inheritance.

Orienting Ourselves After Having Traversed Polymorphism

We have passed the point of no return on our journey from Procedureton to Objectropolis, and now, having completed our traversal through the object-oriented district known as Polymorphism we are familiar with its principles and now are fluent in the language spoken by its residents. Now, it is onward to Objectropolis or bust!

As we found with Inheritance, Polymorphism also offers no recognizable guideposts or familiar terrain; this is a foreign landscape with no counterpart in our home town of Procedureton. Nonetheless, we are now as familiar with this district as the residents who live here and we are as capable as the native population in navigating our way around Polymorphism.

Refer again to the chart in Appendix A, illustrating the comparison between function groups and classes of how each one facilitates the capabilities of the principles of object-oriented programming. Row 16 shows how these two programming formats support the principles of polymorphism. We can see that function groups offer no support for this principle; it also is unique to classes.

Summary

In this chapter, we became more familiar with the object-oriented concept of polymorphism. We learned there are two kinds of polymorphism, static and dynamic, and that only dynamic polymorphism applies to the ABAP language through a process known as dynamic dispatch. We learned that a significant reason for using polymorphism is to reduce the conditional logic we might otherwise require, having the beneficial effect of simplifying our maintenance efforts since such conditional logic no longer becomes scattered across multiple objects.

Polymorphism Exercises

Refer to Chapter 6 of the functional and technical requirements documentation (see Appendix B) for the accompanying ABAP exercise programs associated with this chapter. Take a break from reading the book at this point to reinforce what you have read by changing and executing the corresponding exercise programs. The exercise programs associated with this chapter are those in the 104 series: ZOOT104A and ZOOT104B.

■ ■ ■

CHAPTER 7

Interfaces

The next stop on our journey to Objectropolis takes us from Polymorphism to a place called Interfaces.

The term *interface* has multiple meanings within the data processing industry. The ubiquitous GUI interface enables people to interact with a software system. Many ABAP programmers are familiar with the acronym RICEF, in which the "I" represents Interfaces and most often is associated with data exchanges with external systems. The signature for function modules is known as its interface. With such ambiguity already associated with this word, it is unfortunate that the word also has a specific meaning in the object-oriented programming context. The word *interface* is qualified sometimes as an *independent interface*[1] to distinguish it from all these other contexts, where its modifier *independent* denotes that the interface is not associated with a GUI, or a process for exchanging data with an external system or for specific signature recognition of function modules, but simply that it is independent, disconnected from any specific use.

Supplementing Public Visibility of Classes

Interface is a description of a feature available in some but not all object-oriented programming environments, and it is one available to both Java and ABAP environments. In the object-oriented context, an interface is a set of *definitions* for data types, constants, and/or methods that can be used by a class as a supplement to its own public visibility. Just as a class can indicate that it inherits from another class, a class similarly can indicate that it uses an interface. A class using an interface is said to *implement* the interface. This concept of implementing an interface arises mostly from the fact that, unlike a class, an interface containing method definitions provides no implementation for those methods, each of which is defined in the interface only to establish the name of the method and its signature. It is the responsibility of the class implementing the interface to provide implementations for every method defined by the interfaces it uses.

Indeed, those methods defined by an interface used by a class *must* be implemented by the class. This is similar to the idea that abstract methods defined in parent classes *must* be implemented by the child classes inheriting from them.

In many ways, an interface definition is similar to a class definition; however, with interface there is no concept of a visibility level for its members, since all members contributed by an interface to a class implicitly have public visibility. Often programmers will assign names to interfaces to denote the new capability that it confers upon a class implementing it. These names frequently end with the suffix "able" (or its cousin "ible").

I am often asked by students why an interface contributes only members with public visibility. Why, they ask, can the class implementing the interface not define implementations for its methods with protected or private visibility? This is a good question. The answer is that the use of interfaces is a

---

[1] It also is known as a "stand-alone interface."

proclamation by the class to other external entities for the types of members it offers *publicly*. Accordingly, all of these other entities can rely on implementations provided by the class to be publicly accessible. For a class to proclaim it implements an interface and then to provide any one of the implementations of the interface's methods with private visibility means the external users of the class would not have access to all the capabilities afforded by the interface. In effect, implementing an interface is a declaration by the class that it is making *all* of the members of the interface accessible to external entities.[2] We will see later in the section on Design Patterns a pattern where multiple classes implementing the same interface are considered interchangeable. Accordingly, we cannot have each class deciding for itself which interface members it will make publicly available, lest they would no longer be interchangeable.

Let's see an example of an interface that provides definitions for attributes and methods to facilitate fuel consumption. The name of this interface is fuelConsumable and it provides the following public data types for use by those classes implementing it:

consumptionRate	type integer
consumptionUnit	type unit of measure
fuelUnit	type unit of measure
fuelType	type string
fuelQuantity	type integer
remainingFuelPercentage	type decimal (five digits representing nnn.nn)
remainingConsumptionUnits	type integer

The fuelConsumable interface defines these data types but not the actual data fields themselves, leaving to the class the responsibility to define corresponding attributes. Accordingly, the class can use the data types from the interface to define the attributes while at the same time retaining control over their visibility. Had the interface itself defined the actual data fields, then they would be publicly visible. By having the interface define only the types of data and relegating to the class the responsibility to define the data fields, the class can now assign these attributes a visibility level other than public.

The fuelConsumable interface also provides the following public setter methods associated with specific attributes, where the type of data to be exchanged is shown in parenthesis following the method name:[3]

setConsumptionRate(consumptionRate)

setConsumptionUnit(consumptionUnit)

setFuelUnit(fuelUnit)

setFuelType(fuelType)

setFuelCapacity(fuelQuantity)

setFuelLevel(fuelQuantity)

---

[2]It is for this reason that I hesitate to include the definitions of variables in the set of components offered by an interface, since they would be publicly visible, hence modifiable by external entities. Although not technically prohibited, the inclusion of variables in interface definitions should be avoided by programmers not wanting to violate the principles of encapsulation.

[3]The format of invoking a method as shown here is intended to be language independent, but closely resembles the format found with both Java and ABAP.

plus the following public getter methods associated with specific attributes:

getConsumptionRate(consumptionRate)

getConsumptionUnit(consumptionUnit)

getFuelUnit(fuelUnit)

getFuelType(fuelType)

getFuelCapacity(fuelQuantity)

getFuelLevel(fuelQuantity)

and the following methods which have no single associated attribute:

calculatePercentageFuelRemaining(remainingFuelPercentage)

estimateFuelExhaustion(remainingConsumptionUnits)

An interface will often provide the data types it uses for parameters in the signatures of the methods it also defines, as we see in the fuelConsumable interface which defines the data type remainingFuelPercentage used with the signature of method calculatePercentageFuelRemaining. This way the caller of those methods can define corresponding parameter exchange fields in terms of the data types defined by the interface. In addition, an interface may provide constants defined using those data types, so that callers of those methods will have predefined and descriptive constants to be used as compatible signature parameter values passed into the methods.

Suppose class Car is defined to implement the fuelConsumable interface. This means that Car *must* provide implementations for all 14 methods defined by the interface. A simple approach to this is to define private attributes in the Car class to correspond to each of the "set" methods contributed by the interface, using data types defined by the interface. Then, the implementation of each set method will copy the value from the method parameter to the private attribute of the class. Each get method will do the reverse of its corresponding set method, copying the value from the private attribute of the class to the method parameter.

Finally, the method calculatePercentageFuelRemaining will return the value for the following expression:

remainingFuelPercentage = currentFuelLevel * 100 / fuelCapacity

The method estimateFuelExhaustion will return the value for the following expression:

remainingConsumptionUnits = currentFuelLevel * consumptionRate

Based on this, Listing 7-1 shows some pseudocode for a program to track the fuel consumption of a car.

Listing 7-1. Pseudocode to Track the Fuel Consumption of a Car

```
unused_fuel_capacity    type fuelConsumable.remainingFuelPercentage
remaining_consumption   type fuelConsumable.remainingConsumptionUnits
consumption_unit        type fuelConsumable.consumptionUnit
this_car                type reference to class car

create new instance of car object into this_car
invoke behavior setConsumptionRate     of this_car with "30"
invoke behavior setConsumptionUnit     of this_car with "Miles"
invoke behavior setFuelUnit            of this_car with "Gallon"
invoke behavior setFuelType            of this_car with "Gasoline"
invoke behavior setFuelCapacity        of this_car with "14"
invoke behavior setFuelLevel           of this_car with "05"
    o
```

```
        o
        o
invoke behavior calculatePercentageRemainingFuel
                                of this_car
                                with unused_fuel_capacity
invoke behavior estimateFuelExhaustion of this_car
                                with remaining_consumption
invoke behavior getConsumptionUnit      of this_car
                                with consumption_unit
display "this_car unused fuel capacity :"
       , unused_fuel_capacity
       , "%"
display "this_car remaining consumption:"
       , remaining_consumption
       , consumption_unit
```

The result of executing this program is the following lines:

```
this_car unused fuel capacity : 36 %
this_car remaining consumption: 150 Miles
```

Let's expand on this idea. Table 7-1 shows an example of the attribute values associated with some additional classes implementing the fuelConsumable interface after the program instantiating them has executed to the point of having invoked the various set methods to set values for all the corresponding attributes associated with fuel consumption defined by each class.

Table 7-1. *Attribute Values Associated with Classes Implementing the fuelConsumable Interface*

	Interface attributes					
Class implementing interface	Consumption rate per 1 fuel unit	Consumption unit	Fuel unit	Fuel type	Capacity in fuel unit	Current level in fuel unit
Car	30	Miles	Gallon	Gasoline	14	5
Truck	6	Miles	Gallon	Diesel	300	200
Cabin	2	Weeks	Cord	Wood	8	8
Cell Phone	60	Minutes	Milli-amp hour	Electricity (Lithium ion battery)	720	120
Gas Grill	91,500	BTU	Gallon	Propane	20	5
Coal-Fired Power Plant[4]	4	Seconds	Ton	Coal	1,296,000	648,000

---

[4]The attribute values shown for this entry represent those for the Navajo Generating Station near Page, Arizona, which consumes about 8 million tons of coal per year. Accordingly, its values shown for capacity in fuel unit and current level in fuel unit represent a 60-day and 30-day supply, respectively.

The column titled "Class implementing interface" describes the type of class that implements the fuelConsumable interface. Subsequent columns represent values for the attributes defined in the class, using the corresponding data types defined by the interface, for tracking fuel consumption. In each case, the corresponding class provides implementations for each of the methods defined by the interface. For our simple example here, the get and set methods can be implemented in each class similarly to how we saw them implemented for the Car class shown in Listing 7-1, with each set method setting the value for its corresponding attribute of the class and each get method getting the value for its corresponding attribute of the class. Indeed, the implementations for methods calculatePercentageFuelRemaining and estimateFuelExhaustion for each of these classes can use the very same implementation as defined for the Car class.

Interface Reference Variables

At this point, it may occur to us that there seems to be no advantage to using an interface; we could have provided all of these fuel consumption attributes and methods directly for these classes. After all, we had to provide an implementation for every method, so we did not gain much in the way of reusing code. While all of this is true, it overlooks one of the most powerful capabilities that interfaces provide for object-oriented programming, which is this:

- As with class, an interface may be defined as the data type defined for a reference variable.

Just as we can define a variable with type reference to a class, we can also define a variable with type reference to an interface. When we do, the corresponding interface reference variable may hold a reference to an instance of any class implementing the interface. A class may define members beyond those defined by the interface; however, when the instance of the class is accessed via an interface reference variable, only those members of the class defined by the interface are accessible.

With only class reference variables, we would need to define six different variables to hold references to the Car, Truck, Cabin, Cell Phone, Gas Grill, and Coal-Fired Power Plant of the preceding chart. By contrast, we could define a single variable as type reference to fuelConsumable and have it hold a reference to any one of the six classes implementing the fuelConsumable interface.

Listing 7-2 shows the pseudocode we saw in Listing 7-1 altered to use an interface reference variable instead of a class reference variable, with differences from Listing 7-1 highlighted.

Listing 7-2. Pseudocode Using an Interface Reference Variable, with Differences from Listing 7-1 Highlighted

```
unused_fuel_capacity    type fuelConsumable.remainingFuelPercentage
remaining_consumption   type fuelConsumable.remainingConsumptionUnits
consumption_unit        type fuelConsumable.consumptionUnit
this_fuel_consumer      type reference to interface fuelConsumable

create new instance of car object into this_fuel_consumer
invoke behavior setConsumptionRate    of this_fuel_consumer with "30"
invoke behavior setConsumptionUnit    of this_fuel_consumer with "Miles"
invoke behavior setFuelUnit           of this_fuel_consumer with "Gallon"
invoke behavior setFuelType           of this_fuel_consumer with "Gasoline"
invoke behavior setFuelCapacity       of this_fuel_consumer with "14"
invoke behavior setFuelLevel          of this_fuel_consumer with "05"
    o
    o
    o
```

```
invoke behavior calculatePercentageRemainingFuel
                              of this_fuel_consumer
                                with unused_fuel_capacity
invoke behavior estimateFuelExhaustion of this_fuel_consumer
                                with remaining_consumption
invoke behavior getConsumptionUnit      of this_fuel_consumer
                                with consumption_unit
display "this_fuel_consumer unused fuel capacity :"
     , unused_fuel_capacity
     , "%"
display "this_fuel_consumer remaining consumption:"
     , remaining_consumption
     , consumption_unit
```

As indicated by the highlighting, we only renamed variable this_car to this_fuel_consumer and changed its definition from "reference to class car" to "reference to interface fuelConsumable." Nothing else needs to change.

Notice we are creating an instance of class car into the variable defined as reference to interface fuelConsumable with the statement:

```
create new instance of car object into this_fuel_consumer
```

Interfaces and Polymorphism

The concept of static type and dynamic type is applicable to interface reference variables in exactly the same way it is applicable to class reference variables. The static type of a reference variable is whatever entity follows it in its definition, which in the case of this_fuel_consumer is "type (reference to) interface fuelConsumable." Its dynamic type becomes "type (reference to) class car" when we create a car instance into this interface reference variable as shown in the statement above. We saw in the chapter on inheritance, where we specified that the car class inherits from the vehicle class, that because car "is a" vehicle it is permissible for a reference to a car object to occupy a vehicle class reference variable. The same concept applies to interfaces, where we say that a class "implements a" interface, such as in this case where the car class "implements a" fuelConsumable interface. Since car "implements a" fuelConsumable, it is permissible for a reference to a car object to occupy a fuelConsumable interface reference variable.

Accordingly, it should come as no surprise that since the static type and dynamic type of an interface reference variable can be different, when they *are* different, then polymorphism is at work. Indeed, with references to interfaces we will find that the static type and dynamic type are *always* different because we cannot create instances of interfaces, but only instances of classes implementing those interfaces. Recall that with polymorphism, the actual method executed for a reference variable is determined at runtime through the technique known as dynamic dispatch. As such, it is at runtime, when the fuelConsumable interface variable is found to be holding a reference to a car instance, that the statement

```
invoke behavior estimateFuelExhaustion of this_fuel_consumer
                                with remaining_consumption
```

will determine it is the implementation of this method in the *car* instance that is to be invoked.

The interface reference variable enables access only to those members of an implementing class that are defined by the interface. So even though our car instance may have methods defined specifically for the car, such as start, stop, accelerate, and turn, these methods are not accessible through the fuelConsumable interface reference variable. This applies equally to all of the other classes implementing fuelConsumable.

A truck class may have defined for it methods load and unload, a cabin class may have methods open_chimney_flue_damper and close_chimney_flue_damper, a cell phone may have method redial, a gas grill may have method adjust_gas_flow, and coal-fired power plant may have method shutdown, but none of these methods are available via a reference variable defined as type reference to fuelConsumable.

In the chapter on polymorphism we saw an example of using a superclass, boat, composed entirely of abstract methods, inherited by classes motorBoat and sailBoat (Listings 6-1 through 6-3). Such a superclass would be a good candidate for definition as an interface instead of a class. Let's examine the implications of this using the same example, but where boat is now defined as an interface.

First, let's change the boat definition from abstract class to interface, as shown in Listing 7-3.

Listing 7-3. Boat Changed from Abstract Class to Interface, with Differences from Listing 6-1 Highlighted

```
interface boat
                method start
                method turnLeft
                method turnRight
                method stop
endinterface
```

The difference between this pseudocode and its superclass counterpart, as indicated by the highlighting, is that we have replaced *abstract class* with *interface* and *endclass* with *endinterface*. Also, we have removed the method qualifiers *public* and *abstract*; both of these qualifiers are implicit in an interface, which always confers public visibility to its members implemented by a class (so no need for the *public* visibility qualifier) and provides no implementations for its methods (so no need for the *abstract* qualifier).

Our motorBoat class from Listing 6-2 no longer inherits from the boat class, but as shown in Listing 7-4 now implements the boat interface and provides an implementation for every method defined by the boat interface just as it needed to provide one for every method defined by boat when it was defined as an abstract class.

Listing 7-4. motorBoat Class Changed from Inheriting from a Superclass to Implementing an Interface, with Differences from Listing 6-2 Highlighted

```
class motorBoat implements boat
  public method start
    engage propeller
  endmethod
  public method turnLeft
    rotate steering wheel counterclockwise
  endmethod
  public method turnRight
    rotate steering wheel clockwise
  endmethod
  public method stop
    disengage propeller
  endmethod
endclass
```

Also, the sailBoat class from Listing 6-3 no longer inherits from the boat class, but as shown in Listing 7-5 now implements the boat interface and provides an implementation for every method defined by the boat interface just as it needed to provide one for every method defined by boat when it was defined as an abstract class.

Listing 7-5. sailBoat Class Changed from Inheriting from a Superclass to Implementing an Interface, with Differences from Listing 6-3 Highlighted

```
class sailBoat implements boat
  public method start
    raise sail
  endmethod
  public method turnLeft
    push tiller to right
  endmethod
  public method turnRight
    push tiller to left
  public endmethod
  method stop
    lower sail
  endmethod
endclass
```

And finally, the marina class from Listing 6-4 changes only to indicate for one of its method signatures that boat is now an interface and no longer a class, as shown in Listing 7-6.

Listing 7-6. Change to Signature of Method of Marina Class to Regard Reference to Interface Instead of Class, with Differences from Listing 6-4 Highlighted

```
class marina
  public method launchMotorBoat
    thisMotorBoat                 type class of motorBoat
    create new instance of motorBoat into thisMotorBoat
    call method maneuverBoat(thisMotorBoat)
  endmethod
  public method launchSailBoat
    thisSailBoat                  type class of sailBoat
    create new instance of sailBoat into thisSailBoat
    call method maneuverBoat(thisSailBoat)
  endmethod
  private method maneuverBoat(thisBoat type interface of boat)
    invoke behavior start     of thisBoat
    invoke behavior turnLeft  of thisBoat
    invoke behavior turnRight of thisBoat
    invoke behavior stop      of thisBoat
  endmethod
endclass
```

In the end, we have transformed the definition for boat from a class to an interface without changing much in the way the components already had been defined. The editing changes we made may seem insignificant, and perhaps at first glance not worth our attention. However, the larger consideration here is that these minor changes resulted in two classes, motorBoat and sailboat, no longer inheriting from a superclass. In environments that do not support multiple inheritance, this can be a significant advantage. It provides more flexibility for classes motorBoat and sailBoat to inherit from some other superclass without affecting their ability to provide visibility to these entities simply as boats.

Indeed, we should consider that the entire set of members defined by the boat interface would also be applicable to entities that are not boats. Accordingly, we might define the interface using a word that does not connote anything about boats – perhaps, *maneuverable* – as in the updated version of pseudocode shown in Listing 7-7, with differences from the components of preceding listings highlighted.

Listing 7-7. Definition of Components to Reduce Reference to Boat Entity, with Changes and Additions to Preceding Listings Highlighted

```
interface maneuverable
                method start
                method turnLeft
                method turnRight
                method stop
endinterface

class motorBoat implements maneuverable
  public method start
    engage propeller
  endmethod
  public method turnLeft
    rotate steering wheel counterclockwise
  endmethod
  public method turnRight
    rotate steering wheel clockwise
  endmethod
  public method stop
    disengage propeller
  endmethod
endclass

class sailBoat implements maneuverable
  public method start
    raise sail
  endmethod
  public method turnLeft
    push tiller to right
  endmethod
  public method turnRight
    push tiller to left
  public endmethod
  method stop
    lower sail
  endmethod
endclass

class boatMover implements maneuverable
  public method start
    release brake
    engage drive wheels
  endmethod
  public method turnLeft
    move joystick to the left
  endmethod
  public method turnRight
    move joystick to the right
  public endmethod
  method stop
```

```
      disengage drive wheels
      apply brake
    endmethod
endclass

class marina
  public method launchMotorBoat
    thisMotorBoat                    type class of motorBoat
    create new instance of motorBoat into thisMotorBoat
    call method maneuver(thisMotorBoat)
  endmethod
  public method launchSailBoat
    thisSailBoat                     type class of sailBoat
    create new instance of sailBoat into thisSailBoat
    call method maneuver(thisSailBoat)
  endmethod
  public method moveBoatToLandStorage
    thisBoatMover                    type class of boatMover
    create new instance of boatMover into thisBoatMover
    call method maneuverBoat(thisBoatMover)
  endmethod
  private method maneuver(thisManeuverable
                               type interface of maneuverable)
    invoke behavior start       of thisManuverable
    invoke behavior turnLeft  of thisManuverable
    invoke behavior turnRight of thisManuverable
    invoke behavior stop        of thisManuverable
  endmethod
endclass
```

As indicated by the highlighted changes, we have done the following:

- Changed the name of the interface from *boat* to *maneuverable*

- Included a new class boatMover defining a boatyard management vehicle which implements the maneuverable interface

- Changed the name of the sole private method of the marina class so it longer suggests applying only to boats

- Included in the marina class a new public method for moving boats from the water to land storage

Accordingly, this interface, with its more generalized name, can now apply to things other than just boats, expanding its usefulness to other classes requiring maneuverability.

Interfaces and Inheritance

One of the primary reasons for using interfaces with classes is to achieve the equivalent of multiple inheritance. There is no limit to the number of interfaces a class can implement, and therefore is one way to effectively inherit from multiple contributors. This may account for why interfaces are not indigenous to all object-oriented environments, since those supporting multiple inheritance would not require interfaces as a means to circumvent the restrictions arising from single inheritance.

Let's see how this might work. In the chapter on inheritance we saw an example of a class inheritance hierarchy diagram (Figure 5-4, presented again here in Figure 7-1), where class dog inherits from multiple classes. We recognized this to be an example of multiple inheritance, where a class has more than one direct ancestor class, with the dog class inheriting from both the canine and domesticPet classes.

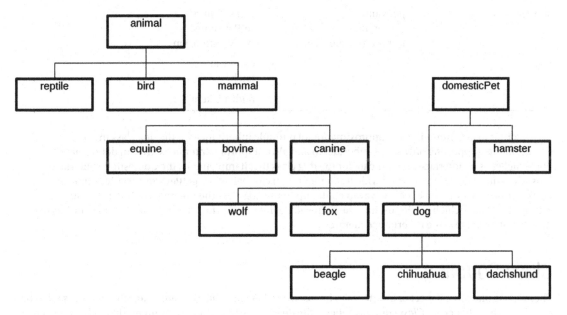

Figure 7-1. *Inheritance hierarchy where class dog illustrates multiple inheritance*

The corresponding chart from Table 5-4, presented again here in Table 7-2, describe some instance attributes and behaviors that might be associated with each class.

Table 7-2. *Classes and Their Members for the Inheritance Hierarchy Described by Figure 7-1*

Class	Attributes	Behaviors
animal	height weight age alacrity	eat sleep speak
mammal		nurseOffspring
canine	furColor	run jump followScentTrail
domesticPet	petName ownerName lastVeterinarianVisit	getPetName setPetName visitVeterinarian
dog		chaseCat fetch
fox		raidChickenCoop

In order to accommodate the approximation of multiple inheritance for the dog class in those environments supporting only single inheritance and also supporting interfaces, we can define class domesticPet as an interface and indicate for the dog class that it implements the domesticPet interface. This will require the dog class to provide implementations for behaviors getPetName, setPetName, and visitVeterinarian, but is an effective way to confer upon the dog class the members defined for both the canine class, from which it inherits, and the domesticPet interface, which it implements, two contributors that do not lie in the same inheritance hierarchy.

Class Coupling

There still is one more aspect of interfaces to be discovered. A class that references another class is said to be *coupled* to the other class. *Class coupling* reflects the degree to which each program module relies on each of the other modules.[5] A class that invokes a method of another class is more tightly coupled to that class than a class that simply has an attribute defined as a reference to the class but calls none of its methods.

Because a variable can be defined as a reference to an interface, this presents the capability of defining signatures for methods that can exchange such interface references. Accordingly, a method signature may indicate that it accepts a parameter defined as a reference to an interface. The implementation of that method may now use the interface reference variable provided through the signature to invoke upon that instance any of the methods defined by the interface *without ever knowing the type of class it is using*. It knows only whatever type of class to which the interface reference variable points, it surely has provided implementations for all of the methods contributed by the interface the class proclaims it implements.

Much of the power of an interface lies in this ability to see only that subset of a class corresponding to the interface definition. Accordingly, our program may not know whether the fuelConsumable interface reference variable holds a reference to an instance of a Car, a Truck, a Cabin, a Cell Phone, a Gas Grill, or a Coal-Fired Power Plant, but it certainly knows that it can invoke its method estimateFuelExhaustion and get an answer. This aspect is known in object-oriented programming as *loose coupling*.

---

[5]See http://courses.cs.washington.edu/courses/cse403/96sp/coupling-cohesion.html.

Loose coupling occurs when one class makes use of another class without explicitly referring to the other class by its class name. That is, class A is able to invoke a behavior of class B without mentioning class B by name. Loose coupling is facilitated when a class uses a reference to an interface instead of a reference to a concrete class.[6]

Refer to Listing 7-7 describing interface maneuverable and a classes sailBoat, motorBoat, boatMover, and marina. Classes sailBoat, motorBoat, and boatMover all implement the maneuverable interface. Class marina has private method called maneuver with a signature accepting a reference to an instance of a class through the maneuverable interface. This private method invokes the start, turnLeft, turnRight, and stop behaviors of an instance of class sailBoat, motorBoat, or boatMover depending on which of the other methods of the marina class invokes the maneuver method. Accordingly, method maneuver is oblivious to which type of class it is using; it only knows that the instance it has been sent by the caller through its signature is a class implementing the maneuverable interface. When method launchSailBoat invokes method maneuver, it sends an instance of class sailBoat as a parameter, but method maneuver regards this merely as an instance of a class implementing the maneuverable interface. As such, method maneuver is capable of invoking behaviors of a sailBoat instance without ever referring to it by its class name.

Loose coupling provides for more flexible design since the class using the interface reference is not bound to any specific type of class. In our fuel consumption example, a program that uses a reference variable to the fuelConsumable interface can work with any type of class implementing this interface. By contrast, had these classes not implemented the fuelConsumable interface, then a program would need to use a reference variable corresponding to the specific type of class to use (Car, Truck, Cabin, etc.) for its processing, and as a consequence would become tightly bound to that class.

Recall the discussion on the topic of cohesion from the chapter on abstraction. Class coupling and class cohesion generally have an inverse relationship to each other. As the cohesion of a class becomes lower, its class coupling usually becomes tighter. That is, low class cohesion usually promotes tight coupling whereas high class cohesion promotes loose coupling. We should strive to define classes having high cohesion and loose coupling, and it is often through the use of interfaces that we can achieve this result.

ABAP Language Support for Interfaces

The object-oriented extensions to the ABAP language accommodate interfaces in the following ways:

- By facilitating the definition of independent interfaces

- By supporting the use of independent interfaces in class definitions

- By supporting aliases within classes for members contributed by interfaces

- By enabling polymorphism through the use of interface reference variables

Interfaces are defined using the *interface* construct, which, unlike the complementary class constructs, requires only one construct to contain its entire definition:

```
interface interface-name.
  [types ...]
  [constants ...]
  [method interface_method_name [signature] ...]
  o
  o
endinterface.
```

---

[6]A case can be made that loose coupling also occurs when an instance of a subclass is referenced as an instance of one of its superclasses; however, such an arrangement depends on class inheritance and limits the flexibility to within the same inheritance hierarchy. By contrast, interfaces are not limited by such constraints.

A class indicates those interfaces it implements by naming them on an *interfaces* statement placed in the public visibility section of the class definition:

```
class class-name definition [options].
  public section.
    interfaces interface-name.
  o
  o
endclass.
```

It should be noted that while a class can indicate only a single class from which it inherits, there is no limit to the number of interfaces a class can implement. Both class and non-class components can access any types and constants defined by the interface through the class component selector (=>):

```
report.
  o
  o
  o
data this_variable type interface_name=>type_name.
  o
  o
  o
if this_variable eq interface_name=>constant_name.
```

Class components can provide implementations for the methods defined by the interface by providing a compound method name using the interface name and method name separated by the interface component selector (~):

```
class class-name implementation.
  method interface_name~method_name.
    o
    o
    o
  endmethod.
  o
  o
  o
endclass.
  o
  o
  o
  call method interface_name~method_name.
```

Use of this compound method name to refer to interface components allows for multiple interfaces implemented by a class to contain the same component names. For instance, class *car* can implement interfaces named maneuverable and fuel_consumable, both of which define method engage_safety_monitor, and by qualifying references to method engage_safety_monitor by its interface name enables both same-named methods to coexist in the car class. A class may also provide alternative names for those members contributed by the interface by naming them on an *aliases* statement, alleviating the need to use the interface selector technique when referencing the member contributed by the interface:

```
class class-name definition [options].
  public section.
    interfaces interface-name.
    aliases alias_name for interface_name~method_name.
  o
  o
endclass.
class class-name implementation.
  method alias_name.
    o
    o
    o
  endmethod.
  o
  o
  o
endclass.
  o
  o
  o
  call method alias_name.
```

Polymorphism also is available through the use of interfaces:

```
interface fuel_consumable.
  methods estimate_fuel_exhaustion [signature].
  o
  o
class car definition.
  public section.
    interfaces fuel_consumable.
  o
  o
  data this_car             type ref to car.
  data this_fuel_consumable type ref to fuel_consumable.
  o
  o
  create object this_car
  this_fuel_consumable      = this_car.
  call method this_fuel_consumable->estimate_fuel_exhaustion [signature].
  o
  o
```

Orienting Ourselves After Having Traversed Interfaces

We have reached the last leg of the path in our journey from Procedureton to Objectropolis, and now, having completed our traversal through the object-oriented district known as Interfaces we are familiar with its principles and now are fluent in the language spoken by its residents.

As we found with both Inheritance and Polymorphism, Interfaces also offers no recognizable guideposts or familiar terrain, appearing to us as yet another exotic landscape with no counterpart in our home town of Procedureton. Nonetheless, we are now as familiar with this district as the residents who live here and we are as capable as the native population in navigating our way around Interfaces.

Refer again to the chart in Appendix A, illustrating the comparison between function groups and classes of how each one facilitates the capabilities of the principles of object-oriented programming. Row 17 shows how these two programming formats support the principles of independent interfaces. We see that function groups have no support for this principle; it also is unique to classes.

Summary

In this chapter, we became more familiar with the object-oriented concept of interfaces, a principle not applicable to all object-oriented environments. We learned that independent interfaces contain definitions for attribute types and method signatures but contain no associated method implementations, and that interfaces can be used to supplement the public visibility section of a class. A class using an interface in this way is said to implement the interface, and as a consequence must provide implementations for all of the methods the interface defines. We learned that variables may be defined as references to interfaces and can hold a pointer to any class implementing the interface, but that classes referenced by a variable defined as an interface reference are restricted to accessing through that variable only those members contributed by the interface. We also learned that polymorphism is always in effect when using interface reference variables for the simple reason that it is not possible to create an instance of an interface but only of a class implementing the interface. We learned that the use of interfaces provides a way to achieve the equivalent of multiple inheritance, and that their use promotes loose coupling between objects, alleviating the need for a component to necessarily know what type of class instance it is using.

Interfaces Exercises

Refer to Chapter 7 of the functional and technical requirements documentation (see Appendix B) for the accompanying ABAP exercise programs associated with this chapter. Take a break from reading the book at this point to reinforce what you have read by changing and executing the corresponding exercise programs. The exercise programs associated with this chapter are those in the 105 series: ZOOT105A through ZOOT105D.

CHAPTER 8

■ ■ ■

Welcome to Objectropolis

It has been a long and winding road from Procedureton, but finally we have reached our destination of Objectropolis.

Establishing Dual Residency

We now are bilingual, having the capability to code using either the procedural or object-oriented paradigms with our work. Now that we understand the basic principles of object-oriented design, we no longer shudder at the thought of having to look at object-oriented code, nor do we recoil from the thought of participating in design discussions where object-oriented concepts are involved.

We have become a full-fledged, object-oriented designers and programmers. Accordingly, we have established dual residency in both Procedureton and Objectropolis. While in Objectropolis we can "talk the talk" and "walk the walk," having not only learned the lingo but also having embraced the culture of the town.

Beyond Objectropolis

So, where do we go from here? Indeed, is there even a place to go to next?

In my Object-Oriented Chalk Talks classes, I usually start the first lecture by drawing a diagram on the white board of a crude outline of the United States. I select a point on the East Coast (usually on the Florida peninsula) to represent Procedureton, select another point on the West Coast (usually at about where San Francisco might be located) to represent Objectropolis, and then I draw a circuitous path between the two, picking locations along the way to represent the districts of Encapsulation, Abstraction, Inheritance, Polymorphism, and Interfaces. This, I tell the class, represents the path of least resistance from our comfort zone of procedural programming through the basic principles of object-oriented design which we will be covering in the first half of the course.

The intent of the diagram is to show that our journey from Procedureton to Objectropolis is reminiscent of the westward expansion of the United States during the 19th century, where intrepid pioneer families traveled in horse-drawn Conestoga wagons across trails leading to the frontier. Upon arriving in Objectropolis, we still may regard our mode of transportation as being similar to the land-based wagons of those early westward pioneers, to whom the thought of manned flight was not even a remote possibility. We, however, being aware of the possibilities of the 21st century, can easily conceive of manned flight since many of us travel this way on a weekly basis, and although there is no terrain beyond Objectropolis over which we could navigate using the land-based wagons, certainly there are vast regions of the galaxy beyond Objectropolis that await our exploration.

Accordingly, next we will be reaching for the stars. Learning the basic principles of object-oriented design has given us a solid foundation upon which we have been able to improve our software development efforts, but with only these skills we remain tethered to the Earth. The difference between the basic

© James E. McDonough 2017
J. E. McDonough, *Object-Oriented Design with ABAP*, DOI 10.1007/978-1-4842-2838-8_8

principles of object-oriented programming and the heights we can reach when we use these basic principles with design patterns is the difference between remaining earthbound and traveling throughout the galaxy.

The basic principles have given us the vocabulary, rules of syntax, semantics, and sentence structure to be found in any language. Design patterns enable us to take these words, phrases, and paragraphs and with them create poetry, inspiring oratory, even great works of literature.

Before we embark on such an adventurous voyage into design patterns, first we will get some flight training by becoming familiar with Unified Modeling Language, which will help us with celestial navigation.

PART II

Communicating Design Through Design Diagrams

CHAPTER 9

■ ■ ■

Introduction to the Unified Modeling Language

We are about to leave the terrain provided by the basic principles of object-oriented design over which we traveled to arrive in Objectropolis and to reach for the stars in the galaxy known as Design Patterns. We need to acquire some expertise with celestial mapping and cosmic diagramming to help us navigate through this expanse. The Unified Modeling Language provides us with this skill.

The Unified Modeling Language (UML) was created in 1996 when James Rumbaugh, Grady Booch, and Ivar Jacobson (a.k.a. The Three Amigos), all working at Rational Software Corporation, consolidated Rumbaugh's Object Modeling Technique (OMT) and Booch's Object-Oriented Design (OOD) into a single non-proprietary general purpose modeling language to support software engineering.[1] UML was adopted in 1997 by the Object Modeling Group, a standards consortium for the computer industry.

With the current official release (2.5, June 2015) UML defines 14 types of diagrams, divided into two categories. Half are known as *structural*; the other half known as *behavioral,* as the hierarchy[2] in Figure 9-1 shows.

---

[1] `www.cs.pomona.edu/classes/cs121/supp/UML%20tutorial/history_of_uml.htm`
[2] Taken from the model appearing at `www.omg.org/spec/UML/2.5/PDF/`, Figure A.5 The taxonomy of structure and behavior diagrams (page 683)

© James E. McDonough 2017
J. E. McDonough, *Object-Oriented Design with ABAP*, DOI 10.1007/978-1-4842-2838-8_9

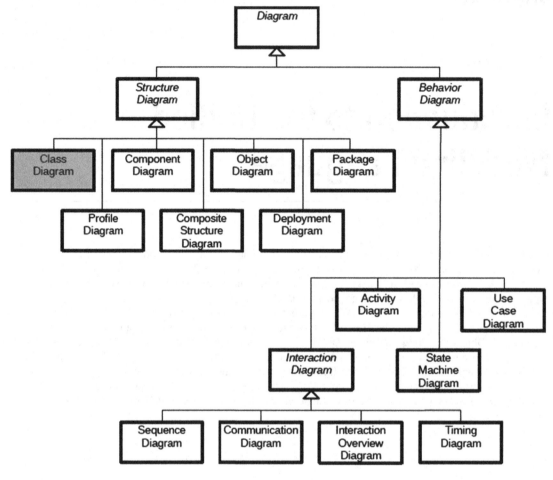

Figure 9-1. *UML diagram hierarchy*

A comprehensive explanation of UML is beyond the scope of this book, so we will explore only the class diagram (shown highlighted in Figure 9-1), since it provides a convenient way for us to organize and depict classes and interfaces, their attributes and behaviors, and the relationships between these entities.

UML Class Diagrams[3]

A UML class diagram represents each class or interface using a box containing three sections and relationship lines connecting these boxes. Within a box, the top section contains the name of the class or interface, the middle section describes its attributes, and the bottom section describes its behaviors. Figure 9-2 shows a class diagram box for a car class with two attributes and two behaviors, and an interface box for simpleNavigation with no attributes and one behavior.

---

[3]For more information, refer to https://msdn.microsoft.com/en-us/library/dd409437.aspx.

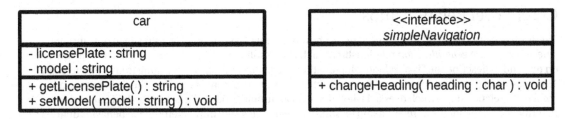

Figure 9-2. *Class diagram representation for class car and interface simpleNavigation*

For class diagrams describing a large number of classes and interfaces, it is commonplace for the box to omit the attributes and behaviors sections.

Entries are typically shown using the *camel case* notation convention,[4] where multiple words of an entry have no intervening space and appear in lowercase with the first letter of each new word appearing in uppercase. Indeed, the convention for text appearing in class diagram boxes is to use *lower camel case*, where the first letter of the first word also appears in lowercase. Abstract entries are shown using the italic font.

The name of the class or interface appearing in the upper box is centered. When it describes an interface, the identifier <<interface>> appears above the interface name.

Attributes are left-justified, showing the name of the attribute and its type, separated by a colon. The type may be followed by an equal sign and a value if the field is to have a default starting value.

Behaviors also are left-justified. The signatures for the behaviors described in the bottom section are enclosed in parenthesis and show the parameter name and parameter type separated by a colon. This is followed by the type of return value,[5] separated from the right parenthesis by a colon, with *void* indicating the absence of a return value.

Each member described in the bottom two sections is preceded by a visibility level setting, which may be any of the following:

+	Public
#	Protected
~	Package
-	Private
/	Derived (can be combined with one of the others)
_	Static (is combined with one of the others)

The relationships between the boxes are shown using lines connecting them, and fall into three categories:

- Class-level relationships
- Instance-level relationships
- General relationships

---

[4]See www.dictionary.com/browse/camelcase.

[5]The presumption here is that a UML class diagram describes a design intended for an object-oriented environment in which the language(s) facilitate only single return values from method invocations. The C++ and Java languages conform to this model, and the ABAP language includes the capability to define a method where the corresponding signature is restricted to a single returning value, but ABAP also accommodates defining a method with a signature that facilitates returning multiple values to the caller.

Class-Level Relationships

There are two class-level relationships to depict how different classes or interfaces relate to one another. One is known as a *generalization* relationship, which uses a solid line with an unfilled triangular arrowhead on one end to describe the "is a" relationship existing between a child class inheriting from a parent class. The arrowhead of a generalization relationship line points to the parent class. The other is known as a *realization* relationship, which uses a dashed line with an unfilled triangular arrowhead on one end to describe the "implements a" relationship existing between one entity implementing the behavior defined by the other entity. The realization relationship usually occurs in the form of a class implementing the behavior of an interface. The arrowhead of a realization relationship line points to the entity contributing the definition of the behavior.

Generalization:

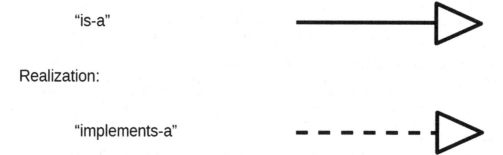

"is-a"

Realization:

"implements-a"

Instance-Level Relationships

Three instance-level relationships, known as *links*, depict how different objects relate to one another, each subsequent term representing a specialization of the one preceding it:

- Association
- Aggregation
- Composition

The *association* link depicts a "relates to" connection between two entities. The following are variations of an association link:

- Unidirectional
- Bidirectional
- Reflexive

A *unidirectional* association implies that only one entity connected on each end of the relationship line knows about the other entity. For instance, a class *vehicle* and class *vehicleRegistrationAgency* are connected via a unidirectional association because vehicleRegistrationAgency knows about vehicle but vehicle does not know about vehicleRegistrationAgency. This is represented by a simple solid line connecting the two entities with an arrowhead pointing to the entity that knows nothing about the other.

A *bidirectional* association implies that the entity connected on each end of the relationship line knows about the other entity. For instance, class patient and class physician are connected via a bidirectional association because each one knows about the other: a patient is treated by a physician, and a physician treats a patient. The patient and physician classes may or may not have relationships with other types of classes, such as patient having a relationship with the diet class and physician having a relationship with the professional organization class, but these other classes can exist independently of the patient and physician classes. Meanwhile, the relationship between patient and physician is symbiotic; neither would exist without the other. This is represented by a simple solid line connecting the two entities.

A *reflexive* association illustrates a class with a relationship to itself. An example of this is an *employee* class having a relationship to a manager, and manager also is represented by the employee class. This type of relationship is represented by a simple solid line starting out from one of the sides of the class box and then making a 270-degree turn to return and connect back to the top or bottom of the class box; effectively, both ends of the line connect to the same class box.

The *aggregation* link depicts a "has a" connection between two entities. This usually means that an attribute of one class is a pointer to the instance of another class; that is, the containing object aggregates pointers to one or more other objects. An aggregation link represents a connection stronger than other variations of an association link. This is represented by a solid line with an unfilled diamond arrowhead on one end. The arrowhead of an aggregation relationship line points to the entity that does the aggregating. The containing object necessarily knows about the contained object, but the reverse is not necessarily true.

The *composition* link depicts an "owns a" connection between two entities. This also usually means that an attribute of one class is a pointer to the instance of another class; that is, the containing object is composed of pointers to one or more other objects. A composition link represents a connection stronger yet than an aggregation link. This is represented by a solid line with a filled diamond arrowhead on one end. The arrowhead of a composition relationship line points to the entity that does the composing. Again, the containing object necessarily knows about the contained object, but the reverse is not necessarily true.

The difference between aggregation and composition lies in the lifespan of the contained objects. Composition implies a dependent relationship by the contained objects to the containing object, whereas aggregation implies an independent relationship between the contained objects to the containing object. With composition, any contained objects are destroyed when the containing object is destroyed. With aggregation, contained objects are left alive when the containing object is destroyed. A good example for this is the following:

- A car instance "owns a" carburetor instance. When the car is destroyed, so is the carburetor. This is an example of composition.

- A pond instance "has a" duck instance. When the pond is drained, the duck is not destroyed, but merely flies away to find another pond. This is an example of aggregation.

The following types of lines are used to depict these relationships:

Association:

uni-directional "relates to"

bi-directional "relates to"

Aggregation:

"has-a"

Composition:

"owns-a"

An instance level relationship also indicates the cardinality (a.k.a. multiplicity) between the connected boxes, and denotes the number of entities at each end that can connect through the relationship. These may be one of the following:

0..1	Zero or one
1	Exactly one
0..*	Zero or more
1..*	One or more

For example, a car instance can own one engine instance, so the composition relationship between the two instances would show an "exactly one" cardinality at both the car and engine ends of the relationship line. Also, a car instance may or may not own a super charger instance, but if it does, it would have only one, so the composition relationship between the two instances would show an "exactly one" cardinality at the car end of the relationship line and a "zero or one" cardinality at the super charger end of the relationship line. Meanwhile, a car parking lot may be empty, partially filled, or full of car instances, so the aggregation relationship between the two instances would show an "exactly one" cardinality at the car parking lot end of the relationship line and a "zero or more" cardinality at the car end of the relationship line.

It is also common to use explicit numbers, when they apply, in place of the zeros, ones, and asterisks appearing in the entries above, as in the following examples:

0..4	Zero to four
5	Exactly five
5..9	Five to nine
6..*	Six or more

General Relationships

There is one general relationship, known as *dependency*. This relationship establishes a connection between an entity that depends on another entity, known as the *supplier*, for its implementation. There are several types of dependencies that can be described by a general relationship, such as *uses*, *calls*, *instantiates*, etc. It is represented by a dashed line with an open arrowhead on one end. For each general relationship, the description of the corresponding dependency, enclosed by guillemet marks (<< and >>), is specified next to the connecting line. The arrowhead of a general relationship line points to the supplier.

Dependency:

"depends on"

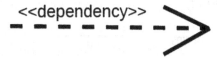

Examples of UML Class Diagrams

So, let's use UML to model our previous examples, as shown in Figure 9-3, starting with our famous fox and dog entities, as enhanced in Table 3-3 in Chapter 3.

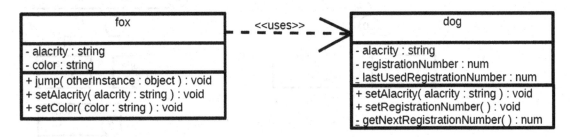

Figure 9-3. *UML class diagram modeling fox and dog classes*

This UML class diagram in Figure 9-3 depicts the following:

- A fox class with two private instance attributes for alacrity (type string) and color (type string), and three public instance behaviors for jump (with signature otherInstance of type object, and returning nothing), setAlacrity (with signature alacrity of type string, and returning nothing), and setColor (with signature color of type string, and returning nothing).

- A dog class with two private instance attributes for alacrity (type string) and registrationNumber (type num), one static private attribute for lastUsedRegistrationNumber (type num), a static private behavior getNextRegistrationNumber (with empty signature and returning a value of type num), and two public instance behaviors for setAlacrity (with signature alacrity of type string, and returning nothing) and setRegistrationNumber (with empty signature and returning nothing).

- A general relationship, called dependency, between the two classes indicating that the fox *uses* the dog. In this case, fox is dependent upon dog; there must be an instance of a dog object over which the fox can jump, but dog is not dependent on fox.

The most recent exercise affords many other types of relationships to be included in its corresponding UML class diagram, as shown in Figure 9-4. The numbered circles are references to the numbered items of explanation that follow the UML class diagram.

Class definitions (7):

car
dead_reckoning
gps
navigator
report
truck
vehicle

Interface definitions (1):

simple_navigation

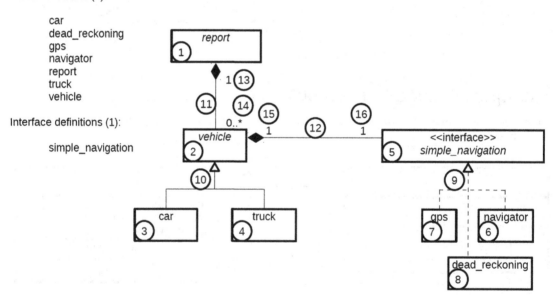

Figure 9-4. UML class diagram describing exercise program ZOOT105D

1. The report class is a static class – it is marked as abstract – so its name is shown using the italic font.

2. The vehicle class is an abstract class, so its name is shown using the italic font.

3. The car class is a concrete class, so its name is shown using the regular font.

4. The truck class is a concrete class, so its name is shown using the regular font.

5. The simple_navigation interface provides definitions for abstract methods which must be implemented in any class using the interface, so its name is shown using the italic font. Also, interface names in class diagram boxes are preceded with the <<interface>> banner.

6. The navigator class is a concrete class, so its name is shown using the regular font.

7. The gps class is a concrete class, so its name is shown using the regular font.

8. The dead_reckoning class is a concrete class, so its name is shown using the regular font.

9. The classes navigator, gps, and dead_reckoning all implement the simple_navigation interface, so the relationship between their boxes and the interface box is shown using the "implements a" relationship, which is a dashed line with an unfilled triangular arrowhead pointing to the interface each of them implements. We could have shown this relationship using three separate relationship lines, one between each of the three class boxes and the interface box, but here they are shown consolidated, with the relationship lines from each class box merging into the single line pointing to the interface box. Also, the UML standard does not require all relationship lines to be oriented vertically and horizontally as shown in this UML class diagram, but can be oriented diagonally as well.

10. The classes car and truck are both child classes inheriting from the vehicle class, so the relationship between their boxes and their parent class is shown using the "is a" relationship, which is a solid line with an unfilled triangular arrowhead pointing to the parent class from which they inherit.

11. The report class owns instances of vehicle classes, so the relationship between their boxes is shown using the "owns a" relationship, which is a solid line with a filled diamond arrowhead pointing to the owning class.

12. The vehicle class owns instances of classes implementing the simple_navigation interface, so the relationship between their boxes is shown using the "owns a" relationship, which is a solid line with a filled diamond arrowhead pointing to the owning class.

13. For the "owns a" relationship between the report class and vehicle class, the cardinality for the report class is set to 1, indicating that there is exactly one report instance involved in this relationship.

14. For the "owns a" relationship between the report class and vehicle class, the cardinality for the vehicle class is set to 0..*, indicating that there are zero or more vehicle instances involved in this relationship.

15. For the "owns a" relationship between the vehicle class and simple_navigation interface, the cardinality for the vehicle class is set to 1, indicating that there is exactly one vehicle instance involved in this relationship.

16. For the "owns a" relationship between the vehicle class and simple_navigation interface, the cardinality for the simple_navigation interface is set to 1, indicating that there is exactly one simple_navigation instance involved in this relationship.

Summary

In this chapter, we learned about the effort in 1996 between James Rumbaugh, Grady Booch, and Ivar Jacobson to produce a general purpose modeling language to support software engineering, which came to be known as the Unified Modeling Language. We learned about the class diagram, where a class is represented as a box consisting of three sections to denote class name, its attributes, and its behaviors; where names typically follow the lower camel case notation convention; attributes and behaviors are marked with visibility indicators; and the italic font is used to denote abstraction. We also learned that relationship lines connect class boxes on a class diagram and fall into three categories:

- Class-level relationships

- Instance-level relationships

- General relationships

We learned that class-level relationships use the generalization ("is a") relationship line to denote inheritance and the realization relationship line ("implements a") to denote implementation of an interface. We also learned that instance-level relationships may be accompanied by a cardinality indication to denote the number of entities at each end that can connect through the relationship, where these relationships use the association ("relates to") relationship line to denote a unidirectional, bidirectional, or reflexive relationship, use the aggregation ("has a") relationship line to denote reference to an entity also known by other entities, and use the composition ("owns a") relationship line to denote reference to an entity known only to the owner. In addition, we learned that general relationships use the dependency ("depends on") relationship line to point from the dependent entity to the independent one, accompanied by a word enclosed within guillemet marks to indicate the type of dependency.

PART III

■ ■ ■

Leveraging Object-Oriented Concepts Through Design Patterns

CHAPTER 10

■ ■ ■

Design Patterns

Now that we know the basic principles of object-oriented design and have become familiar with the class diagrams offered by the Unified Modeling Language, we are now ready to begin our exploration of the galaxy known as Design Patterns.

Those of us who write code for living occasionally experience a sense of *déjà vu* – that we have already written something identical or similar once before in some other program, but can't remember exactly where or when. Some of us may remember where and when we did something similar; and some of us may even have a collection of code snippets (or entire programs) from which we can copy and paste sections of code and tailor them to the specific task at hand. Whether we recognize a programming challenge as one for which we have a handy snippet of code available or simply one for which we have a sense of *déjà vu*, the common denominator between the two is that we recognize a *pattern* that we have seen before. These patterns with which we are familiar and for which we might have a handy snippet of code available to use as a model enable us to reuse a proven solution in the new *design* on which we are working. These constitute our personal collection of *design patterns*.

These design patterns are not the same as callable utilities that can produce some desired result. For instance, I often find myself writing classes to hold a cache of records read from a persistent data storage device, the idea being that if I need the same record more than once during processing I can obtain it faster from the cache than by reading it again from the slower persistent data storage device. Accordingly, these caching classes are customized for a specific type of persistent storage record and for a specific set of columns from that type of record. It is not practical to write a single callable utility that can handle any set of columns from many different types of records. So I find myself devising multiple small classes to handle the specifics I need, but all of them use the same basic design pattern for retaining a subset of columns of records read from the persistent data storage device. The design pattern lays out the type of solution to build, and writing a new caching class is the manifestation of that design pattern applied to a specific use.

Other programmers we encounter during our careers will also have their personal collection of design patterns they use to solve their design challenges. Some design patterns are so pervasive in data processing that many different programmers have recognized the same patterns and have exchanged ideas with each other on the best ways to implement solutions using the pattern. Indeed, there are those in the data processing industry who believe virtually every programming challenge has already been encountered and solved by someone else.

© James E. McDonough 2017
J. E. McDonough, *Object-Oriented Design with ABAP*, DOI 10.1007/978-1-4842-2838-8_10

The Gang of Four

In 1995, Erich Gamma, Richard Helm, Ralph Johnson, and John Vlissides compiled a set of 23 such common design patterns into their now-famous book *Design Patterns: Elements of Reusable Object-Oriented Software*.[1] It was the first generally available catalog of design patterns applicable to computer programming. They did for data processing what Christopher Alexander and his colleagues did nearly 20 years earlier for architecture.[2] The book had a significant impact on the software development industry and, more than 20 years later, remains the definitive compendium of design patterns for use in computer programming. It not only describes 23 of the most commonly recurring patterns, but defines a *language* for speaking about design patterns. The four authors have collectively become known as the "Gang of Four," and many software designers now refer to the book simply by the acronym for this moniker: *GoF*.

GoF defines a template for describing a design pattern, and all the design patterns it contains are all described using this same template. The template includes, among others, the name of the pattern, a short statement describing the pattern, advice on where the pattern is applicable, example code, and related patterns. The example code primarily uses C++ and Smalltalk, which can present a challenge to those who are unfamiliar with these languages. However, the catalog is so thorough that it has been embraced by software designers specializing in many other object-oriented languages.

GoF classifies its 23 design patterns using two criteria: *purpose* and *scope*.

- *Purpose* reflects what the pattern does, and is subdivided into three categories: *creational*, *structural*, and *behavioral*.

  "Creational patterns concern the process of object creation. Structural patterns deal with the composition of classes or objects. Behavioral patterns characterize the ways in which classes or objects interact and distribute responsibility."[3]

- *Scope* has two categories: *class* and *object*.

  "Scope specifies whether the pattern applies primarily to classes or to objects. Class patterns deal with relationships between classes and their subclasses. These relationships are established through inheritance, so they are static – fixed at compile-time. Object patterns deal with object relationships, which can be changed at runtime and are more dynamic. Almost all patterns use inheritance to some extent. So the only patterns labeled 'class patterns' are those that focus on class relationships."[4]

The combinations of the two criteria provide a convenient way to perceive patterns.

  "Creational class patterns defer some part of object creation to subclasses, while creational object patterns defer it to another object."

  "The Structural class patterns use inheritance to compose classes, while the Structural object patterns describe ways to assemble objects."

  "The Behavioral class patterns use inheritance to describe algorithms and flow of control, whereas the Behavioral object patterns describe how a group of objects cooperate to perform a task that no single object can carry out alone."[5]

---

[1]Erich Gamma, Richard Helm, Ralph Johnson, and John Vlissides, *Design Patterns: Elements of Reusable Object-Oriented Software*, Addison-Wesley, 1995.
[2]Refer to `A Pattern Language: Towns, Buildings, Construction` by Christoper Alexander, Sara Ishikawa, Murray Silverstein, Max Jacobson, Ingrid Fiksdahl-King, ShlomoAngel; Oxford University Press, 1977.
[3]GoF, p. 10
[4]GoF, p. 10
[5]GoF, p. 10

Table 10-1 represents the organization of the 23 GoF design patterns.[6]

Table 10-1. *Organization of the 23 GoF Design Patterns*

		Purpose		
		Creational	Structural	Behavioral
Scope	Class	Factory Method	Adapter (class)	Interpreter Template Method
	Object	Abstract Factory Builder Prototype Singleton	Adapter (object) Bridge Composite Decorator Façade Flyweight Proxy	Chain of Responsibility Command Iterator Mediator Memento Observer State Strategy Visitor

Notice that Adapter is the only one of the GoF patterns that has both a class scope as well as an object scope.[7]

The GoF book establishes the outline used to describe each design pattern:[8]

1. Pattern name and classification: The classification represents the purpose and scope as shown in Table 10-1.

2. Intent: Essentially a sentence or two describing the pattern.

3. Also Known As: Other names, if any, by which the pattern is known.

4. Motivation: A scenario describing a design challenge suited for the pattern.

5. Applicability: Advisory on situations when the pattern is appropriate as well as inappropriate.

6. Structure: A diagram of the design pattern showing the interaction of the participants.

7. Participants: The types of individual classes and interfaces used in the pattern.

8. Collaborations: The interaction between the participants.

9. Consequences: Both positive and negative aspects of using the pattern.

10. Implementation: Details about how the pattern is to be implemented.

---

[6]From Table 1.1: Design pattern space, GoF, p. 10

[7]One pattern not included amongst the 23 GoF design patterns is known as the Model-View-Controller pattern (a.k.a. MVC), the name of which may already be familiar to many ABAP programmers due to its repeated mention in the book *ABAP Objects: ABAP Programming in SAP NetWeaver* (Horst Keller, Sascha Krüger; 2nd edition, Galileo Press, 2007), in addition to the plethora of articles available via the Internet on the topic of MVC with ABAP. Indeed, the GoF book describes MVC (pp. 4-6) as a compound design pattern consisting of an Observer, a Composite, and a Strategy pattern all working in cooperation with each other.

[8]GoF, p. 6.

11. Sample Code: GoF uses C++ and Smalltalk.

12. Known Uses: Examples of real software packages using the pattern.

13. Related Patterns: Other design patterns exhibiting similarities, highlighting the significant differences between them, and other patterns that are particularly suitable in multi-pattern collaborative designs.

The Design Pattern Name

In my Object-Oriented Chalk Talks, I usually start the section on design patterns by telling the class that I am going to play the role of a business analyst, and share with them all the information about a new application I want them to implement in ABAP. I use the white board to list various capabilities I want included as I speak about the new application, which is to show those rows from a specific persistence repository database which are missing values for certain columns:

> "This application is to produce a report that needs to allow the user to scroll forward and backward through the list of applicable rows, as well as scroll left and right when the columns all cannot fit on the screen at the same time. The user needs to be able to print the report as well as save the results to a local file. The user needs to be able to get totals for numeric columns as well as have the ability to produce control breaks for selected columns. It would be nice if the report also provided the user with the capability to select a row, push a button, and see the values for all of the columns of that row shown in a pop-up box. It also would be helpful to the user if they were able to rearrange the order of the columns at will, change the width of a column by dragging a column boundary, left to shorten and right to lengthen, as well as hide selected columns from the report, which can be unhidden later. Another feature the users require is the ability to sort the rows by a specific column value as well as filter out those rows which do or do not conform to some criteria value or range the user could specify for the column. Also, a find feature is necessary to locate rows in the report which contain some specified value or partial value. It would be great if we could present the report such that it enables users to manipulate the content similar to the way a spreadsheet works. In addition, it would be nice if users were able to save the display settings of the report after they had applied sorting and filtering criteria, so they could recall that format with each new use. It would be nicer still if these saved display settings could be presented in a list, enabling the user to select the display settings they need at that moment. ... "

I continue this narrative for a while until someone eventually interrupts me.

"Jim," they say, "why don't you simply tell us to use ALV,[9] which already provides all of those capabilities?"

"Yes," I tell them, "that is exactly the point for having a good *name* for a design pattern." A name enables us simply to state the name of the design pattern during design discussions and everyone immediately knows all the implications associated with that name. It is similar to the proverbial cliché about a picture being worth a thousand words. Refer back to the long business analyst narrative above where I used over 300 words to describe a process which could be described very succinctly by this two-word statement:

> Use ALV.

---

[9]ALV is the acronym for the SAP Application List Viewer, and has become the definitive technique for producing reports in ABAP programs.

Patterns exist in other fields of endeavor besides architecture and software design, with each field having its own named patterns to be used to facilitate discussions between people who both are familiar with the field of endeavor and know the relevant pattern names. The *Karo-Cann Defense* immediately connotes a king pawn opening while the *Albin Counter Gambit* indicates a queen pawn opening,[10] but each name alleviates the need for further explanation about the opening sequence of moves in chess matches where these patterns are used. The names *derecho, tornado,* and *hurricane* describe severe weather patterns, each of which carries its own implications about wind speeds and precipitation that require no elaboration. Similarly, the *alternate merge* pattern is familiar to drivers who find themselves in the situation where two lanes of traffic are converging into a single lane, while the *holding stack* pattern is familiar to commercial airline pilots waiting to land at heavy-traffic airports. *Fibonacci, prime number,* and *Mandelbrot set* describe number patterns, while textile patterns include *argyle, glen plaid,* and *houndstooth. Flemish, monk,* and *sussex* are variations of load-bearing bond brickwork patterns, whereas *basket weave, herringbone,* and *della robia* are variations of non-load-bearing bond brickwork patterns. In each case, simply using the *name* of the pattern instantly conveys a wealth of information that might otherwise require many paragraphs of explanation and much time expended.

Patterns Explored in this Book

The following list of names covers the patterns we will be exploring over the next few chapters:

1. Singleton
2. Strategy
3. Observer
4. Factory
5. Adapter
6. Decorator
7. Chain of Responsibility
8. Iterator
9. Template Method
10. Command
11. Null Object
12. State
13. Lazy Initialization
14. Flyweight
15. Memento
16. Visitor

Of these, Null Object (11) and Lazy Initialization (13) are not included in the GoF book.

---

[10]Fred Reinfeld, *The Complete Chess Course*, Doubleday, 1953.

Use of UML Class Diagrams to Illustrate Design Patterns

The GoF book was published a year before UML was invented. Accordingly, although GoF provides a class diagram for each design pattern, these diagrams do not use the UML notation. Instead, each one is illustrated using James Rumbaugh's Object Modeling Technique (OMT). The UML class diagrams accompanying the design patterns covered over the next few chapters approximate the OMT structure diagrams included in GoF.

Also, because design patterns are general solutions to recurring design challenges, the class diagrams themselves are somewhat generalized to accommodate variations on different ways in which the design patterns can be manifested. Amongst others, the following liberties were taken with the UML class diagrams:

- The relationship lines representing aggregation ("has a;" ◇—) and composition ("owns a;" ◆—) differ from each other in their designation for whether or not the referenced object is destroyed when the referring object is destroyed. The UML diagrams in the following chapters do not distinguish between them, and are illustrated using only the aggregation relationship line.

- Aggregation relationship lines are usually accompanied by multiplicity indications on both ends of the lines. To allow for more general combinations, these numbers have been omitted in some cases.

- The designation by GoF that a participant is or provides an *interface* is interpreted in the broadest sense, and is not taken to mean that the participant is defined specifically as a stand-alone interface, for which the UML notation normally would include a <<interface>> banner along with the entity name in the name box. Instead, the interpretation of the word *interface* is in the context of the *public interface* provided by the entity, which could be furnished using either a class or an interface component. Therefore, unless otherwise required for clarity, classes are not shown implementing an interface, but instead are shown inheriting from a superclass. When it contributes only abstract methods, the superclass entity should be regarded as a general place holder for either a class or a stand-alone interface, and its connecting *generalization* relationship lines used to denote inheritance should be regarded as proxies for the connecting *realization* relationship lines used to denote the implementation of stand-alone interfaces.

Summary

In this chapter, we learned that there are names for those general algorithms we find ourselves using over and over again in different situations: design patterns. We also learned that other programmers also have their own collection of such patterns, and that in 1995 the Gang of Four compiled the first published catalog of 23 design patterns applicable to computer programming. We now understand the importance of having a good name for a design pattern since it simplifies communications we have with our colleagues about software designs.

■ ■ ■

CHAPTER 11

Singleton Design Pattern

The first stop on our voyage through the Design Patterns galaxy takes us to the Singleton design pattern, one of the design patterns found in the GoF catalog. We will find this design pattern useful when we need to guarantee that there is only a single instance of a class available during execution.

We may have multiple instances of a class, with each instance having its own unique attribute values. However, there are some classes that are intended to have one and only one instance per program execution. Some examples are the following devices through which a user interacts with a computer:

- Monitor

- Keyboard

- Mouse

Although possible, it is unlikely we will ever need more than one monitor,[1] one mouse, and one keyboard per user per program. We can define classes corresponding to these devices, but we may elicit some user consternation and frustration if our program were to create multiple instances to correspond to them, eventually losing track of which instance has the current information for the user.

In these cases, we can avoid such problems by creating only one instance of the class. Although this sounds simple enough, there is a difference between *intending* and *insuring* we have only one instance.

One and Only One

The Singleton design pattern is used when we need to insure that a class has one and only one instance. It is categorized by GoF with a *creational* purpose and an *object* scope. The intent behind this design pattern is the following:

Ensure a class only has one instance, and provide a global point of access to it.[2]

---

[1]Though not a need, many users now prefer a multiple-monitor configuration.
[2]GoF, p. 127.

© James E. McDonough 2017
J. E. McDonough, *Object-Oriented Design with ABAP*, DOI 10.1007/978-1-4842-2838-8_11

This design pattern has the simplest UML class diagram of all, shown in Figure 11-1.

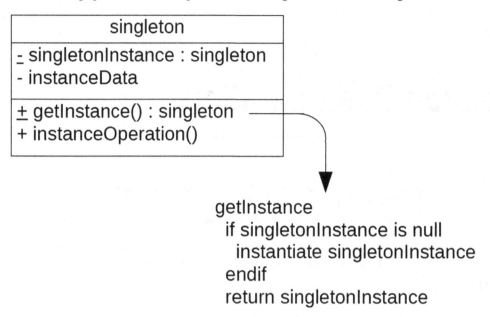

Figure 11-1. *UML class diagram for Singleton design pattern*

This is one of the few design patterns where only one class box is represented in its UML class diagram. Notice that the class is defined with both static and instance members: singletonInstance is marked as a private static attribute of type singleton, whereas instanceData is marked as a private instance attribute; also, instanceOperation is marked as a public instance method while getInstance is marked as a public static method. As shown in Figure 11-1, public static method getInstance returns a reference to the instance of singleton found in static attribute singletonInstance, creating an instance if one has not yet been created.

Many programmers notice the similarity between a singleton and a static class since they share the same trait of insuring that only a single class entity is available at execution time; however, that is about all they share. They differ in the following ways:

- Whereas instantiation does not apply to a static class, a singleton requires instantiation.

- Whereas a static class is composed solely of static members, a singleton is composed of a combination of instance members and static members.

- Whereas polymorphism cannot be used with the methods of a static class, it can be used with the instance methods of a singleton, where a singleton subclass can override the methods provided by its superclass.

The question naturally arises of how to insure that a class has one and only one instance. The most common way to achieve this is to define the class with *private* instantiability; that is, only the class itself may create instances of the class. Although this may seem to be counterintuitive (how can instances of a class be created when only the class itself is capable of creating such instances?), it is solved easily by defining the class as a hybrid class, meaning it has both static and instance members.

Recall that static members of a class are available to external entities even when no instances of the class exist. One of those static members will be an attribute defined as a reference to an instance of the class itself, and another of those static members will be a public method that can be invoked by external entities to get an instance of the class. When invoked, this public static method will check whether or not the static attribute holding a reference to the class already points to an instance, and, if not, create an instance and then pass a reference to this instance to the caller. The first time this public static method is invoked will result in an instance of the class being created and placed into the static reference attribute. Subsequent invocations will not need to create another instance because one already exists, and this same instance will be used again.

Figure 11-2 shows a UML diagram for a mouse class as a singleton, showing how the singleton instance is made available to external entities.

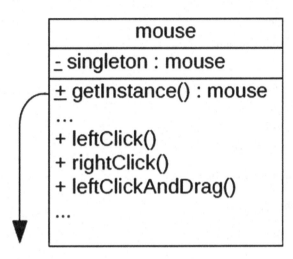

```
getInstance
  if singleton is null
    instantiate singleton
  endif
  return singleton
```

Figure 11-2. *UML diagram for a singleton mouse class*

Here we see a public static method getInstance by which external entities can get a reference to the singleton instance of the mouse class. Because it is a static method, getInstance can be invoked even when no instance of a mouse class exists. The implementation of the getInstance method checks to determine whether or not the private static attribute named singleton, which holds a reference to a mouse instance, is bound to an instance of a mouse object. If not, one is created. A reference to this object is passed back to the caller.

There are variations on this theme but all follow the same principle. We define a class to have a static constructor that creates the instance upon first access, in which case the public static method to get an instance of the class does not need to check whether or not an instance exists (it will always exist by the time it can make such a check since the static constructor will have completed its processing before the public static method starts its processing). Also, in those languages where a public attribute can be marked as publicly readable but not changeable (there are ways of doing this in Java, and ABAP provides the "read-only" qualifier for public attributes), then access to instance members of the singleton can simply be calls through the read-only static attribute of the class, provided a static constructor is in control of creating an instance of the class.

Singleton in ABAP

An ABAP example using the get_instance technique is shown below with a singleton for a screen manager, an entity of which we would not want to have more than one, since our program most likely would use only one monitor screen to manage interaction with the user.

First, Listing 11-1 shows the definition for class screen_manager.

Listing 11-1. Definition for class screen_manager

```
class screen_manager definition final create private.
  public section.
    class-methods: get_instance
                     returning value(instance)
                       type ref to screen_manager
                     .
    methods      : get_screen_height
                       exporting screen_height type int4
                   , get_screen_width
                       exporting screen_width  type int4
                   , set_screen_height
                       importing screen_height type int4
                   , set_screen_width
                       importing screen_width  type int4
                   .
  private section.
    class-data  : singleton      type ref
                                   to screen_manager
                   .
    data        : screen_height type int4
                   , screen_width  type int4
                   .
endclass.
```

Notice the screen_manager class has a combination of both static and instance members. Notice also the *create private* instantiability level qualifying the class definition statement, which also includes the qualifier final[3] to indicate the class may have no inheritors. The implementation for the methods of class screen_manager might look like the code shown in Listing 11-2.

Listing 11-2. Implementation for class screen_manager

```
class screen_manager implementation.
  method get_instance.
    if screen_manager=>singleton is not bound.
      create object screen_manager=>singleton.
    endif.
    instance                  = screen_manager=>singleton.
  endmethod.
```

---

[3]In ABAP, a class marked as *create private* will confer *create none* upon any subclasses, preventing them from both being instantiated and creating instances of the superclass. Accordingly, SAP recommends including the *final* qualifier in the definition of those classes that are assigned *create private* instantiability.

```
method get_screen_height.
  screen_height                    = me->screen_height.
endmethod.
method get_screen_width.
  screen_width                     = me->screen_width.
endmethod.
method set_screen_height.
  me->screen_height                = screen_height.
endmethod.
method set_screen_width.
  me->screen_width                 = screen_width.
endmethod.
endclass.
```

Listing 11-3 shows a snippet of code describing how a program would make use of this type of singleton.

Listing 11-3. Report Program Using class screen_manager

```
o
o
data             : report_screen_height type int4
                 , report_screen_width  type int4
                 , screen_manager_ref   type ref
                                        to screen_manager
                 .
o
o
report_screen_height          = 30.
report_screen_width           = 120.
o
o
screen_manager_ref            = screen_manager=>get_instance( ).
call method screen_manager_ref->set_screen_height
  exporting
    screen_height             = report_screen_height.
call method screen_manager_ref->set_screen_width
  exporting
    screen_width              = report_screen_width.
o
o
call method screen_manager_ref->get_screen_height
  importing
    screen_height             = report_screen_height.
call method screen_manager_ref->get_screen_width
  importing
    screen_width              = report_screen_width.
```

In Listing 11-3, the programmer needs to insure that a call to method get_instance of class screen_manager, which sets a reference to the singleton into global variable screen_manager_ref, is performed before that global variable is used to access the singleton instance.

The following listings show an ABAP example using the same screen manager where the singleton reference is made available by the singleton class itself. It alleviates the need for the user of the singleton instance to provide a reference variable into which a reference to the singleton can be held, in this case one to hold the reference to the screen manager instance. This example also illustrates the use of compound references, where a reference to a member uses more than one class and/or instance selector.

Listing 11-4 shows the definition for class screen_manager, with differences from Listing 11-1 highlighted.

Listing 11-4. Class screen_manager with Differences from Listing 11-1 Highlighted

```
class screen_manager definition final create private.
  public section.

class screen_manager definition final create private.
  public section.
      class-data   : singleton        type ref
                                       to screen_manager
                                       read-only.
      class-methods: class_constructor
                     get_instance
                       returning value (instance)
                         type ref to screen_manager
                     .
      methods      : get_screen_height
                       exporting screen_height type int4
                   , get_screen_width
                       exporting screen_width  type int4
                   , set_screen_height
                       importing screen_height type int4
                   , set_screen_width
                       importing screen_width  type int4
                     .
  private section.
      class-data   : singleton        type ref
                                       to screen_manager
                     .
      data         : screen_height    type int4
                   , screen_width     type int4
                     .
endclass.
```

Notice that the static attribute singleton has been moved from the private section to the public section, and is now accompanied by the *read-only* qualifier. Notice also that static method *get_instance* has been replaced by a static constructor. Listing 11-5 shows the implementation, again with differences from Listing 11-2 highlighted.

Listing 11-5. Class screen_manager with Differences from Listing 11-2 Highlighted

```
class screen_manager implementation.
  method get_instance class_constructor.
    if screen_manager=>singleton is not bound.
     create object screen_manager=>singleton.
    endif.
    instance                  = screen_manager=>singleton.
  endmethod.
  method get_screen_height.
    screen_height             = me->screen_height.
  endmethod.
  method get_screen_width.
    screen_width              = me->screen_width.
  endmethod.
  method set_screen_height.
    me->screen_height         = screen_height.
  endmethod.
  method set_screen_width.
    me->screen_width          = screen_width.
  endmethod.
endclass.
```

Listing 11-6 shows how a report program would make use of the singleton defined within the screen manager class through statements using compound references, again with differences from Listing 11-3 highlighted.

Listing 11-6. Report Program Using class screen_manager with Differences from Listing 11-3 Highlighted

```
  o
  o
  data          : report_screen_height type int4
                , report_screen_width  type int4
                , screen_manager_ref   type ref
                                          to screen_manager
                .
  o
  o
  report_screen_height      = 30.
  report_screen_width       = 120.
  o
  o
  screen_manager_ref              = screen_manager=>get_instance( ).
  call method screen_manager_ref=>singleton->set_screen_height
    exporting
      screen_height             = report_screen_height.
  call method screen_manager_ref=>singleton->set_screen_width
    exporting
      screen_width              = report_screen_width.
  o
  o
  call method screen_manager_ref=>singleton->get_screen_height
```

```
  importing
    screen_height              = report_screen_height.
call method screen_manager_ref=>singleton->get_screen_width
  importing
    screen_width               = report_screen_width.
```

Let's look more closely at what is taking place in Listing 11-6 with these compound references using both the class component selector (=>) and instance component selector (->) in a single operand. The first reference to class screen_manager is the statement invoking its instance method set_screen_height through its static attribute singleton:

```
call method screen_manager=>singleton->set_screen_height
  exporting
    screen_height              = report_screen_height.
```

Here we see the highlighted string of characters following the "call method" statement to be composed of the name of a class (screen_manager), followed by a class component selector, followed by the name of a public static attribute of the class (singleton), followed by an instance component selector, followed by the name of a public instance method (set_screen_height), all with no intervening spaces between them. This constitutes a compound reference.[4] Indeed, here we are accessing an instance method of a class for which our report does not even have a reference to a corresponding instance. How is this even possible? Let's explore this in more detail.

Although the runtime environment does not behave exactly this way, it is helpful to conceive the execution of this statement in the following way:

1. After moving past the "call method" words starting this statement, the statement parser facilitating program execution reaches the portion of the statement operand containing "screen_manager=>". Recognizing that the class selector => denotes a reference to a class name, the statement parser at that point requests the runtime environment to load into storage, if not already loaded, the class name that precedes the class selector, in this case screen_manager. Indeed, since this is the first reference to this class, this will be the point at which the runtime environment loads class screen_manager. At that moment, its static constructor will be invoked, which, according to the implementation for this method, will initialize static attribute singleton with a reference to an object of type screen_manager.

2. Next, the statement parser will reach the portion of the statement operand containing "singleton->". Recognizing that the instance selector -> denotes an instance reference, the reference field preceding the instance selector, in this case singleton, defined as a static attribute of the screen_manager class, is inspected to determine the dynamic type of the instance it holds, in this case a reference to a screen_manager instance. By this time, a corresponding object of type screen_manager already will have been instantiated into this static attribute through the completion of the static constructor method, invoked during the parsing of the previous portion of this statement operand.

---

[4]Such references, where any one of the three components could use up to the full 30-character maximum length of its respective component name, would not have been possible years ago in releases of SAP environments such as R/3 where the ABAP editor restricted the width of a single line to 72 characters. Extending this editor line width restriction, which now stands at 255 characters, made it possible to construct such long compound references without having to resort to cumbersome techniques to avoid overrunning the line end barrier.

3. Next, the statement parser will reach the portion of the statement operand containing "set_screen_height", which it will recognize as the instance method of class screen_manager to be invoked through the instance reference held in reference field singleton, and will parse the remainder of the statement to resolve the parameters to be exchanged with this instance method.

4. The statement "call method screen_manager=>singleton->set_screen_width ..." will be subject to the same type of statement parsing as its predecessor. The difference this time is that class screen_manager has already been loaded during the processing of the preceding statement, and so its static constructor will not be invoked again.

Summary

In this chapter, we learned how to define a class in such a way as to insure that only one instance of it will ever exist during execution, discovering two ways in which a singleton object makes the reference to its single instance available to external entities. We now understand the similarities and differences between a singleton object and a purely static class. We also know that a singleton is a hybrid class, having both static and instance members, and that private instantiability is one of its significant characteristics.

Singleton Exercises

Refer to Chapter 8 in the functional and technical requirements documentation (see Appendix B) for the accompanying ABAP exercise programs associated with this chapter. Take a break from reading the book at this point to reinforce what you have read by changing and executing the corresponding exercise programs. The exercise programs associated with this chapter are those in the 301 series: ZOOT301A through ZOOT301B.

■ ■ ■

CHAPTER 12

Strategy Design Pattern

The next stop on our voyage through the Design Patterns galaxy takes us to the Strategy design pattern, another of the design patterns found in the GoF catalog. We will find this design pattern useful when we need to be able to regard each class in a family of related classes as interchangeable. The Strategy design pattern exemplifies the power of independent interfaces.

The Right Tool for the Job

A Swiss Army Knife is a versatile, foldable, pocket-sized, multi-tool utility containing a variety of pivoting attachments suitable for use in everyday circumstances. Its handle is shaped to offer both comfort and dexterity to the person using it. Although there are many different models, a small version with only a few attachments might include the following:

- Large knife blade
- Small knife blade
- Can opener
- Straight-head screwdriver

More robust models offer additional attachments, including

- Bottle cap remover
- Phillips-head screwdriver
- Nail file
- Saw blade
- Pliers
- Scissors
- Corkscrew
- Compass
- Magnifying lens

To use one of the many tools, simply unfold the corresponding attachment from its closed position into its locked open position and maneuver the tool by its handle. What makes this tool so comfortable to use is that each tool has the same *handle*, enabling the user to apply the same grip regardless of the actual function the tool is providing.

© James E. McDonough 2017

J. E. McDonough, *Object-Oriented Design with ABAP*, DOI 10.1007/978-1-4842-2838-8_12

Imagine we are having dinner with family and friends and the time has come to open a bottle of wine. The wine bottle has a cork seal with a plastic outer wrapper to protect the cork. Our Swiss Army Knife becomes useful to help us open the bottle. We unfold the small knife blade attachment and use it to cut away the plastic outer wrapper protecting the cork. Once completed, the small knife blade gets folded back to its closed position and the corkscrew attachment is opened to assist us in removing the cork from the bottle. We grip the handle of the Swiss Army Knife the same way for each of these attachments.

Object-oriented programming offers us something similar to the design of a Swiss Army Knife. We can define object-oriented classes to correspond to each one of the Swiss Army Knife tool attachments, and indicate that each one implements the same interface. This interface then acts as the *handle* by which we can grip and manipulate the corresponding tool attachment.

A Family of Interchangeable Features

The Strategy design pattern encapsulates a set of features that all offer the same interface for their access. Strategy is categorized by GoF with a *behavioral* purpose and an *object* scope. The intent behind this design pattern is the following:

> **Define a family of algorithms, encapsulate each one, and make them interchangeable. Strategy lets the algorithm vary independently from clients that use it.[1]**

Strategy makes use of these participants[2] working in collaboration with each other:

1. Strategy: Declares an interface common to all supported algorithms. Context uses this interface to call the algorithm defined by a ConcreteStrategy.

2. ConcreteStrategy: Implements the algorithm using the Strategy interface.

3. Context: Is configured with a ConcreteStrategy object. Maintains a reference to a Strategy object. May define an interface that lets Strategy access its data.

The UML class diagram for Strategy is shown in Figure 12-1.

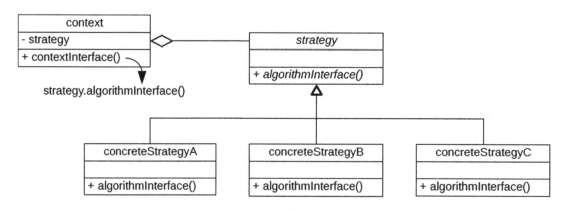

Figure 12-1. UML class diagram for the Strategy design pattern

---

[1]GoF, p. 315.
[2]GoF, p. 317.

Notice that the Context participant does not access any ConcreteStrategy participant directly, but does so through the interface provided by the Strategy participant.

The definitive word of the intent is *interchangeable*. By providing clients an interface by which to access the implementations of its methods, each class of the family can be referenced through a corresponding interface reference variable. Furthermore, restricting the methods of each family class only to those it gains through the interface is what makes each class *interchangeable* with all other classes in the same family. Accessing any of the family classes through the interface using an interface reference variable constitutes the optimal way to access the class. Accordingly, a client will have no dependencies on any particular class in this family of classes. This allows us to adhere to one of the principles of reusable object-oriented design espoused by GoF:

- Program to an interface, not an implementation.[3]

The definitive phrase of the intent is *vary independently*. Since access to one of the interchangeable classes of the family is best achieved via interface reference variables, then the classes that comprise the family members are not accessed directly by any clients. This leaves each of the classes in the family free to have their implementations changed however and whenever a developer sees fit. It removes the obstacle of searching for direct callers of the class to determine the impact any changes would have upon those callers. Since each class in the family implements the same interface, and *only* that interface, and as long as the interface doesn't change, then the search for external callers is rendered unnecessary, thus simplifying the maintenance process.

The use of the Strategy design pattern illustrates an example of using *class composition*. In the UML diagram above, the context entity is shown to include both a private attribute named strategy and a public method named contextInterface. The relationship between the strategy entity and the private attribute of the context entity is depicted using an *aggregation* instance level relationship line. This means a strategy entity is among those objects *composing* the context entity. In effect, the context *has a* strategy, one that is determined and created during program execution.

To return to our Swiss Army Knife analogy, as long as a new foldable attachment can be properly fitted into a specific model, the attachment can be manipulated through the same handle as all of its other attachments.

The UML class diagram for the Strategy pattern adapted to the Swiss Army Knife is shown in Figure 12-2.

---

[3]GoF, p. 18.

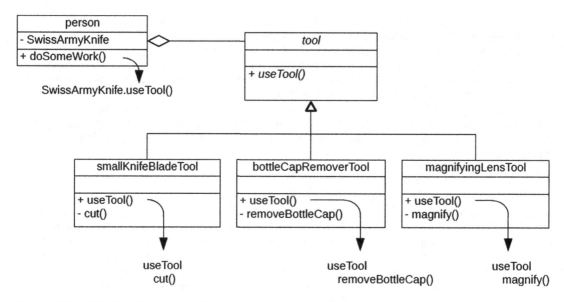

Figure 12-2. *UML class diagram for Strategy design pattern applied to the Swiss Army Knife*

Here we see that a person can have a Swiss Army Knife. Furthermore, the person interacts with the Swiss Army Knife through the tool interface, enabling each of the tool attachments to be handled the same way. The person merely *uses* the tool attachment. The details associated with what *use* entails for each of the individual tool attachments are implemented in those respective concrete classes implementing the tool interface. Regardless of which tool happens to be open at the time, the person grasps the tool handle the same way for all of them.

Strategy in ABAP

Here is how we might implement the Strategy design pattern UML class diagram illustrated above into functioning ABAP code. The tool interface, shown in Listing 12-1, plays the role of the Strategy participant.

Listing 12-1. Tool Interface

```
interface tool.
  methods        : use_tool.
endinterface.
```

The following three classes play the roles of the ConcreteStrategy participants. As shown in Listing 12-2, the small_knife_blade_tool class definition indicates in its public section that it implements the tool interface and that has defined an alias for the use_tool method provided by the tool interface, while its private section defines the cut method. Its implementation shows public method use_tool invoking private method cut.

Listing 12-2. small_knife_blade Class

```
class small_knife_blade_tool definition.
  public section.
    interfaces    : tool.
    aliases       : use_tool for tool~use_tool.
  private section.
    methods       : cut.
endclass.
class small_knife_blade_tool implementation.
  method use_tool.
    call method me->cut.
  endmethod.
  method cut.
    message 'cutting' type 'I'.
  endmethod.
endclass.
```

As shown in Listing 12-3, the bottle_cap_remover_tool class definition is defined similarly to the small_knife_blade_tool class except for the name of its private method. Its implementation shows public method use_tool invoking private method remove_bottle_cap.

Listing 12-3. bottle_cap_remover Class

```
class bottle_cap_remover_tool definition.
  public section.
    interfaces    : tool.
    aliases .     : use_tool for tool~use_tool.
  private section.
    methods       : remove_bottle_cap.
endclass.
class bottle_cap_remover_tool implementation.
  method use_tool.
    call method me->remove_bottle_cap.
  endmethod.
  method remove_bottle_cap.
    message 'removing bottle cap' type 'I'.
  endmethod.
endclass.
```

As shown in Listing 12-4, the magnifying_lens_tool class definition is also defined similarly to the small_knife_blade_tool class except for the name of its private method. Its implementation shows public method use_tool invoking private method magnify.

Listing 12-4. magnifying_lens_tool Class

```
class magnifying_lens_tool definition.
  public section.
    interfaces    : tool.
    aliases       : use_tool for tool~use_tool.
  private section.
    methods       : magnify.
endclass.
```

```
class magnifying_lens_tool implementation.
  method use_tool.
    call method me->magnify.
  endmethod.
  method magnify.
    message 'magnifying' type 'I'. Strategy
  endmethod.
endclass.
```

As shown in Listing 12-5, the person class definition, playing the role of the Context participant, shows a private attribute swiss_army_knife defined as a reference to the tool interface. It also defines a public method called do_some_work. Also included here is a constructor method for providing a new person instance with a reference to a swiss_army_knife. The implementation for the constructor shows initializing the private attribute with the reference to the swiss_army_knife provided by the instantiator, meaning that at the completion of creating an instance of a person it will also have a reference to an instance of a swiss_army_knife. Its implementation for the public method do_some_work invokes method use_tool through its private attribute reference to the instance of a swiss_army_knife.

Listing 12-5. person Class

```
class person definition.
  public section.
    methods      : constructor
                     importing swiss_army_knife
                       type ref to tool
                 , do_some_work
                     .
  private section.
    data         : swiss_army_knife type ref to tool.
endclass.
class person implementation.
  method constructor.
    me->swiss_army_knife          = swiss_army_knife.
  endmethod.
  method do_some_work.
    call method me->swiss_army_knife->use_tool.
  endmethod.
endclass.
```

Finally, unrelated to the UML diagram but illustrating how the UML components would be used, a report program shown in Listing 12-6 defines a data field bartender as a reference to the person class and a data field bartender_tool as a reference to the tool interface. Subsequent processing shows creating an instance of a tool into the bartender_tool reference (specifically, one of class type bottle_cap_remover_tool), creating an instance of person into the bartender reference (passing the bartender_tool on the create statement), then finally invoking the do_some_work of the person instance through the bartender reference variable.

Listing 12-6. Report Program Snippet Using the Entities Defined Above

```
o
o
data            : bartender          type ref to person
```

```
                , bartender_tool          type ref to tool
                  .
o
o
create object bartender_tool type bottle_cap_remover_tool.
create object bartender
  exporting swiss_army_knife = bartender_tool.
call method bartender->do_some_work.
```

When this report is executed we should expect to see "removing bottle cap" appear on the screen as an informational message.

Indeed, at some point we might expect a bar patron to approach the bartender with a request for a glass of wine, requiring the bartender to open a new bottle. So it is not too difficult for us to imagine a class defining a corkscrew tool also implementing the tool interface, such as shown in Listing 12-7.

Listing 12-7. corkscrew_tool Class

```
class corkscrew_tool definition.
  public section.
    interfaces    : tool.
    aliases       : use_tool for tool~use_tool.
  private section.
    methods       : uncork_bottle.
endclass.
class corkscrew_tool implementation.
  method use_tool.
    call method me->uncork_bottle.
  endmethod.
  method uncork_bottle.
    message 'uncorking bottle' type 'I'.
  endmethod.
endclass.
```

Accordingly, we might expect something similar to the snippet of code in Listing 12-8 to be added to the report program to facilitate the request by a patron to the bartender for a glass of wine.

Listing 12-8. Report Program Snippet Using the New Class Defined in Listing 12-7

```
o
o
create object bartender_tool type corkscrew_tool.
create object bartender
  exporting swiss_army_knife = bartender_tool.
call method bartender->do_some_work.
```

Notice that the requests to open a bottle of beer or to open a bottle of wine both use the very same statement,

```
call method bartender->do_some_work.
```

but result in different behaviors depending on which attachment of the bartender's Swiss Army Knife is open.

With this additional code, now when this report is executed we should see the message "removing bottle cap" appear on the screen followed by the message "uncorking bottle." It is through its abilities to invoke the behaviors of the tool interface for different classes implementing the tool interface and get a different result with each behavior that makes the Strategy design pattern so powerful.

Summary

In this chapter, we learned the benefits of accessing a class through an interface reference. We now are familiar with the way in which we can define a family of interchangeable classes where each family member implements the same interface, enabling us to decide during execution which class of the family is the most appropriate one to be used for the task at hand. The use of the Strategy design pattern enhances our ability to provide more flexible software designs because through its use we are able to apply maintenance changes to a class independently from the clients using it.

Strategy Exercises

Actually, there are no new exercise programs associated with this chapter since the Strategy design pattern has already been used with the exercise programs since Chapter 7, which covered interfaces. Refer to Chapter 9 of the associated functional and technical requirements documentation (see Appendix B) for more details.

CHAPTER 13

■ ■ ■

Observer Design Pattern

The next stop on our voyage through the Design Patterns galaxy takes us to the Observer design pattern, another of the design patterns found in the GoF catalog. We will find this design pattern useful in situations where one class needs to be kept aware of changes occurring in another class.

The Observer design pattern often is described as a *publish* and *subscribe* arrangement between entities. A good example of this is the process of getting a daily newspaper delivered to you. You, as the customer, subscribe to the newspaper. The newspaper publishes a new edition every day. Since you are a subscribing customer, a copy is delivered to you every day. Copies also are delivered to all of the other subscribers. After a while you decide you no longer want to receive this newspaper, so you cancel your subscription. The newspaper continues to be published daily, but you no longer get a copy delivered to you.

To further explain the Observer design pattern, I'll start with a business scenario, introduce a new business requirement, and then show how the Observer design pattern addresses the new requirement.

Transportation Business Scenario

In the early 1980s I spent 15 months as a driver for Carretta Trucking, Incorporated of Paramus, New Jersey, which specialized in hauling produce from the west coast to the east coast of the United States using trucks with a team of two drivers, where one would drive while the other slept. This was a 24-hours-per-day, 365-days-per-year operation. The company maintained two dispatch centers: one on the east coast in Paramus, New Jersey and one on the west coast in Brea, California. At any given time, there were some trucks headed west, some headed east, and some that had already delivered the westbound load but had not yet loaded with an eastbound load.

My co-driver Ed and I eventually settled into a comfortable routine where each of us would drive for a full 10-hour shift[1] followed by a 2-hour stop for food, fuel, and relaxation before changing drivers. We usually found ourselves stopping between the hours of 10:00 and 12:00. We could average about 50 miles per hour when moving[2] and usually we were able to complete a combined 20 hours of driving in a 24-hour period, meaning that a 3,000 mile trip from coast to coast would take about 72 hours.

Ed and I made many runs to the west coast and back over the months we spent together as a team. A typical run for us is described in Table 13-1, which shows us hauling a load of cosmetics leaving Hillside, New Jersey at 4:00 p.m. Friday, January 8, 1982, and, 67 hours later, delivering it to Los Angeles California at 11:00 a.m. Monday, January 11, 1982, and then heading empty to Salinas, California to pick up a load of lettuce leaving at 6:30 p.m., and, 72 hours later, delivering it to Bronx, New York at 6:30 p.m. Thursday, January 14, 1982, with all times shown using Eastern Standard Time.

---

[1]At that time, Interstate Commerce Commission (ICC) regulations allowed for a driver to drive continuously for up to 10 hours, after which the driver must take an 8-hour break.
[2]In those days, the nationwide maximum speed limit on U.S. interstate highways was 55 miles per hour.

© James E. McDonough 2017
J. E. McDonough, *Object-Oriented Design with ABAP*, DOI 10.1007/978-1-4842-2838-8_13

Each morning between 8:00 a.m. and noon, east coast time, we were required to call the dispatcher on the coast to which we were heading, state our location and, if eastbound, the pulp temperature of the produce we were hauling.

I left the company in June, 1982 just as they were about to install a computerized system to enable better tracking of their trucks.[3]

Table 13-1. *Round-Trip Hauling Freight Between the East Coast and West Coast of the United States*

Tractor: 440 Trailer: R227	Location	Arrive	Depart	Miles to destination	Miles between stops	Pulp Temp
Start date: 01/08/1982 Load id:cosmetics Co-drivers: E. Kading J. McDonough	Hillside, New Jersey	2:45 p.m. Fri	4:00 p.m. Fri	2890		
					297	
	Toms Brook, Virginia	10:00 p.m. Fri	12:00mid Fri	2593		
					503	
	Cookeville, Tennessee	10:00 a.m. Sat	12:00m Sat	2090		
					495	
	Russellville, Arkansas	10:00 p.m. Sat	12:00mid Sat	1595		
					522	
	Amarillo, Texas	10:00 a.m. Sun	12:00m Sun	1073		
					518	
	Holbrook, Arizona	10:00 p.m. Sun	12:00mid Sun	555		
					555	
	Los Angeles, California	11:00 a.m. Mon		0		
Start date: 01/11/1982 Load id:empty Co-drivers: E. Kading J. McDonough	Los Angeles, California		11:30 a.m. Mon	303		
					303	
	Salinas, California	6:00 p.m. Mon		0		

(*continued*)

---

[3]This was a career change for me. Three days after returning from my final run I attended my first class of the summer semester at my local community college, where I began to study computer programming.

Table 13-1. (*continued*)

Tractor: 440 Trailer: R227	Location	Arrive	Depart	Miles to destination	Miles between stops	Pulp Temp
Start date: 01/11/1982 Load id: lettuce Co-drivers: E. Kading J. McDonough	Salinas, California		6:30 p.m. Mon	3009		34°F
					175	
	West Sacramento, California	10:00 p.m. Mon	12:00mid Mon	2834		34°F
					527	
	West Wendover, Nevada	10:00 a.m. Tue	12:00m Tue	2307		33°F
					511	
	Laramie, Wyoming	10:00 p.m. Tue	12:00mid Tue	1796		33°F
					491	
	Lincoln, Nebraska	10:00 a.m. Wed	12:00m Wed	1305		34°F
					495	
	Joliet, Illinois	10:00 p.m. Wed	12:00mid Wed	810		34°F
					500	
	Brookville, Pennsylvania	10:00 a.m. Thu	12:00m Thu	310		34°F
					310	
	Bronx, New York	6:30 p.m. Thu		0		34°F

New Business Requirement[4]

The dispatchers complained to company management that although the new computers enabled better managing and tracking of the trucks, they had up-to-date information about the location of the trucks only at the moment the drivers made their daily morning call. As the day progressed, the dispatchers were uncertain whether the trucks were moving at all, and if so, whether they still were moving at the expected 50 miles per hour average. They felt the new computerized tracking was not much better than the old manual methods they used prior to the new computer system. They prevailed upon management to improve the computer system so the information on individual trucks was closer to real-time.

---

[4]Whereas the business scenario is historically accurate, the new business requirement is merely hypothetical; I had left the company before the computerized tracking system was installed.

After agreeing to improve the computer system, management contacted the computer services company responsible for the software maintenance and explained the challenge. The developers devised a way to eliminate the need for drivers to call dispatchers, and instead had the drivers, via on-board communication links, simply log into the system anytime they stopped for an extended break, indicating they were no longer moving and giving their location, and again just before getting underway, indicating they had begun moving once again.

This enabled the dispatchers to approximate real-time information about the trucks, allowing them to determine at any hour of the day or night the location of each truck. They always knew which trucks were stopped and where they were located. The location of the moving trucks could now be estimated by multiplying the number of hours since the time the truck last got underway by the average speed of 50 miles per hour.[5]

Under Observation

The Observer design pattern is one where instances of classes *observe* changes in instances of other classes and take action based on the change. Observer is categorized by GoF with a *behavioral* purpose and an *object* scope. The intent behind this design pattern is the following:

> **Defines a one-to-many dependency between objects so that when one object changes state, all of its dependents are notified and updated automatically.**[6]

Observer makes use of these participants[7] working in collaboration with each other:

1. Subject: Knows its observers. Any number of Observer objects many observe a subject. Provides an interface for attaching and detaching Observer objects.

2. Observer: Defines an updating interface for objects that should be notified of changes in a subject.

3. ConcreteSubject: Stores state of interest to ConcreteObserver objects. Sends a notification to its observers when its state changes.

4. ConcreteObserver: Maintains a reference to a ConcreteSubject object. Stores state that should stay consistent with the subject's. Implements the Observer updating interface to keep its state consistent with the subject's.

The UML class diagram for Observer is shown in Figure 13-1.

---

[5]These days, GPS tracking technology makes this estimation technique unnecessary, and companies such as Qualcomm specialize in providing up-to-the-moment commercial fleet tracking systems.
[6]GoF, p. 293.
[7]GoF, p. 295.

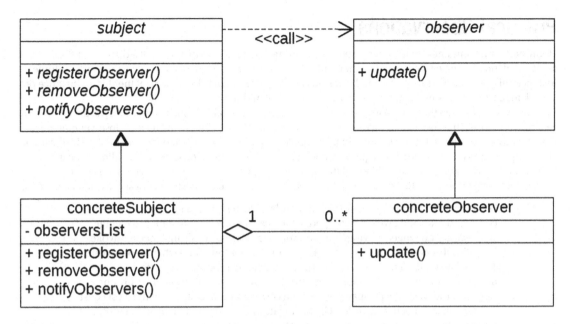

Figure 13-1. *UML class diagram for the Observer design pattern*

The concrete observer is an instance of a class that needs to be aware of changes taking place in an instance of another class. The concrete subject is an instance of a class to which the concrete observer needs to be aware of changes.

The concrete observer implements the Observer interface. This means it needs to provide an implementation for the update method.

The concrete subject implements the Subject interface. This means it needs to provide implementations for methods registerObserver, removeObserver, and notifyObserver.

During execution, the concrete observer invokes the registerObserver method of the concrete subject, effectively indicating to the concrete subject that it wants to be made aware of its changes. The concrete subject retains the address of the concrete observer. This constitutes a "has a" relationship between the concrete subject and the concrete observer; the concrete subject "has a" concrete observer. Indeed, the concrete subject may have zero to unlimited concrete observers, and the address of each one will be retained in a list of observers.

When the subject changes its state, it invokes its own notifyObservers method. The processing here is to loop through the list of addresses for concrete observers, and for each one invoke its update method. The concrete subject does not need to know anything about the type of class the concrete observer is; it merely relies on the fact that the concrete subject implements the Observer interface, which means the concrete subject must provide an implementation for the update method.

When the concrete observer no longer needs to be aware of changes in the subject, it invokes method removeObserver of the subject, which will cause the address of the observer to be removed from the list of observers.

The relationship between a concrete observer and a concrete subject is one of *loose coupling*. The communication between these two objects occurs at the level of the interface defined by the subject and observer entities. Accordingly, there is no direct communication between either concrete class; each one invokes the methods of the other via its respective public interface. It also illustrates another example of *class composition*, since a concrete subject *has a* list of concrete observers to be notified when its state changes.

Let's see how this applies to a business scenario.

Practical Observations

Upon starting the enhanced computer system for Carretta Trucking, two instances of a dispatcher class are created: one for the east coast dispatcher and one for the west coast dispatcher. Also, there are multiple instances of the truck class to represent the various trucks carrying their loads. One of them is an instance of a truck to represent the one Ed and I are driving: tractor 440 and trailer R227.

Upon being notified that truck 440 is on its way to pick up a westbound load, the west coast dispatcher issues a command causing the corresponding west coast dispatcher instance to invoke the registerObserver method for truck instance 440, the one Ed and I are driving. The implementation of the registerObserver method by the truck class simply places the address of the requesting observer class into its list of observers. Accordingly, the instance representing truck 440 now has the address of the west coast dispatcher as an entry in its list of observers.

Follow along using Table 13-1 as Ed and I drive truck 440 from the east coast to the west coast and back again.

- Upon arriving in Hillside, NJ at 2:45 p.m. Friday, we log into the system and issue a command indicating we have stopped, which causes our truck instance to change state; we are no longer moving. This command causes our truck instance to invoke its notifyObservers method, which calls the update method for each of its observers. The update method implemented in the dispatcher class simply records the date, time, and the new location of our truck. At this point, our truck has only one observer, the west coast dispatcher, and the corresponding instance of the west coast dispatcher, upon being so notified by having its update method invoked, records that we have stopped in Hillside, New Jersey at 2:45pm Friday.

- At 4:00 p.m. Friday Ed and I are loaded and ready to get underway. We log into the system and issue a command indicating we have started, causing our truck instance again to change state: we are now moving. This command causes our truck instance to invoke its notifyObservers method again and calls the update method for each of its observers. Our truck still has only one observer, and the corresponding instance of the west coast dispatcher, upon being so notified, records that we have started.

- At 10:00 p.m. Friday we arrive in Toms Brook, Virginia. We log into the system and issue a command indicating we have stopped. Again, this command causes our truck instance to invoke its notifyObservers method. We still have only one observer and its corresponding instance is notified that we have stopped in Toms Brook, Virginia.

- At midnight Friday we change drivers and are ready to get underway again. Once more we log into the system and issue a command indicating we have started, which again causes our truck instance to invoke its notifyObservers method, which again notifies the west coast dispatcher instance that we have started.

- At 10:00 a.m. Saturday we arrive in Cookeville, Tennessee and depart 2 hours later. We logged onto the system with each change of status, stopping and then starting again, and each time our truck instance invoked its notifyObservers method to update the west coast dispatcher with our location and state.

- At 10:00 p.m. Saturday we arrive in Russellville, Arkansas and depart 2 hours later. We follow the same process we did 12 hours earlier.

By this time, we have been westbound for 32 hours. We logged onto the system each time we started and stopped, so the west coast dispatcher was notified with each change in our status.

At 8:00am Sunday morning the west coast dispatcher checks to see where Ed and I are located. The last notification our truck instance gave to the west coast dispatcher instance was 8 hours earlier when we indicated we were departing Russellville, Arkansas. Upon seeing this information, the west coast dispatcher can extrapolate that we are still moving and, based on our approximate rate of 50 miles per hour when moving, are located about 400 miles west of Russellville, Arkansas, which would put us in the vicinity of Sayre, Oklahoma.

- At 10:00 a.m. Sunday we arrive in Amarillo, Texas and depart 2 hours later. With each change, our truck instance invokes its notifyObservers method to update the west coast dispatcher instance accordingly.

- At 10:00 p.m. Sunday we arrive in Holbrook, Arizona and depart 2 hours later. Again, we follow the same process we did 12 hours earlier.

- At 11:00 a.m. Monday we arrive in Los Angeles, California where we stop and unload.[8] Upon logging onto the system to issue the command indicating we have stopped, our truck instance invokes its notifyObservers method to update the west coast dispatcher instance with the location where we have stopped.

After our cargo has been unloaded, we notify the west coast dispatcher, who sends us 300 miles north to Salinas, California to pick up an eastbound load of lettuce.

At this point, the west coast dispatcher no longer has any interest in being an observer of our truck, so it issues a command causing the west coast dispatcher instance to invoke the removeObserver method of our truck instance. The implementation of the removeObserver method by the truck class simply discards the address of the requesting observer class from its list of observers. Accordingly, the instance of our truck now has no addresses in its list of observers.

Meanwhile, the east coast dispatcher is now interested in being an observer to our truck. Similarly, the east coast dispatcher issues a command causing the corresponding east coast dispatcher instance to invoke the registerObserver method for the instance of the truck we are driving. Accordingly, the instance of our truck now has the address of the east coast dispatcher in its list of observers.

- At 6:00 p.m. Monday we arrive in Salinas, California, and, following the same process, our truck instance invokes its notifyObservers method to update the east coast dispatcher instance that we have stopped here.

- At 6:30 p.m. Monday we depart Salinas, and our truck instance invokes its notifyObservers method to update the east coast dispatcher instance that we have started.

- At 10:00 p.m. Monday we arrive in West Sacramento, California and depart 2 hours later. With each change, our truck instance invokes its notifyObservers method to update the east coast dispatcher instance accordingly, including our pulp temperature of 34°F.

- At 10:00 a.m. Tuesday we arrive in West Wendover, Nevada and depart 2 hours later. With each change, our truck instance invokes its notifyObservers method to update the east coast dispatcher instance accordingly, including our pulp temperature of 33°F

This process continues as we change drivers again

- between 10:00 p.m. and midnight Tuesday in Laramie, Wyoming (pulp temperature 33°F)

- between 10:00 a.m. and noon Wednesday in Lincoln, Nebraska (pulp temperature 34°F)

- between 10:00 p.m. and midnight Wednesday in Joliet, Illinois (pulp temperature 34°F)

- between 10:00 a.m. and noon Thursday in Brookville, Pennsylvania (pulp temperature 34°F)

until finally arriving at 6:30 p.m. Thursday in Bronx, New York where we stop and unload, and, following the same process, our truck instance invokes its notifyObservers method to update the east coast dispatcher instance that we have stopped here and that our pulp temperature is 34°F.

---

[8]Somewhere before arriving in Los Angeles Ed and I would have changed drivers, but we would not have made our usual 2-hour stop to do this.

At this point, the east coast dispatcher no longer has any interest in being an observer of our truck, so it issues a command causing the east coast dispatcher instance to invoke the removeObserver of our truck instance.

Now consider that both the east and west coast dispatchers need to track not only the truck Ed and I are driving, but all of the other trucks as well. Accordingly, each dispatcher instance will be an observer to many truck instances at the same time.

Consider also that this computer system may also be made accessible (with the proper security authorizations in place, of course) to both shippers and customers interested in tracking their loads and by unloading crews who may want to know whether a truck is still on schedule. They would translate into instances of shippers, customers, and loading crews, which would register and remove themselves as observers to specific trucks.

This constitutes quite an improvement over the old process where drivers called the dispatcher only once a day. Figure 13-2 shows the corresponding UML diagram showing the relationship between the west coast dispatcher and truck 440.

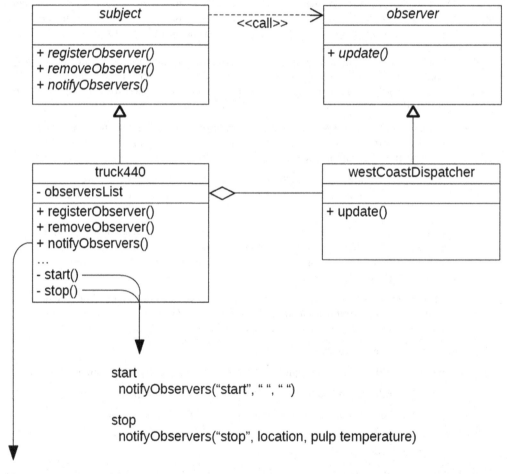

Figure 13-2. *UML class diagram for the Observer design pattern applied to the transportation scenario*

Uses of the Observer Pattern in Technology Today

These days, in the realm of personal computing, the Observer pattern can be recognized in the RSS feed model, where you decide which feeds you want to subscribe to and the publisher keeps you informed of changing information. In the realm of social media, the Observer pattern can be recognized in the Twitter model, where you establish an account on Twitter and then decide to *follow* (subscribe) the *tweets* (publications) of another user. It can even be recognized with email, where broadcast messages are sent to a list of email addresses, often with a statement notifying the recipient how to unsubscribe from the broadcasts.

Exchanging Information Between Subject and Observer

With the Observer design pattern, there are two techniques by which a subject can exchange information with its observers:

- The *push* technique
- The *pull* technique

With *push*, the subject sends (pushes) its state values with the invocation of the update method of the observer. The observer gets all of its information through the update method. This is the technique we saw used with the Carretta Trucking system, where each time the truck stopped, its corresponding truck instance would invoke the update method of each of its observer instances and push to them the location of the truck and the pulp temperature of the cargo.

With *pull*, the subject essentially sends no state information when invoking the update method of the observer. Upon getting notified of a change in state through its update method, the observer instance makes a call to the subject to request (pull) the state information it seeks.

Many object-oriented scholars regard the pull technique as more elegant and flexible than the push technique. With push, every observer must accept all information the subject chooses to send it, regardless whether the observer needs that information. With pull, each observer can pick and choose which fragments of information it wants to know, but needs to make a subsequent call to get them. Both techniques have an impact on the signature of the update method, and pull has a subsequent effect on defining additional methods by which an observer can request change-of-state information from the subject. A case can be made to use the pull technique with our Carretta Trucking example when one considers that an unloading crew, registering itself as an observer, is interested only in whether the truck is running on time, and not with the pulp temperature of the cargo.

Observer Design Pattern in ABAP

It is entirely unnecessary to define Subject and Observer interfaces and to implement them in respective concrete subject and concrete observer classes in ABAP. This is because the Observer design pattern is implemented directly into the ABAP language itself, through *events* defined for classes. This is not to suggest that we are prohibited from using these Observer design pattern concepts to define such entities and interactions if we so choose, but only that doing so gains very little beyond the capabilities offered through the corresponding ABAP language statements.

Table 13-2 shows a comparison of the elements composing the Observer design pattern and for each of its counterparts in the ABAP language.

Table 13-2. *Comparison of the Elements Composing the Observer Design Pattern and Counterparts in the ABAP Language*

Observer design pattern element	ABAP language statement equivalent
Implementing the update method in the observer class	METHODS meth FOR EVENT evt OF cif IMPORTING parm1 parm2 … This statement appears in the definition of the observer class or interface and references an event (evt) triggered by the subject class or interface (cif). Here, the name of the method does not need to be known to the subject, as is the case with the update method defined by the Observer interface of the Observer design pattern. Instead, this statement enables associating the name of any method of an observer class with an event raised by a subject class. The signature of the method is dependent on the signature of the corresponding event it is observing. A reference to the invoking subject class is available in the implicit parameter SENDER and does not need to be defined in the method signature. A method signature facilitates the push technique. A corresponding implementation must be provided for this method. This statement correlates to the design-time preparation for subscribing.
Invoking the subject method registerObserver by the observer class	SET HANDLER handler1 handler 2 … ACTIVATION "X" Here, handler is the name of a method defined on a METHODS … FOR EVENT statement, which qualifies the type of subject class and its specific event to be observed. With this statement the observer class not only registers as an observer of the subject but also indicates the names of the update methods to be invoked when the subject notifies its observers. If not otherwise specified, ACTIVATION "X" is the default. This statement correlates to the runtime request to subscribe.
Invoking subject method removeObserver by observer class	SET HANDLER handler1 handler 2 … ACTIVATION " " This statement correlates to the runtime request to unsubscribe.
(No counterpart in Observer design pattern)	EVENTS evt EXPORTING … This statement is defined in the subject class and advertises to potential observer classes those events it is capable of triggering. Observer classes may pick and choose those events of the subject class it is interested in observing. This statement correlates to the design-time preparation for publishing.
Invoking subject method notifyObservers by subject class	RAISE EVENT evt EXPORTING … This statement is how a subject class indicates a change in state, causing all of its observers to be notified accordingly. This statement correlates to the runtime request to publish.

There is one significant difference between the Observer design pattern and the corresponding implementation provided by ABAP language statements. With the Observer design pattern, each subject class retains its own list of observers, each observer to have its update method invoked when the subject class changes state. Accordingly, the subject class is aware of its observers. By contrast, subject classes using the ABAP statements EVENTS and RAISE EVENT are oblivious to the presence of any observer classes they may have. All of the management required to facilitate the Observer design pattern through the ABAP language statements takes place in the runtime environment. This is why with ABAP, a subject class does not need to provide the ABAP equivalent of implementations for the registerObserver, removeObserver, and notifyObservers methods.

Because ABAP provides statements to facilitate the observation of one instance by another, there is no need for us to define the subject and observer classes shown in the UML diagram above, but Listings 13-1 through 13-4 illustrate how we can define the truck and dispatcher classes in such a way that the dispatcher instance can respond to events raised by the truck instance.

The definition of the truck class, shown in Listing 13-1, plays the role of the *ConcreteSubject* participant, specifying public events for starting and stopping along with public methods start and stop.

Listing 13-1. Definition of truck Class

```
class truck definition.
  public section.
    events      : starting
                    exporting
                      value(current_driver)
                        type string
                , stopping
                    exporting
                      value(location)
                        type string
                      value(pulp_temperature)
                        type int4
                  .
    methods     : constructor
                    importing
                      truck_id
                        type string
                , start
                    importing
                      current_driver
                        type string
                , stop
                    importing
                      location
                        type string
                      pulp_temperature
                        type int4
                  .
  private section.
    data        : truck_id        type string
                , current_driver type string
                , location        type string
                , pulp_temperature
                                  type int4
                  .
endclass.
```

The implementation of these public methods is shown in Listing 13-2, where each method raises its corresponding public event.

Listing 13-2. Implementation of truck Class

```
class truck implementation.
  method constructor.
    me->truck_id                = truck_id.
  endmethod.
  method start.
    me->current_driver          = current_driver.
    " Notify observers this truck is now moving:
    raise event starting
      exporting
        current_driver          = me->current_driver.
  endmethod.
  method stop.
    me->current_driver          = space.
    me->location                = location.
    me->pulp_temperature        = pulp_temperature.
    " Notify observers this truck is no longer moving:
    raise event stopping
      exporting
        location                = location
        pulp_temperature        = pulp_temperature .
  endmethod.
endclass.
```

The definition of the dispatcher class is defined to track trucks and plays the role of the *ConcreteObserver* participant. As shown in Listing 13-3, its definition provides public methods to initiate and terminate the observation of truck instances. Notice that its private section defines an internal table for retaining information about trucks it is tracking as well as methods for responding to the starting and stopping events raised by the truck class.

Listing 13-3. Definition of dispatcher Class

```
class dispatcher definition.
  public section.
    methods     : constructor
                    importing
                      dispatcher_id
                        type string
                , show_tracked_trucks
                , start_observing_truck
                    importing
                      truck_instance
                        type ref to truck
                , stop_observing_truck
                    importing
                      truck_instance
                        type ref to truck

                  .
```

```
private section.
  types          : begin of truck_row
                 ,    truck_instance
                                  type ref
                                   to truck
                 ,   driver       type string
                 ,   last_date    type string
                 ,   last_time    type string
                 ,   last_location
                                  type string
                 ,   last_pulp_temperature
                                  type int4
                 , end    of truck_row
                 , truck_list     type standard table
                             of dispatcher=>truck_row
                 .
  data           : dispatcher_id  type string
                 , trucks_being_tracked
                                  type dispatcher=>truck_list
                 .
  methods        : respond_to_truck_starting
                     for event starting
                           of truck
                     importing
                       current_driver
                       sender
                 , respond_to_truck_stopping
                     for event stopping
                           of truck
                     importing
                       location
                       pulp_temperature
                       sender
                 .
endclass.
```

Implementations for the methods of the dispatcher class are shown in Listing 13-4.

Listing 13-4. Implementation of dispatcher Class

```
class dispatcher implementation.
  method constructor.
    me->dispatcher_id            = dispatcher_id.
  endmethod.
  method respond_to_truck_starting.
    data          : truck_entry   type dispatcher=>truck_row
                  .
    " Indicate corresponding truck entry is now moving:
    truck_entry-driver           = current_driver.
    truck_entry-last_date        = sy-datum.
    truck_entry-last_time        = sy-uzeit.
    modify me->trucks_being_tracked
```

```
      from truck_entry
      transporting driver
                  last_date
                  last_time
    where truck_instance         eq sender.
  endmethod.
  method respond_to_truck_stopping.
    data          : truck_entry    type dispatcher=>truck_row
                   .

    " Indicate corresponding truck entry is no longer moving:
    truck_entry-driver          = space.
    truck_entry-last_date       = sy-datum.
    truck_entry-last_time       = sy-uzeit.
    truck_entry-last_location   = location.
    truck_entry-last_pulp_temperature
                                = pulp_temperature.
    modify me->trucks_being_tracked
      from truck_entry
      transporting driver
                  last_date
                  last_time
                  last_location
                  last_pulp_temperature
      where truck_instance        eq sender.
  endmethod.
  method show_tracked_trucks.
    data          : truck_entry    type dispatcher=>truck_row
                   .

    write: /01 'Dispatcher id:'
         , me->dispatcher_id
                   .

    loop at me->trucks_being_tracked
       into truck_entry.
      write: /05     truck_entry-driver                 .
           , 25      truck_entry-last_date
           , 35      truck_entry-last_time
           , 45      truck_entry-last_pulp_temperature
           , 55      truck_entry-last_location
                   .
    endloop.
  endmethod.
  method start_observing_truck.
    data          : truck_entry    type dispatcher=>truck_row
                   .

    " Prepare new truck entry:
    truck_entry-truck_instance   = truck_instance.
    " Register this dispatcher instance as an observer to this truck:
    set handler me->respond_to_truck_starting
                me->respond_to_truck_stopping
           for truck_entry-truck_instance.
    " Place new truck entry into the list:
```

```
      append truck_entry
          to me->trucks_being_tracked.
  endmethod.
  method stop_observing_truck.
    data          : truck_entry      type dispatcher=>truck_row
                      .
    " Find corresponding truck entry in the list:
    read table me->trucks_being_tracked
      into truck_entry
      with key truck_instance     = truck_instance .
    " Remove this dispatcher instance as an observer to this truck:
    set handler me->respond_to_truck_starting
                me->respond_to_truck_stopping
          for truck_entry-truck_instance
              activation space.
    " Discard corresponding truck entry from the list:
    delete table me->trucks_being_tracked
      from truck_entry.
  endmethod.
endclass.
```

Notice the use of the set handler statement indicating both the instance of the truck for which observation is to begin or end as well as the names of the private methods to be invoked in response to the public events raised by instances of the truck class. These private methods have been defined with the *for event* clause indicating the applicable event to which each one is to respond. Although defined in the private section, both methods can be invoked externally once they have been registered to respond to external events. This is because their non-public visibility only prevents external entities from directly accessing these methods, but direct method calls are not occurring when events processing is being used.

Notice also the use of *sender* with the private methods. Sender is an undeclared signature parameter implicitly available to any method having a *for events* clause and will hold a reference to the instance raising the event. In the code above, it is used to determine which of the many truck instances is raising the starting or stopping event.

The snippet of report code shown in Listing 13-5 shows an example of using the components defined above.

Listing 13-5. Snippet of Report Code to Demonstrate Using the Events of Classes

```
o
o
data          : truck_440     type ref to truck
              , truck_441     type ref to truck
              , truck_442     type ref to truck
              , west_coast_dispatcher
                              type ref to dispatcher
                      .
create object truck_440
  exporting truck_id        = '440'.
create object truck_441
  exporting truck_id        = '441'.
create object truck_442
  exporting truck_id        = '442'.
o
```

```
o
create object west_coast_dispatcher
  exporting dispatcher_id      = 'west'.
o
o
call method west_coast_dispatcher->start_observing_truck
  exporting: truck_instance    = truck_440
           , truck_instance    = truck_441
           , truck_instance    = truck_442
             .
o
o
call method truck_440->stop
  exporting location            = 'Las Vegas, NV'
           pulp_temperature     = 35
             .
call method truck_441->stop
  exporting location            = 'Chicago, IL'
           pulp_temperature     = 34
             .
call method truck_442->stop
  exporting location            = 'Boston, MA'
           pulp_temperature     = 33
             .
call method truck_440->start
  exporting current_driver      = 'Kading'.
o
o
call method west_coast_dispatcher->show_tracked_trucks.
```

Notice first in Listing 13-5 the creation of three truck objects and a single dispatcher object into their respective class reference variables. This is followed by the request by the dispatcher instance to start observing all three of the truck instances. One by one, each truck instance has its stop behavior invoked, indicating the truck's location and the corresponding pulp temperature of the freight. This is followed by the start behavior of truck instance 440, indicating the name of the driver behind the wheel as the truck gets underway. Finally, the show_tracked_trucks method of the dispatcher instance is invoked to show the current status of all trucks being tracked.

Notice also there are only two invocations to methods of the dispatcher instance: one for it to start observing trucks and another for it to produce a report on the current status of the trucks it is tracking. In between these two method invocations are nothing but calls to behaviors of truck instances, yet with each call, the dispatcher instance was notified of the change and was able to update its tracking information, which subsequently is shown in the report produced by the call to method show_tracked_trucks of the dispatcher instances.

In addition, notice that the truck instances remained oblivious to the fact that they each had observers, and that the dispatcher instance makes no direct calls to any methods of any of the truck instances.

Summary

In this chapter, we learned how one class can establish itself as the observer of the changes taking place in another class, and that, unlike the design patterns we have already explored and others we'll explore later, this observation capability is built into the ABAP language itself, alleviating the need for us to define our own set of classes to provide it. We're now familiar with both the push and pull techniques characteristic of the Observer design pattern. In addition, we saw some examples of the practical uses of the Observer design pattern in current technology.

Observer Exercises

Refer to Chapter 10 of the functional and technical requirements documentation (see Appendix B) for the accompanying ABAP exercise programs associated with this chapter. Take a break from reading the book at this point to reinforce what you have read by changing and executing the corresponding exercise programs. There is one exercise program associated with this chapter: ZOOT303A.

■ ■ ■

CHAPTER 14

Factory Design Patterns

The next stop on our voyage through the Design Patterns galaxy takes us to the Factory patterns, a collection of three distinct patterns (only two of which are found in the GoF catalog). We will find these design patterns useful to simplify the creation of class instances.

Every day we use things to assist us in our endeavors, from the computer we use at work, to the shoes we wear to work, to the mode of transportation we use to commute between home and work. Although many of us might be adept at and take pride in building some of these things for ourselves, most of the things we use have been manufactured elsewhere, and we are the consumers of these products. Indeed, this is a fairly good model: we leave the creation of things we need to the experts who are most experienced in producing them. The benefits are numerous, from continuous improvements in the durability, reliability, and effectiveness of the products to the economic cost of their production. Accordingly, we seek the manufacturer who can offer the best product for the best price.

The same concept applies to creating instances of classes. We can delegate this task to a manufacturer of objects, one that can take into consideration all the nuances of class instantiation on behalf of our program. This allows the program itself to avoid creating the objects it needs and, instead, simply acquire these objects from a manufacturer that has the resources to create what is needed. In short, we obtain the objects we need from an *object factory*.

Varieties of Manufacturers

The idea behind the Factory design patterns is to *encapsulate* the creation of instances of classes, the responsibility for which is delegated to classes specializing in the creation of such instances. There are three different varieties of Factory design patterns, but the primary purpose of all of them is to *create instances of classes*. They are

1. Simple Factory:[1] More idiom than design pattern

2. Factory Method: Uses class inheritance ("is a")

3. Abstract Factory: Uses class composition ("has a")

Whereas the Simple Factory is not covered by GoF, both the Factory Method and Abstract Factory are categorized by GoF with a *creational* purpose; they differ in that Factory Method has a *class* scope while Abstract Factory has an *object* scope.

---

[1]Simple Factory is not one of the 23 GoF patterns. This name comes from the book *Head First Design Patterns* (Freeman, Robson, Sierra, Bates; O'Reilly, 2004), p. 119.

© James E. McDonough 2017

J. E. McDonough, *Object-Oriented Design with ABAP*, DOI 10.1007/978-1-4842-2838-8_14

Simple Factory Design Pattern

A Simple Factory for creating classes is characterized by the following:

- The class definition includes the "create private" qualifier, meaning no entity other than the class itself can create instances of the class.

- The class is defined with a publicly visible static method by which external entities may request an instance of the class be created.

Providing the "create private" qualifier to a class confers complete control to the class over the creation of any of its instances, forcing other entities requiring an instance of the class *to request an instance* instead of creating one themselves.

Simple Factory in ABAP

Listing 14-1 shows an example of using the Simple Factory pattern to control the instantiation of car classes.

Listing 14-1. Simple Factory Pattern Controlling the Instantiation of car Classes

```
class car definition create private.
  public section.
    class-methods: get_instance
                     exporting instance type ref to car.
    methods      : start
                 , stop
                     o
                     o
endclass.
class car implementation.
  method get_instance.
    create object instance.
  endmethod.
  method start.
    o
    o
  endmethod.
  method stop.
    o
    o
  endmethod.
    o
    o
endclass.
```

The operative phrase for the car definition above is *create private*. It means that no entities other than the car class are capable of creating instances of cars. The implementation for the static method get_instance shows that it will create an instance of a car to be returned to the caller. Once created and returned to the caller via the instance reference parameter, the caller can now use the instance reference to invoke the public instance methods defined by the car class.

A good example of this is the standard SAP class cl_salv_table, one of the collection of classes that makes up the ALV Object Model framework. If you look at the definition of this global class via the SE24 transaction, you can see that it is marked as create private by virtue of the value "private" assigned to the Instantiation property on its Properties tab. It is also accompanied by a publicly visible static method named factory, by which instances of cl_salv_table can be requested by external entities. Indeed, the accompanying exercise programs have been invoking this static method to create ALV table instances since the very first exercise.

Simple Factory Similarity with Singleton

Simple Factory and Singleton both include the *create private* qualifier on the class definition statement, insuring that only the class itself is capable of creating its own instances. They differ in that Singleton has a mechanism by which to insure that only one instance ever becomes available during execution, while Simple Factory allows unlimited instances of its class to be created.[2]

Factory Method Design Pattern

The intent behind the Factory Method design pattern is the following:

> **Define an interface for creating an object, but let subclasses decide which class to instantiate. Factory Method lets a class defer instantiation to subclasses.**[3]

Unlike with Simple Factory, where the class itself is accompanied by the "create private" qualifier, the Factory Method is structured where one type of class, a Creator, is creating instances of a different type of class, a Product.

Factory Method makes use of these participants[4] working in collaboration with each other:

1. Product: Defines the interface of objects the factory method creates.

2. ConcreteProduct: Implements the Product interface.

3. Creator: Declares the factory method, which returns an object of type Product. Creator may also define a default implementation of the factory method that returns a default ConcreteProduct object. It may call the factory method to create a Product object.

4. ConcreteCreator: Overrides the factory method to return an instance of a ConcreteProduct.

The following are characteristics of a Factory Method design pattern:

- It is known as *factory method* because a creator superclass defines an abstract method for creating the product instance, a method that must be implemented by an inheriting concrete creator subclass. This abstract method *is* the factory method, the method in which a concrete product gets instantiated.

---

[2]With such similarities it is curious that GoF included Singleton as a design pattern but not Simple Factory.
[3]GoF, p. 107.
[4]GoF, p. 108.

- A creator superclass also defines other non-abstract methods used to control the final state of the object it is creating.

- A public method is defined for the creator superclass, called by external entities to acquire an instance of a product. This public method invokes its own abstract method to have the concrete product created for it by the concrete creator subclass.

The UML class diagram for the Factory Method is shown in Figure 14-1.

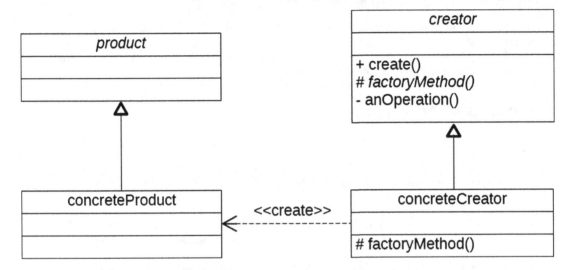

Figure 14-1. *UML class diagram for the Factory Method design pattern*

The diagram shows that the concreteCreator participant will determine what type of concreteProduct is created. This is what is meant by letting the subclass *decide* which class to instantiate. Although multiple concreteCreator subclasses may inherit from the creator superclass, each one of them will follow the same *process*, defined by the public method *create*, for creating instances of product participants. The concreteCreator subclass merely determines which type of concreteProduct will be created. Methods *create* and *anOperation* defined in the creator superclass are oblivious to the actual concreteProduct made available to them by method factoryMethod, working with the concreteProduct merely as a *product* and passing back to the caller an instance of a *product*.

Figure 14-2 shows a UML class diagram illustrating how these components interact in a factory for creating the GPS navigation units we have been using in the accompanying exercise programs.

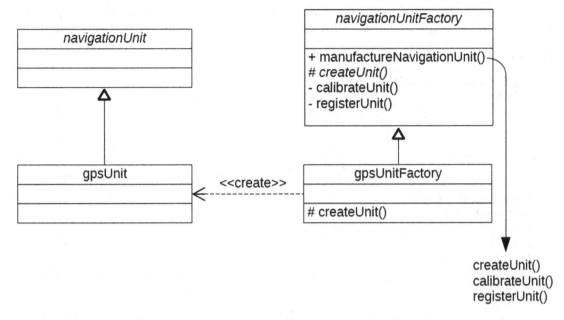

Figure 14-2. *UML class diagram for the Factory Method design pattern applied to a navigation scenario*

Here we see concrete creator gpsUnitFactory inheriting from creator navigationUnitFactory. Class gpsUnitFactory provides an implementation for abstract method createUnit it inherits from its superclass. Its implementation of createUnit creates a navigationUnit, specifically one of type instance of class gpsUnit. To get an instance of a navigationUnit, external entities invoke method manufactureNavigationUnit, defined by the navigationUnitFactory superclass, which invokes private methods calibrateUnit and registerUnit after invoking abstract method createUnit, whose implementation is provided by the gpsUnitFactory subclass. Methods calibrateUnit and registerUnit work with an instance defined at the navigationUnit level of abstraction, and in this particular case are oblivious that they are actually working with a gpsUnit instance.

Factory Method in ABAP

The following code shows how we might implement the Factory Method design pattern UML class diagram illustrated above into functioning ABAP code. First, the classes are defined to represent the product to be produced by the Factory Method. Listing 14-2 shows the code for the navigation_unit class.

Listing 14-2. Code for the navigation_unit Class

```
class navigation_unit definition abstract.
  public section.
    types        : compass_point  type char1.
    methods      : get_heading abstract
                      exporting heading type compass_point
                 , set_heading abstract
                      importing heading type compass_point
                 .
endclass.
```

This code shows the abstract class for the navigation_unit playing the role of the *Product* participant. In Listing 14-3, we see the gps class inheriting from it, playing the role of the *ConcreteProduct* participant.

Listing 14-3. Code for the gps Class

```
class gps definition inheriting from navigation_unit.
  public section.
    methods       : get_heading redefinition
                  , set_heading redefinition
                  .
  private section.
    data          : heading type navigation_unit=>compass_point.
endclass.
class gps implementation.
  method get_heading.
    heading                       = me->heading.
  endmethod.
  method set_heading.
    me->heading                   = heading.
  endmethod.
endclass.
```

Next, Listing 14-4 contains the classes that define the components representing the factory.

Listing 14-4. Classes That Define the Components Representing the Factory

```
class navigation_unit_factory definition abstract.
  public section.
    methods       : manufacture_navigation_unit
                      exporting navigator type ref to navigation_unit.
  protected section.
    methods       : create_unit abstract
                      exporting navigator type ref to navigation_unit.
  private section.
    methods       : calibrate_unit
                      importing navigator type ref to navigation_unit
                  , register_unit
                      importing navigator type ref to navigation_unit
                  .
endclass.
class navigation_unit_factory implementation.
  method manufacture_navigation_unit.
    call method me->create_unit
      importing navigator        = navigator.
    call method me->calibrate_unit
      exporting navigator        = navigator.
    call method me->register_unit
      exporting navigator        = navigator.
  endmethod.
```

```
method calibrate_unit.
  calibrate the navigator
endmethod.
method register_unit.
  register the navigator
endmethod.
endclass.
```

In Listing 14-4, we see the abstract class for navigation_unit_factory playing the role of the *Creator* participant. Notice that it defines abstract protected method create_unit, which requires this entire class to be defined as abstract as well as relieving it from providing an implementation for this method. Its private methods facilitate calibrating and registering a navigation unit. Its public method, enabling callers to get a new instance of a fully calibrated and registered navigation unit returned to them, invokes the methods create_unit, calibrate_unit, and register_unit, in that sequence. The abstract method create_unit, implemented by a subclass, is responsible for creating a concrete instance of a navigation unit, which is then calibrated and registered by the methods of this class. Accordingly, the processing taking place in this class knows nothing about the specific concrete class of navigation_unit it is calibrating and registering.

In Listing 14-5, we see the gps_unit_factory class inheriting from the navigation_unit_factory class, playing the role of the *ConcreteProduct* participant. Notice that it provides an implementation for the abstract method create_unit defined by its superclass. Notice also that the implementation for the create_unit method simply creates an instance of a navigation unit of type GPS.

Listing 14-5. Class gps_unit_factory

```
class gps_unit_factory definition
                      inheriting from navigation_unit_factory.
  protected section.
    methods      : create_unit redefinition.
endclass.
class gps_unit_factory implementation.
  method create_unit.
    create object navigator type gps.
  endmethod.
endclass.
```

In this example, the create_unit method *is* the factory method, the method resulting in the creation of a concrete instance of a navigation_unit. Listing 14-6 shows how these components might be used by other entities.

Listing 14-6. Class car Using the Classes Defined Above

```
class car definition.
  o
  o
  private section.
    data         : navigator type ref to navigation_unit.
    methods      : get_navigation_unit
                      importing navigation_type type char1.
  o
  o
```

179

```
endclass.
class car implementation.
  o
  o
  method get_navigation_unit.
    data        : navigator_factory type ref to navigation_unit_factory
                , manufacturer      type seoclsname
                .

    case navigation_type.
      o
      o
      when global_positioning.
        manufacturer              = 'GPS_UNIT_FACTORY'.
    endcase.
    create object navigator_factory type (manufacturer).
    call method navigator_factory->manufacture_navigation_unit
      importing navigator        = me->navigator.
  endmethod.
endclass.
```

We see in Listing 14-6 that the car class has a private method get_navigation_unit, which handles determining the relevant type of navigation unit manufacturer, creating an instance of a ConcreteCreator participant of the Factory Method design pattern using the relevant type of navigation unit manufacture, and then invoking a method of that ConcreteCreator to create for it an instance of a navigator product to be used with the car instance.

Abstract Factory Design Pattern

The Abstract Factory design pattern is the last of the factory patterns to be covered, and, as its UML diagram shows, is much more involved than what we have seen so far. It may, at first glance, appear too daunting to comprehend this pattern, but fear not, because we will see an example of its use to help us better understand its power.

The intent behind the Abstract Factory design pattern is the following:

> **Provide an interface for creating families of related or dependent objects without specifying their concrete classes.**[5]

Abstract Factory makes use of these participants[6] working in collaboration with each other:

1. AbstractFactory: Declares an interface for operations that create *abstract product* objects.

2. ConcreteFactory: Implements the operations to create *concrete product* objects.

3. AbstractProduct: Declares an interface for a type of product object.

4. ConcreteProduct: Defines a product object to be created by the corresponding concrete factory. Implements the AbstractProduct interface.

5. Client: Uses only interfaces declared by AbstractFactory and AbstractProduct classes.

---

[5]GoF, p. 87.
[6]GoF, p. 89.

The following are characteristics of an Abstract Factory design pattern:

- It is known as *abstract factory* because the client accesses the factory *abstractly* through an interface instead of working directly with a concrete factory.

- It uses composition; the client "has a" reference to an abstract factory instance. This reference can point to any one of the several different concrete factories inheriting from abstract factory, each of which is capable of creating a family of related products.

- Once the factory has created instances of the concrete products, the client accesses these instances through an interface, enabling the client to work with the instances created by any one of the concrete factories the same as the instances of any other concrete factory.

The UML class diagram for Abstract Factory is shown in Figure 14-3.

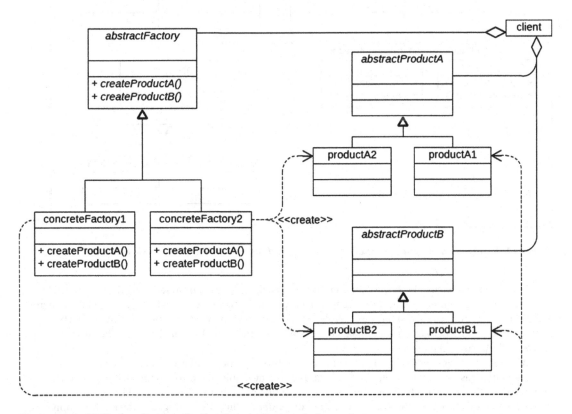

Figure 14-3. *UML class diagram for the Abstract Factory design pattern*

Notice the client "has a" reference to an instance of an abstractFactory. It also "has a" reference to instances of each abstract product, which will contain a reference to a product produced by the abstractFactory instance. The client interacts with the abstractions and not directly with any of the concrete instances.

The UML class diagram shown in Figure 14-4 is a copy of Figure 14-3 but shows how an abstract factory pattern can be established to create widgets used to compose the windows for presenting content by different internet browsers.

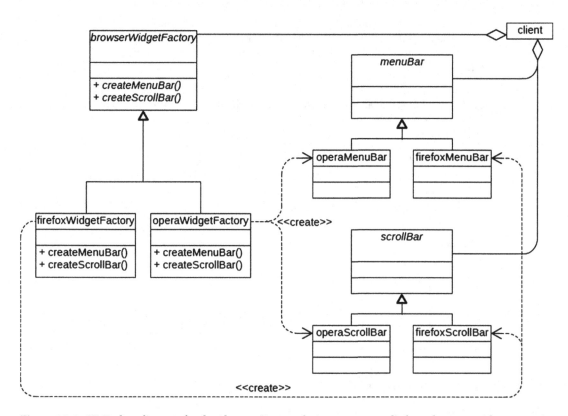

Figure 14-4. *UML class diagram for the Abstract Factory design pattern applied to a browser widget scenario*

As illustrated in Figure 14-4, the client has a reference to an abstract browserWidgetFactory as well as references to abstract menuBar and ScrollBar widgets produced by this abstract factory. One of the concrete widget factories produces menu bars and scroll bars to be used with the Firefox Internet browser, while another produces menu bars and scroll bars to be used with the Opera Internet browser. The client interacts only with the abstract references.

When a computer user decides to open the Firefox browser, the client program managing this interaction has a concrete Firefox widget factory made available to it through the abstract browserWidgetFactory. This factory produces menu bar and scroll bar widgets for the Firefox family. Accordingly, the user of the browser sees window components composed using only the Firefox family members. This assures a consistent appearance of the windows produced by the Firefox browser during web surfing.

Later, the user decides to close the Firefox browser and open the Opera browser. Now the client program managing this interaction has a concrete Opera widget factory made available to it through the abstract browserWidgetFactory, producing menu bar and scroll bar widgets for the Opera family. Accordingly, the user of the browser sees window components composed using only the Opera family members, assuring a consistent appearance of the windows produced by the Opera browser during web surfing.

As long as the client program uses the abstract factory to supply its menu bars and scroll bars, there is little chance of a browser window being displayed with both a Firefox menu bar and an Opera scroll bar.

Abstract Factory in ABAP

The following code shows how we might implement the Abstract Factory design pattern UML class diagram illustrated above into functioning ABAP code. First, we define an abstract class corresponding to the menuBar abstract class illustrated in the UML diagram in Figure 14-4, playing the role of the *AbstractProduct* participant and shown in Listing 14-7 with some general public methods applicable to menu bars.

Listing 14-7. Abstract Class menu_bar

```
class menu_bar definition abstract.
  public section.
    methods     : hover_over_menu_item abstract
                , left_click_on_menu_item abstract
                , right_click_on_menu_item abstract
                .

endclass.
```

All of these methods are defined as abstract, meaning the class must also be defined as abstract (this would be necessary even if only one method had been defined as abstract) and contains no implementation due to the absence of any non-abstract methods. Listing 14-8 shows the classes inheriting from it, each of which plays the role of the *ConcreteProduct* participant and provides implementations for the abstract methods defined by the superclass.

Listing 14-8. Concrete menu_bar Classes for Firefox and Opera Browsers

```
class firefox_menu_bar definition
                       inheriting from menu_bar.
  public section.
    methods     : hover_over_menu_item redefinition
                , left_click_on_menu_item redefinition
                , right_click_on_menu_item redefinition
                .
endclass.
class firefox_menu_bar implementation.
  method hover_over_menu_item.
    do menu bar hovering applicable to firefox
  endmethod.
  method left_click_on_menu_item.
    do menu bar left-click applicable to firefox
  endmethod.
  method right_click_on_menu_item.
    do menu bar right-click applicable to firefox
  endmethod.
endclass.
```

```
class opera_menu_bar definition
                        inheriting from menu_bar.
  public section.
    methods      : hover_over_menu_item redefinition
                 , left_click_on_menu_item redefinition
                 , right_click_on_menu_item redefinition
                 .
endclass.
class opera_menu_bar implementation.
  method hover_over_menu_item.
    do menu bar hovering applicable to opera
  endmethod.
  method left_click_on_menu_item.
    do menu bar left-click applicable to opera
  endmethod.
  method right_click_on_menu_item.
    do menu bar right-click applicable to opera
  endmethod.
endclass.
```

Next are the abstract classes corresponding to the scrollBar abstract class illustrated in the UML diagram in Figure 14-4, also playing the role of the *AbstractProduct* participant and shown in Listing 14-9 with some general public methods applicable to scroll bars. In this case, there are two classes so we can distinguish between horizontal and vertical scroll bars.

Listing 14-9. Abstract Classes horizontal_scroll_bar and vertical_scroll_bar

```
class horizontal_scroll_bar definition abstract.
  public section.
    methods      : scroll_left abstract
                 , scroll_right abstract
                 .
endclass.
class vertical_scroll_bar definition abstract.
  public section.
    methods      : scroll_back abstract
                 , scroll_forward abstract
                 .
endclass.
```

Listing 14-10 shows the classes inheriting from them, each of which again plays the role of the *ConcreteProduct* partcipant.

Listing 14-10. Concrete Scroll Bar Classes for Firefox and Opera Browsers

```
class firefox_horizontal_scroll_bar definition
                        inheriting from horizontal_scroll_bar.
                 .
  public section.
    methods      : scroll_left redefinition
                 , scroll_right redefinition
                 .
endclass.
```

```
class firefox_horizontal_scroll_bar implementation.
  method scroll_left.
    do scroll left applicable to firefox
  endmethod.
  method scroll_right.
    do scroll right applicable to firefox
  endmethod.
endclass.

class firefox_vertical_scroll_bar definition
                        inheriting from vertical_scroll_bar.

  public section.
    methods     : scroll_back redefinition
                , scroll_forward redefinition
                .

endclass.
class firefox_vertical_scroll_bar implementation.
  method scroll_back.
    do scroll back applicable to firefox
  endmethod.
  method scroll_forward.
    do scroll forward applicable to firefox
  endmethod.
endclass.

class opera_horizontal_scroll_bar definition
                        inheriting from horizontal_scroll_bar.
  public section.
    methods     : scroll_left redefinition
                , scroll_right redefinition
                .

endclass.
class opera_horizontal_scroll_bar implementation.
  method scroll_left.
    do scroll left applicable to opera
  endmethod.
  method scroll_right.
    do scroll right applicable to opera
  endmethod.
endclass.

class opera_vertical_scroll_bar definition
                        inheriting from vertical_scroll_bar.
  public section.
    methods     : scroll_back redefinition
                , scroll_forward redefinition
                .

endclass.
```

```
class opera_vertical_scroll_bar implementation.
  method scroll_back.
    do scroll back applicable to opera
  endmethod. "line 100
  method scroll_forward.
    do scroll forward applicable to opera
  endmethod.
endclass.
```

Listing 14-11 shows the definition of an abstract class corresponding to the browserWidgetFactory abstract class illustrated in the UML diagram in Figure 14-4, playing the role of the *AbstractFactory* participant.

Listing 14-11. Class browser_widget_factory

```
class browser_widget_factory definition abstract.
  public section.
    methods      : create_menu_bar abstract
                      exporting menu type ref to menu_bar
                 , create_horizontal_scroll_bar abstract
                     exporting
                       scroller type ref to horizontal_scroll_bar
                 , create_vertical_scroll_bar abstract
                     exporting
                       scroller type ref to vertical_scroll_bar
                 .
endclass.
```

Listing 14-12 shows the classes inheriting from it, each playing the role of the *ConcreteFactory* participant.

Listing 14-12. Concrete Widget Factory Classes for Firefox and Opera Browsers

```
class firefox_widget_factory definition
                            inheriting from browser_widget_factory.
  public section.
    methods      : create_menu_bar redefinition
                 , create_horizontal_scroll_bar redefinition
                 , create_vertical_scroll_bar redefinition
                 .
endclass.
class firefox_widget_factory implementation.
  method create_menu_bar.
    create object menu type firefox_menu_bar.
  endmethod.
  method create_horizontal_scroll_bar.
    create object scroller type firefox_horizontal_scroll_bar.
  endmethod.
  method create_vertical_scroll_bar.
    create object scroller type firefox_vertical_scroll_bar.
  endmethod.
endclass.
```

```
class opera_widget_factory definition
                            inheriting from browser_widget_factory.
  public section.
    methods      : create_menu_bar redefinition
                 , create_horizontal_scroll_bar redefinition
                 , create_vertical_scroll_bar redefinition
                 .
endclass.
class opera_widget_factory implementation.
  method create_menu_bar.
    create object menu type opera_menu_bar.
  endmethod.
  method create_horizontal_scroll_bar.
    create object scroller type opera_horizontal_scroll_bar.
  endmethod.
  method create_vertical_scroll_bar.
    create object scroller type opera_vertical_scroll_bar.
  endmethod.
endclass.
```

Listing 14-13 shows the definition for a browser manager class making use of the preceding classes and playing the role of the *Client* participant.

Listing 14-13. Definition of Class browser_manager

```
class browser_manager definition.
  public section.
    methods      : constructor
                 , hover_over_menu_item
                 , left_click_on_menu_item
                 , right_click_on_menu_item
                 , scroll_back
                 , scroll_forward
                 , scroll_left
                 , scroll_right
                 .
  private section.
    data         : menu_bar          type ref to menu_bar
                 , horizontal_scroll_bar
                                      type ref
                                        to horizontal_scroll_bar
                 , vertical_scroll_bar
                                      type ref
                                        to vertical_scroll_bar
                 , widget_factory    type ref
                                        to browser_widget_factory
                 .
    methods      : get_widget_factory
                      exporting widget_factory
                        type ref to browser_widget_factory
                 .
endclass.
```

The definition of the browser manager includes some public methods for responding to user actions as well as a public constructor. Its private members include references to a menu bar, a horizontal scroll bar, and a vertical scroll bar, in addition to a reference to the browser widget factory that will create these browser widgets, each of which correlates to the aggregation relationship lines of Figure 14-4 leading to the client entity from the menuBar, scrollbar, and browserWidgetFactory abstract entities. Notice that the data definitions for the menu bar and horizontal and vertical scroll bars are references to abstract classes, enabling the client to invoke menu clicking and scrolling for the browser without ever having to know the specific type of browser for which these widgets are associated. Notice also that the data definition for the widget factory is a reference to an abstract class, enabling the client to invoke methods of the factory to create menu bars and scroll bars also without ever having to know the specific type of browser for which this factory makes widgets.

Listing 14-14 shows the implementation of the browser manager class.

Listing 14-14. Implementation of Class browser_manager

```
class browser_manager implementation.
  method constructor.
    " create instance of abstract factory:
    call method me->get_widget_factory
      importing widget_factory    = me->widget_factory.
    " use abstract factory to create 1 menu bar and 2 scroll bars:
    call method me->widget_factory->create_menu_bar
      importing menu              = me->menu_bar.
    call method me->widget_factory->create_horizontal_scroll_bar
      importing scroller          = me->horizontal_scroll_bar.
    call method me->widget_factory->create_vertical_scroll_bar
      importing scroller          = me->vertical_scroll_bar.
  endclass.
  method get_widget_factory.
    data          : widget_manufacturer type seoclsname.
    determine type of browser.
    case type of browser.
      when 'firefox'.
        widget_manufacturer = 'FIREFOX_WIDGET_FACTORY'.
      when 'opera'.
        widget_manufacturer = 'OPERA_WIDGET_FACTORY'.
      when others.
        o
        o
    endcase.
    create object widget_factory
          type (widget_manufacturer).
  endmethod.
  method hover_over_menu_item.
    call method menu_bar->hover_over_menu_item.
  endmethod.
  method left_click_on_menu_item.
    call method menu_bar->left_click_on_menu_item.
  endmethod.
```

```
method right_click_on_menu_item.
  call method menu_bar->right_click_on_menu_item.
endmethod.
method scroll_back.
  call method vertical_scroll_bar->scroll_back.
endmethod.
method scroll_forward.
  call method vertical_scroll_bar->scroll_forward.
endmethod.
method scroll_left.
  call method horizontal_scroll_bar->scroll_left.
endmethod.
method scroll_right.
  call method horizontal_scroll_bar->scroll_right.
endmethod.
endclass.
```

The public constructor invokes the private method get_widget_factory, which will instantiate a browser widget factory based on the active browser. Once the browser widget factory has been instantiated, it is invoked by the constructor to create a menu bar and two scroll bars. The remaining methods react to subsequent user actions, such as clicking a menu item and scrolling, each one of which invokes a corresponding method of the menu bar or scroll bar widget instance created by the browser widget factory.

Finally, Listing 14-15 shows an entity that creates and uses the instance of the browser manager class.

Listing 14-15. Entity Creating and Using an Instance of Class browser_manager

```
class screen_manager definition abstract final.
  public section.
    class-methods: class_constructor
                 , scroll_right
                     o
                     o
                     .
  private section.
                     o
                     o
    class_data   : internet_browser type ref to browser_manager.
endclass.
class screen_manager implementation.
  method class_constructor.
    create object internet_browser.
  endmethod.

  method scroll_right.
    call method internet_browser->scroll_right.
  endmethod.
    o
    o
endclass.
```

Notice in all of the preceding ABAP code the absence of conditional logic with the exception of the case statement in the get_widget_factory of class browser_manager, where the determination is made for the type of active browser so the correct type of concrete widget factory can be identified. Once identified and an instance of a browser widget factory is created, we no longer need to check the type of browser for which widgets need to be made nor for the type of browser the user actions correspond to, all of which is implicit based upon the concrete widget factory instantiated and all the widget instances this factory will produce.

Summary

In this chapter, we learned about the multiple variations of the Factory design pattern, and that all variations are dedicated to the task of creating instances of classes. The Simple Factory relies on private instantiability to restrict solely to the class itself the ability to create instances of the class, while the Factory Method design pattern relies on class inheritance for instance creation, and the Abstract Factory design pattern relies on class composition to facilitate creating instances. Another significant difference between them is that the Simple Factory facilitates creating instances of the same class, the Factory Method facilitates creating instances of other classes (where the class to be created is controlled by a subclass), and the Abstract Factory facilitates creating instances of other classes that all have a family relationship.

Factory Exercises

Refer to Chapter 11 of the functional and technical requirements documentation (see Appendix B) for the accompanying ABAP exercise programs associated with this chapter. Take a break from reading the book at this point to reinforce what you have read by changing and executing the corresponding exercise programs. The exercise programs associated with this chapter are those in the 304 series: ZOOT304A through ZOOT304D.

■ ■ ■

CHAPTER 15

Adapter Design Pattern

The next stop on our voyage through the Design Patterns galaxy takes us to the Adapter design pattern, another of the design patterns found in the GoF catalog. We will find this design pattern most useful once the maintenance cycle has begun on software components.

Since a software component spends most of its life in the maintenance phase, it is inevitable that changes will need to be applied to existing components. Often times a developer will recognize that some new capability recently becoming available makes a better solution than the current solution. This could result from a variety of reasons, amongst them improved performance, improved reliability, the need to port existing software to a new platform, a change in the underlying relational database, a new data exchange protocol, enhanced data security or some other disruptive technology presenting a new business opportunity to be exploited. As is often the case with maintenance programming, we would endeavor to make as few changes as necessary to enable the software with the enhanced capability.

Change is Inevitable

Suppose we have a program written years ago containing many locations at which requests for a service are made to a service provider. The original service provider expects its requesters to use the "wedge" interface, so named because of its interface shaped like a wedge, as illustrated on the left side of Figure 15-1. If we were to move the graphics on the left toward each other so they touch, as illustrated on the right side of Figure 15-1, we would find that the "point" of the service requester fits perfectly into the "notch" of the service provider, resulting in a tight fit. If these had been bricks used in building a brick wall, they would form a solid bond upon which other bricks could be laid.

© James E. McDonough 2017

J. E. McDonough, *Object-Oriented Design with ABAP*, DOI 10.1007/978-1-4842-2838-8_15

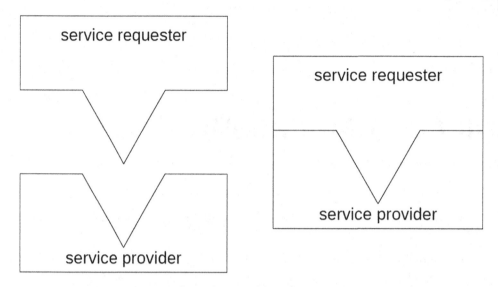

Figure 15-1. *Illustration of wedge interface used by both service requester and service provider*

Let's suppose a new more robust service provider has become available, and we have been given the task of changing an existing program to replace requests to the old service provider with requests to the new service provider. The challenge we face is that the new service provider does not recognize the "wedge" interface we have been using with the old service provider – instead, it uses the "semicircle" interface, so named because of its interface shaped like a semicircle, as illustrated on the left side of Figure 15-2. If we were to move the graphics on the left toward each other so they touch, as illustrated on the right side of Figure 15-2, we would find that the "point" of the service requester does not make a secure fit into the "semicircle depression" of the service provider. If these had been bricks used in building a brick wall, they would not form a solid bond, and our attempt to lay other bricks upon them in their current alignment would compromise the stability and integrity of our brick wall.

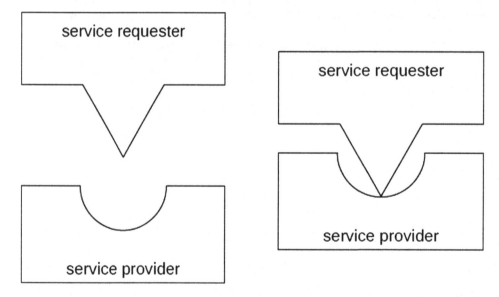

Figure 15-2. *Illustration of wedge interface used by service requester and semicircle interface used by service provider*

One solution we might consider is to embark on the task of changing all the callers to the service provider from using the "wedge" interface to using the "semicircle" interface. When there are only a few locations where a request is placed to the service provider, this approach seems reasonable. However, when we find there are many such locations, then the prospect of applying the same type of change to all those locations becomes much more involved, perhaps even daunting.

Minimizing the Effects of Change

Another solution we might consider is one where we let the service requester continue to use the "wedge" interface, but place between the service requester and the new service provider, which now expects the use of the "semicircle" interface, a component capable of resolving the differences between the interfaces. That is, the component converts the "wedge" interface used by the service requester into the "semicircle" interface expected by the service provider, as illustrated on the left side of Figure 15-3[1] where the intervening gray component facilitates the different interfaces.

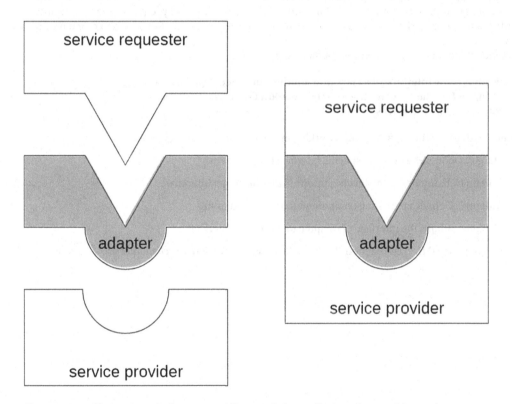

Figure 15-3. *Illustration of adapter providing notch for wedge interface used by service requester and bump for semicircle interface used by service provider*

---

[1]This set of shapes is based on those used with the explanation of the Adapter pattern found in the book Head First Design Patterns by Eric Freeman, et al. (O'Reilly, 2004).

If we were to move the graphics on the left toward each other so they touch, as illustrated on the right side of Figure 15-3, we would find that the "point" of the service requester fits perfectly into the "notch" of the adapter, and that the "semicircle bump" of the adapter fits perfectly into the "semicircle depression" of the service provider, resulting in a tight fit across all 3 components.

This may be the simpler change as it requires only that the service requester change the object it is invoking and not the interface it is using to make the invocation. The service requester interacts with a new interface *adapter* component, and the adapter component interacts with the service provider, effectively enabling components with dissimilar interfaces to work together through an intermediary component.

Adapting to Change

The Adapter design pattern is categorized by GoF with a *structural* purpose. Though all other design patterns covered by GoF have either a *class* scope or an *object* scope, Adapter is the only one applicable to both of these scopes. The *class* Adapter uses inheritance while the *object* Adapter uses composition. It should be noted that the conventional wisdom within the object-oriented programming community now considers a design based on class composition to be superior and more flexible than one based on class inheritance.

The intent behind this design pattern is the following:

> **Converts the interface of a class into another interface the client expects. Adapter lets classes work together that couldn't otherwise because of incompatible interfaces.**[2]

Adapter makes use of these participants[3] working in collaboration with each other:

1. Target: Defines the domain-specific interface that Client uses.

2. Client: Collaborates with objects conforming to the Target interface.

3. Adaptee: Defines an existing component that needs adapting.

4. Adapter: Adapts the interface of Adaptee to the Target interface.

The corresponding UML class diagrams for both the *class* adapter and *object* adapter are shown in Figure 15-4.[4]

---

[2]GoF, p. 139.
[3]GoF, p. 141.
[4]According to GoF, the *class* Adapter facilitates multiple inheritance (GoF, p. 141). This UML class diagram for the adapter component shows only the use of single inheritance in combination with an interface.

Class adapter:

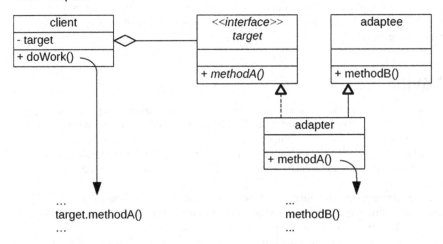

Object adapter:

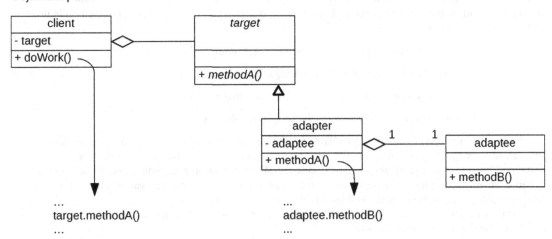

Figure 15-4. *UML class diagrams showing both the class and object variations of the Adapter design pattern*

In the *class* adapter example, the call by adapter to methodB is a call to a method provided to adapter through *inheritance* (adapter "is a" adaptee). With this arrangement, the adapter inherits from the adaptee.

In the *object* adapter example, the call by adapter to adaptee.methodB is a call to a method of an instance contributing to the *composition* of adapter (adapter "has a" adaptee). With this arrangement, the adapter "wraps" an instance of the adaptee.

Notice that in the diagrams for both variations shown in Figure 15-4 the Client participant remains the same – its use of the Adapter design pattern does not require it to know whether the Target participant is using the class scope or object scope implementation. Indeed, the Client participant typically remains oblivious to the fact that the Target participant has implemented an adapter.

Adaptive Behavior

Let's see an example of how this would work in practice. The Liberty Bell Tours Company operates a single tour bus in Philadelphia, Pennsylvania. The bus is outfitted with an Aquarius brand navigation mechanism, and this has been working well now for some years. The owners of the company recently became aware of the new Capricorn brand navigation mechanism, which offers much more reliability and less periodic maintenance than Aquarius. They decided to replace the Aquarius unit with a Capricorn unit during the next scheduled maintenance of the bus.

Aquarius supports the NavigationUnit interface, which enables tracking the direction the bus is heading based on the four main compass points: north, south, east and west. Accordingly, the bus had been configured to make use of the Aquarius unit through the NavigationUnit interface.

The new Capricorn unit is based not on a heading but on a bearing, a number of degrees of a circle between 00 and 360 to represent the direction of travel. Capricorn does not support the NavigationUnit interface and provides no support for compass point headings. So, in order for it to be used with the tour bus of the Liberty Bell Tours Company, there would need to be a way for the heading used by the bus to be converted to and from the bearing used by Capricorn. The correlation between a compass point heading and its equivalent bearing is as follows:

- A heading of **north** is equivalent to a bearing of **00 degrees**.

- A heading of **east** is equivalent to a bearing of **90 degrees**.

- A heading of **south** is equivalent to a bearing of **180 degrees**.

- A heading of **west** is equivalent to a bearing of **270 degrees**.

Rather than convert all the existing software for the bus to facilitate bearings, we have decided to write an adapter class which can accept the heading requests made by the bus and convert them into the corresponding bearing requests required by Capricorn. When a request is made for the current heading, the adapter will request from Capricorn the current bearing and then change this value in degrees into a corresponding compass heading to send back to the bus.

Figure 15-5 shows the corresponding UML class diagram for the *class* scope of the Adapter in the context of the Capricorn navigation unit.

Class adapter:

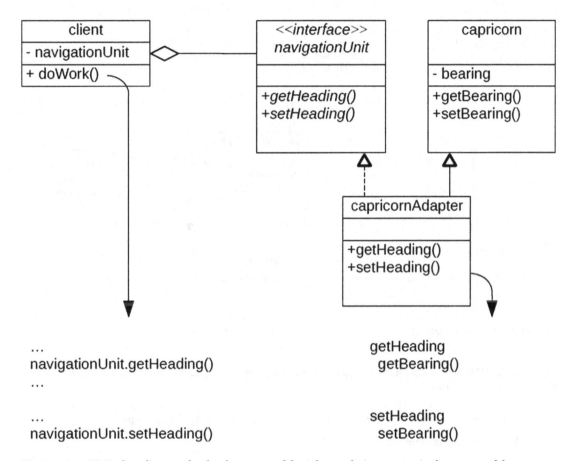

Figure 15-5. *UML class diagram for the class scope of the Adapter design pattern in the context of the Capricorn navigation unit*

Figure 15-6 shows the corresponding UML class diagram for the *object* scope of the Adapter in the context of the Capricorn navigation unit.

Object adapter:

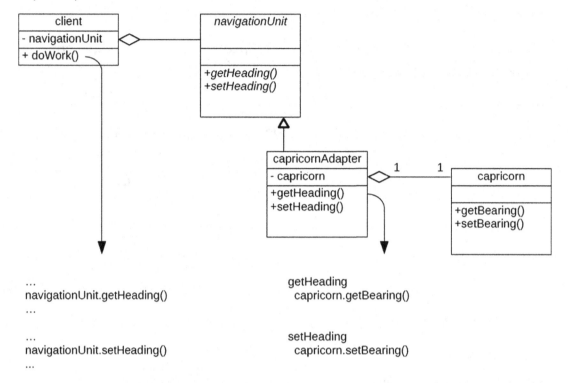

Figure 15-6. *UML class diagram for the object scope of the Adapter design pattern in the context of the Capricorn navigation unit*

Let's also show the roles the various class types play as participants in this design pattern:

1. Target: navigationUnit

2. Client: bus

3. Adapter: capricornAdapter

4. Adaptee: capricorn

Regardless which of these variations we opt to use, we find the Client participant in this design pattern having a reference to a navigationUnit, the Target participant. This Target participant interface is implemented by the capricornAdapter concrete class, representing the Adapter participant. The capricornAdapter either "is a" (class adapter) or "has a" reference to (object adapter) capricorn, the Adaptee participant.

Adapter in ABAP

Let's explore how we might implement the Adapter design pattern UML class diagrams illustrated above in Figure 15-5 (class adapter) and Figure 15-6 (object adapter) into functioning ABAP code. First, let's establish the code as it would exist prior to the need to use the Adapter design pattern, as shown in Listing 15-1, which shows interface navigation_unit being implemented by class aquarius.

Listing 15-1. Interface navigation_unit is implemented by class aquarius

```
interface navigation_unit.
  types          : compass_point  type char1.
  constants      : north               type compass_point value 'N'
                 , south               type compass_point value 'S'
                 , east                type compass_point value 'E'
                 , west                type compass_point value 'W'
                 .
  methods        : get_heading
                      exporting heading type compass_point
                 , set_heading
                      importing heading type compass_point
                 .
endinterface.

class aquarius definition.
  public section.
    interfaces   : navigation_unit.
    aliases      : get_heading for navigation_unit~get_heading
                 , set_heading for navigation_unit~set_heading
                 .
  private section.
    data         : heading type navigation_unit=>compass_point.
endclass.
class aquarius implementation.
  method get_heading.
    heading                    = me->heading.
  endmethod.
  method set_heading.
    me->heading                = heading.
  endmethod.
endclass.
```

In the example in Listing 15-1, interface navigation_unit defines two methods to be implemented by those classes implementing this interface, and class aquarius is shown implementing the navigation_unit interface and providing implementations for those methods. Listing 15-2 shows a bus class whose constructor method creates for it an instance of an Aquarius type of navigation_unit and whose head_north method invokes the set_heading method of the Aquarius navigation unit.

Listing 15-2. Class bus creates and uses an instance of aquarius via interface navigation_unit

```
class bus definition.
  public section.
    methods      : constructor
                 , head_north
                 .
  private section.
    data         : navigation_device type ref to navigation_unit.
endclass.
```

```
class bus implementation.
  method constructor.
    create object me->navigation_device type aquarius.
  endmethod.
  method head_north.
    call method me->navigation_device->set_heading
      exporting heading         = navigation_unit=>north.
  endmethod.
endclass.
```

This is how the code would look when first placed into production.

Eventually we would get a chance to change the bus class so that it now uses the Capricorn navigation unit instead of the Aquarius unit. The class representing the Capricorn navigation unit is shown in Listing 15-3.

Listing 15-3. Class capricorn

```
class capricorn definition.
  public section.
    types       : degrees       type n length 3.
    methods     : get_bearing
                      exporting bearing type degrees
                , set_bearing
                      exporting bearing type degrees
  private section.
    data        : bearing type degrees.
endclass.
class capricorn implementation.
  method get_bearing.
    bearing                   = me->bearing.
  endmethod.
  method set_bearing.
    me->bearing               = bearing.
  endmethod.
endclass.
```

The capricorn class plays the role of the *Adaptee* participant and is intended to replace the aquarius class. Typical for an Adaptee participant is that it knows nothing about its use in the Adapter design pattern. Notice that it is based on bearings and not headings. Accordingly, the only way it can replace class aquarius is for it to be fitted with an adapter capable of converting between headings and bearings.

Adapter in ABAP Using *class* Scope

Since Capricorn does not facilitate navigation via compass points, but uses bearings instead, here is an example of how we would change the ABAP code to introduce the class scope variation of the adapter.

Interface navigation_unit shown in Listing 15-1, now to play the role of of the *Target* participant, requires no changes for use in the *class* scope variation of the Adapter design pattern.

The aquarius class is replaced by the capricorn_adapter class, shown in Listing 15-4, which plays the role of the *Adapter* participant. Though the entire class is new, only those lines that differ from the aquarius class it is replacing, described in Listing 15-1, are shown with highlighting. Notice that this class both implements the navigation_unit interface (as did the aquarius class) as well as inherits from class capricorn. This adapter class accommodates converting from headings used by the caller to bearings used by superclass capricorn.

Listing 15-4. Class capricorn_adapter; differences with aquarius class defined in Listing 15-1 shown highlighted

```
class capricorn_adapter definition inheriting from capricorn.
  public section.
    interfaces    : navigation_unit.
    aliases       : get_heading for navigation_unit~get_heading
                  , set_heading for navigation_unit~set_heading
                  .
  private section.
    constants     : bearing_north   type capricorn=>degrees value 000
                  , bearing_east    type capricorn=>degrees value 090
                  , bearing_south   type capricorn=>degrees value 180
                  , bearing_west    type capricorn=>degrees value 270
                  .
    data          : heading type navigation_unit=>compass_point.
endclass.
class capricorn_adapter implementation.
  method get_heading.
    data          : bearing         type capricorn=>degrees.
    call method me->get_bearing
      importing bearing             = bearing.
    " convert capricorn bearing to corresponding compass heading:
    case bearing.
      when capricorn_adapter=>bearing_north.
        heading                     = navigation_unit=>north.
      when capricorn_adapter=>bearing_south.
        heading                     = navigation_unit=>south.
      when capricorn_adapter=>bearing_east.
        heading                     = navigation_unit=>east.
      when capricorn_adapter=>bearing_west.
        heading                     = navigation_unit=>west.
    endcase.
  endmethod.
  method set_heading.
    data          : bearing         type capricorn=>degrees.
    " convert compass heading to corresponding capricorn bearing:
    case heading.
      when navigation_unit=>north.
        bearing                     = capricorn_adapter=>bearing_north.
      when navigation_unit=>south.
        bearing                     = capricorn_adapter=>bearing_south.
      when navigation_unit=>east.
        bearing                     = capricorn_adapter=>bearing_east.
      when navigation_unit=>west.
        bearing                     = capricorn_adapter=>bearing_west.
    endcase.
    call method me->set_bearing
      importing bearing             = bearing.
  endmethod.
endclass.
```

Notice that the capricorn_adapter class provides constants to represent the correlation between the four main compass points and their equivalent bearing values. Notice also that its implementations for the get_heading and set_heading methods includes case statements to determine the bearing equivalent to a heading. With this class scope adapter arrangement of these components we can say that class capricorn_adapter "implements a" interface navigation_unit and "is a" class capricorn.

Listing 15-5 shows the bus class, playing the role of the *Client* participant, with changes to use class capricorn_adapter instead of class aquarius shown highlighted. None of the method invocations to the navigation device require changing even though the class recording the heading – capricorn – is based not on headings but on bearings.

Listing 15-5. Class bus, with differences from Listing 15-2 shown highlighted

```
class bus definition.
  public section.
    methods     : constructor
                , head_north
                .
  private section.
    data        : navigation_device type ref to navigation_unit.
endclass.
class bus implementation.
  method constructor.
    create object me->navigation_device type capricorn_adapter.
  endmethod.
  method head_north.
    call method me->navigation_device->set_heading
      exporting heading        = navigation_unit=>north.
  endmethod.
endclass.
```

Adapter in ABAP Using *object* Scope

Here is an example of how we would change the ABAP code to introduce the object scope variation of the adapter. Again we have the same capricorn class shown in Listing 15-3 still playing the role of the *Adaptee* participant as we had with the class scope example, and again the navigation_unit interface shown in Listing 15-1 still playing the role of the *Target* participant.

As illustrated in Listing 15-6, the aquarius class is replaced with the capricorn adapter class, still playing the role of the *Adapter* participant. Though the entire class is new, only those lines that differ from the aquarius class described in Listing 15-1 are shown with highlighting. The significant difference between this *object* scope adapter and the corresponding *class* scope adapter shown in Listing 15-4 is that the object scope adapter does not inherit from class capricorn, but is composed with an instance of a capricorn class.

Listing 15-6. Class capricorn_adapter; differences with aquarius class defined in Listing 15-1 shown highlighted

```
class capricorn_adapter definition.
  public section.
    interfaces : navigation_unit.
    aliases    : get_heading for navigation_unit~get_heading
               , set_heading for navigation_unit~set_heading
               .
```

```
    methods        : constructor
                     .
  private section.
    constants      : bearing_north   type capricorn=>degrees value 000
                   , bearing_east    type capricorn=>degrees value 090
                   , bearing_south   type capricorn=>degrees value 180
                   , bearing_west    type capricorn=>degrees value 270
                     .
    data           : capricorn_unit type ref to capricorn.
    data           : heading type navigation_unit=>compass_point.
endclass.
class capricorn_adapter implementation.
  method constructor.
    create object capricorn_unit.
  endmethod.
  method get_heading.
    data        : bearing        type capricorn=>degrees.
    call method me->capricorn_unit->get_bearing
      importing bearing         = bearing.
    " convert capricorn bearing to corresponding compass heading:
    case bearing.
      when capricorn_adapter=>bearing_north.
        heading                 = navigation_unit=>north.
      when capricorn_adapter=>bearing_south.
        heading                 = navigation_unit=>south.
      when capricorn_adapter=>bearing_east.
        heading                 = navigation_unit=>east.
      when capricorn_adapter=>bearing_west.
        heading                 = navigation_unit=>west.
    endcase.
  endmethod.
  method set_heading.
    data        : bearing        type capricorn=>degrees.
    " convert compass heading to corresponding capricorn bearing:
    case heading.
      when navigation_unit=>north.
        bearing                 = capricorn_adapter=>bearing_north.
      when navigation_unit=>south.
        bearing                 = capricorn_adapter=>bearing_south.
      when navigation_unit=>east.
        bearing                 = capricorn_adapter=>bearing_east.
      when navigation_unit=>west.
        bearing                 = capricorn_adapter=>bearing_west.
    endcase.
    call method me->capricorn_unit->set_bearing
      importing bearing         = bearing.
  endmethod.
endclass.
```

Notice that whereas the class scope adapter version shown in Listing 15-4 invokes method get_bearing of capricorn via the statement

```
call method me->get_bearing ...
```

the object scope adapter version shown in Listing 15-6 invokes it via the statement

```
call method me->capricorn_unit->get_bearing ...
```

The same concept applies to calling method set_bearing. Notice also that the object scope adapter has a constructor defined for it, which will create an instance of class capricorn into its private attribute capricorn_unit. With this object scope adapter arrangement of these components we can say that class capricorn_adapter "implements a" interface navigation_unit and "has a" class capricorn. Compare this with the class scope adapter which also "implements a" interface navigation_unit but "is a" class capricorn.

The code for the bus class, shown in Listing 15-5, still plays the role of the *Client* participant for the object scope of the Adapter class, and requires no changes from those shown in Listing 15-5.

A Variation on a Theme

Let us suppose the navigation_unit interface defined in Listing 15-1 had been defined not as an interface but as an abstract class, as shown in Listing 15-7.

Listing 15-7. Abstract class navigation_unit is inherited by class aquarius

```
class navigation_unit definition abstract.
  public section.
    types      : compass_point  type char1.
    constants  : north             type compass_point value 'N'
               , south             type compass_point value 'S'
               , east              type compass_point value 'E'
               , west              type compass_point value 'W'
               .
    methods    : get_heading abstract
                   exporting heading type compass_point
               , set_heading abstract
                   importing heading type compass_point
               .
endclass.

class aquarius definition inheriting from navigation_unit.
  public section.
    methods    : get_heading redefinition
               , set_heading redefinition
               .
  private section.
    data       : heading type navigation_unit=>compass_point.
endclass.
class aquarius implementation.
  method get_heading.
```

```
    heading                        = me->heading.
  endmethod.
  method set_heading.
    me->heading                    = heading.
  endmethod.
endclass.
```

Other than the navigation_unit entity now defined as an abstract class with abstract methods instead of an interface, and the public section of the aquarius class changed accordingly to reflect the absence of the interfaces and aliases statements and the presence of the *inheriting from* phrase on the class aquarius definition statement, the code is basically the same as shown in Listing 15-1. This could just as easily have been the original way the code had been placed into production for the Liberty Bell Tours Company.

With navigation_unit defined as an abstract class as shown in Listing 15-7 instead of as an interface as shown in Listing 15-1, could we have followed either of the component relationships described by the class scope adapter UML diagram in Figure 15-5 and the object scope adapter UML diagram in Figure 15-6 in replacing the aquarius class with the capricorn_adapter class? Specifically, would both adapter scope variations – the class adapter and the object adapter – still be available to us as options?

Here is a hint: Notice in Listing 15-7 that class aquarius includes the phrase *inheriting from navigation_ unit* on its class definition statement.

Here is another hint: Notice in Listing 15-4 that class capricorn_adapter, modeled using the class scope adapter, includes the phrase *inheriting from capricorn* on its class definition statement.

Here is yet another hint: Class capricorn_adapter is intended to replace class aquarius.

The answer to the question whether both adapter scope variations still would be available to us as options is No. The class scope variation would not be available because this would require class capricorn_ adapter to inherit from both class navigation_unit as well as from class capricorn. Since ABAP does not support multiple inheritance, the class scope variation cannot be used when, as shown in Listing 15-7, class aquarius already inherits from class navigation_unit. Meanwhile, the object scope variation could be used since even though it still would require class capricorn_adapter to inherit from class navigation_unit to replace aquarius it would not require it also to inherit from class capricorn – instead, an instance of class capricorn would be composed as part of class capricorn_adapter. In short, when class aquarius "implements a" navigation_unit interface, as shown in Listing 15-1, then either the class scope or object scope adapter may be used with its replacement class capricorn_adapter; but when class aquarius "is a" class navigation_ unit, as shown in Listing 15-7, then only the object scope adapter may be used with its replacement class capricorn_adapter.

Summary

In this chapter we learned that our maintenance efforts can be simplified by minimizing the effects of change, enabling classes with dissimilar interfaces to communicate with each other through an intervening component capable of converting the interface a caller uses into the one a receiver expects, rendering their interface incompatibilities moot. We can choose whether it is the class scope or object scope variation of the Adapter design pattern that best suits our requirements.

Adapter Exercises

Refer to Chapter 12 of the functional and technical requirements documentation (see Appendix B) for the accompanying ABAP exercise programs associated with this chapter. Take a break from reading the book at this point to reinforce what you have read by changing and executing the corresponding exercise programs. The exercise programs associated with this chapter are those in the 305 series: ZOOT305A and ZOOT305B.

■ ■ ■

CHAPTER 16

Decorator Design Pattern

The next stop on our voyage through the Design Patterns galaxy takes us to the Decorator design pattern, another of the design patterns found in the GoF catalog. We will find this design pattern useful in dynamically applying additional responsibilities to objects.

The Decorator design pattern simplifies the task of assigning additional capabilities to an object. Many times its advantages become evident only during maintenance efforts, in situations where additional capabilities are assigned to an object that does not yet use the Decorator pattern. It addresses a problem that has become all too common as new features are added to existing software. First, let's explore the problem it addresses, and then see how the Decorator design pattern solves the problem.

The Practical Limits of Inheritance

The current exercise program with its classes named car and truck inheriting from class vehicle has been working just fine, but now the users are requesting new capabilities. They want to be able to indicate that car and truck objects have either or both of two specific types of optional equipment:

- Vehicle locator (VL): A high-tech device used to find the vehicle after it has been stolen

- Cold climate (CC): A package of equipment for operating in cold weather, including such things as heavy-duty battery, fuel anti-coagulation system, upgraded deicing and defrosting unit, etc.

Our first inclination might be to change our UML class diagram to include new specialization subclasses to car and truck that include one or both of these features. This seems to be a perfectly reasonable approach since a car with a vehicle locator option represents a specialization of a car without such an option, and inheritance is well suited to reusing an existing class as the parent to one offering a more specialized level of abstraction. Our UML diagram might look like the one shown in Figure 16-1.

© James E. McDonough 2017
J. E. McDonough, *Object-Oriented Design with ABAP*, DOI 10.1007/978-1-4842-2838-8_16

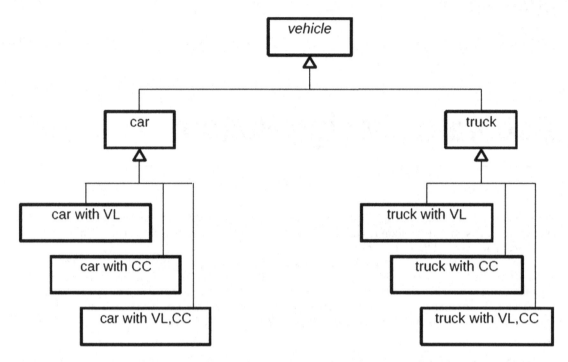

Figure 16-1. *UML diagram with hierarchy of classes facilitating two vehicle options*

For these two new vehicle options features, we added three new subclasses inheriting from car and another three new subclasses inheriting from truck. We can now accommodate either a car or a truck with both features, only one feature, or neither feature. Indeed, this might work well for a while.

Sometime later we find the users returning with a request for "just one more" vehicle option:

- Corrosion resistance (CR): An under-body coating on exposed metal parts to inhibit rust

Following the design we used to implement the previous two vehicle options, we begin by extending the UML class diagram to include new specialization subclasses to car and truck, and it is during this process where the maintenance problem inherent in this design becomes apparent. It will take eight new subclasses to handle all the unique combinations of vehicle options, as illustrated in the updated UML class diagram in Figure 16-2.

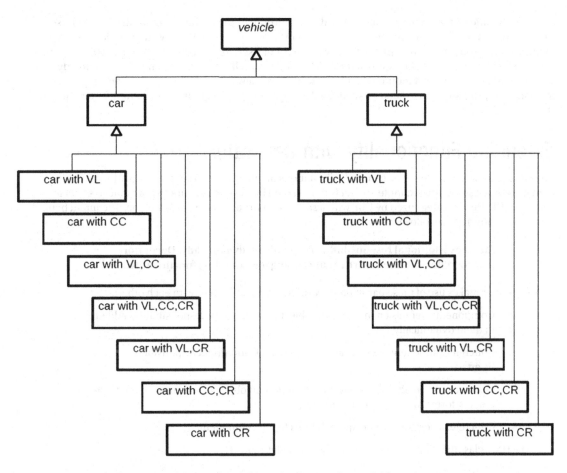

Figure 16-2. *UML diagram with hierarchy of classes facilitating three vehicle options*

Although we might be able to handle this with some effort, the next user request for "just one more" vehicle option will require 16 new subclasses to handle all the unique combinations, and the one after that will require 32 more. At some point during maintenance it will require far too much time and effort to build the new subclasses required to accommodate all the unique combinations for "just one more" vehicle option. There is a name for this phenomenon: it is called *class explosion.*

Accordingly, it is during maintenance efforts where we are likely to realize that this class design based solely on inheritance is not scalable for handling subsequent requests for new vehicle options. As currently organized, we can determine the total number of classes that would be required to represent any type of vehicle with any combination of vehicle options with the formula

$$2^n m$$

where the exponent n denotes the number of vehicle options we may select for a vehicle (including none at all) and m represents the different type of vehicle subclasses upon which we may apply those vehicle options. The combination of three vehicle options (vehicle locator, cold climate, and corrosion resistance) and the two different types of vehicles (car and truck) produces the requirement for the 16 subclasses to the vehicle class as illustrated in the UML class diagram in Figure 16-2. Were we to include a new type of vehicle at this point, it would require 8 more vehicle subclasses, for a total of 24. If at that point we provide a new vehicle option, it would require a total of 48 vehicle subclasses, twice the number we already have available. Imagine the effort required just to write all these new classes. It becomes a daunting task even for seasoned programmers to keep up with the development requirements for each new feature added to the mix.

Extending Functionality with Decorator

The Decorator design pattern overcomes the limitations of inheritance to support the various combinations of members of a set. In this example, the set is represented by the extra features we are able to select for the vehicles. Decorator is categorized by GoF with a *structural* purpose and an *object* scope. The intent behind this design pattern is the following:

> **Attaches additional responsibilities to an object dynamically. Decorators provide a flexible alternative to subclassing for extending functionality.**[1]

Decorator makes use of these participants[2] working in collaboration with each other:

1. Component: Defines an interface for objects that can have responsibilities added to them dynamically.

2. ConcreteComponent: Defines an object to which additional responsibilities can be attached.

3. Decorator: Maintains a reference to a Component object and defines an interface that conforms to Component's interface.

4. ConcreteDecorator: Adds responsibilities to the component.

The UML class diagram for Decorator is shown in Figure 16-3.

---

[1]GoF, p. 175.
[2]GoF, p. 177.

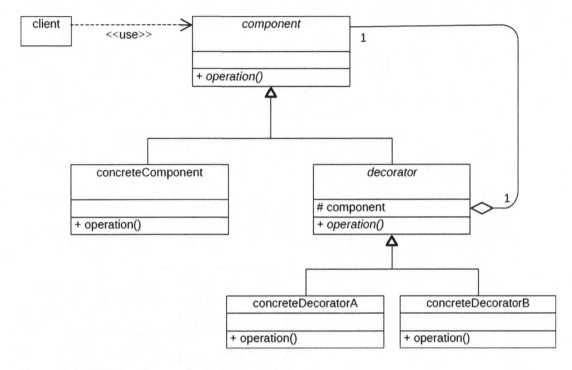

Figure 16-3. *UML class diagram for the Decorator design pattern*

Notice the relationship between decorator and component. Their cardinality indicates one decorator will have one component. This recursive relationship between decorator and component will continue indefinitely as long as the component object is a concreteDecorator, and will be terminated when a component object is a concreteComponent.

Although class inheritance is used in this design pattern, its flexibility is derived from its use of *class composition*. Its definitive characteristic is that the abstract decorator "has a" abstract component; a decorator class is *composed of,* among other things, an instance of another *component* class. This feature is what enables *composing* a series of these objects *at execution time*. Think of each concrete decorator as a "wrapper"[3] wrapping an instance of either a concrete component or another concrete decorator. Within the implementation for each decorator of the public behavior *operation*, it is imperative that there be an invocation of the public behavior *operation* of the wrapped component, either before or after performing its own behavior, guaranteeing that each decorator in the series gets a chance to contribute its own additional responsibility.

Figure 16-4 shows this general UML class diagram describing a specific set of classes to facilitate a windowing presentation service.

---

[3]GoF offers Wrapper as the name by which the Decorator is "also known as;" GoF, p. 175.

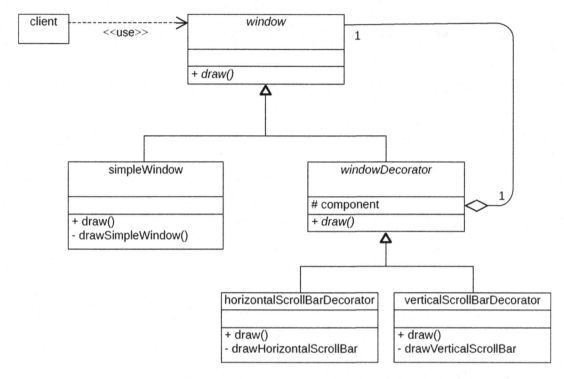

Figure 16-4. *UML class diagram for the Decorator design pattern applied to windowing presentation service scenario*

In each case above where there are multiple behaviors shown for a class, the public behavior *draw* invokes the private behaviors of the same class. Also, the public behavior *draw* implemented for both the horizontalScrollBarDecorator and verticalScrollBarDecorator will at some point invoke the public behavior *draw* of their wrapped component.

Let's create some scenarios to show how the Decorator pattern would be used to facilitate attaching additional responsibilities dynamically. We'll assume that the window frame is 10 centimeters in height and 15 centimeters in width, and that the client uses a window to display content.

1. In this first scenario, the content of the information to be presented fits completely within the 10x15 centimeter window frame. In this case, we don't need scroll bars, so we create an instance of class simpleWindow and provide this to the client, who then could invoke its public method *draw* to have the content displayed within the window frame.

2. In this next scenario, the content of the information to be presented is 8x20. Here is a case where we need a horizontal scroll bar to be able to move the window frame left and right to see all of the content. Accordingly, we create an instance of a class simpleWindow wrapped within an instance of class horizontalScrollBarDecorator, as illustrated in Figure 16-5.

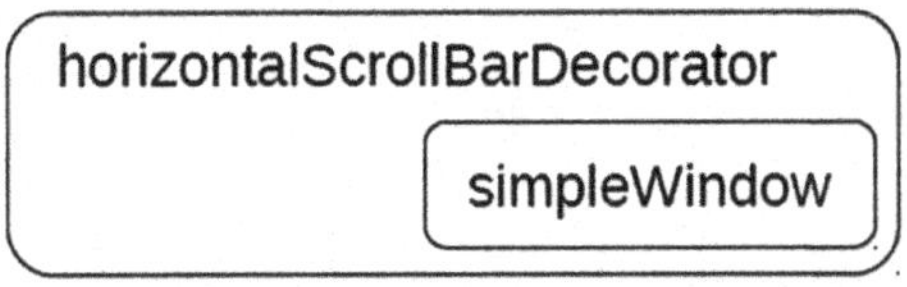

Figure 16-5. *simpleWindow wrapped by horizontalScrollBarDecorator*

The horizontalScrollBarDecorator instance is provided to the client, who then can invoke its public method *draw*. The implementation of *draw* for horizontalScrollBarDecorator first invokes the public method *draw* of its wrapped Component, simpleWindow. The implementation of public method *draw* for simpleWindow merely presents the content to be displayed and then passes control back to the caller. When control returns to the *draw* method of horizontalScrollBarDecorator, it invokes its private method *drawHorizontalScrollBar*, which causes a horizontal scroll bar to appear in the window frame, enabling the user to scroll the frame left and right to view all the content.

3. In this next scenario, the content of the information to be presented is 12x12. Here is a case where we need a vertical bar to be able to move the window frame up and down to see all of the content. Accordingly, we create an instance of a class simpleWindow wrapped within an instance of class verticalScrollBarDecorator, as illustrated in Figure 16-6.

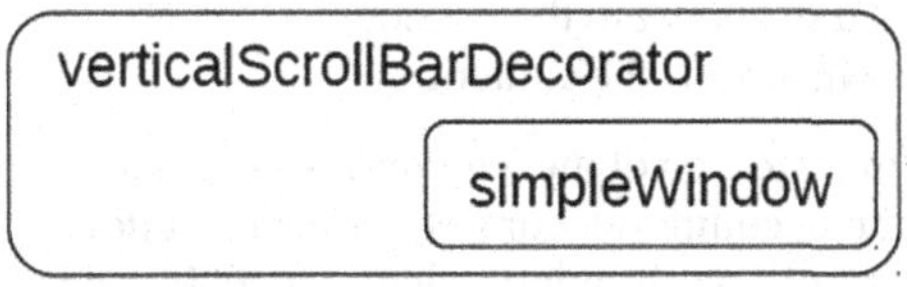

Figure 16-6. *simpleWindow wrapped by verticalScrollBarDecorator*

The verticalScrollBarDecorator instance is provided to the client, who then can invoke its public method *draw*. The implementation of *draw* for verticalScrollBarDecorator first would invoke the public method *draw* of its wrapped Component, simpleWindow. The implementation of public method *draw* for simpleWindow mercly would present the content to be displayed and then pass control back to the caller. When control returns to the *draw* method of verticalScrollBarDecorator, it invokes its private method *drawVerticalScrollBar*, which causes a vertical scroll bar to appear in the window frame, enabling the user to scroll the frame up and down to view all the content.

4. In this next scenario, the content of the information to be presented is 30x30. Here is a case where we need both horizontal and vertical scroll bars to be able to move the window frame left, right, up, and down to see all of the content. Accordingly, we create an instance of a class simpleWindow wrapped within an instance of class horizontalScrollBarDecorator, itself wrapped within an instance of verticalScrollBarDecorator, as illustrated in Figure 16-7.

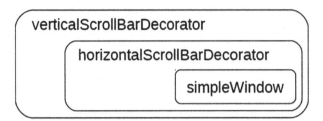

Figure 16-7. *simpleWindow wrapped by horizontalScrollBarDecorator wrapped by verticalScrollBarDecorator*

The verticalScrollBarDecorator instance is provided to the client, who can then invoke its public method *draw*. The implementation of *draw* for verticalScrollBarDecorator first would invoke the public method *draw* of its wrapped Component, horizontalScrollBarDecorator, which first would invoke the public method *draw* of its wrapped Component, simpleWindow. The implementation of public method *draw* for simpleWindow merely would present the content to be displayed and then pass control back to the caller. When control returns to the *draw* method of horizontalScrollBarDecorator, it invokes its private method *drawHorizontalScrollBar*, which causes a horizontal scroll bar to appear in the window frame, enabling the user to scroll the frame left and right to view the content, and then pass control back to the caller. When control returns to the *draw* method of verticalScrollBarDecorator, it invokes its private method *drawVerticalScrollBar*, which causes a vertical scroll bar to appear in the window frame, enabling the user to scroll the frame up and down to view the content.

Notice that in each scenario the client merely invokes the *draw* method of the *window* instance it has been provided, and is oblivious to whether that instance is a concrete component or a concrete decorator. Notice also in each scenario the innermost (or only) instance is one of class simpleWindow, which does not have any component upon which to invoke any behaviors. In addition, notice that the wrapping decorator instances always wrap an object of class *window*, a more general abstraction level in the decorator's very own inheritance hierarchy, and insure that the *draw* method of their wrapped component gets invoked, lest the wrapped component not have an opportunity to contribute the additional responsibility it attaches to the object. And finally, notice that the set of wrapped instances are *built at execution time*, when it can be known which decorators are required to contribute the additional responsibility necessary to enable the user to view the content.

There are two distinct phases when using the Decorator design pattern:

- Construction

- Execution

Construction is the process of arranging for a simpleWindow to be wrapped by a windowDecorator, which itself may be wrapped by yet another windowDecorator, a process that continues during construction until all of the necessary decorators have been included in the mix. The process begins with the instantiation of a simpleWindow. This instance is then provided as the component to be wrapped with the instantiation of a new windowDecorator, which itself is then provided as the component to be wrapped with the instantiation of yet another windowDecorator, and continues until a windowDecorator is instantiated which is not wrapped by any other windowDecorator.

Execution is the process of invoking the public *operation* method on the final instance created during construction. The implementation of this method in each windowDecorator component will invoke the same named method of its wrapped component, a process that will continue until the same named method of the simpleWindow instance contained at the center of these wrapping instances finally is invoked.

Wow! That is a lot to digest. Let's put this into context with the vehicle options and see how using the Decorator pattern overcomes the limitations of inheritance. With Decorator, we do not need to define all the different combinations of vehicles and their various options as independent classes, as we tried to do until we realized that this model would result in class explosion as new options were added. We simply need to define each vehicle option as a single concrete decorator class. Then, at execution time, we *compose* a series of objects to represent the combination of vehicle options requested by the user. Each vehicle option becomes a *decorator* to the vehicle, attaching to the vehicle the additional responsibility provided by the vehicle option. The UML class diagram shown in Figure 16-8 illustrates this.

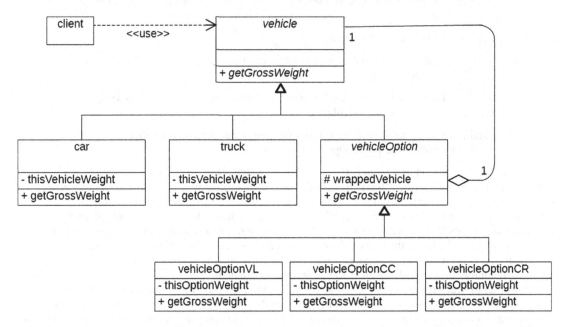

Figure 16-8. *UML class diagram for the Decorator design pattern applied to the vehicle options scenario*

Let's also show the roles the various class types play as participants in this design pattern:

1. Component: vehicle

2. ConcreteComponent: car, truck

3. Decorator: vehicleOption

4. ConcreteDecorator: vehicleOptionVL, vehicleOptionCC, vehicleOptionCR

The following pseudocode represents the implementation for method getGrossWeight in the concrete component:

```
grossWeight = thisVehicleWeight
```

Also, the following pseudocode represents the implementation for method getGrossWeight in the concrete decorator, where in this case it will invoke the getGrossWeight behavior of the "wrapped" component before performing this behavior itself:

```
invoke method getGrossWeight
             of instance wrappedVehicle
             returning grossWeight
add thisOptionWeight to grossWeight
```

As shown above, the implementation of getGrossWeight in the decorator class passes control on to its wrapped object, from which it receives a gross weight, and then adds its own vehicle option weight to this gross weight, which is sent back to the caller.

Suppose during execution we encounter a scenario where a user wants a truck with all three of these vehicle options. The series of classes would be composed in the following way:

- First, we create an instance of a truck class.

- Next, we create an instance of a vehicleOptionVL class and indicate that its wrapped vehicle is the truck object.

- Next, we create an instance of a vehicleOptionCC class and indicate that its wrapped vehicle is the vehicleOptionVL object.

- Finally, we create an instance of a vehicleOptionCR class and indicate that its wrapped vehicle is the vehicleOptionCC object.

When complete, the vehicleOptionCR instance "has a" vehicleOptionCC instance, which "has a" vehicleOptionVL instance, which "has a" truck instance. Stated another way, one concrete component, truck, is wrapped by a concrete decorator, vehicleOptionVL, which is wrapped by another concrete decorator, vehicleOptionCC, which is wrapped by yet another concrete decorator, vehicleOptionCR. Invoking the getGrossWeight on the vehicleOptionCR instance results in a gross weight returned that is the sum of the weight of the truck, the weight of the VL option, the weight of the CC option, and the weight of the CR option. The client merely invokes the getGross Weight of the outermost class. It does not need to know anything about the way in which the gross weight is being calculated.

The order in which these concrete decorators wrap other objects hardly matters since each decorating object will get a chance to perform its decorating behavior, but the innermost object is always a concrete component. Accordingly, we can mix and match a vehicle concrete component with various selected vehicle decorator concrete components at execution time to create what amounts to a single vehicle object with all the necessary vehicle options. This is how the Decorator design pattern helps us to avoid the pitfalls of class explosion; we simply compose at execution time a combination of objects from those classes available to us, instead of trying during design and coding time to accommodate all the various combinations into single classes.

Decorator in ABAP

First, we will cover how to define the components participating in the Decorator design pattern, and then we will cover how to construct those components into a usable set of objects.

Defining the Decorator

Here is how we might implement the Decorator design pattern UML class diagram illustrated above into functioning ABAP code. First up, playing the role of the *Component* participant, is abstract class vehicle, shown in Listing 16-1.

Listing 16-1. Abstract Class vehicle

```
class vehicle definition abstract.
  public section.
    methods       : get_gross_weight abstract
                      returning value(gross_weight) type int4.
endclass.
```

Notice that the public method it defines, get_gross_weight, is abstract. Next, playing the roles of *ConcreteComponent* participants, are the definitions for class car, shown in Listing 16-2, and class truck, shown in Listing 16-3.

Listing 16-2. Class car

```
class car definition inheriting from vehicle.
  public section.
    methods       : get_gross_weight redefinition.
  private section.
    constants     : this_vehicle_weight type int4 value 2208.
endclass.
class car implementation.
  method get_gross_weight.
    gross_weight                = me->this_vehicle_weight.
  endmethod.
endclass.
```

Listing 16-3. Class truck

```
class truck definition inheriting from vehicle.
  public section.
    methods       : get_gross_weight redefinition.
  private section.
    constants     : this_vehicle_weight type int4 value 8802.
endclass.
class truck implementation.
  method get_gross_weight.
    gross_weight                = me->this_vehicle_weight.
  endmethod.
endclass.
```

Notice that both the car and truck classes inherit from the abstract class vehicle. Notice also that each one contains a constant indicating the weight of the car or truck vehicle, and that each provides an implementation for the inherited abstract method get_gross_weight, implemented to return the car or truck vehicle weight as the gross weight.

Next, shown in Listing 16-4 and playing the role of the *Decorator* participant, is the definition for abstract class vehicle_option.

Listing 16-4. Abstract Class vehicle_option

```
class vehicle_option definition abstract inheriting from vehicle.
  protected section.
    data          : wrapped_object type ref to vehicle.
endclass.
```

Notice for this class that it has a protected section defining field wrapped_object as a reference to a vehicle object. Furthermore, notice that it indicates method get_gross_weight also is abstract in this class, meaning that this class is deferring an implementation for this inherited abstract method to its subclasses.

Next, shown below and playing the roles of *ConcreteDecorator* participants, are the three classes vehicle_option_vl (vehicle locator), vehicle_option_cc (cold climate), and vehicle_option_cr (corrosion resistance). Each inherits from class vehicle_option and each provides an implementation for the abstract method get_gross_weight. In addition, each has a constructor method that accepts a reference to a vehicle object it is to wrap. Each class also contains a constant holding the weight for the particular vehicle option. Listing 16-5 shows the code for class vehicle_option_vl.

Listing 16-5. Class vehicle_option_vl

```
class vehicle_option_vl definition inheriting from vehicle_option.
  public section.
    methods      : get_gross_weight redefinition
                 , constructor
                     importing object_to_wrap type ref to vehicle
                 .
  private section.
    constants    : this_option_weight type int4 value 55.
endclass.
class vehicle_option_vl implementation.
  method constructor.
    call method super->constructor.
    me->wrapped_object           = wrapped_object.
  endmethod.
  method get_gross_weight.
    gross_weight = me->wrapped_object->get_gross_weight( ).
    add me->this_option_weight to gross_weight.
  endmethod.
endclass.
```

Notice that the constructor method takes the reference it is provided for the object it is to wrap and places this into its own field wrapped_object, a field it inherits from its superclass. Accordingly, each ConcreteDecorator has a reference to the vehicle instance it is wrapping. Notice also that in its implementation for the get_gross_weight method it first invokes the get_gross_weight method of the object it is wrapping, receiving from it a gross weight value, and then adds its own vehicle option weight to this gross weight.

Compare the definition for class vehicle_option_vl in Listing 16-5 with class vehicle_option_cc shown in Listing 16-6. They are identical with the exception of the class name and the value specified for the option weight.

Listing 16-6. Class vehicle_option_cc

```
class vehicle_option_cc definition inheriting from vehicle_option.
  public section.
    methods      : get_gross_weight redefinition
                 , constructor
                     importing wrapped_object type ref to vehicle
                 .
  private section.
    constants    : this_option_weight type int4 value 404.
endclass.
```

```
class vehicle_option_cc implementation.
  method constructor.
    call method super->constructor.
    me->wrapped_object          = wrapped_object.
  endmethod.
  method get_gross_weight.
    gross_weight = me->wrapped_object->get_gross_weight( ).
    add me->this_option_weight to gross_weight.
  endmethod.
endclass.
```

Class vehicle_option_cr, shown in Listing 16-7, also is identical to the previous two classes other than the same exceptions.

Listing 16-7. Class vehicle_option_cr

```
class vehicle_option_cr definition inheriting from vehicle_option.
  public section.
    methods       : get_gross_weight redefinition
                  , constructor
                      importing wrapped_object type ref to vehicle
                  .
  private section.
    constants     : this_option_weight type int4 value 26.
endclass.
class vehicle_option_cr implementation.
  method constructor.
    call method super->constructor.
    me->wrapped_object          = wrapped_object.
  endmethod.
  method get_gross_weight.
    gross_weight = me->wrapped_object->get_gross_weight( ).
    add me->this_option_weight to gross_weight.
  endmethod.
endclass.
```

At this point, we have ABAP code examples for all of the participants of the Decorator design pattern described by the preceding UML. However, this only facilitates the execution of the pattern. We still need to assemble these objects into a set of wrapped components.

Constructing the Decorator

The UML diagram in Figure 16-8, for which we have been providing all this code, has an entity called client, which is shown using the Component of this pattern, class vehicle. The client uses the vehicle by invoking its get_gross_weight method. Before this can occur, we need a mechanism to construct the various participants into a usable state. This may be done by the client or by some other component on behalf of the client. The code shown in Listing 16-8 provides an example of how we might define a class that can construct a decorated vehicle for a caller that can indicate the type of vehicle as well as the set of decorators with which it is to be adorned.

Listing 16-8. Definition of Class to Construct the Decorated Vehicle

```
class vehicle_builder definition abstract final.
  public section.
    class-methods: build_car
                    importing
                      vehicle_locator_option       type abap_bool
                      cold_climate_option          type abap_bool
                      corrosion_resistance_option type abap_bool
                    exporting
                      car type ref to vehicle
                  , build_truck
                    importing
                      vehicle_locator_option       type abap_bool
                      cold_climate_option          type abap_bool
                      corrosion_resistance_option type abap_bool
                    exporting
                      truck type ref to vehicle
                  .
  private section.
    class-methods: apply_options
                    importing
                      basic_vehicle type ref to vehicle
                      vehicle_locator_option       type abap_bool
                      cold_climate_option          type abap_bool
                      corrosion_resistance_option type abap_bool
                    exporting
                      vehicle type ref to vehicle
                  .
endclass.
```

The definition of this static class, shown in Listing 16-8, simply provides two public static methods, one to create a car and one to create a truck, accepting flags indicating whether each of the possible vehicle options is to be included. The private static method facilitates applying the specified options.

The implementation of this class is presented in Listing 16-9.

Listing 16-9. Implementation of Class to Construct the Decorated Vehicle

```
class vehicle_builder implementation.
  method build_car.
    data         : basic_car type ref to vehicle.
    create object basic_car type car.
    call method vehicle_builder=>apply_options
      exporting
        basic_vehicle                = basic_car
        vehicle_locator_option       = vehicle_locator_option
        cold_climate_option          = cold_climate_option
        corrosion_resistance_option = corrosion_resistance_option
      importing
        vehicle                      = car.
  endmethod.
```

```
method build_truck.
    data            : basic_truck type ref to vehicle.
    create object basic_truck type truck.
    call method vehicle_builder=>apply_options
      exporting
        basic_vehicle              = basic_truck
        vehicle_locator_option     = vehicle_locator_option
        cold_climate_option        = cold_climate_option
        corrosion_resistance_option = corrosion_resistance_option
      importing
        vehicle                    = truck.
endmethod.
method apply_options.
    data            : options_list type standard table of seoclsname
                    , option like line of options_list
                    , object_to_be_wrapped type ref to vehicle
                    .
    if vehicle_locator_option eq abap_true.
      append 'VEHICLE_OPTION_VL' to options_list.
    endif.
    if cold_climate_option eq abap_true.
      append 'VEHICLE_OPTION_CC' to options_list.
    endif.
    if corrosion_resistance_option eq abap_true.
      append 'VEHICLE_OPTION_CR' to options_list.
    endif.
    vehicle = basic_vehicle.
    loop at options_list
       into option.
      object_to_be_wrapped = vehicle.
      create object vehicle type (option)
        exporting wrapped_object = object_to_be_wrapped.
    endloop.
  endmethod.
endclass.
```

Each of the public methods creates its respective car or truck instance. Each of these methods then invokes the apply_options method, which simply makes a list of the class names applicable to the vehicle options chosen, and then loops through this table creating instances of these classes, each one wrapping the initial car or truck instance and then the vehicle_option instance created during any previous loops.

Listing 16-10 describes a fragment of code showing how a client might use this class to create for it a decorated vehicle.

Listing 16-10. Code to Use Class vehicle_builder to Create an Instance of a Decorated Car

```
o
o
data            : rental_car type ref to vehicle
                , rental_car_gross_weight type int4
                .
o
o
```

```
call method vehicle_builder=>build_car
  exporting
    vehicle_locator_option    = abap_true
    cold_climate_option       = abap_true
    corrosion_resistance_option = abap_true
  importing
    vehicle                   = rental_car.
o
o
```

Listing 16-11 shows how to use the instance of vehicle it creates to find its gross_weight.

Listing 16-11. Code to Use the Decorated vehicle_builder Instance to Get Its Gross Weight

```
o
o

rental_car_gross_weight      = rental_car->get_gross_weight( ).
```

After the client makes use of the vehicle_builder class shown above to provide it with an instance of a vehicle in its field rental_car, it may remain completely oblivious to the dynamic type of the instance it has been provided. The client is unconcerned with the actual type of class used to instantiate the outer wrapper of all the instances used in constructing this decorated vehicle; it simply regards it as an instance of the static type offered by the field holding its reference. We see this with the statement above invoking method get_gross_weight of the rental_car, a behavior available to an instance of vehicle; that is, while the dynamic type of the rental_car may be vehicle_option_cr, it is referenced simply as static type vehicle.

Variation on Decorator Theme

A closer examination of the implementations shown above of method get_gross_weight for those classes inheriting from class vehicle_option reveals that they are identical. In a case like this, we might consider having the superclass vehicle_option itself provide the implementation for this method on behalf of the subclasses. We can do this, but we also need to consider that the implementation of this method can use only those attributes available to it. In their current implementations, the methods refer to their constant this_option_weight, a field provided only by each vehicle_option subclass. To elevate this processing to the superclass, we need a way to inform the superclass the value for the weight of the specific option, known only to the subclass.

This can be achieved easily by providing the superclass with a protected data field into which the value for the weight of the specific option is moved during processing of the constructor method. Listing 16-12 shows how to change the abstract class vehicle_option code to facilitate this, with differences from Listing 16-4 highlighted.

Listing 16-12. Abstract class vehicle_option, Which Also Provides Implementation of Methods for Its Subclasses

```
class vehicle_option definition abstract inheriting from vehicle.
  public section.
    methods    : get_gross_weight redefinition.
  protected section.
    data      : wrapped_object type ref to vehicle.
    data      : option_weight  type int4.
endclass.
```

222

```
class vehicle_option implementation.
  method get_gross_weight.
    gross_weight = me->wrapped_object->get_gross_weight( ).
    add me->option_weight to gross_weight.
  endmethod.
endclass.
```

In Listing 16-12 we see the new protected data field that will hold the option weight applicable to the subclass. Notice that the class now provides an implementation for method get_gross_weight, which has been elevated from its subclasses to this superclass, but has its add statement changed to refer to the protected data field option_weight defined by this class instead of the constant provided by the subclass, since the subclass constant would be unavailable to the superclass.

Using subclass vehicle_option_v1 as a proxy for all of the subclasses inheriting from class vehicle_option, we see that its redefinition of method get_gross_weight has been removed, now that this functionality is being provided by the superclass itself. Listing 16-13 shows how to change the code from Listing 16-5 to facilitate the implementation of method get_gross_weight in the superclass.

Listing 16-13. Class vehicle_option_v1 Now with an Implementation for Method get_gross_weight Provided by the Superclass

```
class vehicle_option_v1 definition inheriting from vehicle_option.
  public section.
    methods    : get_gross_weight redefinition
               , constructor
                   importing object_to_wrap type ref to vehicle
                 .
  private section.
    constants  : this_option_weight type int4 value 55.
endclass.
class vehicle_option_v1 implementation.
  method constructor.
    call method super->constructor.
    me->wrapped_object             = wrapped_object.
    me->option_weight              = me->this_option_weight.
  endmethod.
  method get_gross_weight.
    call method me->wrapped_object->get_gross_weight
      importing gross_weight.
    add me->this_option_weight to gross_weight.
  endmethod.
endclass.
```

In addition, the constructor sets option_weight, the protected field provided by the superclass, to the value of the this_option_weight constant defined in the subclass. This is how the superclass has access to the weight of the specific vehicle option; although it cannot reference the constants defined in the subclasses, it certainly can reference a protected field it defines on behalf of those subclasses.

As long as all subclasses of vehicle_option require the same implementation for get_gross_weight, then all of them can simply rely on the superclass vehicle_option to provide it. In those cases where a subclass requires some other processing, it is a simple matter for that subclass to override the superclass implementation and provide its own applicable processing.

Uses of the Decorator Pattern in Technology Today

Open any web page using your favorite Internet browser. A drop-down context menu will appear by right-clicking the mouse pointer on the blank area at the top of the Internet browser window. This context menu usually includes some entries with such titles as Menu Bar, Favorites Bar, Command Bar, Status Bar, and Bookmarks Toolbar. These entries typically have a check mark appearing to the left of them to indicate whether or not the corresponding feature appears within the Internet browser window, and can be toggled on and off simply by clicking their corresponding entry on this drop-down menu.

It is easy to imagine a Decorator design pattern at work controlling the presentation of the Internet browser window. The main window itself is defined by a class representing the concrete component. Each of these additional features, controlled by a click on the drop-down menu, is defined by a class representing a concrete decorator. Each time you click an entry to include or exclude it from the Internet browser window, the supporting software goes through a process of rebuilding the composition of class instances corresponding to the active selections that need to appear on the window.

Try this and see how your Internet browser window is altered as you change these settings. Consider how simple it might be for a new menu option to be included in the drop-down list and for its corresponding class to be included in the Decorator pattern controlling the appearance of the Internet browser window. In many cases, the classes corresponding to these features may be browser add-ons or plug-ins supplied by third-party software vendors complying with public method signatures and established protocols to insure compatibility with the browser software. Indeed, in using a Decorator design pattern, the designers of the software controlling the Internet browser window have assured the capability for "attach[ing] additional responsibilities to an object dynamically," to the extent that there is no need even to know all the classes that eventually might become involved in the presentation, exemplifying the idea of "provid[ing] a flexible alternative to subclassing for extended functionality."

Summary

In this chapter, we learned that there are practical limitations to using class inheritance, often resulting in class explosion, a scourge of software design not often discovered until the initial design has gone to production and we find ourselves faced with subsequent maintenance challenges. Since the Decorator design pattern relies on class composition for combining selected capabilities dynamically, it avoids the pitfalls associated with the class explosion evolving out of designs based primarily on inheritance. We now know there are two phases associated with the use of the Decorator design pattern: one phase for the construction of the pattern and another phase for the execution of the pattern.

Decorator Exercises

Refer to Chapter 13 of the functional and technical requirements documentation (see Appendix B) for the accompanying ABAP exercise programs associated with this chapter. Take a break from reading the book at this point to reinforce what you have read by changing and executing the corresponding exercise programs. The exercise programs associated with this chapter are those in the 306 series: ZOOT306A through ZOOT306C.

■ ■ ■

CHAPTER 17

Chain of Responsibility Design Pattern

The next stop on our voyage through the Design Patterns galaxy takes us to the Chain of Responsibility design pattern, another of the design patterns found in the GoF catalog. We will find this design pattern useful when we need to perform specific processing but want to avoid tight coupling between the requester and the servicer.

The Chain of Responsibility design pattern shares some characteristics with the Decorator design pattern explored in the previous chapter. Both of these design patterns rely on an object composed with another object of a type found in its own inheritance hierarchy, with each containing object invoking the same-named method of its contained object. Both also have the same two phases applicable: construction and execution.

The Decorator design pattern presents the possibilities for an object to have a multitude of additional responsibilities. The operative concept with Decorator is "and;" through the concrete decorators, the concrete component gains a new responsibility through *this* decorator object *and* another new responsibility through *that* decorator object *and* still another new responsibility through *some other* decorator object, *and* so on, *and* so forth. Each decorator contributes a different responsibility to a decorated object.

The operative concept with the Chain of Responsibility design pattern is "or;" a request is handled by *this* object *or that* object *or some other* object. Only one object will be identified as the object to handle the request, which is passed from object to object along a chain of objects until one of them handles it.

Lost in Translation

Issue a web search for "language translators" and you will get hits for a variety of web applications capable of translating text from one language to another. One potential UML class diagram design for an application for translating between English and Spanish is shown in Figure 17-1.

© James E. McDonough 2017

J. E. McDonough, *Object-Oriented Design with ABAP*, DOI 10.1007/978-1-4842-2838-8_17

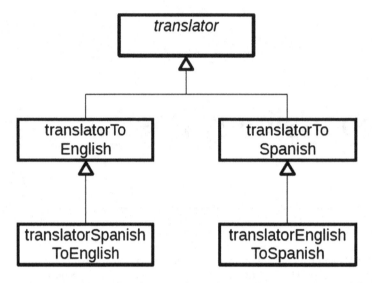

Figure 17-1. *UML class diagram design for translating between English and Spanish*

Here there are five classes for handling all the translation between English and Spanish. Of course, no sooner would we have completed this design than surely we would get a request to include "just one more language," perhaps French. Then our potential UML class diagram would expand accordingly, as shown in Figure 17-2.

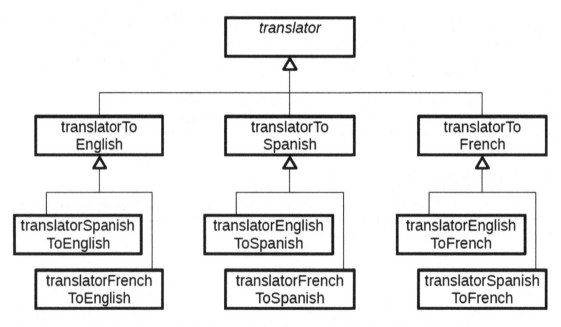

Figure 17-2. *UML class diagram design for translating between English, Spanish, and French*

Note that the number of classes has doubled, from five to ten, just to handle one additional language. Include yet another language in the design, perhaps German, and the UML class diagram would expand yet again, as shown in Figure 17-3.

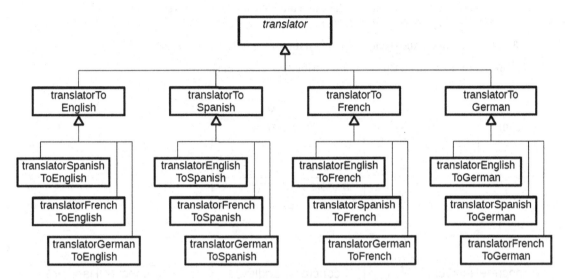

Figure 17-3. *UML class diagram design for translating between English, Spanish, French, and German*

At 17 classes, this is not quite double the number of classes we had before, but now we know that with this design each additional language exposes us to the same *class explosion* problem we encountered with the Decorator pattern. In this case, our formula for calculating the number of required classes is

$$n^2 + 1$$

where the exponent n denotes the number of languages our translator could handle. We need a design that is not going to succumb to the pitfalls associated with class explosion. Since usually we only need to translate from one language to another, we need a flexible way to identify the source and target languages during execution instead of trying to create classes to accommodate every possible combination of languages.

Loose Coupling with Chain of Responsibility

The Chain of Responsibility design pattern is categorized by GoF with a *behavioral* purpose and an *object* scope. The intent behind this design pattern is the following:

> **Avoid coupling the sender of a request to its receiver by giving more than one object a chance to handle the request. Chain the receiving objects and pass the request along the chain until an object handles it.**[1]

Chain of Responsibility makes use of these participants[2] working in collaboration with each other:

---

[1]GoF, p. 223.
[2]GoF, p. 225.

1. Handler: Defines an interface for handling requests. It optionally implements the successor link.

2. ConcreteHandler: Handles requests for which it is responsible. Can have a successor. If the ConcreteHandler can handle the request, it does so; otherwise, it forwards the request to its successor.

3. Client: Initiates the request to a ConcreteHandler object on the chain.

The UML class diagram for Chain of Responsibility is shown in Figure 17-4.

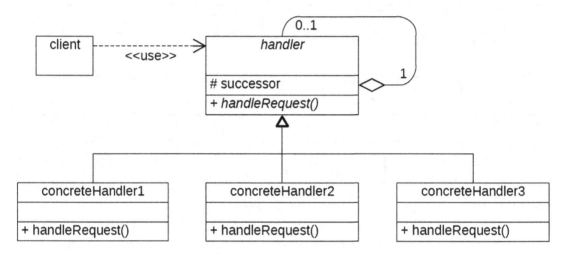

Figure 17-4. *UML class diagram for the Chain of Responsibility design pattern*

Notice the handler object "has a" different handler object, known as the successor. This is the essence of the "chain" in Chain of Responsibility; it is a series of handler objects with each one linked to another via its successor object reference. Notice also the cardinality of the relationship between successor and handler, which indicates that a handler "has" zero to one handlers. This means a handler object does not necessarily need to have a successor handler object, and this *will be* the case for the final link in the chain. Indeed, this self-recursive relationship of a handler object having its own handler object is terminated only by a null value for the successor.

A characteristic of the Chain of Responsibility design pattern is that there is a specific sequence of objects built into a chain, each of which has a unique responsibility compared with the other objects in the chain. Starting with the first link in the chain, each object is given a chance to handle a request, with each handling object "wrapping" a subsequent handling object, except for the final link in the chain, which does not wrap any other handler. When an object determines that the request to be handled is the one it is capable of handling, it does so; otherwise, it sends the request along to the next link in the chain. It promotes *loose coupling* because the caller does not know which of the objects in the chain is the one to handle the request. Indeed, the caller would not even need to know which objects compose the chain of responsibility.

One variation on this theme is that the request is not handled by any of the objects composing the Chain of Responsibility, and so the request falls off the end of the chain with no corresponding processing occurring. Another variation is one where the final link in the chain handles the request anyway, whether or not the request matches the capability it has to offer. The actual requirements of processing will determine which of these variations is implemented.

Figure 17-5 shows the UML class diagram for the Chain of Responsibility adapted to our language translation application.

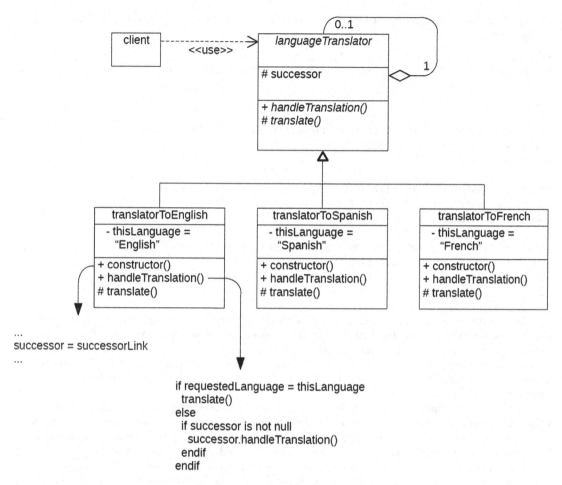

Figure 17-5. *UML class diagram for the Chain of Responsibility design pattern applied to a language translation application*

The implementations for the methods constructor and handleTranslation of each of the languageTranslator subclasses are identical, while their respective translate methods contain the necessary processing to convert the text into the language for which the subclass is responsible. The client merely needs to invoke the handleTranslation method on the object representing the first link in the chain, sending along the text and the requested language into which the text should be translated. Thereafter, the chain of objects themselves check for which amongst them, if any, is the object responsible for handling translations into the requested language. Indeed, since they all should be identical, containing the conditional logic described above, we could dispense entirely with separate implementations in each subclass for the handleTranslation method and implement this only once at the superclass level. This means that the very same method containing the check to determine whether the current object is the one responsible for the requested language translation is used by every subclass, alleviating any need for adjusting this logic to facilitate any new subclasses assigned a specific language for which they are responsible.

However, this only shows how easy it is to facilitate the language translation. One additional step required is to *build* the chain of objects representing the Chain of Responsibility. To do this, we must create a series of languageTranslator subclasses with each one indicating its successor in the chain, as described in the snippet of pseudocode shown in Listing 17-1.

Listing 17-1. Snippet of Pseudocode for Constructing the Chain of Objects Representing the Chain of Responsibility

```
firstLinkInChain      type languageTranslator
successorLink         type languageTranslator initial value is null

  ...

create new instance of object translatorToFrench into firstLinkInChain
  with successor object = successorLink
successor = firstLinkInChain

create new instance of object translatorToSpanish into firstLinkInChain
  with successor object = successor
successor = firstLinkInChain

create new instance of object translatorToEnglish into firstLinkInChain
  with successor object = successor

  ...
```

At this point, we have built a chain of three language translator objects, where each one except the final link has a successor translator object. Also, we used the same object reference variable, first_link_in_chain, as the receiver for each new object created, and indicated with each new object the identity of the object it is to use as its successor language translator. In addition, each new translator object became the successor object for the next new translator object to be created, which is how we facilitated creating this series of objects into a chain.

The end result is that reference variable first_link_in_chain is pointing to the first translator object in a Chain of Responsibility of translation objects. To include additional language translators, we simply include them in this series of object creations. Using the logic shown above, the first translator object created is the final link in the chain and the last translator object created is regarded as the first link in the chain.

The task of building the Chain of Responsibility is usually delegated to a class that can facilitate this activity on behalf of all client callers, and typically is not left up to the client to actually build the chain it will use. Creating the chain is often managed by a factory-type class that can not only build the chain but can also be invoked by clients to obtain a reference to the first link in the chain. The client uses this first link object to initiate language translation, as shown in the following snippet of pseudocode:

```
firstLinkInChain = LanguageTranslationManager.getFirstLink()
firstLinkInChain.handleTranslation()
```

Figure 17-6 illustrates the nesting of these language translator objects composing the Chain of Responsibility, with each outer object wrapping its successor translator object.

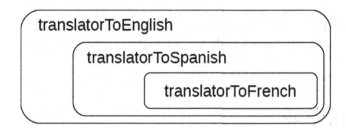

Figure 17-6. Nesting of language translator objects making up the Chain of Responsibility

When the first object in the chain, the one invoked directly by the client, is not the one responsible for the requested translation, it means the client had no direct contact with the object that eventually facilitated the translation. Again we see the advantages of loosely coupled objects: the client has no knowledge of all the language translators composing the Chain of Responsibility; it has access only to the first link in this chain.

So, let's redesign the class hierarchy for our language translation application to make Latin the common language to be used for all translations, meaning that to facilitate a translation from language A to language B, we first translate language A into Latin and then translate the resulting Latin into language B. The client entity facilitates receiving the source language, text, and target language, and then invokes the two translators to facilitate translation of the source text into Latin and then translation of that Latin text into the target language. The UML diagram for this design is shown in Figure 17-7.

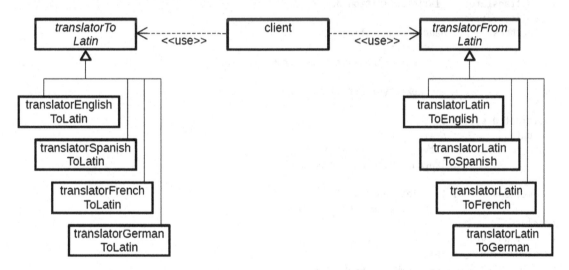

Figure 17-7. UML diagram for the language translator using Latin as a base language

With this design we can build one Chain of Responsibility using all the inheriting subclasses of translatorToLatin and build another Chain of Responsibility using all the inheriting subclasses of translatorFromLatin. One of the objects in the first chain will translate the text from its original language into Latin, and then one of the objects in the second chain will translate that Latin text into the requested language. Each one of these subclasses checks whether or not it is the translation handler for the requested language, and if not, sends the request on to its successor object.

During maintenance cycles we could find ourselves with the requirement to create new translator objects to facilitate translations to and from additional languages. With this hierarchy, we only need to add two new translator classes with each new language: one to translate the new language into Latin and another to translate Latin into the new language. This averts the class explosion complications with which we otherwise might have been confronted.

Chain of Responsibility in ABAP

First, we will learn how to define the components participating in the Chain of Responsibility design pattern, and then we will learn how to construct those components into a usable set of objects.

Defining the Chain

Here is how we might implement the Chain of Responsibility design pattern UML class diagram illustrated in Figure 17-7 into functioning ABAP code. We're using the same format variation shown with the Decorator pattern where the superclass provides the bulk of programming for the subclass. Listing 17-2 describes the abstract class providing translation of some source text into Latin.

Listing 17-2. Abstract class translator_to_latin

```
class translator_to_latin definition abstract.
  public section.
    methods      : handle_translation
                     importing
                        source_language type string
                     changing
                        text type string
                     .
  protected section.
    data         : next_in_chain
                     type ref to translator_to_latin.
                   , language_specialty type string
                     .
    methods      : translate abstract
                     changing text type string.
endclass.
class translator_to_latin implementation.
  method handle_translation.
    if source_language eq me->language_specialty.
      call method me->translate
        changing text = text.
    else.
      if me->next_in_chain is bound.
        call method me->next_in_chain->handle_translation
          exporting source_language = source_language
          changing  text            = text.
      endif.
    endif.
  endmethod.
endclass.
```

It provides an implementation for the handle_translation method, but that method invokes abstract method translate defined by this class. The expectation is that the subclass will provide the implementation for this method to contain the ability to translate the source text into Latin. Notice that method handle_translation determines whether to invoke abstract method translate by checking the source language against a language specialty defined as a protected attribute. The expectation is that the constructor of the subclass will populate this attribute with the language it is capable of translating.

A corresponding class is shown in Listing 17-3 to handle translating from Latin.

Listing 17-3. Abstract class translator_from_latin

```
class translator_from_latin definition abstract.
  public section.
    methods      : handle_translation
                     importing
                       target_language type string
                     changing
                       text type string
                     .
  protected section.
    data         : next_in_chain
                     type ref to translator_from_latin.
                 , language_specialty type string
                     .
    methods      : translate abstract
                     changing text type string.
endclass.
class translator_from_latin implementation.
  method handle_translation.
    if target_language eq me->language_specialty.
      call method me->translate
        changing text = text.
    else.
      if me->next_in_chain is bound.
        call method me->next_in_chain->handle_translation
          exporting target_language = target_language
          changing  text            = text.
      endif.
    endif.
  endmethod.
endclass.
```

The abstract classes defined in Listings 17-2 and 17-3 play the role of *Handler* participants in the Chain of Responsibility design pattern. Listing 17-4 shows the definition of the subclass playing the role of a *ConcreteHandler* participant facilitating translation from Latin to English.

Listing 17-4. Class translator_latin_to_english

```
class translator_latin_to_english definition
                             inheriting from translator_from_latin.
  public section.
    methods      : constructor
                     importing next_translator
```

```
                         type ref to translator_from_latin
                      .
  protected section.
    methods       : translate redefinition.
  private section.
    constants     : this_language_specialty type string value 'English'.
endclass.
class translator_latin_to_english implementation.
  method constructor.
    call method super->constructor.
    me->next_in_chain             = next_translator.
    me->language_specialty        = me->this_language_specialty.
  endmethod.
  method translate.
    statements to facilitate translation of text
  endmethod.
endclass.
```

Similar to what we saw with examples of ABAP code with the Decorator pattern, the constructor of this subclass sets the values of protected attributes provided by the superclass, enabling the superclass to make decisions on behalf of the subclass without needing to know anything about the specific subclass. The implementation of method translate is where the processing needs to be placed to accommodate a translation.

Listing 17-5 shows the definition of the subclass also playing the role of a *ConcreteHandler* participant facilitating translation from English to Latin.

Listing 17-5. Class translator_english_to_latin

```
class translator_english_to_latin definition
                                  inheriting from translator_to_latin.
  public section.
    methods       : constructor
                      importing next_translator
                        type ref to translator_to_latin
                      .
  protected section.
    methods       : translate redefinition.
  private section.
    constants     : this_language_specialty type string value 'English'.
endclass.
class translator_english_to_latin implementation.
  method constructor.
    call method super->constructor.
    me->next_in_chain             = next_translator.
    me->language_specialty        = me->this_language_specialty.
  endmethod.
  method translate.
    statements to facilitate translation of text
  endmethod.
endclass.
```

The other subclasses for translating between Latin and Spanish, French, and German are constructed similarly to these two ConcreteHandlers facilitating Latin and English. Notice that none of these

ConcreteHandler subclasses contains any conditional logic for determining whether it is the one handling the applicable language. All of the translator determination is implemented only once in the handle_ translation method provided by the superclass.

But we are not yet finished. The class definitions noted above will facilitate execution of the Chain of Responsibility once it has been constructed. We still need to construct it.

Constructing the Chain

Constructing the chain of objects necessary for using the Chain of Responsibility design pattern is slightly different than what we saw with the construction of the Decorator design pattern. With Chain of Responsibility there is usually no need to determine up front which objects are required in the chain, since only one of them will provide the necessary processing. Compare this with the set of objects for the Decorator, where every one of them provides its bit of processing.

The static class shown in Listing 17-6 handles creating translators on behalf of clients needing language translation.

Listing 17-6. Static Class Constructing the Objects Composing the Chain of Responsibility

```
class translator_builder definition abstract final.
  public section.
    class-methods: create_translator_from_latin
                     exporting
                       translator
                         type ref to translator_from_latin
                 , create_translator_to_latin
                     exporting
                       translator
                         type ref to translator_to_latin
                   .
endclass.
class translator_builder implementation.
  method create_translator_from_latin.
      data        : translators_list type standard table of seoclsname
                  , translator_class like line of translators_list
                  , next_translator_in_chain
                      type ref to translator_from_latin
                    .

    append 'TRANSLATOR_LATIN_TO_ENGLISH' to translators_list.
    append 'TRANSLATOR_LATIN_TO_SPANISH' to translators_list.
    append 'TRANSLATOR_LATIN_TO_FRENCH'  to translators_list.
    append 'TRANSLATOR_LATIN_TO_GERMAN'  to translators_list.
    loop at translators_list
       into translator_class.
      next_translator_in_chain = translator.
      create object translator type (translator_class)
        exporting next_in_chain = next_translator_in_chain.
    endloop.
  endmethod.
  method create_translator_to_latin.
      data        : translators_list type standard table of seoclsname
                  , translator_class like line of translators_list
```

```
                  , next_translator_in_chain                    .
                      type ref to translator_to_latin
                     .
    append 'TRANSLATOR_ENGLISH_TO_LATIN' to translators_list.
    append 'TRANSLATOR_SPANISH_TO_LATIN' to translators_list.
    append 'TRANSLATOR_FRENCH_TO_LATIN'  to translators_list.
    append 'TRANSLATOR_GERMAN_TO_LATIN'  to translators_list.
    loop at translators_list
       into translator_class.
      next_translator_in_chain = translator.
      create object translator type (translator_class)
        exporting next_in_chain = next_translator_in_chain.
    endloop.
  endmethod.
endclass.
```

Notice that the names of the concrete translators are appended to the internal table translators_list in random sequence. When a chain of objects is to be composed of many links, an argument can be made that it matters which link of the chain should be the first and which should be the last. For instance, when using the components defined above, there is an expectation for most of the language translations to occur between English and Spanish, so having their respective concrete translators occupy the first two links of their respective chains may provide for some performance optimization. As constructed above, these two translators will be the final links in their respective chains; the final object created will represent the first link in the chain. However, other than for reasons of performance optimization, there is no need for these links to appear in any specific sequence.

Now, as new languages are added and need to be handled by the translators, this requires only the definition of a two new classes—one for handling translation from the new language to Latin and a counterpart for translating Latin to the new language—and a change to the translator_builder class to include these new translation classes as links in the Chain of Responsibility.

An entity playing the role of the *Client* participant, requiring language translation of its text, might use code like that shown in Listing 17-7.

Listing 17-7. Client Participant

```
  o
  o
data         : translator_of_source_language
                 type ref to translator_to_latin
             , translator_to_target_language
                 type ref to translator_from_latin
             , assembly_instructions type string
               .
  o
  o
call method translator_builder=>create_translator_to_latin
  importing translator = translator_of_source_language.
call method translator_builder=>create_translator_from_latin
  importing translator = translator_to_target_language.
  o
  o
call method translator_of_source_language->handle_translation
  exporting source_language = 'English'
```

236

```
  changing  text              = assembly_instructions.
call method translator_to_target_language->handle_translation
  exporting target_language = 'Spanish'
  changing  text              = assembly_instructions.
  o
  o
```

As shown, the client requests two language translators from static class translator_builder, one for translating to Latin and another for translating from Latin. It then invokes these translators one after the other, providing both the applicable language as well as the text content. In the case illustrated above, the assembly instructions are translated from English to Spanish.

Notice the absence of conditional logic in the client to facilitate the source and target languages. It is oblivious to the objects composing the chain of translators, and simply needs to supply the text along with the source and target languages on two method invocations for a complete translation to occur. Translating text from and into other languages is as simple as changing the designations of the source and target languages.

Summary

In this chapter, we learned more about class explosion and how we can steer clear of it. The Chain of Responsibility design pattern relies on class composition for combining selected capabilities during execution. The result is a set of loosely coupled class instances arranged in a chain, with each instance capable of invoking the next instance in the chain, and where only one of them will be selected to perform the associated processing. Like the Decorator design pattern explored in the previous chapter, Chain of Responsibility also avoids the pitfalls associated with the class explosion problem evolving from designs based primarily on inheritance, it also has both a construction and execution phase associated with it, and it similarly simplifies our maintenance efforts.

Chain of Responsibility Exercises

Refer to Chapter 14 of the functional and technical requirements documentation (see Appendix B) for the accompanying ABAP exercise programs associated with this chapter. Take a break from reading the book at this point to reinforce what you have read by changing and executing the corresponding exercise programs. The exercise programs associated with this chapter are those in the 307 series: ZOOT307A through ZOOT307C.

CHAPTER 18

■ ■ ■

Iterator Design Pattern

The next stop on our voyage through the Design Patterns galaxy takes us to the Iterator design pattern, another of the design patterns found in the GoF catalog. We will find this design pattern useful when we need to access the elements of a structure sequentially without having to know the representation of those elements.

One of the things we should endeavor to avoid when writing code is having our programs know too much about how other entities manager their information. These other entities expose this information externally by not adhering sufficiently to the principle of encapsulation. The Iterator design pattern assists us in enforcing encapsulation by enabling external entities to obtain information without needing to know anything about how that information is organized internally.

Programming on a Need-to-Know Basis

The Ajax Company provides financial services for other corporations. One of these services is to facilitate managing contributions to the pensions of employees of their corporate customers. These customers provide Ajax with an electronic address of a class instance representing their company, from which Ajax's proprietary pension contribution management software retrieves the pertinent information about each employee of the customer corporation as it manages the pension contributions by that corporation to its employees.

Ajax started with only a few small corporations as customers. Each of them provides electronic access to their list of employees, which has always been organized in a simple spreadsheet format. This has worked fine for quite a while. Over the years Ajax has added a few more small corporations as customers, and these companies were able to provide electronic access to their list of employees in the same spreadsheet format.

The sales organization of Ajax recently got a tip about a very large corporation that was considering using its services. This potential customer has a policy of organizing human resources information in the xml format. They have agreed to contract with Ajax for the pension contribution management if Ajax agrees to change its software to access their employee list in the xml format. Not willing to miss such a lucrative sales opportunity, the Ajax management pressed its software development staff to find a way to facilitate this. Eventually the upgraded software became available, which relies on conditional logic in the processing program checking the customer identifier to determine the format of the data to be accessed.

This worked fine for while ... until one day when the program crashed while processing the pension contributions for one of the smaller Ajax customers. An investigation revealed that this small corporation no longer stored its employee data in a spreadsheet format, but recently migrated to the same xml format used by the large corporate customer. Since the software was already capable of processing this format, the change only required some more conditional logic to include this small company in the list of those that managed their data in xml format.

© James E. McDonough 2017

J. E. McDonough, *Object-Oriented Design with ABAP*, DOI 10.1007/978-1-4842-2838-8_18

A crisis was averted, but it served as a wake-up call to Ajax management. Although its pension contribution management processing program was based on needing to know the format of the employee data of its customers, a change to that data format could be implemented at any time by any of its customers. Ajax needed a better way to facilitate accessing the list of employees of its customers, one that did not rely on any specific data format.

Iterator Helps Out

The Iterator design pattern is uniquely suited to enable sequential access by a caller to a list of items held by another entity without the requirement for the caller to know anything about the format of the list. The Iterator design pattern is categorized by GoF with a *behavioral* purpose and an *object* scope. The intent behind this design pattern is the following:

> **Provide a way to access the elements of an aggregate object sequentially without exposing its underlying representation.**[1]

With Iterator, we do not need to access an entire list. We merely need to know whether or not there are any remaining entries in the list, and, if so, to be able to retrieve the next entry. Accordingly, the format of the list provided by the external entity becomes irrelevant. The Ajax customers can store their employee data in any format they see fit. The Ajax pension contribution management processing program merely needs to request the next employee entry from the list, if one remains to be processed.

The definitive phrase of the intent is *without exposing,* since Iterator facilitates the adherence of a class to the principle of encapsulation by allowing it to keep the underlying representation of its aggregates hidden from external entities, a representation that without an Iterator might require the class to assign public visibility to an aggregate for it to become accessible to those external entities. As a consequence, it promotes *loose coupling* because a caller does not need to know how a callee defines the underlying representation for an aggregate; the caller merely receives a new object that can provide aggregate elements one after the other using a representation declared by an interface available to both caller and callee.

Iterator makes use of these participants[2] working in collaboration with each other:

1. Iterator: Defines an interface for accessing and traversing elements

2. ConcreteIterator: Implements the iterator interface; keeps track of the current position in the traversal of the aggregate

3. Aggregate: Defines an interface for creating an iterator object

4. ConcreteAggregate: Implements the iterator creation interface to return an instance of a ConcreteIterator

Essentially, a concrete aggregate creates an instance of a concrete iterator, which contains a list of items and a pointer to the current item. The concrete iterator provides method implementations for traversing the list of items. There are variations for the methods provided by the iterator interface, but what might be considered a minimum set of methods for the iterator is illustrated in the UML class diagram shown in Figure 18-1.

---

[1]GoF, p. 257.
[2]GoF, p. 259.

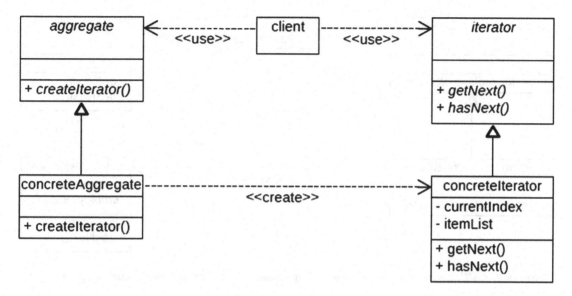

Figure 18-1. UML class diagram for the Iterator design pattern

The client accesses the concrete aggregate through the aggregate interface to request the creation of an instance of an iterator, which the concrete aggregate creates and passes back to the client. The concrete iterator created by the concrete aggregate contains a copy of the item list and has a pointer to the next item in the list. The client then accesses the concrete iterator through the iterator interface to determine whether there is an item remaining on the list (via the hasNext method) and to retrieve the next item on the list (via the getNext method). Although the client is able to retrieve sequentially the list items of the concrete iterator, throughout this entire process it remains oblivious to the way in which the items are stored, either the original items themselves or the copy of those items created for the new iterator instance.

More robust implementations of the Iterator design pattern could include additional abstract methods defined for the iterator and implemented by the concrete iterator, to enable such capabilities as resetting the pointer to the beginning of the list or the end of the list, and moving either forward or backward in the list.

Figure 18-2 shows the UML class diagram for Iterator adapted to the processing required by the Ajax Company for managing pension contributions for its customers.

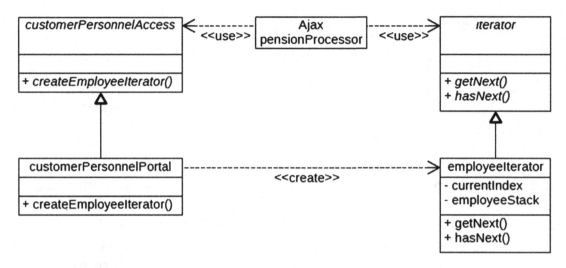

Figure 18-2. *UML class diagram for the Iterator design pattern applied to pension processor scenario*

Ajax has changed its pension management system software to retrieve employee information from its customers using the model described above. The Ajax pension processing program requests a list of employees from the customer personnel portal, which creates for the Ajax requester an iterator object containing a list of employees. The Ajax pension processing program can now simply issue the hasNext and getNext calls against the iterator to retrieve information about the next employee, oblivious to how the list entries are being managed either by the customer personnel department or by the iterator object it has been provided.

Iterator in ABAP

The following code shows how we can implement the Iterator design pattern UML class diagram illustrated in Figure 18-2 into functioning ABAP code. We start with a definition of the employee class, as shown in Listing 18-1. We don't show the full definition and implementation of this class since that level of information it is not pertinent to the operation of the Iterator pattern, instead merely indicating that its definition precedes the definition of other classes that will reference it.

Listing 18-1. Class employee

```
class employee definition.
  o
  o
endclass.
class employee implementation.
  o
  o
endclass.
```

Next, shown in Listing 18-2, is the definition of the abstract class iterator, playing the role of the *Iterator* participant.

Listing 18-2. Abstract Class iterator

```
interface iterator.
    methods      : get_next
                      returning value(next)
                        type ref to object
                 , has_next
                      returning value(more)
                        type abap_bool
                 .
endinterface.
```

The abstract class iterator, shown above, indicates *ref to object* as the type of parameter returned by the get_next method. This means it can return a reference to any type of instance since all classes implicitly inherit from object. It is also used as the superclass for class employee_iterator, shown in Listing 18-3, a class playing the role of the *ConcreteIterator* participant and one that makes reference to the employee class previously defined in Listing 18-1.

Listing 18-3. Class employee_iterator

```
class employee_iterator definition.
  public section.
    interfaces   : iterator
                 .
    aliases      : get_next
                      for iterator~get_next
                 , has_next
                      for iterator~has_next
                 .
    types        : employee_list   type standard table
                                      of ref to employee
                 .
    methods      : constructor
                      importing employee_stack
                        type employee_iterator=>employee_list
                 .
  private section.
    data         : current_index type i
                 , employee_entries type i
                 , employee_stack type employee_iterator=>employee_list
                 .
endclass.
class employee_iterator implementation.
  method constructor.
    call method super->constructor.
    me->employee_stack = employee_stack.
    describe table me->employee_stack lines me->employee_entries.
    me->current_index = 1.
  endmethod.
  method get_next.
    read table me->employee_stack
         into next index me->current_index.
```

```
      add 1 to me->current_index.
    endmethod.
    method has_next.
      if me->current_index le me->employee_entries.
        more = abap_true.
      else.
        more = abap_false.
      endif.
    endmethod.
endclass.
```

Notice the presence of a constructor method, the processing for which will copy the list of references to employee objects from the signature parameter to private attribute employee_stack, and then will set instance attribute employee_entries to the number of entries in the employee_stack and set instance attribute current_index to 1, leaving the instance in a state where it can iterate through the stack from the first entry to the last.

This is followed by the definition of the customer_personnel_access abstract class, shown in Listing 18-4, which plays the role of the *Aggregate* participant.

Listing 18-4. Class customer_personnel_access

```
interface customer_personnel_access.
    methods      : create_employee_iterator
                      returning value(iterator) type ref to iterator
                 .
endinterface.
```

Next, shown in Listing 18-5, is the definition for class customer_personnel_portal, playing the role of the *ConcreteAggregate* participant, a class that inherits from customer_personnel_access.

Listing 18-5. Class customer_personnel_portal

```
class customer_personnel_portal definition.
  public section.

    interfaces   : customer_personnel_access
                 .
    aliases      : create_employee_iterator
                      for customer_personnel_access~create_employee_iterator
                 .
endclass.
class customer_personnel_portal implementation.
  method create_employee_iterator.
    data         : employee_stack type standard table
                                  of ref to employee
                 .
    invoke processing capable of creating into employee_stack
      a list of references to employee objects
    create object iterator type employee_iterator
      exporting employee_stack = employee_stack.
  endmethod.
endclass.
```

Its implementation for method create_employee_iterator consists of getting a list of references to employee instances and using this list to create an instance of an employee_iterator.

The Ajax pension processor code can now iterate through the list of employees simply by using the iterator created for it by an instance of customer_personnel_access, as shown in Listing 18-6.

Listing 18-6. Class ajax_pension_processor

```
class ajax_pension_processor definition.
  public section.
    methods    : iterate
               , handle_pension_contribution
                   importing
                     employee
                       type ref to employee
                 .
  private section.
    data       : aggregate      type ref to customer_personnel_access
               , iterator       type ref to iterator
               , next_object    type ref to object
               , next_employee  type ref to employee
                 .
  method handle_pension_contribution.
    perform pension contribution activities
  endmethod.
  method iterate.
    create object aggregate type customer_personnel_portal.
    iterator = aggregate->create_employee_iterator( ).
    while iterator->has_next( ) eq abap_true.
      next_object            = iterator->get_next( ).
      try.
        next_employee          ?= next_object.
        call me->handle_pension_contribution(next_employee).
      catch cx_sy_move_cast_error.
        continue. " ignore this entry
      endtry.
    endwhile.
  endmethod.
endclass.
```

There are a few things to notice about this ajax_pension_processor class. First, notice that its method iterate creates into field aggregate, defined with static type ref to customer_personnel_access, an instance of class customer_personnel_portal. Accordingly, the static type of field aggregate and dynamic type of reference to which it points are not the same.

Next to notice is that it defines field next_object as type ref to object. This will be the receiving field with the call to the get_next method of the iterator instance since the signature of the get_next method indicates that it returns a reference to object. In ABAP, a field defined as reference to object can point to any object but can access none of its members. Accordingly, if we want to refer to this object as an employee, we first need to move the pointer to a field defined as type ref to employee. Field next_employee is defined this way.

Recall from the discussion on inheritance that moving a pointer from a more generalized reference field to a more specialized one constitutes a specializing cast; the move may or may not succeed depending on whether the dynamic type of the sending field is compatible with the static type of the receiving field. In this case, we expect it to work because all of the object references returned by the iterator are references

245

to employees. Despite our expectation, the ABAP compiler will require that we use the move-cast operator (?=) to set field next_employee from field next_object. If the move does not succeed, the move-cast operator will throw a move-cast exception, specifically, one of type cx_sy_move_cast_error. Accordingly, if we want to intercept this exception, we need to embed the move-cast operation in a try-endtry block, one that indicates exception class cx_sy_move_cast_error on a catch clause. This was implemented in Listing 18-6, so should the move-cast operation ever fail, we have indicated to ignore the error and continue on with the next iteration.

The last thing to notice is the call to method has_next of the iterator instance. The signature of this method indicates that it will be *returning* a parameter rather than changing or exporting one. Such methods are known as functional methods and are capable of being used as the logical expression in conditional statements when the value being returned is compatible with the type of logical expression applicable to the conditional statement. In the case shown in Listing 18-6, it is used to determine when the while loop should terminate since eventually it will return a condition of false, ending the while loop.

It may appear to some that the Iterator design pattern represents too much fuss about accessing the entries of a list sequentially. After all, in ABAP we can simply loop through the entries in a table without requiring all these classes to do it for us. Yes, this is true, but the benefit of the pattern is not that it can access list entries sequentially so much that it can do it without violating the principle of encapsulation, and when it comes to maintaining source code, this may mean the difference between having to change only the component responsible for holding the table entries and also having to change all the external entities that are accessing that table.

Summary

In this chapter, we learned there are ways a class can make the elements of an internal structure available sequentially to external entities without compromising its adherence to the principle of encapsulation. The Iterator design pattern reduces the amount of information classes need to know about each other and enables the maintenance of such interacting classes to proceed independently from each other. We also learned how the Iterator design pattern promotes loose coupling between classes.

Iterator Exercises

Refer to Chapter 15 of the functional and technical requirements documentation (see Appendix B) for the accompanying ABAP exercise programs associated with this chapter. Take a break from reading the book at this point to reinforce what you have read by changing and executing the corresponding exercise programs. The exercise programs associated with this chapter are those in the 308 series: ZOOT308A through ZOOT308D.

CHAPTER 19

■ ■ ■

Template Method Design Pattern

The next stop on our voyage through the Design Patterns galaxy takes us to the Template Method design pattern, another of the design patterns found in the GoF catalog. We will find this design pattern useful when we need to establish a fixed sequence of steps while allowing for some flexibility in their implementation.

Every day we encounter situations where we must perform a sequence of steps in a certain order. We put on socks before we put on shoes; we open a car door before we get into or out of a car and we close it behind us; we carefully compare food items at the market, select some to buy, pay for them, prepare a meal with them, and clean up after the meal. None of the steps in these sequences can be done in a different order. For more complicated operations, we often use some type of modeling device to help us maintain the correct sequence in which to perform a series of tasks. We often refer to these modeling devices using words such as steps, recipe, and *template*.

Let's consider what is required to prepare a favorite breakfast dish enjoyed by programmers around the world: oatmeal. Here are the steps to make a single serving of piping hot oatmeal cereal using a stovetop:

Stovetop directions for oatmeal:

- Gather ingredients: oats, water, salt.
- Place water and salt into small pot.
- Bring water to boil.
- Stir in oats.
- Cook over medium heat for 5 minutes, stirring occasionally.
- Transfer oatmeal from pot to cereal bowl.
- Stir before serving.

This process has been used for centuries; today we can prepare oatmeal using a microwave oven instead of a stovetop. The associated steps are slightly different:

Microwave directions for oatmeal:

- Gather ingredients: oats, water, salt.
- Place oats, water, and salt into microwave-safe cereal bowl.
- Set microwave oven to cook for 3 minutes on high.
- Start microwave oven.
- Stir before serving.

© James E. McDonough 2017
J. E. McDonough, *Object-Oriented Design with ABAP*, DOI 10.1007/978-1-4842-2838-8_19

There's also a variation of standard oatmeal called *instant* oatmeal, for which the preparation is slightly different for both the stovetop and microwave alternatives:

Stovetop directions for instant oatmeal:

- Gather ingredients: instant oatmeal, water, salt.

- Place oatmeal and salt into cereal bowl.

- Place water into small pot.

- Bring water to boil.

- Pour water into cereal bowl.

- Stir before serving.

Microwave directions for instant oatmeal:

- Gather ingredients: instant oatmeal, water, salt.

- Place oatmeal, salt, and water into microwave-safe cereal bowl.

- Set microwave oven to cook for 2 minutes on high.

- Start microwave oven.

- Stir before serving.

Here we see four different sets of directions for preparing a hearty oatmeal breakfast, but they all conform to the following general sequence of steps:

- Gather oatmeal ingredients

- Prepare oatmeal

- Cook oatmeal

- Serve oatmeal

Before you can enjoy oatmeal for breakfast, each of these steps needs to be completed in the order shown, but the details involved within each of these steps depends on whether or not we are using a microwave oven and whether or not we are using instant oatmeal. Accordingly, these general steps represent a template for the operations associated with preparing oatmeal, but each step affords us some flexibility in its execution.

With software we similarly encounter situations where we need certain processes to occur in a specific order, but the details of those processes are dependent upon other influencing factors. The Template Method design pattern enables us to establish the sequence of steps, yet leaves some flexibility in the details of their implementation.

Providing Flexibility While Enforcing a Specific Sequence of Operations

The Template Method design pattern is categorized by GoF with a *behavioral* purpose and a *class* scope. The intent behind this design pattern is the following:

> **Define the skeleton of an algorithm in an operation, deferring some steps to subclasses. The Template Method lets subclasses redefine certain steps of an algorithm without changing the algorithm's structure.**[1]

The Template Method makes use of these participants[2] working in collaboration with each other:

1. AbstractClass: Defines abstract primitive operations that concrete subclasses define to implement steps of an algorithm. Implements a template method defining the skeleton of an algorithm. The template method calls primitive operations as well as operations defined in AbstractClass or those of other objects.

2. ConcreteClass: Implements the primitive operations to carry out subclass-specific steps of the algorithm.

The UML class diagram for the Template Method is shown in Figure 19-1.

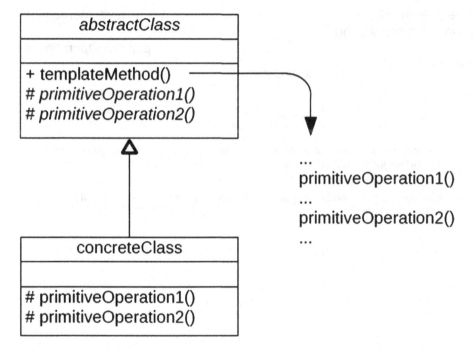

Figure 19-1. *UML class diagram for the Template Method design pattern*

Notice the primitiveOperations specified by the abstractClass are shown using an italic font, meaning they represent abstract methods that must be implemented by a subclass. Notice also the templateMethod itself is shown using a non-italic font, meaning abstractClass is also providing the implementation for it. The templateMethod is usually marked as a *final* method, preventing subclasses from overriding it and reordering the sequence of operations to be performed. This is how the Template Method design pattern gets its name: a method provides a template of steps describing a specific sequence of operations to be performed while leaving some flexibility for subclasses to contribute to or override the activities to be performed for a given step.

---

[1]GoF, p 325.
[2]GoF, p 327.

As shown in Figure 19-2, a variation on the UML class diagram for the Template Method is one where there are no abstract methods defined by the superclass; the superclass provides default implementations for the primitive operations, each of which can be extended or overridden by the subclass as necessary.[3] GoF refers to them as *hook* operations when they contain a default implementation that does nothing.

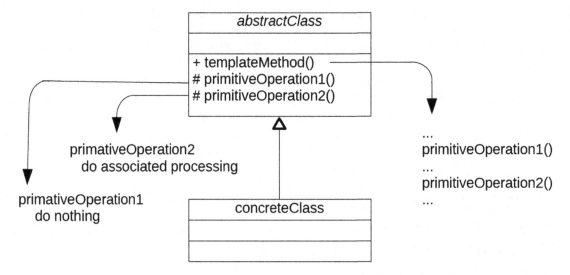

Figure 19-2. *UML class diagram for the Template Method design pattern where an abstract superclass provides method implementations for primitive operations*

Figure 19-3 shows how the Template Method design pattern might apply to making oatmeal for breakfast.

---

[3]Technically, when no abstract methods are defined in the superclass, it loses the requirement to be regarded as an abstract class. Most likely, however, there are multiple inheritors, each extending or overriding the methods defined in the superclass, since without these subclasses to distinguish one sequence of template steps from another there would be no reason for establishing a template method.

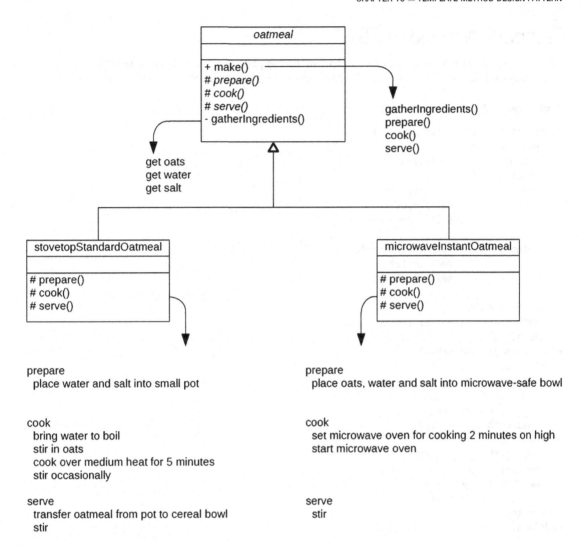

Figure 19-3. *UML class diagram for the Template Method design pattern applied to oatmeal breakfast scenario*

Here we see an oatmeal class defined with public method make, protected abstract methods named prepare, cook, and serve, and a private method called gatherIngredients. Method make is the template method, invoking the other methods defined by the oatmeal class in a specific order. The subclasses stovetopStandardOatmeal and microwaveInstantOatmeal supply implementations for each of the abstract methods defined by the superclass. Whereas the subclasses control the details of what constitutes preparing, cooking, and serving oatmeal, they do not alter the sequence of these steps in any way. Indeed, this would be enforced by assigning final to the make method of the oatmeal class, thus preventing the subclasses from changing its sequence of steps.

Template Method in ABAP

The following code shows how we might implement the Template Method design pattern UML class diagram illustrated above into functioning ABAP code. Listing 19-1 shows the abstract class oatmeal.

Listing 19-1. Abstract Class oatmeal

```
class oatmeal definition abstract.
  public section.
    methods      : make final.
  protected section.
    data         : oats type cup
                 , water type cup
                 , salt type pinch
                 .
    methods      : prepare abstract
                 , cook abstract
                 , serve abstract
                 .
  private section.
    methods      : gather_ingredients.
endclass.
class oatmeal implementation.
  method make.
    call method me->gather_ingredients.
    call method me->prepare.
    call method me->cook.
    call method me->serve.
  endmethod.
  method gather_ingredients.
    me->oats = get oats
    me->water = get water
    me->salt = get salt
  endmethod.
endclass.
```

The oatmeal class shown in Listing 19-1 plays the role of the *AbstractClass* participant. Notice that its public method is marked as final, meaning subclasses cannot override it. Notice also that all of the protected methods are abstract, delegating implementations for them to the subclasses.

The subclass associated with making standard oatmeal using a stovetop, shown in Listing 19-2 and playing the role of the *ConcreteClass* participant, inherits from the oatmeal class above and provides implementations for the abstract methods defined in the superclass.

Listing 19-2. Class stovetop_standard_oatmeal

```
class stovetop_standard_oatmeal definition inheriting from oatmeal.
  protected section.
    methods      : prepare redefinition
                 , cook    redefinition
                 , serve   redefinition
                 .
endclass.
```

```
class stovetop_standard_oatmeal implementation.
  method prepare.
    place me->water and me->salt into small pot
  endmethod.
  method cook.
    bring me->water to boil
    stir in me->oats
    cook over medium heat for 5 minutes
    stir occasionally
  endmethod.
  method serve.
    transfer oatmeal from pot to cereal bowl
    stir
  endmethod.
endclass.
```

The subclass associated with making instant oatmeal using a microwave, shown in Listing 19-3, also plays the role of a *ConcreteClass* participant, also inherits from the oatmeal class above, and also provides implementations for the abstract methods defined in the superclass.

Listing 19-3. Class microwave_instant_oatmeal

```
class microwave_instant_oatmeal definition inheriting from oatmeal.
  protected section.
    methods     : prepare redefinition
                , cook    redefinition
                , serve   redefinition
                .
endclass.
class microwave_instant_oatmeal implementation.
  method prepare.
    place me->oats, me->water and me->salt into microwave-safe bowl
  endmethod.
  method cook.
    set microwave oven for cooking 2 minutes on high
    start microwave oven
  endmethod.
  method serve.
    stir
  endmethod.
endclass.
```

Compare the implementations of the abstract methods provided by both of the subclasses above. Each one implements the methods according to the constraints imposed upon it by the type of oatmeal and type of cooking device with which it is associated. Additional subclasses can be defined to handle the remaining two combinations of oatmeal type and cooking device.

A client intending to use this set of classes might provide code such as shown in Listing 19-4.

Listing 19-4. Code for Client Intending to Use the Classes Defined Above

```
o
o
data             : breakfast type ref to oatmeal.
o
o
if cooking_device eq 'microwave'.
  if type_of_oatmeal eq 'instant'.
    create object breakfast type microwave_instant_oatmeal.
  else.
    create object breakfast type microwave_standard_oatmeal.
  endif.
else.
  if type_of_oatmeal eq 'instant'.
    create object breakfast type stovetop_instant_oatmeal.
  else.
    create object breakfast type stovetop_standard_oatmeal.
  endif.
endif.
call method breakfast->make.
o
o
```

Notice in this code that once it is determined the type of class to instantiate, no subsequent conditional logic is required with the call to its make method, with the invoked instance assuming complete control over the process by which an oatmeal breakfast is made.

Summary

In this chapter, we learned how a superclass defines a fixed sequence of steps to be performed while leaving some flexibility for how those steps are facilitated by subclasses. The Template Method design pattern is characterized by a superclass that defines a public method that invokes its own protected methods in a specific order. These protected methods can be marked abstract, requiring their implementation by subclasses, or they can be fully implemented by the superclass containing processing to be performed on behalf of its subclasses, or they can be empty methods, known as hooks, which do nothing except provide a place where subclasses can override the empty method and supply extra processing to be performed. A defining characteristic of the Template Method design pattern is that subclasses have the option to override certain steps of a process but cannot override the sequence in which those steps are performed.

Template Method Exercises

Refer to Chapter 16 of the functional and technical requirements documentation (see Appendix B) for the accompanying ABAP exercise programs associated with this chapter. Take a break from reading the book at this point to reinforce what you have read by changing and executing the corresponding exercise programs. There is one exercise program associated with this chapter: ZOOT309A.

■ ■ ■

CHAPTER 20

Command Design Pattern

The next stop on our voyage through the Design Patterns galaxy takes us to the Command design pattern, another of the design patterns found in the GoF catalog. We will find this design pattern useful when we want to trigger the execution of an activity without having to know what the activity is.

The Command design pattern is most applicable in situations where the requester for an activity is to remain oblivious to the implementation details for completing the activity, and contributes to enabling objects to remain only loosely coupled.

Plumbing Business Scenario

Acme Plumbing and Heating has 50 plumbing, heating, ventilation, and air conditioning technicians who service the plumbing and heating needs of the residents of Ottawa, Ontario. Although Acme often is awarded large jobs, such as installing the plumbing infrastructure into a new office building under construction, which can take many weeks, it primarily offers scheduled and emergency plumbing services to city residents. Calls for services are handled through a service call center, with each call for service resulting in the creation of a service work order.

These technicians average about three stops per day per technician throughout the week, with their daily schedules arranged by a central dispatching office and consisting of a queue of service work orders to be completed, arranged in a sequence based on the priority of the work. Of course, this only represents the expected work for the day, as emergency calls can be assigned to the technician throughout the day, and these emergency service work orders take priority over the scheduled stops.

The work schedules are available to each technician via an electronic list, available either by an on-board computer in the truck or by a mobile phone application. Upon arriving at work each day, each technician pulls the first work order from their queue. The work order includes the address where the work is to be performed and a description of the work to be completed. Although the service call center operators and technician dispatchers have some working knowledge of plumbing and heating considerations, enough to be able to arrange the priorities for the scheduled jobs and to communicate *what* is to be done, they do not include detailed information for *how* to do the job, the details of which are left up to the technician assigned the work order.

The following are some of the more common activities included in work orders assigned to the Acme technicians:

- Fix leaky faucet.
- Clear clogged drain.
- Replace broken pipe.
- Bleed all radiators.

© James E. McDonough 2017
J. E. McDonough, *Object-Oriented Design with ABAP*, DOI 10.1007/978-1-4842-2838-8_20

- Inspect furnace.

- Install water heater.

The following is a typical winter scenario. The technician working the northwest section of the city has a list of four work orders in the queue, and is already nearly complete with the first one. Meanwhile, a resident in that area who finds one of the pipes in the house has frozen and burst open places a call to Acme for emergency service. The service call center agent creates a work order for the technician who works that section of the city. When that technician notifies the dispatcher that the current job has been completed, the dispatcher issues the next work order assigned to that technician, which now happens to be the emergency call to fix a burst pipe. The technician attends to this emergency as the next task, deferring the other regularly scheduled work orders. Upon completing the emergency call, the technician continues with the next work order in the queue.

A service work order represents a *command* for the service technician to perform some task. The service call center creates these work orders and the dispatcher assigns them in a sequence to make the most efficient use of the service technician's time. Other than an estimate for how much time a work order should take to complete, the dispatcher does not require any details about the service activities that make up the work order. Accordingly, the dispatcher merely *commands* the service technician to do some work at a specific time, but does not need to know what that work entails.

This is the essence of the Command design pattern: the requester entity (dispatcher) who requests a provider entity (service technician) to perform some task (work order) may have no knowledge of the action to be performed by the provider entity. It enables a caller to trigger an activity without knowing any details about the activity itself.

A Command Performance

The Command design pattern is categorized by GoF with a *behavioral* purpose and an *object* scope. The intent behind this design pattern is the following:

> **Encapsulate a request as an object, thereby letting you parameterize clients with different requests, queue or log requests, and support undoable operations.**[1]

Command makes use of these participants[2] working in collaboration with each other:

1. Command: Declares an interface for executing an operation.

2. ConcreteCommand: Defines a binding between a Receiver object and an action. Implements the Execute method by invoking the corresponding operation(s) on the Receiver.

3. Client: Creates a ConcreteCommand object and sets its receiver.

4. Invoker: Asks the command to carry out the request.

5. Receiver: Knows how to perform the operations associated with carrying out a request. Any class may serve as a Receiver.

The UML class diagram for the Command design pattern is shown in Figure 20-1.

---

[1]GoF, p. 233.
[2]GoF, p. 236.

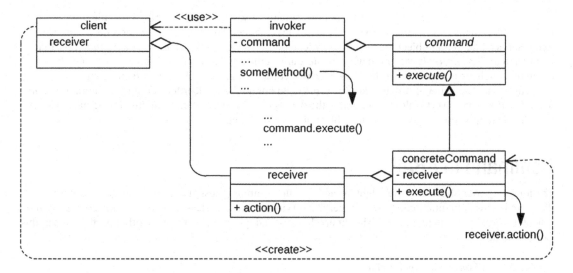

Figure 20-1. *UML class diagram for the Command design pattern*

Notice that the Invoker participant merely calls the execute method of its Command participant. It is unaware of the action the Command participant will cause to be performed. Notice also that the ConcreteCommand participant invokes the action method upon the receiver instance with which it is constructed. In addition, notice that it is the Client participant that creates the instance of a ConcreteCommand participant.

Figure 20-2 shows the UML class diagram for the Command design pattern as it would apply to Acme Plumbing and Heating.

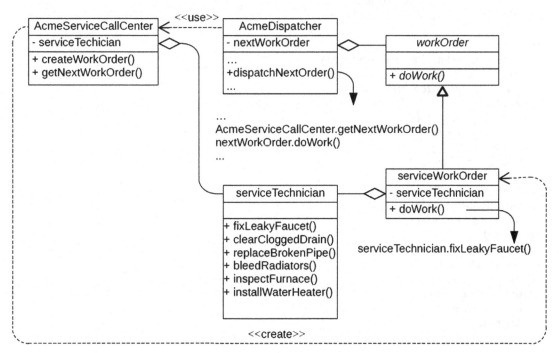

Figure 20-2. *UML class diagram for the Command design pattern applied to plumbing services scenario*

We see that the Acme Service Call Center object creates a service work order for a specific service technician based upon receiving a service call to fix a leaky faucet. The Acme dispatcher requests of the Acme Service Call Center object the next work order assigned to that technician, and then *commands* that technician to *do some work,* without having to know any of the details of the work to be performed, the details of which are encapsulated into the service work order assigned to the service technician.

The Acme dispatcher always invokes the same behavior on the work order: the simple command to *do work.* It is the service work order that contains the details to convert this command into the actual behavior to be invoked upon the service technician object: fix a leaky faucet.

Command in ABAP

The following code shows how we might implement the Command design pattern UML class diagram illustrated above into functioning ABAP code. The service_technician class, shown in Listing 20-1, plays the role of the *Receiver* participant and is shown first because it depends on none of the other participants in this Command design.

Listing 20-1. Class service_technician

```
class service_technician definition.
  public section.
    methods      : go_to_worksite
                      importing worksite type string
                 , fix_leaky_faucet
                 , clear_clogged_drain
                 , replace_broken_pipe
                 , bleed_radiators
                 , inspect_furnace
                 , install_water_header
                 .
endclass.
class service_technician implementation.
  method go_to_worksite.
    travel to specified worksite
  endmethod.
  method fix_leaky_faucet.
    fix leaky faucet
  endmethod.
  method clear_clogged_drain.
    clear clogged drain
  endmethod.
  method replace_broken_pipe.
    replace broken pipe
  endmethod.
  method bleed_radiators.
    bleed radiators
  endmethod.
  method inspect_furnace.
    inspect furnace
  endmethod.
```

```
  method install_water_header.
    install water heater
  endmethod.
endclass.
```

Notice that the service_technician class has a method to instruct the technician where to go to provide the service and other methods to tell the technician what to do upon arriving.

Next is the work_order abstract class, shown in Listing 20-2, playing the role of the *Command* participant; it simply provides the abstract public method do_work.

Listing 20-2. Abstract class work_order

```
class work_order definition abstract.
  public section.
    methods     : do_work abstract.
endclass.
```

Class service_work_order, shown in Listing 20-3, inherits from the work_order class shown above and plays the role of the *ConcreteCommand* participant.

Listing 20-3. Class service_work_order

```
class service_work_order definition inheriting from work_order.
  public section.
    methods     : constructor
                    importing technician type ref to service_technician
                              problem    type string
                              worksite   type string
                    .
  private section.
    data        : technician type ref to service_technician
                , problem    type string
                , worksite   type string
                .
endclass.
class service_work_order implementation.
  method constructor.
    call method super->constructor.
    me->technician              = technician.
    me->problem                 = problem.
    me->worksite                = worksite.
  endmethod.
  method do_work.
    call method technician->go_to_worksite
      exporting worksite = me->worksite.
    case me->problem.
      when 'leaky faucet'.
        call method me->technician->fix_leaky_faucet.
      when 'clogged drain'.
        call method me->technician->clear_clogged_drain.
      when 'broken pipe'.
        call method me->technician->replace_broken_pipe.
```

```
      when 'radiators'.
        call method me->technician->bleed_radiators.
      when 'furnace'.
        call method me->technician->inspect_furnace.
      when 'water header'.
        call method me->technician->install_water_heater.
    endcase.
  endmethod.
endclass.
```

Notice in Listing 20-3 the definition of a constructor for the service_work_order class, by which the instance retains information about its technician instance, the problem to be fixed, and the location of the work site. Its implementation of the do_work method first sends the technician to the work site and then issues the command associated with the problem to the technician.

Listing 20-4 shows the definition of class acme_service_call_center, playing the role of the *Client* participant.

Listing 20-4. Class acme_service_call_center

```
class acme_service_call_center definition.
  public section.
    constants   : priority_emergency type char1 value '1'
                , priority_high      type char1 value '2'
                , priority_medium    type char1 value '3'
                , priority_low       type char1 value '4'
                .
    methods     : constructor
                , create_work_order
                    importing requested_technician type string
                              problem              type string
                              worksite             type string
                , get_next_work_order
                    importing requested_technician type string
                    exporting work_order type ref to work_order
                .
  private section.
    types       : begin of technician_entry
                ,   technician_name type string
                ,   technician_instance type ref
                                to service_technician
                , end   of technician_entry
                , begin of work_order_entry
                ,   priority        type char1
                ,   technician_name type string
                ,   work_order type ref
                                to work_order
                , end   of work_order_entry
                .
    data        : technician_stack type standard table
                                of technician_entry
```

```
                , work_order_stack type sorted table
                                of ref to work_order
                                with non-unique key priority
                    .
endclass.
class acme_service_call_center implementation.
  method constructor.
    data          : technician_entry like line of me->technician_stack.
    technician_entry-name = 'Smith'.
    create object technician_entry-technician_instance.
    append technician_entry to me->technician_stack.
    technician_entry-name = 'Jones'.
    create object technician_entry-technician_instance.
    append technician_entry to me->technician_stack.
      o
      o
  endmethod.
  method create_work_order.
    data          : technician_entry like line of me->technician_stack
                  , work_order_entry like line of me->work_order_stack
                    .
    read table me->technician_stack
         into technician_entry
         with key technician_name = requested_technician.
    work_order_entry-technician_name = technician_entry-technician_name.
    work_order_entry-priority = priority.
    create object work_order_entry-work_order
             type service_work_order
      exporting technician = technician_entry-technician_instance
                problem    = problem
                worksite   = worksite.
    append work_order_entry to me->work_order_stack.
  endmethod.
  method get_next_work_order.
    data          : work_order_entry like line of me->work_order_stack
                    .
    read table me->work_order_stack into work_order
      with key technician_name = requested_technician.
    delete table me->work_order_stack index sy-tabix.
  endmethod.
endclass.
```

The constructor method shown in Listing 20-4 builds the list of technicians into the internal table technician_stack. The create_work_order method facilitates placing a new work order into the internal table work_order_stack after finding from table technician_stack the technician instance for the requested technician. The get_next_work_order method retrieves from the internal table work_order_stack the next entry associated with the requested technician and then deletes this entry from the table.

Finally, the acme_dispatcher class, shown in Listing 20-5, plays the role of the *Invoker* participant.

Listing 20-5. Class acme_dispatcher

```
class acme_dispatcher definition.
  public section.
    methods      : constructor
                     importing service_call_center
                       type ref to acme_service_call_center
                 , dispatch_next_work_order
                     importing technician_name type string
                 .
  private section.
    data         : service_call_center type ref to acme_service_call_center
                 , next_work_order     type ref to work_order
                 .
endclass.
class acme_dispatcher implementation.
  method constructor.
    me->service_call_center      = service_call_center.
  endmethod.
  method dispatch_next_work_order.
    call method me->service_call_center->get_next_work_order
      exporting requested_technician = technician_name
      importing work_order            = me->next_work_order.
    call me->next_work_order->do_work.
  endmethod.
endclass.
```

Notice in Listing 20-5 that the acme_dispatcher class has a constructor method accepting a reference to an instance of an acme_service_call_center. It needs a reference to this service call center so it can invoke its method to get the next work order. Notice the implementation for method dispatch_next_work_order, which calls upon the service call center to provide it the next work order for the technician and then simply invokes the do_work method on that work order instance. The dispatcher instance is oblivious to the service to be performed by the service technician it is dispatching; all the information regarding the location of the work site and the work to be done is contained within the work order.

An entity to make use of these participants might contain code that looks similar to Listing 20-6.

Listing 20-6. Entity Making Use of Participants Defined Above

```
o
o
data          : service_call_center
                  type ref to acme_service_call_center
              , service_dispatcher
                  type ref to acme_dispatcher
              .
o
o
" 1
create object service_call_center.
" 2
create object service_dispatcher
  exporting service_call_center = service_call_center.
```

```
o
o
" 3
call method service_call_center->create_work_order
  exporting requested_technician = `Jones`
            problem               = `leaky faucet`
            priority              = acme_service_call_center=>priority_low
            worksite              = `105 Sycamore Street`.
o
o
" 4
call method service_call_center->create_work_order
  exporting requested_technician = `Smith`
            problem               = `broken pipe`
            priority              = acme_service_call_center=>priority_high
            worksite              = `2296 Ontario Blvd.`.
o
o
" 5
call method service_dispatcher->dispatch_next_work_order
  exporting technician_name = `Smith`.
call method service_dispatcher->dispatch_next_work_order
  exporting technician_name = `Jones`.
o
o
```

In the fragment of code in Listing 20-6 we see the following:

1. An instance of class acme_service_call_center is created.

2. An instance of class acme_dispatcher is created.

3. The instance of class acme_service_call_center is used to create a service work order for technician Jones to fix a leaky faucet.

4. The instance of class acme_service_call_center is used to create a service work order for technician Smith to fix a broken pipe.

5. The instance of acme_dispatcher is used to dispatch the next work order to technician Smith and the following work order to technician Jones.

Dependencies and Dependency Injection

Refer back to the private section defined for class acme_dispatcher shown in Listing 20-5. Notice it defines two attributes: one is a reference to an instance of class acme_service_call_center and the other is a reference to an instance of class work_order. Anytime an entity defines a storage field as a reference to an instance of some other class, the entity becomes dependent upon that type of class; indeed, it is coupled to that class. Accordingly, class acme_dispatcher is dependent upon classes acme_service_call_center and work_order. It means, among other things, that when both classes are defined as local classes, as illustrated in the code above, the definition of the dependent class must follow that of the class upon which it is dependent. It also means that code changes made to the class upon which it is dependent can have syntax or execution ramifications upon the dependent class.

Now refer back to the public section defined for class acme_dispatcher shown in Listing 20-5. Notice it defines a constructor method accepting a reference to an instance of a class. Anytime a method signature indicates that it accepts a reference to an instance of a class, *dependency injection* is at work. Dependency injection means that the caller is providing a reference to an instance of a class for the called method to use. The caller essentially injects the instance to be used into the called method through its signature.

Compare dependency injection with the scenario where a class or its methods facilitates creating its own instances of classes to be used, or requests other objects to provide it with a reference to an instance of a class. Neither constitutes injection since the class or method is actively requesting a reference to an instance. It is only when a method signature accepts a reference to an instance of a class that injection occurs.

Summary

In this chapter, we learned how to define a set of classes where the class initiating the request for some activity to be executed knows nothing about the process associated with completing that activity. The Command design pattern promotes flexible designs, including the instantiation of classes that can facilitate reversible operations and reduces the information classes need to know about each other.

Command Exercises

Refer to Chapter 17 of the functional and technical requirements documentation (see Appendix B) for the accompanying ABAP exercise programs associated with this chapter. Take a break from reading the book at this point to reinforce what you have read by changing and executing the corresponding exercise programs. The exercise programs associated with this chapter are those in the 310 series: ZOOT310A through ZOOT31C.

■ ■ ■

CHAPTER 21

Null Object Pattern

The next stop on our voyage through the Design Patterns galaxy takes us to the Null Object design pattern, the first of two design patterns we'll encounter that are not registered in the GoF catalog. We will find this design pattern useful in reducing conditional logic.

While using a program, a user may be able to issue commands for actions prior to having selected the type of object upon which those actions are applicable. Without having selected an object, the reference to the object is not yet bound to an actual object. We might find ourselves implementing conditional logic in the program to check whether or not an object is bound before attempting to use one of its methods to facilitate the action selected by the user.

The Placebo Effect

A *null object* is one defined to be a surrogate for another object, providing *null* implementations for all the behaviors of the object for which it is a surrogate. With a null object, we can dispense with the conditional logic in the program testing whether or not an actual object is bound to an object reference. Instead, we insure that a null object is bound to the object reference from the time the program begins executing until the time the user makes an object selection, which can then replace the null object. Any actions the user issues prior to selecting an object for those actions will be issued against the null object, which will do ... *nothing*.

The Null Object design pattern is not covered by GoF. The intent behind this design pattern is the following:

> **Provide an object as a surrogate for the lack of an object of a given type. The Null Object pattern provides intelligent do-nothing behavior, hiding the details from its collaborators.**[1]

This pattern becomes useful in situations where we do not yet have available to us an object that can provide any actual "do" behaviors. Since the null object is designed to provide empty behaviors for every behavior available through an object for which it acts as a surrogate, an object reference can be bound to a null object during the initialization phase of the entity holding a reference to the object. This alleviates the need for the conditional logic to test for a bound reference; it will always be bound to some object.

The UML class diagram for the Strategy pattern adapted to the Swiss Army Knife we saw in a previous chapter is shown in Figure 21-1, this time using a null object to handle the cases where one of the various attachments has not yet been chosen.

---

[1]This definition is taken from www.oodesign.com/null-object-pattern.html.

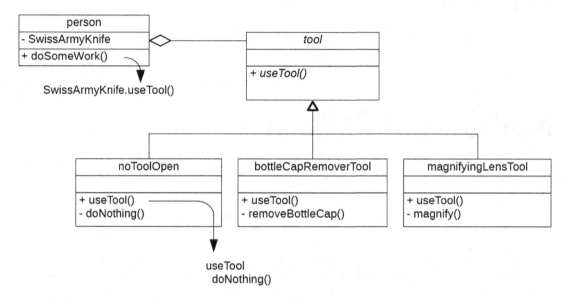

Figure 21-1. *UML class diagram for the Strategy design pattern, expanded to include null object class noToolOpen*

In this case, we instantiate an object of class person, a class that "has a" Swiss Army Knife as one of its attributes. Instead of placing conditional logic into the implementation of the doSomeWork method of the person class, testing whether or not there is a bound instance of a tool ready for use, a Swiss Army Knife instance is instantiated during the initialization of the person object, and it holds a reference to a noToolOpen object. If the doSomeWork method is then invoked prior to having created an instance of a specific tool of the Swiss Army Knife, the corresponding invocation of the useTool method results in no activity. In this way, there is always a bound reference to the SwissArmyKnife attribute upon which its public method useTool can be invoked, alleviating the need to include conditional logic throughout the code checking for the presence of a bound reference before attempting to invoke its methods.

Null Object in ABAP

Here is how we might implement the Null Object design pattern UML class diagram illustrated above in Figure 21-1 into functioning ABAP code. The following definitions for the interface tool and classes bottle_cap_remover_tool and magnifying_lens_tool, shown in Listing 21-1, were copied unchanged from Listings 12-1, 12-3, and 12-4 of the section describing the Strategy design pattern in Chapter 12.

Listing 21-1. Interface Tool and Classes bottle_cap_remover and magnifying_lens_tool

```
interface tool.
  methods        : use_tool.
endinterface.

class bottle_cap_remover_tool definition.
  public section.
    interfaces   : tool.
    aliases      : use_tool for tool~use_tool.
```

```
  private section.
    methods      : remove_bottle_cap.
endclass.
class bottle_cap_remover_tool implementation.
  method use_tool.
    call method me->remove_bottle_cap.
  endmethod.
  method remove_bottle_cap.
    message 'removing bottle cap' type 'I'.
  endmethod.
endclass.

class magnifying_lens_tool definition.
  public section.
    interfaces   : tool.
    aliases      : use_tool for tool~use_tool.
  private section.
    methods      : magnify.
endclass.
class magnifying_lens_tool implementation.
  method use_tool.
    call method me->magnify.
  endmethod.
  method magnify.
    message 'magnifying' type 'I'.
  endmethod.
endclass.
```

The no_tool_open class shown in Listing 21-2 represents a null object.

Listing 21-2. Class no_tool_open, Implemented as a Null Object

```
class no_tool_open definition.
  public section.
    interfaces   : tool.
    aliases      : use_tool for tool~use_tool.
endclass.
class no_tool_open implementation.
  method use_tool.
  endmethod.
endclass.
```

Notice the implementation shown in Listing 21-2 for method use_tool is empty. Accordingly, should this object ever be instantiated and its use_tool method invoked, no action will occur.

The person class shown in Listing 21-3 also was copied from Listing 12-5 of the Strategy section in Chapter 12, but its constructor signature has been changed to make instantiating a corresponding Swiss Army Knife optional. Differences from Listing 12-5 are highlighted.

Listing 21-3. Class person, with Differences from Listing 12-5 Highlighted

```
class person definition.
  public section.
    methods      : constructor
                     importing swiss_army_knife
                       type ref to tool optional
                  , do_some_work
                     .
  private section.
    data        : swiss_army_knife type ref to tool.
endclass.
class person implementation.
  method constructor.
    if swiss_army_knife is supplied.
      me->swiss_army_knife       = swiss_army_knife.
    else.
      create object me->swiss_army_knife
        type no_tool_open.
    endif.
  endmethod.
  method do_some_work.
    call method me->swiss_army_knife->use_tool.
  endmethod.
endclass.
```

The report shown in Listing 21-4 instantiates a person object as a reference to a baby, a type of person we should expect to have no access to a Swiss Army Knife. Accordingly, the instantiation of the baby object omits the optional swiss_army_knife parameter applicable to its constructor, leaving the constructor method of the person class to create an instance of a null object for the Swiss Army Knife attribute of this person object.

Listing 21-4. Report That Creates an Instance of class Person and Then Invokes Its do_some_work Method Without First Invoking a Method to Select a Tool of the Swiss Army Knife

```
report.
  data          : baby type ref to person.
  o
  o
  create object baby.
  o
  o
  call method baby->do_some_work.
```

Notice that the create object statement in Listing 21-4 specifies no importing parameter for the baby object. As a consequence, the baby object is created with a Swiss Army Knife with no tool open due to the conditional check for a supplied parameter in the constructor method of the person class, which, as shown in Listing 21-3, is now marked optional. A call to method do_some_work of the baby instance, shown in Listing 21-4 as the final statement of the report, will result in no action taking place by the corresponding Swiss Army Knife instance.

Summary

In this chapter, we learned a way to avoid the necessity of providing conditional logic to check for the presence of a bound object reference, simplifying the logic and having a positive effect on maintenance efforts. The Null Object design pattern provides a way to create instances of classes that do nothing but can be used like any other class instance.

Null Object Exercises

Refer to Chapter 18 of the functional and technical requirements documentation (see Appendix B) for the accompanying ABAP exercise programs associated with this chapter. Take a break from reading the book at this point to reinforce what you have read by changing and executing the corresponding exercise programs. There is one exercise program associated with this chapter: ZOOT311A.

■ ■ ■

CHAPTER 22

State Design Pattern

The next stop on our voyage through the Design Patterns galaxy takes us to the State design pattern, another of the design patterns found in the GoF catalog. We will find this design pattern useful when we need to make an object behave differently based on its internal state.

One aspect of an entity is its current condition. A person can be healthy or sick. A door can be open or closed. Water can exist as solid, liquid, or gas. Another name for this condition is the *state* of the entity. Often we refer to the entity as being "in a state" to describe its condition, such as a person being "in a state of good health" or a door being "in a closed state."

Not only is an entity considered in a state, but it can also transition to a different state. A healthy person can become sick. A closed door can be opened. Ice can melt.

In addition, an entity has its own behaviors, some of which are affected by its current state. For instance, a person can run and jump, but only when the person is in a healthy state; and can fight infection, but only when the person is in a sick state. Similarly, water can flow, but only when it is liquid, and can maintain a shape, but only when it is solid. Meanwhile, an entity may have other behaviors unaffected by its state, such as a person breathing, which can be done whether healthy or sick.

State Diagram

States and their transitions for an entity are often depicted in what is known as a *state diagram,* as illustrated in Figure 22-1, where

- A *state* is represented by a circle containing the description of the state.

- A *state transition* is represented by a single-headed arrow line connecting the state circles between which a transition is valid from the old state to the new state.

- A *transition condition* is represented by a word or phrase to indicate what must occur for a transition from one state to another, and appears close to the state transition connecting line with which it is associated.

© James E. McDonough 2017
J. E. McDonough, *Object-Oriented Design with ABAP*, DOI 10.1007/978-1-4842-2838-8_22

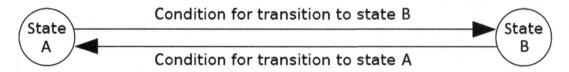

Figure 22-1. *State diagram*

For example, the state diagram illustrated in Figure 22-2 represents the transition of water between the solid and liquid states.

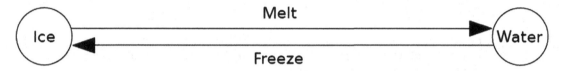

Figure 22-2. *State diagram applied to ice changing state to water and water changing state to ice*

The state diagram assists us in visualizing the various states and the valid transitions between them. To explore this further, let's consider the various states applicable to an aircraft.

Aerial Maneuvers

Any large commercial airliner company has a multitude of airplanes in its fleet. At any given time, some of these airplanes will be flying, others will be on the ground taxiing to or from a runway, and still others will be on the ground stopped at an airport terminal gate loading or unloading passengers. These are only three of the possible states of the aircraft:

- Flying
- On tarmac
- At gate

Some typical behaviors a captain may invoke for a commercial aircraft are

- Take off
- Ascend
- Increase speed
- Maintain level flight
- Decrease speed
- Descend
- Land
- Turn left
- Turn right
- Stop at gate
- Load

- Unload

- Leave gate

- Communicate with tower

- Communicate with passengers

Some of these behaviors result in a change of state, while others are dependent on the current state, and still others are independent of the state. A state diagram to describe the states and transitions might look like the one shown in Figure 22-3.

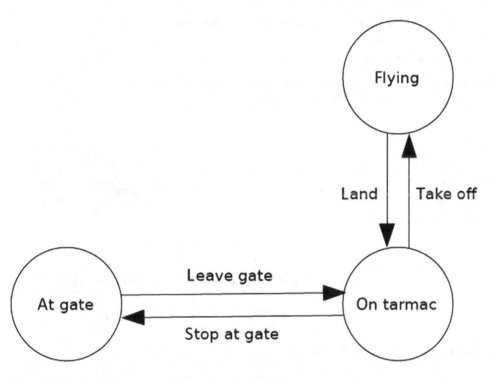

Figure 22-3. *State diagram applied to commercial airplanes*

Here we see the three aircraft states and all the valid transitions between them. For instance, the leave gate behavior is a valid transition from the at gate state to the on tarmac state, and is valid only for transitioning between these two states. There are no valid direct transitions between the states of at gate and flying.

The behaviors named ascend, maintain level flight, and descend seemingly apply only when the aircraft is in the flying state. Similarly, behaviors load and unload apply only when the aircraft is in the at gate state. Behaviors increase speed, decrease speed, turn left, and turn right apply equally to both the flying and on tarmac states, but not to the at gate state. Meanwhile, behaviors *communicate with tower* and *communicate with passengers* apply irrespective of the current state.

With these states influencing whether a behavior is applicable, imagine the conditional logic we would need to implement for the aircraft instance to insure that a behavior cannot be applied inappropriately, such as allowing the unload behavior to occur while the aircraft is in the flying state, or the turn right behavior to occur when the aircraft is in the at gate state. Although we may be able to write the initial logic to facilitate all the various checks and balances for the behaviors of the aircraft, this conditional logic begins to spiral out of control as we add more states and more behaviors during subsequent maintenance cycles.

Maintaining Control Over State Conditional Logic

The State design pattern is categorized by GoF with a *behavioral* purpose and an *object* scope. The intent behind this design pattern is the following:

> **Allow an object to alter its behavior when its internal state changes. The object will appear to change its class.**[1]

State makes use of these participants[2] working in collaboration with each other:

1. Context: Defines the interface of interest to clients

2. State: Defines an interface for encapsulating the behavior associated with a particular state of Context

3. ConcreteState: Subclasses

Each subclass implements a behavior associated with a state of the Context. The UML class diagram for State is shown in Figure 22-4.

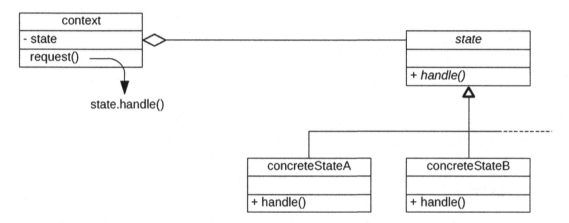

Figure 22-4. *UML class diagram for the State design pattern*

Notice that the Context participant delegates a request to an instance of the State participant to which it holds a reference. Each of the ConcreteState subclass participants provides the request handling applicable to the state it represents by providing an implementation for the abstract handle method defined by the State participant.

Figure 22-5 shows this general UML class diagram describing a specific set of classes to facilitate airline service.

---

[1]GoF, p. 305.
[2]GoF, p. 306.

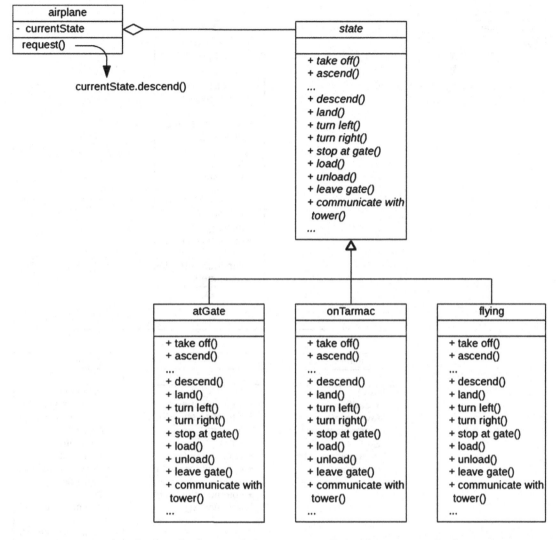

Figure 22-5. UML class diagram for the State design pattern applied to the commercial airline scenario

As illustrated in Figure 22-5, each of the subclasses inheriting from the state class implements each of the abstract methods. In the case of the descend method, this is implemented in both the atGate and onTarmac classes as an empty method; it does nothing.

Indeed, it often becomes the case for the subclass to implement an empty behavior for many of the methods. Accordingly, a variation of this UML diagram is one where the state class provides empty implementations for each of its methods on behalf of the subclasses, leaving the subclasses to override only those behaviors for which some non-empty implementation is warranted, as illustrated in the UML class diagram shown in Figure 22-6.

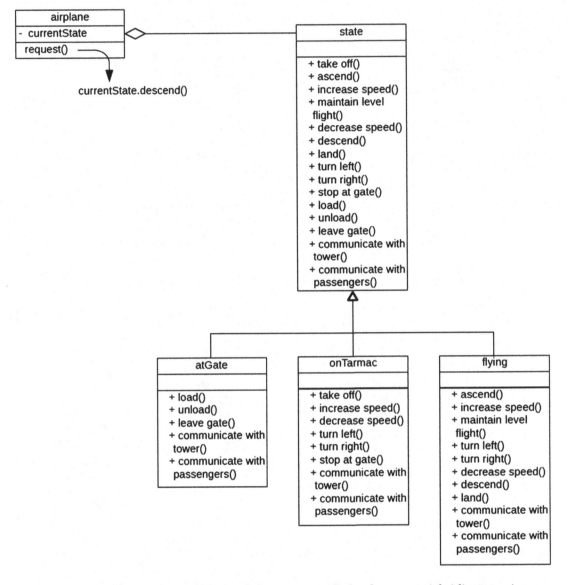

Figure 22-6. *UML class diagram for the State design pattern applied to the commercial airline scenario, where a superclass provides empty method implementations for all methods*

Notice that the state class and its methods shown in Figure 22-6, contrary to the diagram shown in Figure 22-5, are using a non-italic font, indicating that each method has an implementation, with each one implemented as an empty method. The state subclasses override only those methods where an implementation other than an empty method is warranted.

If the currentState attribute points to an instance of the atGate or onTarmac class, the command to descend does nothing since this will result in invoking the empty method implementation provided by the state superclass. On the other hand, if the currentState attribute points to an instance of the flying class, the overriding implementation for method descend provided by the flying class takes precedence.

With this arrangement, state methods implicitly provide no action unless explicitly overridden by the subclass to provide some action.

Regardless of which of the preceding UML diagrams are used to model the state design pattern, they all serve to eliminate all the conditional logic otherwise required to determine whether or not a method is applicable to a specific state. This means that as new state subclasses become necessary, it requires only that we 1) provide applicable implementations for its behaviors and 2) provide a way for the context entity to acquire one of these new subclasses as a state object.

You might recognize the similarity the state class in the diagram in Figure 22-6 has with the null object pattern from the previous chapter. In both cases, the classes provide empty implementations for each of their methods. The significant difference between them is that the state class is intended to be subclassed by a family of classes representing the various states through which an entity can transition, with each subclass overriding only those methods where a non-empty implementation is warranted, while the null object simply provides a valid reference to an object with empty implementations until such time as it can be replaced with a class that can provide non-empty implementations.

State in ABAP

The following code shows how we might implement the State design pattern UML class diagram illustrated above into functioning ABAP code, using the variation shown in Figure 22-6 where state is defined as a class providing no-action implementations for each of its methods, with each method corresponding to an action an airplane may make during normal operations. For brevity, Listing 22-1 shows only a subset of these methods.

Listing 22-1. Class state Showing All Methods Implemented as Empty Methods

```
class state definition.
  public section.
    methods      : leave_gate
                 , stop_at_gate
                 , take_off
                 , land
                 , turn_left
                 , turn_right
                 , ascend
                 , descend
                 , load
                 , unload
                 .
endclass.
class state implementation.
  method leave_gate.
  endmethod.
  method stop_at_gate.
  endmethod.
  method take_off.
  endmethod.
  method land.
  endmethod.
  method turn_left.
  endmethod.
  method turn_right.
```

```
    endmethod.
    method ascend.
    endmethod.
    method descend.
    endmethod.
    method load.
    endmethod.
    method unload.
    endmethod.
endclass.
```

The state class, shown above in Listing 22-1, plays the role of the *State* participant and the implementation for each of its methods is empty. This insures that no action will be taken for that corresponding command unless it is overridden in a subclass providing some specific action.

The following three classes play the role of the *ConcreteState* participants, each inheriting from the state class. Listing 22-2 shows the code for the class at_gate_state.

Listing 22-2. Class at_gate_state

```
class at_gate_state definition inheriting from state.
  public section.
    methods      : constructor
                     importing aircraft type ref to airplane
               , leave_gate    redefinition
               , load          redefinition
               , unload        redefinition
                     .
  private section.
    data        : airplane      type ref to airplane.
endclass.
class at_gate_state implementation.
  method constructor.
    call method super->constructor.
    me->airplane                 = aircraft.
  endmethod.
  method leave_gate.
    call methods of me->airplane facilitating this
      method in this state
    call method me->airplane->switch_to_on_tarmac_state.
  endmethod.
  method load.
    call methods of me->airplane facilitating this
      method in this state
  endmethod.
  method unload_gate.
    call methods of me->airplane facilitating this
      method in this state
  endmethod.
endclass.
```

The at_gate_state class shown in Listing 22-2 overrides the definitions for only those methods of its superclass for which it intends to offer an activity other than the no-action provided by the superclass method. In this case, the only actions applicable to an airplane in the at_gate state are the leave_gate, load, and unload actions. Notice that the implementation for each of these methods invokes methods of the airplane instance, the reference to which is provided to the constructor method when this state object is instantiated.

Listing 22-3 shows the class on_tarmac_state.

Listing 22-3. Class on_tarmac_state

```
class on_tarmac_state definition inheriting from state.
  public section.
    methods        : constructor
                       importing aircraft type ref to airplane
                 , stop_at_gate  redefinition
                 , take_off      redefinition
                 , turn_left     redefinition
                 , turn_right    redefinition
                 .
  private section.
    data           : airplane       type ref to airplane.
endclass.
class on_tarmac_state implementation.
  method constructor.
    call method super->constructor.
    me->airplane                  = aircraft.
  endmethod.
  method stop_at_gate.
    call methods of me->airplane facilitating this
       method in this state
    call method me->airplane->switch_to_at_gate_state.
  endmethod.
  method take_off.
    call methods of me->airplane facilitating this
       method in this state
    call method me->airplane->switch_to_flying_state.
  endmethod.
  method turn_left.
    call methods of me->airplane facilitating this
       method in this state
  endmethod.
  method turn_right.
    call methods of me->airplane facilitating this
       method in this state
  endmethod.
endclass.
```

The on_tarmac_state class overrides the definitions for only those methods of its superclass for which it intends to offer an activity other than the no-action provided by the superclass method. In this case, the only actions applicable to an airplane in the on_tarmac state are the stop_at_gate, take_off, turn_left, and turn_right actions.

The same concept applies to the flying_state class, shown in Listing 22-4.

Listing 22-4. Class flying_state

```
class flying_state definition inheriting from state.
  public section.
    methods      : constructor
                     importing aircraft type ref to airplane
               , land          redefinition
               , turn_left     redefinition
               , turn_right    redefinition
               , ascend        redefinition
               , descend       redefinition
                 .
  private section.
    data         : airplane      type ref to airplane.
endclass.
class flying_state implementation.
  method constructor.
    call method super->constructor.
    me->airplane               = aircraft.
  endmethod.
  method land.
    call methods of me->airplane facilitating this
      method in this state
    call method me->airplane->switch_to_on_tarmac_state.
  endmethod.
  method turn_left.
    call methods of me->airplane facilitating this
      method in this state
  endmethod.
  method turn_right.
    call methods of me->airplane facilitating this
      method in this state
  endmethod.
  method ascend.
    call methods of me->airplane facilitating this
      method in this state
  endmethod.
  method descend.
    call methods of me->airplane facilitating this
      method in this state
  endmethod.
endclass.
```

Finally, the airplane class shown in Listing 22-5, playing the role of the *Context* participant, has a constructor method that creates an instance of each of the states to which it may transition. It determines the command it is to execute in its request method, the implementation for which is a case statement invoking a corresponding method of its current state object.

Listing 22-5. Class airplane

```
class airplane definition.
  public section.
    methods     : constructor
                , request
                    importing action type string
                , switch_to_at_gate_state
                , switch_to_on_tarmac_state
                , switch_to_flying_state
                .
  private section.
    data        : current_state    type ref to state
                , at_gate_state     type ref to state
                , on_tarmac_state   type ref to state
                , flying_state      type ref to state
                .
endclass.
class airplane implementation.
  method constructor.
    create object at_gate_state
            type at_gate_state
      exporting aircraft = me.
    create object on_tarmac_state
            type on_tarmac_state
      exporting aircraft = me.
    create object flying_state
            type flying_state
      exporting aircraft = me.
    call method me->switch_to_at_gate_state.
  endmethod.
  method switch_to_at_gate_state.
    me->current_state              = me->at_gate_state.
  endmethod.
  method switch_to_on_tarmac_state.
    me->current_state              = me->on_tarmac_state.
  endmethod.
  method switch_to_flying_state.
    me->current_state              = me->flying_state.
  endmethod.
  method request.
    case action.
      when 'leave gate'.
        call method current_state->leave_gate.
      when 'stop at gate'.
        call method current_state->stop_at_gate.
      when 'take off'.
        call method current_state->take_off.
      when 'land'.
        call method current_state->land.
```

```
      when 'turn left'.
        call method current_state->turn_left.
      when 'turn right'.
        call method current_state->turn_right.
      when 'ascend'.
        call method current_state->ascend.
      when 'descend'.
        call method current_state->descend.
      when 'load'.
        call method current_state->load.
      when 'unload'.
        call method current_state->unload.
    endcase.
  endmethod.
endclass.
```

The actual processing associated with the action identified in the case statement of method request is dependent upon which concrete state class reference is occupying the current_state attribute. For instance, when the command unload is encountered while in the flying state, the absence of a redefinition in the flying_state class for the unload method means that the no-action method provided by the superclass will be invoked, resulting in the command being ignored.

Notice also that any state change required by the processing of the command is handled by the concrete state object; other than setting its initial state, the airplane class no longer controls setting its own state. The responsibility for changing the state of the airplane has been delegated to the corresponding concrete state objects; for example, method land of concrete state object flying_state invokes method switch_to_on_ tarmac_state of its airplane instance attribute.

ABAP Class Interdependency Considerations

All of the classes defined in Listings 22-1 through 22-5 are conceptually correct, but notice that most of them are interdependent upon each other. The definition for class at_gate_state shown in Listing 22-2 has a private attribute defined as ref to type airplane, a class not defined until Listing 22-5. This same dependency applies to the on_tarmac_state class shown in Listing 22-3 and the flying_state class shown in Listing 22-4, both of which also have a private attribute defined as reference to the airplane defined in Listing 22-5. Class airplane has references to the state class defined in Listing 22-1. Indeed, the state class is the only one defined without any dependencies on any of these other classes.

It is under class interdependency scenarios such as this that we need to consider other implications of the ABAP repository that were first mentioned in Chapter 3 in the "Managing Class Encapsulation Units in the ABAP Repository" section. Let's explore the implications this class interdependency has on the decision whether to designate the set of classes shown in Listings 22-1 through 22-5 as global classes or local classes.

Let's start with implications of global classes. If each of the classes shown in Listings 22-1 through 22-5 were defined as a global class, then using the source code-based editor of the Class Builder, we could, with one exception, define them as they are shown in the listings above. Five distinct global classes would be defined to correspond to each of the five listings. The one exception is the name of the class. Due to the ABAP repository naming restrictions applying to custom development objects, each class needs to start with a Y or Z. Furthermore, it is customary for global classes to be defined with the leading characters CL_, meaning that all of our classes defined globally would now assume the class names zcl_state, zcl_airplane, etc. Once this is done, the classes can exist as independent entities despite their interdependency, although it may require that the interdependent classes be activated simultaneously.

With local classes it's a different story. All of these class definitions would reside in a single ABAP repository object. Since the ABAP compiler is a single-pass compiler, it will expect to already have parsed through the source code representing a class when it encounters a reference to that class in the source code. Notice in the classes defined in Listings 22-2 through 22-4 their respective references to class airplane, which, if the classes were arranged in the sequence shown by the listings, would not yet have been by the compiler parsing the source code during its single pass. The ABAP language provides a statement that enables a class to be referenced in the code before the compiler encounters its actual definition: the *class definition deferred* statement, the syntax of which is

```
class <class name> definition deferred.
```

This statement needs to be placed in the source code prior to the first reference to the class. Accordingly, we would place

```
class airplane definition deferred.
```

between Listing 22-1 and Listing 22-2, so that the reference by class at_gate_state to class airplane will be accepted by the compiler, despite not yet having parsed through the code defining the airplane class, as shown in Listing 22-6.

Listing 22-6. Classes state, at_gate_state, on_tarmac_state, flying_state, and airplane with Deferred Definition Statement for Class airplane Preceding the First Class to Reference It

```
class state definition.
  o
  o
endclass.
class state implementation.
  o
  o
endclass.

class airplane definition deferred.

class at_gate_state definition.
  o
  o
  private section.
    data        : airplane      type ref to airplane.
endclass.
class at_gate_state implementation.
  o
  o
endclass.

class on_tarmac_state definition.
  o
  o
endclass.
class on_tarmac_state implementation.
  o
  o
endclass.
```

```
class flying_state definition.
  o
  o
endclass.
class flying_state implementation.
  o
  o
endclass.

class airplane definition.
  o
  o
endclass.
class airplane implementation.
  o
  o
endclass.
```

This is often sufficient to resolve references to declarations of classes defined later in a single repository object. However, this still is not enough for Listings 22-2 through 22-5. Whereas the definition deferred statement will permit the reference to a class not yet encountered by the compiler, it will not defer references to the members defined by the deferred class. Look again at Listing 22-2, where the implementation for method leave_gate of class at_gate_state invokes a method of the airplane class with the statement

```
call method me->airplane->switch_to_on_tarmac_state.
```

This means there is a reference not just to class airplane but to one of its members, and the statement will be flagged by the compiler as an invalid reference.

A way to get around this with local classes is to separate the definition portion of the class from its implementation portion, similar to the arrangement shown in Listing 22-7.

Listing 22-7. Classes state, at_gate_state, on_tarmac_state, flying_state, and airplane with Deferred Definition Statement for Class airplane Preceding the First Class to Reference It and Where Definition Portions for All Classes Precede the Implementation Portion of Any Class

```
class state definition.
  o
  o
endclass.
```

class airplane definition deferred.

```
class at_gate_state definition.
  o
  o
endclass.

class on_tarmac_state definition.
  o
  o
endclass.
```

```
class flying_state definition.
  o
  o
endclass.

class airplane definition.
  public section.
    methods     : constructor
                , request
                    importing action type string
                , switch_to_at_gate_state
                , switch_to_on_tarmac_state
                , switch_to_flying_state
                .
  o
  o
endclass.

class state implementation.
  o
  o
endclass.

class at_gate_state implementation.
  o
  o
  method leave_gate.
    o
    o
      call method me->airplane->switch_to_on_tarmac_state.
  endmethod.
endclass.

class on_tarmac_state implementation.
  o
  o
endclass.

class flying_state implementation.
  o
  o
endclass.

class airplane implementation.
  o
  o
endclass.
```

The fact that the airplane class definition portion now precedes the at_gate_state class implementation portion now makes it possible for the at_gate_state class to reference a member of the airplane class. The example in Listing 22-7 is one where all class definition portions precede any class implementation portions. In this case, there is no reason the definition and implementation portions of class state cannot remain adjacent, since there are no references to its members by any other classes, but it is shown separated in Listing 22-7 just for consistency in keeping all class definition portions adjacent to each other. The definition deferred statement is still necessary in this arrangement because it resolves the references in classes at_gate_state, on_tarmac_state, and flying state to the class definition for airplane that the compiler still would not yet have encountered.

Summary

In this chapter, we learned the concept of state, how to create state diagrams to represent states and state transitions, how the state of a class is represented by the values of its attributes, and how instances of classes can alter their behavior as their internal state changes. The State design pattern reduces the conditional logic necessary to determine the manifestation of a behavior by encapsulating behavior implementations into state objects. It assists us in preventing subsequent maintenance cycles from spiraling out of control. We also learned two variations of providing implementations for these behaviors: one variation relies on an interface or abstract superclass to provide the definitions for all methods that are then implemented by subclasses and the other variation relies on a superclass also providing empty implementations for all of its methods, leaving the subclasses to override only those where a non-empty method is applicable.

State Exercises

Refer to Chapter 18 of the functional and technical requirements documentation (see Appendix B) for the accompanying ABAP exercise programs associated with this chapter. Take a break from reading the book at this point to reinforce what you have read by changing and executing the corresponding exercise programs. The exercise programs associated with this chapter are those in the 312 series: ZOOT312A through ZOOT312L.

CHAPTER 23

■ ■ ■

Lazy Initialization Technique

The next stop on our voyage through the Design Patterns galaxy takes us to the Lazy Initialization technique, the second of two design patterns we'll encounter that is not registered in the GoF catalog. We will find this design pattern useful in optimizing components.

Initializing components used during the execution of programs is a common housekeeping task applicable to both procedural and object-oriented programming. We may find that initializing these components at the beginning of execution incurs performance and storage consumption penalties when later we determine that some initialized components are never used.

Let There Be Light

Imagine you have completed your work day and have finally arrived home after sunset. Upon entering your home through the front door, you reach over to the light switch and click it into the "on" position. Most likely this will illuminate a light or two near the front door. It would be unlikely that your home is configured such that every light in your home is controlled by this single light switch by the front door. Although such an arrangement might save you the trouble of clicking other light switches as you move through your home, chances are you will not have a reason to move into every room in your home. Even if you did visit every room, it would probably be unnecessary for all rooms in your home to be illuminated at the same time, which would constitute a colossal waste of energy in addition to the high electric bills.

Instead, most homes are configured such that each room has its own light switch to control the light in the room. We can turn the light on as we enter a room and off as we leave, making much more efficient use of energy. In short, we do not consume the energy it takes to light a room unless we actually are using the room.

The same concept is applicable to programming: do not initialize a component until the component will be used. Unlike lights in homes, where the cost to operate the light is fairly constant, the cost to initialize program components is dependent on the component itself, and some are expensive to make available for use.

Delay Tactics

Lazy initialization is not categorized by GoF. Indeed, it is not so much a design pattern as it is a programming technique. The intent behind it is the following:

> **Delay the creation of an object or performance of an expensive operation until the moment it is needed.**

Used judiciously, this technique has the potential to improve performance dramatically and to avoid the excessive consumption of storage.

Lazy initialization is the antithesis of what is known as eager initialization, a technique by which a component is initialized early in the execution of a program under the expectation that the component will always need to be available at some time during processing.

© James E. McDonough 2017
J. E. McDonough, *Object-Oriented Design with ABAP*, DOI 10.1007/978-1-4842-2838-8_23

An example of using lazy initialization is the way in which we might create the various aircraft states explored in the previous chapter. The eager initialization technique is when you create three state objects (atGate, onTarmac, and flying) for each aircraft. The assumption is that each aircraft for which we have created these states is expected to transition to each of these states at some time during its operation.

Suppose we were to board a flight on one of these aircraft while it is in the atGate state. The doors close after everyone has boarded and the aircraft pushes away from the gate, transitioning to the onTarmac state. At this point the aircraft has transitioned between two of its three possible states. As we settle in while the pilot taxis the aircraft toward the runway, we hear the dreaded announcement coming over the intercom:

> "This is your captain speaking. We are experiencing mechanical difficulties and will be returning to the gate."

Moments later the aircraft transitions from the onTarmac state to the atGate state, at which point all passengers disembark, followed again by the aircraft transitioning to the onTarmac state as it is towed to the hangar for repairs. It never gets a chance to transition to the flying state. Accordingly, the flying state object never gets used by this hapless aircraft object.

With lazy initialization, each of the state objects is instantiated at the moment it becomes known that there will be a transition to the corresponding state. An onTarmac state instance is created only upon pushing away from the gate. Accordingly, there would be no flying state object created for an aircraft forced to return to the gate due to mechanical difficulties.

Lazy Initialization in ABAP

Here is how we might implement the lazy initialization technique into the code for the UML diagram described in Figure 22-6 of the previous chapter, where the classes at_gate_state, on_tarmac_state, and flying_state all inherit from the state class, and where an airplane class is composed with references to state objects.

Listing 23-1 shows the definition of the airplane class from Listing 22-5. Its three public "switch" methods are intended to update the current_state attribute with a reference to the applicable state class.

Listing 23-1. Class airplane

```
class airplane definition.
  public section.
    methods      : constructor
                 , request
                     importing action type string
                 , switch_to_at_gate_state
                 , switch_to_on_tarmac_state
                 , switch_to_flying_state
                 .
  private section.
    data         : current_state    type ref to state
                 , at_gate_state     type ref to state
                 , on_tarmac_state type ref to state
                 , flying state      type ref to state
                 .
endclass.
class airplane implementation.
  method constructor.
    create object at_gate_state
            type at_gate_state
```

```
      exporting aircraft = me.
    create object on_tarmac_state
            type on_tarmac_state
      exporting aircraft = me.
    create object flying_state
            type flying_state
      exporting aircraft = me.
    call method me->switch_to_at_gate_state.
  endmethod.
  method switch_to_at_gate_state.
    me->current_state              = me->at_gate_state.
  endmethod.
  method switch_to_on_tarmac_state.
    me->current_state              = me->on_tarmac_state.
  endmethod.
  method switch_to_flying_state.
    me->current_state              = me->flying_state.
  endmethod.
    o
    o
endclass.
```

Notice that the constructor for the airplane immediately creates instances to state classes for all of the states through which it could transition during processing. This may mean that instances of state objects are being created that will never be used during processing. Listing 23-2 shows how the airplane class of Listing 23-1 is changed to use the lazy initialization technique, with differences highlighted.

Listing 23-2. Class airplane with Differences from Listing 23-1 Highlighted

```
class airplane definition.
      o
      o
endclass.
class airplane implementation.
  method constructor.
    create object at_gate_state
            type at_gate_state
      exporting aircraft = me.
    create object on_tarmac_state
            type on_tarmac_state
      exporting aircraft = me.
    create object flying_state
            type flying_state
      exporting aircraft = me.
    call method me->switch_to_at_gate_state.
  endmethod.
  method switch_to_at_gate_state.
    if me->at_gate_state is not bound.
      create object at_gate_state
              type at_gate_state
          exporting aircraft = me.
    endif.
```

289

```
    me->current_state              = me->at_gate_state.
  endmethod.
  method switch_to_on_tarmac_state.
    if me->on_tarmac_state is not bound.
      create object on_tarmac_state
              type on_tarmac_state
          exporting aircraft = me.
    endif.
    me->current_state              = me->on_tarmac_state.
  endmethod.
  method switch_to_flying_state.
    if me->flying_state is not bound.
      create object flying_state
              type flying_state
          exporting aircraft = me.
    endif.
    me->current_state              = me->flying_state.
  endmethod.
    o
    o
endclass.
```

Here we no longer have the constructor creating instances of state objects that may never be used. Instead, each method implementing a switch to a new state checks whether there is a bound reference to the new state, and if one does not exist, it is created. The result is that a state object is not created until the moment it is known that it needs to exist.

Summary

In this chapter, we learned how to avoid unnecessarily creating instances of classes that might never be used. The lazy initialization technique allows us to reduce the wasteful utilization of resources, consuming storage and performing processing only when it is known that an entity will be needed. This is one of the techniques by which we can optimize the performance of the components we create through software design.

Lazy Initialization Exercises

Refer to Chapter 20 of the functional and technical requirements documentation (see Appendix B) for the accompanying ABAP exercise programs associated with this chapter. Take a break from reading the book at this point to reinforce what you have read by changing and executing the corresponding exercise programs. The exercise programs associated with this chapter are those in the 313 series: ZOOT313A and ZOOT313B.

CHAPTER 24

Flyweight Design Pattern

The next stop on our voyage through the Design Patterns galaxy takes us to the Flyweight design pattern, another of the design patterns found in the GoF catalog. We will find this design pattern useful in optimizing components.

Imagine you live in Procedureton and work in Objectropolis, with about 20 kilometers distance separating the two towns. Now imagine your commute between work and home is facilitated by a roadway with a lane dedicated exclusively to your use; no other commuters can use your lane. This would be a boon to those of us who have ever dealt with delays due to heavy traffic or anxiety due to aggressive commuting behaviors. We could arrive and leave work at any time we choose without regard to the commuting habits of others. No longer would we suffer the stress of a tailgating commuter encroaching upon us from behind and creating a dangerous situation.

Now imagine all the residents of Procedureton also work in Objectropolis, and each one of them also has their own dedicated lane of roadway for their exclusive use. The benefits of such an arrangement would be many, but unfortunately this is completely impractical. Aside from the cost to build such a roadway, which would be prohibitive, it would also allocate all the land between the two towns for the sole purpose of surface transportation between them.

In the real world, we are more pragmatic with such matters. We avoid the exorbitant cost and wasteful use of land resources toward building and maintaining such a utopian arrangement by *sharing*, with all other commuters, a single roadway with perhaps only one lane dedicated for travel in each direction, and, as a consequence, enduring some inconvenience once in a while.

This same concept applies to programming. Some objects require the use of other objects to perform services. Though conceivable for one object to "own" another object, thus restricting it to servicing only the needs of the owning object, we can reap the benefits of improved performance and reduced resource consumption by having fewer of these service objects shared amongst all the objects requiring their services.

Sharing Resources

The Flyweight design pattern reduces the number of objects required for processing by arranging for many objects to *share* some of the other objects they require instead of each one having its own objects.

© James E. McDonough 2017
J. E. McDonough, *Object-Oriented Design with ABAP*, DOI 10.1007/978-1-4842-2838-8_24

The Flyweight design pattern is categorized by GoF with a *structural* purpose and an *object* scope. The intent behind this design pattern is the following:

Use sharing to support large numbers of fine-grained objects efficiently.[1]

The definitive word of the intent is *sharing*. In order to facilitate sharing, a shared object needs to be designed in such a way that eliminates any attribute values that would prevent it from being used by more than one other object. Attribute values that can be shared become known as *intrinsic* data and can reside in the shared object because the value is relevant to all sharing objects. Those values that cannot be shared constitute *extrinsic* data and must be passed to the shared object by each sharing object with each call for services.

Flyweight makes use of these participants[2] working in collaboration with each other:

1.   Flyweight: Declares an interface through which flyweights can receive and act on extrinsic state.

2.   ConcreteFlyweight: Implements the Flyweight interface and adds storage for intrinsic state, if any. A ConcreteFlyweight object must be shareable. Any state it stores must be intrinsic; that is, it must be independent of the ConcreteFlyweight object's context.

3.   UnsharedConcreteFlyweight: Not all Flyweight subclasses need to be shared. The Flyweight interface *enables* sharing; it doesn't enforce it. It's common for UnsharedConcreteFlyweight objects to have ConcreteFlyweight objects as children at some level in the flyweight object structure.

4.   FlyweightFactory: Creates and manages flyweight objects. Ensures that flyweights are shared properly. When a client requests a flyweight, the FlyweightFactory object supplies an existing instance or creates one, if none exists.

5.   Client: Maintains a reference to flyweight(s). Computes or stores the extrinsic state of flyweight(s).

The UML class diagram for the Flyweight design pattern is shown in Figure 24-1.

---

[1]GoF, p. 195.
[2]GoF, p. 198.

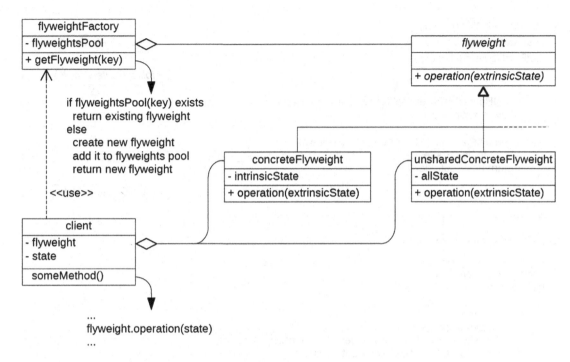

Figure 24-1. *UML class diagram for the Flyweight design pattern*

Notice that the FlyweightFactory participant retains a pool of instances of ConcreteFlyweight and UnsharedConcreteFlyweight participants, each of which uses the interface provided by the Flyweight participant. The implementation for its getFlyweight method will determine whether or not an instance of a flyweight by the requested key value already exists, and if one does not exist, will create a new flyweight instance using that key value and add it to the flyweight pool, returning to the caller the new or existing flyweight instance.

Notice also that the ConcreteFlyweight participants retain attributes representing intrinsic state, representing information that can be shared amongst all its users, but that it accepts extrinsic state information through the method signature of the public operation method, requiring all users to provide any information that cannot be shared by all its users.

The UML class diagram for the Flyweight design pattern describing the practical means by which to find the best route for commuting between Procedureton and Objectropolis is shown in Figure 24-2.

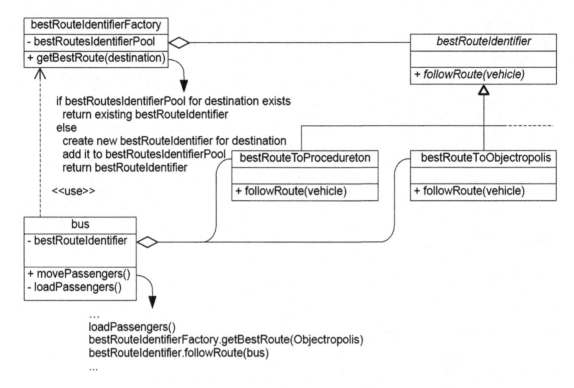

Figure 24-2. UML class diagram for the Flyweight design pattern applied to a best route scenario

Although we may have many buses simultaneously moving passengers between Procedureton and Objectropolis, each bus does not require its own unique bestRouteIdentifier object. We need a maximum of only two instances of the bestRouteIdentifier class, which could be *shared* by all of the buses: one describing the best route to Procedureton and the other describing the best route to Objectropolis.

Flyweight in ABAP

Here is how we might implement the Flyweight design pattern UML class diagram illustrated in Figure 24-2 into functioning ABAP code. First, shown in Listing 24-1, is the definition of the vehicle class. We do not show the full definition and implementation of this class since that level of information is not pertinent to the operation of the Flyweight pattern, instead merely indicating that its definition would precede the definition of other classes that will reference it.

Listing 24-1. Class vehicle

```
class vehicle definition.
  o
  o
endclass.
```

Listing 24-2 shows the abstract class best_route_identifier, playing the role of the Flyweight participant and defining an abstract method follow_route and accepting an instance of vehicle to follow the route.

Listing 24-2. Abstract class best_route_identifier

```
class best_route_identifier definition abstract.
  public section.
    methods      : follow_route abstract
                     importing route_follower type ref to vehicle.
endclass.
```

Notice the absence of any attributes that would prevent instances of this class from being shared amongst multiple vehicles.

Listing 24-3 shows two subclasses, best_route_to_procedureton and best_route_to_objectropolis, inheriting from class best_route_identifier, each playing the role of the ConcreteFlyweight participant. Each one provides an implementation for the abstract follow_route method, inherited from the superclass, providing the best route to its respective destination.

Listing 24-3. Subclasses Inheriting from best_route_identifier

```
class best_route_to_procedureton definition
                                inheriting from best_route_identifier.
  public section.
    methods      : follow_route redefinition.
endclass.
class best_route_to_procedureton implementation.
  method follow_route.
    statements go here indicating best route to Procedureton
  endmethod.
endclass.

class best_route_to_objectropolis definition
                                inhering from best_route_identifier.
  public section.
    methods      : follow_route redefinition.
endclass.
class best_route_to_objectropolis implementation.
  method follow_route.
    statements go here indicating best route to Objectropolis
  endmethod.
endclass.
```

Listing 24-4 shows the static route_identifier_factory class with its public static method get_best_route. This class plays the role of the FlyweightFactory participant. Notice that its implementation of this public method searches for an existing entry in the best_route_identifier_pool, and if one is not found for the desired destination, an object of type best_route_identifier is created and is used to populate a new entry in the best_route_identifier_pool.

Listing 24-4. Static Class best_route_identifier_factory

```
class best_route_identifier_factory definition abstract final.
  public section.
    class-methods: get_best_route
                     importing desired_destination
                       type string
                     exporting best_route
                       type ref to best_route_identifier.
```

```
  private section.
    types         : begin of route_identifier_entry
                  ,   destination   type string
                  ,   best_route    type ref to best_route_identifier
                  , end    of route_identifier_entry
                  .
    class-data    : best_route_identifier_pool
                        type standard table of route_identifier_entry.

    class-methods: create_best_route_instance
                        importing destination
                          type string
                        exporting best_route
                          type ref to best_route_identifier.
endclass.
class best_route_identifier_factory definition.
  method get_best_route.
    data          : route_identifier
                        like line of best_route_identifier_pool.
    read table best_route_identifier_pool
        into route_identifier
        with key destination = desired_destination.
    if route_identifier-destination is initial.
      route_identifier-destination = desired_destination.
      call method create_best_route_instance
        exporting destination = desired_destination
        importing best_route  = route_identifier-best_route.
      append route_identifier
          to best_route_identifier_pool.
    endif.
    best_route = route_identifier-best_route.
  endmethod.
  method create_best_route_instance.
    statements go here to create new instance of best_route_identifier
      subclass to facilitate travel to the specified destination
  endmethod.
endclass.
```

Notice the definition of the pool of flyweights holding various instances of best_route_identifiers, each one accompanied by the destination for which the flyweight instance represents the best route. This means that vehicle instances that would make a request to best_route_identifier_factory to get the best route to its destination will all share the same set of best_route_identifiers; none of them are associated with any specific vehicle instance.

Listing 24-5 shows the definition of the bus class, playing the role of the Client participant, using the best_route_identifier_factory.

Listing 24-5. Class bus

```
class bus definition inheriting from vehicle.
  public section.
    methods      : move_passengers.
  private_section
    methods      : load_passengers.
endclass.
class bus implementation.
  method move_passengers.
    data         : fastest_path type ref to best_route_identifier.
    call method me->load_passengers.
    call method best_route_identifier_factory=>get_best_route
      exporting desired_destination = 'Objectropolis'.
      importing best_route          = fastest_path.
    call method fastest_path->follow_route( me ).
  endmethod.
  method load_passengers.
    statements go here indicating how to load passengers
  endmethod.
endclass.
```

Notice that method move_passengers of the bus class invokes method get_best_route of static class best_route_identifier_factory, passing the name of the destination and receiving an instance of best_route_identifier holding the best path to that destination. It then invokes method follow_route of the instance best_route_identifier, passing itself via the *me* current instance reference to the bus. Any vehicle instances that call method get_best_route of class best_route_identifier_factory using the same destination will receive a reference to the very same instance of best_route_identifier as all other vehicle instances making this call.

Summary

In this chapter, we learned about intrinsic and extrinsic information, and that we can reduce the number of objects required in a design if we can create classes that retain only intrinsic information, leaving it to users of the class to provide whatever extrinsic information might be necessary. This pattern provides us with another way in which we can share objects among many users, utilize resources more efficiently, reduce storage consumption, and optimize the performance of the components we require.

Flyweight Exercises

Refer to Chapter 21 of the functional and technical requirements documentation (see Appendix B) for the accompanying ABAP exercise programs associated with this chapter. Take a break from reading the book at this point to reinforce what you have read by changing and executing the corresponding exercise programs. The exercise programs associated with this chapter are those in the 314 series: ZOOT314A through ZOOT314C.

CHAPTER 25

■ ■ ■

Memento Design Pattern

The next stop on our voyage through the Design Patterns galaxy takes us to the Memento design pattern, another of the design patterns found in the GoF catalog. We will find this design pattern useful when we need to be able to reset the internal state of an object to some previous setting.

We will explore the Memento design pattern through an example where resetting attributes of a class to some previous values might become necessary during the normal use of an application.

Chess Anyone?

Computer chess games are available via chess game applications that can be downloaded to a machine (e.g. Chess Titans) as well as interactive chess games found on the Internet; simply searching for "chess game" will produce a list of websites providing this service. These applications and websites let you play against either a live opponent or the machine. With these games a chess board is presented in the starting position and we choose whether to play white or black. Moves are recorded as a sequence of entries by each player and are reflected in the arrangement of pieces on the board.

The chess game move recording system currently in use regards the chess board as a set of 64 named squares with columns from left to right marked as a through h and rows from bottom to top marked as 1 through 8, as shown in Figure 25-1.

© James E. McDonough 2017

J. E. McDonough, *Object-Oriented Design with ABAP*, DOI 10.1007/978-1-4842-2838-8_25

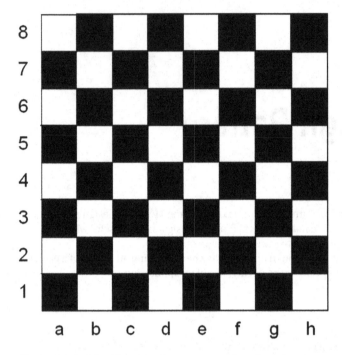

Figure 25-1. *Identification of squares on a chess board*

Each square in Figure 25-1 is identified by its column and row coordinates. For example, the lower right square is identified as h1 (column h, row 1). A game begins with the white pieces arranged as described below, showing the piece abbreviations in parenthesis:

- King (K) at e1
- Queen (Q) at d1
- Bishops (B) at c1 and f1
- Knights (N) at b1 and g1
- Rooks (R) at a1 and h1
- Pawns occupying all the row 2 squares

The black pieces are arranged in the same columns as the white pieces but occupy rows 7 and 8.

The format for representing the series of moves is simply to indicate the piece to be moved and the destination square, except for pawns, which simply indicate the destination square. An x following the piece abbreviation is used to indicate a piece is taken, and ch following the destination square indicates that the move has placed the opponents king in check. The move sheet shown in Table 25-1 provides an example of moves made during a chess game, with the corresponding description of the moves shown in Table 25-2.

Table 25-1. *Chess Moves*

Move	White	Black
1	e4	e5
2	f4	exf4
3	Bc4	Qh4ch
4	Kf1	b5
5	Bxb5	Nf6
6	Nf3	Qh6
7	d3	Nh5
8	Nh4	Qg5
9	Nf5	c6
10	g4	Nf6
...	...	...

Table 25-2. *Description of Moves from Table 25-1*

Description of moves
White pawn at e2 moves to e4; Black pawn at e7 moves to e5.
White pawn at f2 moves to f4; Black pawn at e5 takes pawn at f4.
White bishop at f1 moves to c4; Black queen moves to h4 – check.
White king moves to f1; Black pawn at b7 moves to b5.
White bishop takes pawn at b5; Black knight at g8 moves to f6.
White knight at g1 moves to f3; Black queen moves to h6.
White pawn at d2 moves to d3; Black knight moves to h5.
White knight moves to h4; Back queen moves to g5.
White knight moves to f5; Black pawn at c7 moves to c6.
White pawn at g2 moves to g4; Black knight moves to f6.
...

The move sheet shown above describes the opening moves of what has come to be known as The Immortal Game, a famous game played in London in 1851 between Adolf Anderssen and Lionel Kieseritsky. For the computer to represent this series of moves on the displayed chess board, it would need to clear the square the moving piece occupies before the move and then apply the icon of the moving piece at the destination square.

Table 25-3 shows a variation of the chess move sheet describing the same opening moves of The Immortal Game, but this time shows only a single move of a piece per row. The indication of how the chess board display would change with each move is shown in Table 25-4.

Table 25-3. *Chess Moves*

Move	White	Black
1	e4	...
1	...	e5
2	f4	...
2	...	exf4
3	Bc4	...
3	...	Qh4ch
4	Kf1	...
4	...	b5
5	Bxb5	...
5	...	Nf6
6	Nf3	...
6	...	Qh6
7	d3	...
7	...	Nh5
8	Nh4	...
8	...	Qg5
9	Nf5	...
9	...	c6
10	g4	...
10	...	Nf6
...	...	...

Table 25-4. *Description of Moves from Table 25-3*

Changes to chess board display
Square e2 is cleared; Square e4 indicates white pawn icon.
Square e7 is cleared; Square e5 indicates black pawn icon.
Square f2 is cleared; Square f4 indicates white pawn icon.
Square e5 is cleared; Square f4 indicates black pawn icon.
Square f1 is cleared; Square c4 indicates white bishop icon.
Square d8 is cleared; Square h4 indicates black queen icon.
Square e1 is cleared; Square f1 indicates white king icon.
Square b7 is cleared; Square b5 indicates black pawn icon.
Square c4 is cleared; Square b5 indicates white king icon.
Square g8 is cleared; Square f6 indicates black knight icon.
Square g1 is cleared; Square f3 indicates white knight icon.
Square h4 is cleared; Square h6 indicates black queen icon.
Square d2 is cleared; Square d3 indicates white pawn icon.
Square f6 is cleared; Square h5 indicates black knight icon.
Square f3 is cleared; Square h4 indicates white knight icon.
Square h6 is cleared; Square g5 indicates black queen icon.
Square h4 is cleared; Square f5 indicates white knight icon.
Square c7 is cleared; Square c6 indicates black pawn icon.
Square g2 is cleared; Square g4 indicates white pawn icon.
Square h5 is cleared; Square f6 indicates black knight icon.
...

The UML class diagram shown in Figure 25-2 illustrates how we might construct the objects to handle the chess board, the chess game, and the moves representing The Immortal Game.

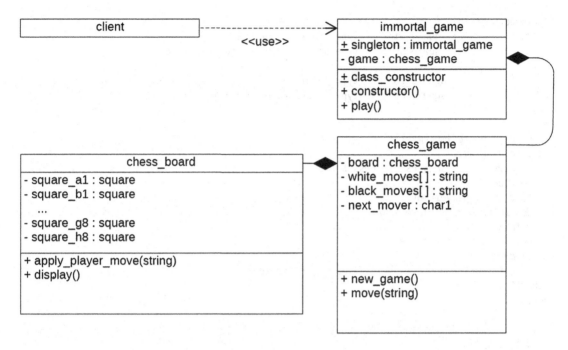

Figure 25-2. *UML class diagram for the computerized chess game design*

In this arrangement, there is a client entity that uses the class immortal_game, a class in which the moves of the immortal game have been captured for replay. Class immortal_game is designed as a singleton instance, providing public behavior play that can be invoked by the client to repeat the moves of the immortal game. It is also composed of a private attribute game, a reference to an instance of class chess_game. Class chess_game provides public behaviors new_game and move. It also has private attributes white_moves, a table of type string; black_moves, also a table of type string; next_mover, a flag to indicate the next mover (white or black); and board, a reference to an instance of class chess_board. Accordingly, the instance of chess_game is composed of an instance of chess_board. Class chess_board provides public behaviors apply_player_move and display in addition to private attributes to represent each of the 64 squares of the chess board.

The ABAP-style pseudocode in Listing 25-1 shows how these classes interact with each other to simulate playing The Immortal Game.

Listing 25-1. Pseudocode for Interaction of Classes Described in Figure 25-2

```
report.
class chess_board definition.
  public section.
    methods     : display
                , apply_player_move
                    importing movement
                    type string
                .
```

```
  private section.
    data          : square_a1      type square value white_rook_icon
                  , square_b1      type square value white_knight_icon
                    ...
                  , square_g8      type square value black_knight_icon
                  , square_h8      type square value black_rook_icon
                  .
endclass.
class chess_board implementation.
  method display.
    display all 64 squares of chess board.
  endmethod.
  method apply_player_move.
    determine moving piece icon.
    determine source square.
    determine target square.
    clear source square.
    target square              = moving piece icon.
  endmethod.
endclass.


class chess_game definition.
  public section.
    constants     : white          type char1 value 'W'
                  , black          type char1 value 'B'
                  .
    methods       : new_game
                  , move
                      importing
                        movement
                          type string
                  .
  private section.
    data          : board          type ref to chess_board
                  , white_moves    type standard table of string
                  , black_moves    type standard table of string
                  , next_mover     type char1
                  .
endclass.
class chess_game implementation.
  method new_game.
    clear: white_moves, black_moves.
    next_mover                 = white.
    create object board.
    board->display( ).
  endmethod.
  method move.
    if next_mover              eq white.
      append movement          to white_moves.
      next_mover               = black.
    else.
```

```
      append movement              to black_moves.
      next_mover                   = white.
    endif.
    board->apply_player_move( movement ).
    board->display( ).
  endmethod.
endclass.

class immortal_game definition.
  public section.
    class-data   : singleton      type ref to immortal_game read-only.
    class-methods: class_constructor.
    methods      : constructor
                 , play
                 .

  private section.
    data         : game           type ref to chess_game.
endclass.
class immortal_game implementation.
  method class_constructor.
    create object immortal_game=>singleton.
  endmethod.
  method constructor.
    create object me->game.
  endmethod.
  method play.
    me->game->new_game( ).
    me->game->move( `e4` ).        " 1    e4    ...
    me->game->move( `e5` ).        " 1    ...   e5
    me->game->move( `f4` ).        " 2    f4    ...
    me->game->move( `exf4` ).      " 2    ...   exf4
    me->game->move( `Bc4` ).       " 3    Bc4   ...
    me->game->move( `Qh4` ).       " 3    ...   Qh4ch
    me->game->move( `Kf1` ).       " 4    Kf1   ...
    me->game->move( `b5` ).        " 4    ...   b5
    me->game->move( `Bxb5` ).      " 5    Bxb5  ...
    me->game->move( `Nf6` ).       " 5    ...   Nf6
    me->game->move( `Nf3` ).       " 6    Nf3   ...
    me->game->move( `Qh6` ).       " 6    ...   Qh6
      ...
  endmethod.
endclass.
start-of-selection.
  immortal_game=>singleton->play( ).
```

Player's Remorse

One feature found with the chess games where the machine can be our opponent is the ability to undo a series of moves. Such backtracking is usually sought after the machine makes a move placing our pieces in a compromising position, and, once the weak position is revealed, enables us to reconsider and redo one or more of our previous moves. A button is usually provided for this capability, called "Previous move" or "Undo," and clicking it once undoes the most recent move. Pressing the button repeatedly continues this process until you reach the starting position of the game.

One of the techniques by which the corresponding display can be changed when the user presses the Undo button is to clear the chess board display back to the starting position for a new game and then to apply each of the moves recorded in the move sheet in succession until reaching the point prior to the most recent move. An alternative to this brute force design is to take a snapshot of the board arrangement after each move and, when an undo is requested, simply retrieve the most recent snapshot and rearrange the board accordingly. The first technique could be regarded as *process* intensive, the second as *storage* intensive; that is, the first technique requires the consumption of CPU time to process all the moves from the start of the game in its quest to reset the board to the corresponding display, whereas the second technique requires the consumption of storage for as many snapshots of the board as there are moves being made as the game progresses. The first technique might result in slow response time while the display is being rebuilt move-by-move, while the second technique will cause storage to be consumed for each snapshot whether or not a specific snapshot is required later. Accordingly, any technique chosen to reset the chess board will have its pros and cons.

Forget-Me-Not

The Memento design pattern facilitates the snapshot technique described above. Specific arrangements of pieces on the chess board are recorded so that the board may be reset to a previous position.

The Memento design pattern is categorized by GoF with a *behavioral* purpose and an *object* scope. The intent behind this design pattern is the following:

> **Without violating encapsulation, capture and externalize an object's internal state so that the object can be restored to this state later.**[1]

Memento makes use of these participants[2] working in collaboration with each other:

1. Memento: Stores the internal state of the Originator object. The memento may store as much or as little of the originator's internal state as necessary at its originator's discretion. Protects against access by objects other than the originator. Mementos have effectively two interfaces. Caretaker sees a *narrow* interface to the memento; it can only pass the memento to other objects. Originator, in contrast, sees a *wide* interface, one that lets it access all the data necessary to restore itself to its previous state. Ideally, only the originator that produced the memento is permitted to access the memento's internal state.

2. Originator: Creates a memento containing a snapshot of its current internal state. Uses the memento to restore its internal state.

3. Caretaker: Is responsible for the memento's safekeeping. Never operates on or examines the contents of a memento.

---

[1]GoF, p. 283.
[2]GoF, p. 285.

In the chess game scenario, class chess_board in Listing 25-1 plays the role of the *Originator* participant. It is the class whose internal state holds the information about how the pieces are arranged on the board at any moment; snapshots of these arrangements need to be made available to reset the pieces to some previous arrangement. It both creates the mementos recording its internal state with each move and uses one or more of these mementos to restore its internal state, effectively resetting the chess board arrangement to represent a previous point in the game.

Class chess_board_memento plays the role of the *Memento* participant. It holds the arrangement of the chess board at a given point in the game.

Class chess_game plays the role of the *Caretaker* participant, requesting chess_board to create an instance of a chess_board_memento that chess_game retains in its internal tables of white and black mementos.

The UML class diagram for the Memento design pattern is shown in Figure 25-3.

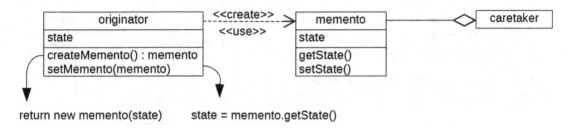

Figure 25-3. UML class diagram for the Memento design pattern

Here we see the originator class providing behaviors createMemento, to create a memento using its own internal state, and setMemento, to reset its internal state using a memento provided through the signature of the behavior. Some external entity requests the originator to create a memento, and when later it is determined that the originator should be set to some previous internal state, again an external entity provides one of the mementos previously created by the originator in requesting the originator reset its own internal state.

The memento class merely facilitates holding a snapshot of the internal state of the originator, providing behaviors getState and setState for getting and setting the state, respectively.

The caretaker class is shown retaining references to the memento instances; that is, caretaker "has a" set of references to mementos. In many cases, the caretaker also is the entity that requests the originator to create the mementos it retains as well as the entity requesting the originator to reset its internal state using one of those mementos.

Notice that the originator class both creates and uses the mementos.

The UML class diagram shown in Figure 25-4 is the same as shown in Figure 25-2 for The Immortal Game but altered to illustrate the use of the memento design pattern, showing the new attributes and methods to be added to existing classes as well as a new class with its relationship to the others; all differences with the UML diagram in Figure 25-2 are highlighted.

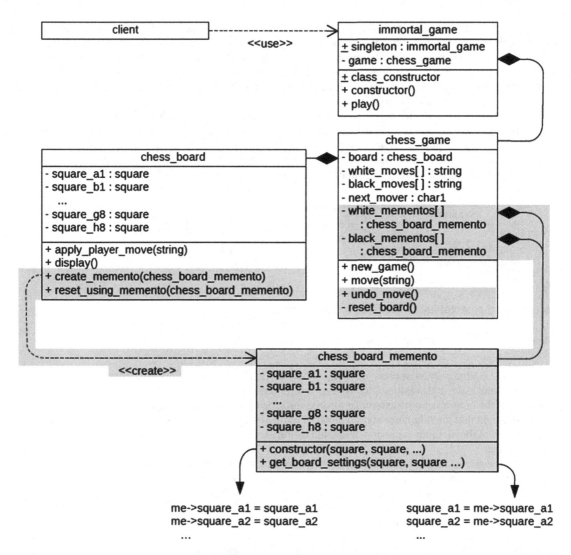

Figure 25-4. UML class diagram for the Memento design pattern applied to the chess game scenario

In this arrangement, the new chess_board_memento class plays the role of the *Memento* participant, class chess_board class plays the role of the *Originator* participant, and the chess_game class plays the role of the *Caretaker* participant. Prior to applying a move, the move method of the chess_game instance now requests the chess_board instance, via method create_memento, to create an instance of chess_board_memento which chess_game alternately will place into its white_mementos or black_mementos table for safe keeping. Upon a request to reverse a chess move, new method undo_move of instance chess_game invokes its private method reset_board, which now will find the appropriate chess_board_memento in its white_mementos and black_mementos tables and request the chess_board instance, via method reset_using_memento, to reset the chess board, after which method undo_move will alter its attributes tracking white and black moves as well as white and black mementos accordingly to discard the undone move and its corresponding memento.

Here we see that the constructor of the chess_board_memento instance provides the capability for its private attribute values to be set to their matching attributes in the chess_board class; that is, when the chess_board instance creates a chess_board_memento instance, it will provide the values of all its 64 private attributes as parameters on the instance constructor, which the constructor will then use to initialize the values of the private attributes of its own instance.

Memento in ABAP

The following ABAP-style pseudocode shows how these modified classes interact with each other to simulate playing The Immortal Game, this time with the ability to undo moves and replay them again. Listing 25-2 shows a new class required to facilitate using the Memento design pattern.

Listing 25-2. Class chess_board_memento

```
class chess_board_memento definition.
  public section.
    methods     : constructor
                      importing square_a1 type square
                                square_b1 type square
                                ...
                                square_g8 type square
                                square_h8 type square
                , get_board_settings
                      exporting square_a1 type square
                                square_b1 type square
                                ...
                                square_g8 type square
                                square_h8 type square
                .
  private section.
    data        : square_a1     type square
                , square_b1     type square
                ...
                , square_g8     type square
                , square_h8     type square
                .
endclass.
class chess_board_memento implementation.
  method constructor.
    me->square_a1              = square_a1.
    me->square_b1              = square_b1.
    ...
    me->square_g8              = square_g8.
    me->square_h8              = square_h8.
  endmethod.
  method get_board_settings.
    square_a1                  = me->square_a1.
    square_b1                  = me->square_b1.
    ...
```

```
      square_g8                = me->square_g8.
      square_h8                = me->square_h8.
    endmethod.
endclass.
```

The chess_board_memento class, shown in Listing 25-2, plays the role of the *Memento* participant. Notice that its sole purpose is to retain the image of all 64 squares on a chess board through its constructor method and then return this information to a caller through the get_board_settings method. Listing 25-3 shows class chess_board, with the differences from Listing 25-1 highlighted.

Listing 25-3. Class chess_board, with Differences from Listing 25-1 Highlighted

```
class chess_board definition.
  public section.
    methods    : display
               , apply_player_move
                   importing movement
                     type string
               , create_memento
                   returning value(memento)
                     type ref to chess_board_memento
               , reset_using_memento
                   importing memento
                     type ref to chess_board_memento
                 .
  private section.
    data       : square_a1     type square value white_rook_icon
               , square_b1     type square value white_knight_icon
                 ...
               , square_g8     type square value black_knight_icon
               , square_h8     type square value black_rook_icon
                 .
endclass.
class chess_board implementation.
  method display.
    display all 64 squares of chess board.
  endmethod.
  method apply_player_move.
    determine moving piece icon.
    determine source square.
    determine target square.
    clear source square.
    target square              = moving piece icon.
  endmethod.
  method create_memento.
    create object memento
      exporting square_a1      = me->square_a1
               square_b1      = me->square_b1
                 ...
               square_g8      = me->square_g8
               square_h8      = me->square_h8.
  endmethod.
```

```
method reset_using_memento.
   call method chess_board_memento->get_board_settings
      importing square_a1          = me->square_a1
                square_b1          = me->square_b1
                   ...
                square_g8          = me->square_g8
                square_h8          = me->square_h8.
endmethod.
endclass.
```

The chess_board class, shown in Listing 25-3, plays the role of the *Originator* participant. It has two additional methods to facilitate the Memento design pattern. Its create_memento method creates an instance of a chess_board_memento, representing its current internal state, which is passed back to the caller, and its reset_using_memento method resets its internal state using the instance of a chess_board_memento provided by the caller. Notice that the chess_board class is not retaining any information about the mementos it creates. Listing 25-4 shows class chess_game, with its differences from Listing 25-1 highlighted.

Listing 25-4. Class chess_game, with Differences from Listing 25-1 Highlighted

```
class chess_game definition.
  public section.
    constants    : white          type char1 value 'W'
                 , black          type char1 value 'B'
                 .
    methods      : new_game
                 , move
                     importing
                       movement
                         type string
                 , undo_move
                 .
  private section.
    data         : board          type ref to chess_board
                 , white_moves    type standard table of string
                 , black_moves    type standard table of string
                 , next_mover     type char1
                 , white_mementos type standard table
                                    of chess_board_memento
                 , black_mementos type standard table
                                    of chess_board_memento
                 .
    methods      : reset_board.
endclass.
class chess_game implementation.
  method new_game.
    clear: white_moves, black_moves, white_mementos, black_mementos.
    next_mover                      = white.
    create object board.
    board->display( ).
  endmethod.
```

```
method move.
    data          : board_memento  type ref to chess_board_memento.
    board_memento = board->create_memento( ).
    if next_mover               eq white.
      append board_memento      to white_mementos.
      append movement           to white_moves.
      next_mover                = black.
    else.
      append board_memento      to black_mementos.
      append movement           to black_moves.
      next_mover                = white.
    endif.
    board->apply_player_move( movement ).
    board->display( ).
endmethod.
method undo_move.
    reset_board( ).
    if next_mover               eq white.
      next_mover                = black.
      delete final row from: black_moves, black_mementos.
    else.
      next_mover                = white.
      delete final row from: white_moves, white_mementos.
    endif.
    board->display( ).
endmethod.
method reset_board.
    data          : board_memento  type ref to chess_board_memento.
    if next_mover               eq white.
      read final row of black_mementos into board_mementos.
    else.
      read final row of white_mementos into board_mementos.
    endif.
    board->reset_using_memento( board_memento ).
endmethod.
endclass.
```

The chess_game class, shown in Listing 25-4, plays the role of the *Caretaker* participant. It has additional attributes and methods to facilitate maintaining a table of memento objects with each new move as well as resetting the board to a previous state. Notice that this class merely requests for and keeps the memento components with each forward move; with a request for a backward move, it simply identifies the most recent memento and then issues a call to its instance of chess_board to reset itself using this memento.

As shown in Listing 25-5, the report has been changed to invoke the new undo_move method of the chess_game class to undo moves 5 and 6 of the Immortal Game and to replay them again, with the differences from Listing 25-1 highlighted.

Listing 25-5. Class immortal_game, with Differences from Listing 25-1 Highlighted

```
class immortal_game definition.
  public section.
    class-data   : singleton      type ref to immortal_game read-only.
    class-methods: class_constructor.
    methods      : constructor
                 , play
                 .
  private section.
    data         : game           type ref to chess_game.
endclass.
class immortal_game implementation.
  method class_constructor.
    create object immortal_game=>singleton.
  endmethod.
  method constructor.
    create object me->game.
  endmethod.
  method play.
    me->game->new_game( ).
    me->game->move( `e4` ).            " 1    e4    ...
    me->game->move( `e5` ).            " 1    ...   e5
    me->game->move( `f4` ).            " 2    f4    ...
    me->game->move( `exf4` ).          " 2    ...   exf4
    me->game->move( `Bc4` ).           " 3    Bc4   ...
    me->game->move( `Qh4` ).           " 3    ...   Qh4ch
    me->game->move( `Kf1` ).           " 4    Kf1   ...
    me->game->move( `b5` ).            " 4    ...   b5
    me->game->move( `Bxb5` ).          " 5    Bxb5  ...
    me->game->move( `Nf6` ).           " 5    ...   Nf6
    me->game->move( `Nf3` ).           " 6    Nf3   ...
    me->game->move( `Qh6` ).           " 6    ...   Qh6
    " Undo moves 5 and 6 and play them over again:
    me->game->undo_move( ). " reset to 6    Nf3   ...
    me->game->undo_move( ). " reset to 5    ...   Nf6
    me->game->undo_move( ). " reset to 5    Bxb5  ...
    me->game->undo_move( ). " reset to 4    ...   b5
    me->game->move( `Bxb5` ).          " 5    Bxb5  ...
    me->game->move( `Nf6` ).           " 5    ...   Nf6
    me->game->move( `Nf3` ).           " 6    Nf3   ...
    me->game->move( `Qh6` ).           " 6    ...   Qh6
    ...
  endmethod.
endclass.
```

Plugging a Security Exposure

Although we now have a working memento capability at our disposal, we're not quite finished. The current relationship between the classes exposes the possibility that any entity could create an instance of a memento, using any values it might choose to provide to represent the internal state of the originator, and then use that bogus memento to request the originator to reset its state accordingly.

To plug this security exposure, we need a way to indicate that memento instances can be created only by the originator participant. At the moment, we have a memento class enabling instantiation by any other entity.

Restricting creation of memento objects to only certain other types of classes can be achieved by using class friendship, whereby a class indicates the names of those classes it considers its friends. Declaring the memento class to offer friendship only to its corresponding originator class in addition to declaring all memento members in the private section and including the create private qualifier on its class definition will restrict the use of mementos only to its originators. Indeed, a portion of the description of the Memento participant states

> Ideally, only the originator that produced the memento would be permitted to access the memento's internal state.[3]

Recall that in the section on friendship it was revealed that friendship has the undesirable effect of breaking encapsulation. Whereas this is generally true with friendship offered between classes, it is not applicable to the Memento design pattern simply because the memento itself exists only in service of the originator. Specifically, the originator creates the memento for the very purpose of holding its internal state, so there is no reason for the originator to make direct changes to the attribute values of the memento since it provided those values in the first place. Not only that, but after creating it the originator typically does not retain a reference to an instance of a memento through which it could make such changes. It is the caretaker that keeps the memento reference safely secured until it is needed later, and the caretaker, not having been offered friendship by the memento, has no access to those members, all of which now are marked privately visible.

Listing 25-6 shows how we would alter the definition of the memento class to insure that only originators can create it and have access to its members, with the differences from Listing 25-2 highlighted.

Listing 25-6. Definition of Class chess_board_memento, with Differences from Listing 25-2 Highlighted

```
class chess_board definition deferred.
class chess_board_memento definition create private friends chess_board.
  private section.
    methods      : constructor
                     importing square_a1 type square
                               square_b1 type square
                                     ...
                               square_g8 type square
                               square_h8 type square
                 , get_board_settings
                     exporting square_a1 type square
                               square_b1 type square
                                     ...
                               square_g8 type square
                               square_h8 type square
                 .
```

---

[3]GoF, p. 285.

```
private section.
    data        : square_a1      type square
                , square_b1      type square
                  ...
                , square_g8      type square
                , square_h8      type square
                .
endclass.
```

With these changes, no entities other than chess_board can create an instance of a chess_board_memento, and even if some other entity, such as an instance of chess_game, were able to get a reference to a chess_board_memento instance, it could not access any of its attributes or invoke any of its methods, since all of them are defined in the private section.

In Listing 25-6 the class statement of the chess_board_memento class is preceded with a class statement deferring definition of the chess_board class. This is necessary only with local definitions of classes when the definition component of a class refers to a class that has not yet been encountered by the compiler; the chess_board_memento class refers in its friends clause to the yet-to-be-encountered chess_board class.

Summary

In this chapter, we learned a way to retain the internal state of an instance in an external component that can be used to reset the internal state at a later time, all while enabling us to adhere to the object-oriented principle of encapsulation. We also learned that there are cases where we might want to restrict only to certain types of classes the ability to create memento objects, and that class friendship can facilitate this for us. Although friendship is a technique that typically results in breaking encapsulation, it can be ignored with the Memento design pattern due to the fact that the memento object is created by and exists solely to service the class it designates as its friend.

Memento Exercises

Refer to Chapter 22 of the functional and technical requirements documentation (see Appendix B) for the accompanying ABAP exercise programs associated with this chapter. Take a break from reading the book at this point to reinforce what we have read by changing and executing the corresponding exercise programs. The exercise programs associated with this chapter are those in the 315 series: ZOOT315A through ZOOT315F.

CHAPTER 26

■ ■ ■

Visitor Design Pattern

The next stop on our voyage through the Design Patterns galaxy takes us to the Visitor design pattern, another of the design patterns found in the GoF catalog. We will find this design pattern most useful once the maintenance cycle has begun on software components.

Before exploring how the Visitor Design Pattern can make our programming lives easier, let's first consider an example of the problem it solves.

Implementation of a New City-Wide Safety Policy

The Public Works Department of the city of Galveston, New York recently implemented a sweeping new safety policy whereby all buildings within the city limits are to be inspected once every five years. A central database retains the addresses of each building along with the inspection certificates and date granted for each type of inspection performed for the building.

When first implemented, the types of inspections to be performed were limited to water quality and air quality. The types of buildings to be inspected were divided into three categories: residential, commercial, and manufacturing. Each type of building had its own requirements for a complete inspection. A residential building inspection usually took one hour; a commercial building inspection required three hours to complete; and a manufacturing building inspection lasted eight hours.

Each business day a Public Works Department agent runs a computer program where the city street and type of inspection is specified on an initial selection screen; the database is searched for the buildings on that street where the most recent inspection date for the specified type of inspection is older than five years; and the resulting addresses are subjected to a new inspection.

Inspections-R-Us

The Ace Business Services Corporation was hired to build the software to facilitate this new safety policy. The designers were fluent in object-oriented principles and immediately recognized the three types of buildings as specializations of a building class. Figure 26-1 shows the UML class diagram they devised to illustrate the hierarchical relationship between these classes.

© James E. McDonough 2017

J. E. McDonough, *Object-Oriented Design with ABAP*, DOI 10.1007/978-1-4842-2838-8_26

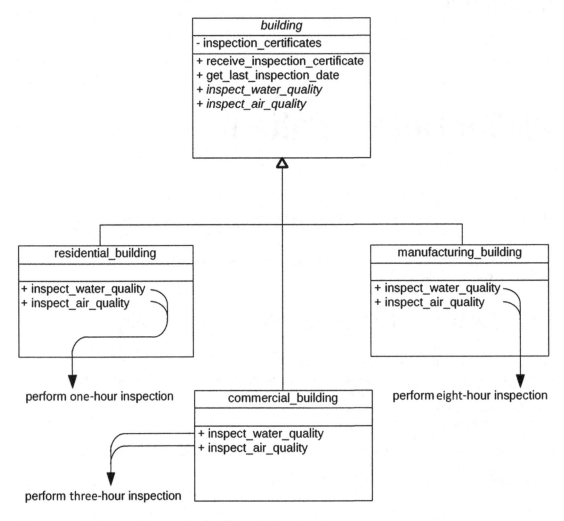

Figure 26-1. *UML class diagram showing hierarchy between classes*

Here we see an abstract class named building, which has a private attribute inspection_certificates, implemented public methods receive_inspection_certificate and get_last_inspection_date, and abstract public methods inspect_water_quality and inspect_air_quality. Classes residential_building, commercial_building, and manufacturing_building each inherit from class building, with each one implementing the abstract methods inspect_water_quality and inspect_air_quality defined by their superclass. One of the programmers quickly wrote some code resembling the ABAP-style pseudocode for the abstract building class, as shown in Listing 26-1.

Listing 26-1. Abstract Class building

```
class building definition abstract.
  public section.
    types          : certificates         type string
                       .
    methods        : receive_inspection_certificate
                         importing inspection type string
                                   date       type sydatum
                   , get_last_inspection_date
                         importing inspection type string
                         exporting date       type sydatum
                   , inspect_water_quality abstract
                         returning value(assessment) type char10
                   , inspect_air_quality abstract
                         returning value(assessment) type char10
                       .
  private section.
    data           : inspection_certificates
                         type standard table of certificates.
endclass.
class building implementation.
  method receive_inspection_certificate.
    o
    o
  endmethod.
  method get_last_inspection_date.
    o
    o
  endmethod.
endclass.
```

The abstract class building shown in Listing 26-1 provides implementations for some of its methods but defers those specific to a type of inspection to subclasses. Shown below are the three classes inheriting from the building class. Listing 26-2 shows the classes inheriting from abstract class building; all are virtually identical in format, the significant difference being the processing involved for each type of inspection.

Listing 26-2. Classes Inheriting from Abstract Class building

```
class residential_building definition inheriting from building.
  public section.
    methods        : inspect_water_quality redefinition
                   , inspect_air_quality redefinition
                       .
endclass.
class residential_building implementation.
  method inspect_water_quality.
    assessment = perform one-hour water quality inspection
  endmethod.
  method inspect_air_quality.
    assessment = perform one-hour air quality inspection
  endmethod.
endclass.
```

```
class commercial_building definition inheriting from building.
  public section.
    methods      : inspect_water_quality redefinition
                 , inspect_air_quality redefinition
                 .
endclass.
class commercial_building implementation.
  method inspect_water_quality.
    assessment = perform three-hour water quality inspection
  endmethod.
  method inspect_air_quality.
    assessment = perform three-hour air quality inspection
  endmethod.
endclass.

class manufacturing_building definition inheriting from building.
  public section.
    methods      : inspect_water_quality redefinition
                 , inspect_air_quality redefinition
                 .
endclass.
class manufacturing_building implementation.
  method inspect_water_quality.
    assessment = perform eight-hour water quality inspection
  endmethod.
  method inspect_air_quality.
    assessment = perform eight-hour air quality inspection
  endmethod.
endclass.
```

Listing 26-3 shows a snippet of code to facilitate inspections by invoking the objects described above.

Listing 26-3. Code for a Component Invoking the Objects Described in Preceding Listings

```
o
o
data street                  type string.
data inspection_type         type string.
data last_inspection_date    type sydatum.
data assessment              type char10.
data buildings               type table of ref to building.
data building                type          ref to building.
o
o
get inspection_type from selection screen
get street          from selection screen
create into buildings instances of all buildings on street
loop at buildings into building.
  call method building->get_last_inspection
    exporting inspection     = inspection_type
    importing date           = last_inspection_date.
  if last_inspection_date older than five years ago.
```

```
case inspection_type.
  when 'water_quality'.
    assessment = building->inspect_water_quality( ).
  when 'air_quality'.
    assessment = building->inspect_air_quality( ).
endcase.
if assessment = 'passed'.
  call method building->receive_inspection_certificate
    exporting inspection     = inspection_type
    date                     = sy-datum.
  endif.
  endif.
endloop.
```

This design worked very well for a while at the Public Works Department in Galveston, New York, but, after a new town council was elected, the decision was made to expand the inspection policy to include inspections for insect infestations. Ace Business Services was awarded the contract to make the necessary changes to the software, and after some brainstorming they drew the UML diagram shown in Figure 26-2, with the differences from the UML diagram in Figure 26-1 highlighted.

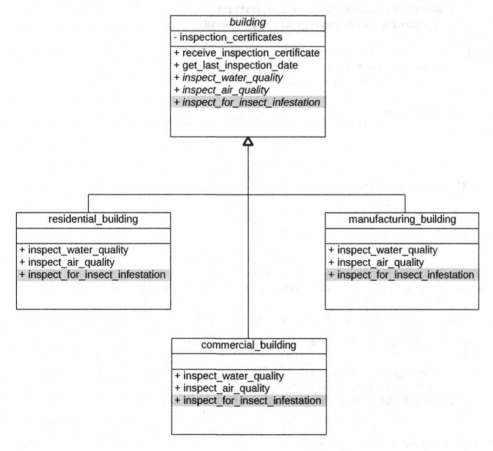

Figure 26-2. *UML class diagram showing how the building class hierarchy handles an additional method, with differences from Figure 26-1 highlighted*

Here we see new abstract method named inspect_for_insect_infestation added to the building superclass, with each of the subclasses providing an implementation for it. Listing 26-4 shows the corresponding code for abstract class building, with differences from Listing 26-1 highlighted.

Listing 26-4. Abstract Class building, with Differences from Listing 26-1 Highlighted

```
class building definition abstract.
  public section.
    types         : certificates           type string
                    .
    methods       : receive_inspection_certificate
                        importing inspection type string
                                  date       type sydatum
                  , get_last_inspection_date
                        importing inspection type string
                        exporting date       type sydatum
                  , inspect_water_quality abstract
                        returning value(assessment) type char10
                  , inspect_air_quality abstract
                        returning value(assessment) type char10
                  , inspect_for_insect_infestation abstract
                        returning value(assessment) type char10
                    .
  private section.
    data          : inspection_certificates
                        type standard table of certificates.
endclass.
class building implementation.
  method receive_inspection_certificate.
    o
    o
  endmethod.
  method get_last_inspection_date.
    o
    o
  endmethod.
endclass.
```

Class building is changed to include a new abstract method for insect infestation inspections. This is implemented in the inheriting classes shown in Listing 26-5, with differences from Listing 26-2 highlighted.

Listing 26-5. Classes Inheriting from Abstract Class building, with Differences from Listing 26-2 Highlighted

```
class residential_building definition inheriting from building.
  public section.
    methods       : inspect_water_quality redefinition
                  , inspect_air_quality redefinition
                  , inspect_for_insect_infestation redefinition
                    .
endclass.
class residential_building implementation.
  method inspect_water_quality.
```

```
      assessment = perform one-hour water quality inspection
    endmethod.
    method inspect_air_quality.
      assessment = perform one-hour air quality inspection
    endmethod.
    method inspect_for_insect_infestation.
      assessment = perform one-hour insect infestation inspection
    endmethod.
endclass.

class commercial_building definition inheriting from building.
  public section.
    methods       : inspect_water_quality redefinition
                  , inspect_air_quality redefinition
                  , inspect_for_insect_infestation redefinition
                  .
endclass.
class commercial_building implementation.
  method inspect_water_quality.
    assessment = perform three-hour water quality inspection
  endmethod.
  method inspect_air_quality.
    assessment = perform three-hour air quality inspection
  endmethod.
  method inspect_for_insect_infestation.
    assessment = perform three-hour insect infestation inspection
  endmethod.
endclass.

class manufacturing_building definition inheriting from building.
  public section.
    methods       : inspect_water_quality redefinition
                  , inspect_air_quality redefinition
                  , inspect_for_insect_infestation redefinition
                  .
endclass.
class manufacturing_building implementation.
  method inspect_water_quality.
    assessment = perform eight-hour water quality inspection
  endmethod.
  method inspect_air_quality.
    assessment = perform eight-hour air quality inspection
  endmethod.
  method inspect_for_insect_infestation.
    assessment = perform eight-hour insect infestation inspection
  endmethod.
endclass.
```

Listing 26-6 shows the invoking snippet of code, also changed to accommodate the new type of inspection, with differences from Listing 26-3 highlighted.

Listing 26-6. Code for a Component Invoking the Objects Described in Preceding Listings, with Differences from Listing 26-3 Highlighted

```
o
o
data street                 type string.
data inspection_type        type string.
data last_inspection_date   type sydatum.
data assessment             type char10.
data buildings              type table of ref to building.
data building               type        ref to building.
o
o
get inspection_type from selection screen
get street          from selection screen
create into buildings instances of all buildings on street
loop at buildings into building.
  call method building->get_last_inspection
    exporting inspection  = inspection_type
    importing date        = last_inspection_date.
  if last_inspection_date older than five years ago.
    case inspection_type.
      when 'water_quality'.
        assessment = building->inspect_water_quality( ).
      when 'air_quality'.
        assessment = building->inspect_air_quality( ).
      when 'insect_infestation'.
        assessment = building->inspect_for_insect_infestation( ).
    endcase.
    if assessment = 'passed'.
      call method building->receive_inspection_certificate
        exporting inspection  = inspection_type
        date                  = sy-datum.
    endif.
  endif.
endloop.
```

This was not difficult for the Ace programmers, but a closer examination reveals that changes to facilitate one new type of inspection resulted in modifications to four classes and one program; indeed, the entire set of components required changes.

The following year the town council of Galveston, New York passed a resolution to include a fire safety inspection in the Public Works Department building inspection policy. Again Ace Business Services was awarded the contract to make the changes and after some brainstorming they drew the UML diagram shown in Figure 26-3, with the differences from the UML diagram in Figure 26-2 highlighted.

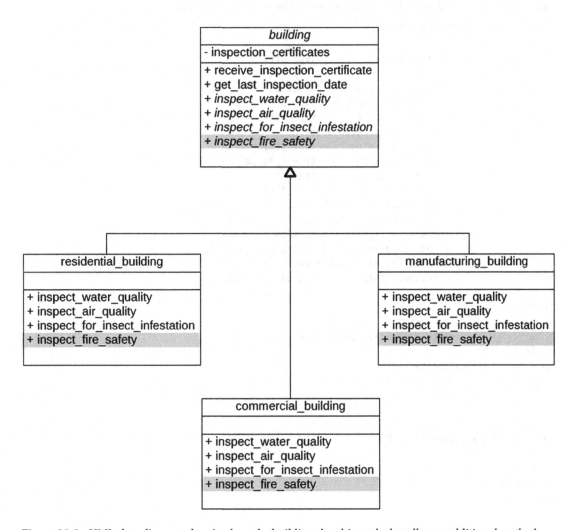

Figure 26-3. *UML class diagram showing how the building class hierarchy handles an additional method, with differences from Figure 26-2 highlighted*

Here we see new abstract method inspect_fire_safety added to the building superclass, with each of the subclasses providing an implementation for it. Listing 26-7 shows the corresponding code for abstract class building, with differences from Listing 26-4 highlighted.

Listing 26-7. Abstract Class building, with Differences from Listing 26-4 Highlighted

```
class building definition abstract.
  public section.
    types       : certificates            type string
                  .
    methods     : receive_inspection_certificate
                     importing inspection type string
                               date        type sydatum
                , get_last_inspection_date
                     importing inspection type string
                     exporting date        type sydatum
                , inspect_water_quality abstract
                     returning value(assessment) type char10
                , inspect_air_quality abstract
                     returning value(assessment) type char10
                , inspect_for_insect_infestation abstract
                     returning value(assessment) type char10
                , inspect_for_fire_safety abstract
                     returning value(assessment) type char10
                  .
  private section.
    data        : inspection_certificates
                     type standard table of certificates.
endclass.
class building implementation.
  method receive_inspection_certificate.
    o
    o
  endmethod.
  method get_last_inspection_date.
    o
    o
  endmethod.
endclass.
```

Again, class building is changed to include a new abstract method for fire safety inspections. This is implemented in the inheriting classes shown in Listing 26-8, with differences from Listing 26-5 highlighted.

Listing 26-8. Classes Inheriting from Abstract Class building, with Differences from Listing 26-5 Highlighted

```
class residential_building definition inheriting from building.
  public section.
    methods      : inspect_water_quality redefinition
                 , inspect_air_quality redefinition
                 , inspect_for_insect_infestation redefinition
                 , inspect_for_fire_safety redefinition
                 .
endclass.
class residential_building implementation.
  method inspect_water_quality.
    assessment = perform one-hour water quality inspection
  endmethod.
  method inspect_air_quality.
    assessment = perform one-hour air quality inspection
  endmethod.
  method inspect_for_insect_infestation.
    assessment = perform one-hour insect infestation inspection
  endmethod.
  method inspect_for_fire_safety.
    assessment = perform one-hour fire safety inspection
  endmethod.
endclass.

class commercial_building definition inheriting from building.
  public section.
    methods      : inspect_water_quality redefinition
                 , inspect_air_quality redefinition
                 , inspect_for_insect_infestation redefinition
                 , inspect_for_fire_safety redefinition
                 .
endclass.
class commercial_building implementation.
  method inspect_water_quality.
    assessment = perform three-hour water quality inspection
  endmethod.
  method inspect_air_quality.
    assessment = perform three-hour air quality inspection
  endmethod.
  method inspect_for_insect_infestation.
    assessment = perform three-hour insect infestation inspection
  endmethod.
  method inspect_for_fire_safety.
    assessment = perform three-hour fire safety inspection
  endmethod.
endclass.
```

```
class manufacturing_building definition inheriting from building.
  public section.
    methods     : inspect_water_quality redefinition
                , inspect_air_quality redefinition
                , inspect_for_insect_infestation redefinition
                , inspect_for_fire_safety redefinition
                .
endclass.
class manufacturing_building implementation.
  method inspect_water_quality.
    assessment = perform eight-hour water quality inspection
  endmethod.
  method inspect_air_quality.
    assessment = perform eight-hour air quality inspection
  endmethod.
  method inspect_for_insect_infestation.
    assessment = perform eight-hour insect infestation inspection
  endmethod.
  method inspect_for_fire_safety.
    assessment = perform eight-hour fire safety inspection
  endmethod.
endclass.
```

Listing 26-9 shows the invoking snippet of code, also changed to accommodate the new type of inspection, with differences from Listing 26-6 highlighted.

Listing 26-9. Code for a Component Invoking the Objects Described in Preceding Listings, with Differences from Listing 26-6 Highlighted

```
o
o
data street                type string.
data inspection_type       type string.
data last_inspection_date  type sydatum.
data assessment            type char10.
data buildings             type table of ref to building.
data building              type         ref to building.
o
o
get inspection_type from selection screen
get street          from selection screen
create into buildings instances of all buildings on street
loop at buildings into building.
  call method building->get_last_inspection
    exporting inspection     = inspection_type
    importing date           = last_inspection_date.
```

```
  if last_inspection_date older than five years ago.
    case inspection_type.
      when 'water_quality'.
        assessment = building->inspect_water_quality( ).
      when 'air_quality'.
        assessment = building->inspect_air_quality( ).
      when 'insect_infestation'.
        assessment = building->inspect_for_insect_infestation( ).
      when 'fire_safety'.
        assessment = building->inspect_for_fire_safety( ).
    endcase.
    if assessment = 'passed'.
      call method building->receive_inspection_certificate
        exporting inspection   = inspection_type
        date                   = sy-datum.
    endif.
  endif.
endloop.
```

This task wasn't difficult for the Ace programmers, but yet again the entire set of components required changes. This design now raised a red flag with one of the Ace programmers, who began to wonder whether the implementation for any subsequent inspection types would also require every component to change.

Sorry, We're Closed

Applying changes to existing components violates what is known as the *Open/Closed Principle*,[1] another of the principles defined by Robert C. Martin. The principle states that once a component has been placed into production, from that point forward it should be *open* for extension but *closed* for modification. Extension means the component can be used as a superclass to a new component seeking to specialize what the component does.[2] Accordingly, to introduce new processing we can use an existing component as a superclass (it is open for extension) for creating a new class, but we should avoid making changes to the existing component itself (it is closed for modification).

This principle recognizes the reality that it is easier and safer *not* to change existing code, code that presumably has already been thoroughly tested prior to being placed into production; to change existing components risks introducing new bugs and possibly making the code harder to understand.

---

[1]See http://butunclebob.com/ArticleS.UncleBob.PrinciplesOfOod.
[2]Presumably the word *extension* is a reference to the Java language, where a subclass indicates its relationship to a superclass by naming the superclass in its class definition following the word *extends,* similar to the way the phrase *inheriting from* denotes this relationship in ABAP.

Just Visiting

The Visitor design pattern enables us to more easily abide by the Open/Closed Principle. Once in place, it simplifies our maintenance efforts when, as we saw with the addition of the insect infestation and fire safety inspections noted above, we need to add new capabilities to an existing process.

The Visitor design pattern is categorized by GoF with a *behavioral* purpose and an *object* scope. The intent behind this design pattern is the following:

> **Represent an operation to be performed on the elements of an object structure. Visitor lets you define a new operation without changing the classes of the elements on which it operates.**[3]

Visitor makes use of these participants[4] working in collaboration with each other:

1. Visitor: Declares a Visit operation for each class of ConcreteElement in the object structure. The operation's name and signature identifies the class that sends the Visit request to the visitor. That lets the visitor determine the concrete class of the element being visited. Then the visitor can access the element directly through its particular interface.

2. ConcreteVisitor: Implements each operation declared by Visitor. Each operation implements a fragment of the algorithm defined for the corresponding class of object in the structure. ConcreteVisitor provides the context for the algorithm and stores its local state. This state often accumulates results during the traversal of the structure.

3. Element: Defines an Accept operation that takes a visitor as an argument.

4. ConcreteElement: Implements an Accept operation that takes a visitor as an argument.

5. ObjectStructure: Can enumerate its elements. May provide a high-level interface to allow the visitor to visit its elements. May either be a composite or a collection such as a list or a set.

---

[3]GoF, p. 331.
[4]GoF, p. 334.

The UML class diagram for the Visitor design pattern is shown in Figure 26-4.

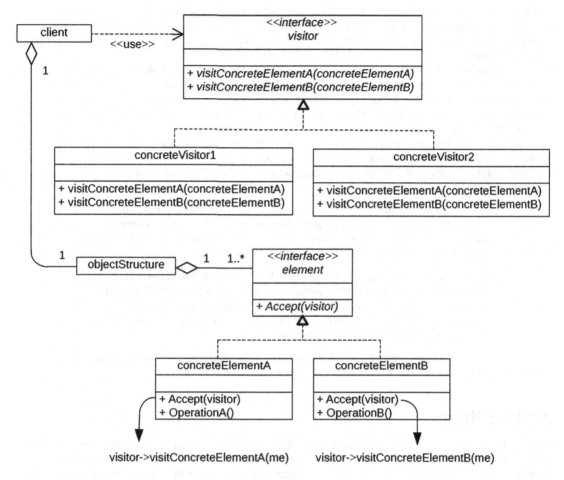

Figure 26-4. *UML class diagram for the Visitor design pattern*

Here we see a client that has an object structure and uses a visitor. The visitor is an interface implemented by concrete visitors. Each concrete visitor has methods to visit each type of concrete element. The object structure also has elements. Each element is an interface implemented by concrete elements. Each of the concrete elements provides an implementation for the Accept method, which is simply to invoke its corresponding visitConcreteElementX method of the visitor interface reference it has been provided.

It may be helpful to think of the *element* participant as a *visitable element*. Accordingly, a client has an object structure composed of visitable elements, and uses visitors to visit its visitable elements. The visitor interface provides a visitConcreteElementX method for each one of the classes implementing the visitable element interface. As such, each concrete visitor has as many visitConcreteElementX method implementations as there are concreteElement classes, one method implementation to correspond to each visitable element class.

The client obtains a reference to a visitor interface. It then loops through its object structure, and for each visitable element invokes its accept method, passing it a reference to the visitor object. The implementation of the accept method of the concrete visitable element, in turn, invokes the relevant visitConcreteElementX method of the visitor object, passing it a reference to the concrete visitable element object making the invocation.

Recall from the discussion on polymorphism that *dynamic dispatch* is the process by which the dynamic type of an object reference is used at execution time to determine the actual method implementation to be invoked. The Visitor design pattern uses what is known as *double dynamic dispatch*. Here is how it works:

> The first dynamic dispatch occurs when the client invokes method accept of the visitable element object, causing the dynamic type of the visitable element interface reference to determine the specific concrete visitable element object whose accept method implementation is to be invoked.

> The second dynamic dispatch occurs when the implementation of the accept method of the visitable element object invokes method visitConcreteElementX of the visitor object it had been passed, causing the dynamic type of the visitor interface reference to determine the specific concrete visitor object whose visitConcreteElementX method is to be invoked.

Accordingly, it is the combination of both the dynamic type of the visitable object and the dynamic type of the visitor object that eventually determines the processing to be performed.

Visiting Hours

Once the Visitor design pattern was brought to their attention, the developers at Ace Business Services spent a few hours devising a new UML class diagram, shown in Figure 26-5, which they intend to use to redesign the processing for the Public Works Department of Galveston, New York so that any additional requests for new types of inspections no longer require changes to existing components.

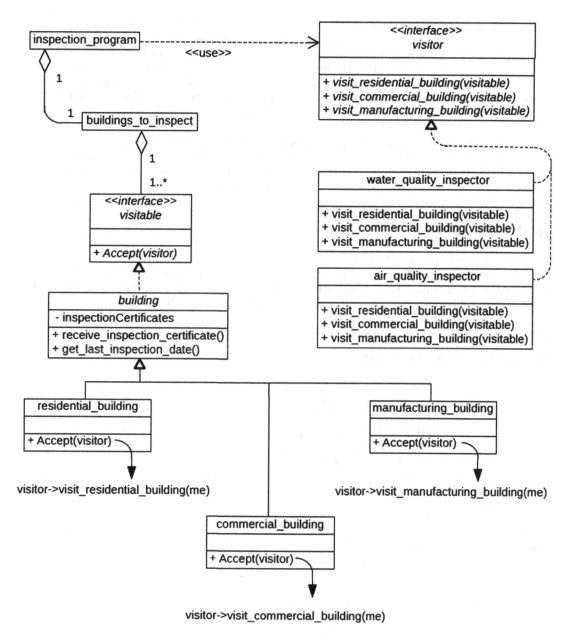

Figure 26-5. *UML class diagram for the Visitor design pattern applied to the building inspection scenario*

Compared with the general UML class diagram for the Visitor design pattern shown in Figure 26-4, we see here exactly the same relationship between the *client (inspection_program)*, *objectStructure (buildings_ to_inspect)*, and *visitor* interface: the inspection_program *uses* the visitor interface and the inspection_ program *has a* structure of buildings_to_inspect. The *element* interface of the general Visitor UML class diagram shown in Figure 26-4 is represented here as the *visitable* interface, but otherwise has the same relationship to the *objectStructure (buildings_to_inspect)*. The *visitor* interface defines three *visit* methods, each of which corresponds to one of the subclasses of *building*: residential, commercial, and manufacturing.

Classes *residential_building*, *commercial_building*, and *manufacturing_building*, all inheriting from superclass *building*, correspond to the *concreteElementX* classes of the general Visitor UML class diagram. Classes *water_quality_inspector* and *air_quality_inspector*, each implementing the *visitor* interface, correspond to the *concreteVisitorN* classes of the general Visitor UML class diagram shown in Figure 26-4.

In the diagram in Figure 26-5, the *building* class is shown implementing the *visitable* interface but does not provide implementations for the *accept* method defined by *visitable*. Instead, the diagram shows that class *building* delegates to its subclasses the responsibility to provide an implementation for the *accept* method.

Indeed, while class *building* still defines and provides implementations for methods *receive_inspection_certificate* and *get_last_inspection_date*, it no longer defines abstract methods *inspect_water_quality*, *inspect_air_quality*, etc.[5] These methods have been rendered obsolete by the presence of the corresponding new concrete visitor classes *water_quality_inspector*, *air_quality_inspector*, etc.

Visitor in ABAP

The Ace developers also rewrote the components to make use of the Visitor design pattern. Listing 26-10 shows the new interfaces, visitor and visitable, facilitating the Visitor design pattern. Notice the presence of the class definition deferred statement naming the building class, referenced by the visitor interface but at this point not yet encountered by the ABAP compiler (it is defined in Listing 26-11).

Listing 26-10. Interfaces Visitor and Visitable

```
class building definition deferred.

interface visitor.
  methods        : visit_residential_building
                     importing building type ref to building
                 , visit_commercial_building
                     importing building type ref to building
                 , visit_manufacturing_building
                     importing building type ref to building
                 .
endinterface.

interface visitable.
  methods        : accept
                     importing visitor type ref to visitor.
endinterface.
```

---

[5]To facilitate brevity in the UML class diagram, we omitted classes corresponding to *insect_infestation_inspector* and *fire_safety_inspector*, which would mimic class *water_quality_inspector* in that each implements the visitor interface and provides implementations for the methods defined by the visitor interface.

Interface visitor plays the role of the *Visitor* participant, while interface visitable plays the role of the *Element* participant. Listing 26-11 shows how abstract class building is changed to indicate that it implements interface visitable, with differences from Listing 26-7 highlighted.

Listing 26-11. Abstract Class building, with Differences from Listing 26-7 Highlighted

```
class building definition abstract.
  public section.
    interfaces    : visitable all methods abstract.
    aliases       : accept for visitable~accept.
    types         : certificates         type string
                  .
    methods       : receive_inspection_certificate
                        importing inspection type string
                                  date       type sydatum
                  , get_last_inspection_date
                        importing inspection type string
                        exporting date       type sydatum
                  , inspect_water_quality abstract
                        returning value(assessment) type char10
                  , inspect_air_quality abstract
                        returning value(assessment) type char10
                  , inspect_for_insect_infestation abstract
                        returning value(assessment) type char10
                  , inspect_for_fire_safety abstract
                        returning value(assessment) type char10
                  .
  private section.
    data          : inspection_certificates
                        type standard table of certificates.
endclass.
class building implementation.
  method receive_inspection_certificate.
    o
    o
  endmethod.
  method get_last_inspection_date.
    o
    o
  endmethod.
endclass.
```

Abstract class building plays the role of a superclass to a *ConcreteElement* participant. Notice that all of its previous abstract methods have been eliminated. Notice also that the method definitions it gets by implementing the visitable interface are marked abstract, through the "... all methods abstract" clause of the interfaces statement, meaning implementations for these methods are delegated to the subclasses.

Listing 26-12 shows how the three inheriting subclasses no longer provide implementations for the abstract methods eliminated from the superclass, with differences from Listing 26-8 highlighted. Each one, playing the role of a *ConcreteElement* participant, provides an implementation for the accept method, which, using the visitor instance provided by the caller through the signature of the accept method, invokes a method of the visitor instance, providing itself, through the self-reference variable *me*, as the visitable entity.

Listing 26-12. Classes Inheriting from Abstract Class building, with Differences from Listing 26-8 Highlighted

```
class residential_building definition inheriting from building.
  public section.
      methods          : inspect_water_quality redefinition
                       , inspect_air_quality redefinition
                       , inspect_for_insect_infestation redefinition
                       , inspect_for_fire_safety redefinition
      methods          : accept redefinition
                       .
endclass.
class residential_building implementation.
  method inspect_water_quality.
    assessment = perform one-hour water quality inspection
  endmethod.
  method inspect_air_quality.
    assessment = perform one-hour air quality inspection
  endmethod.
  method inspect_for_insect_infestation.
    assessment = perform one-hour insect infestation inspection
  endmethod.
  method inspect_for_fire_safety.
    assessment = perform one-hour fire safety inspection
  endmethod.
  method accept.
    visitor->visit_residential_building( me ).
  endmethod.
endclass.

class commercial_building definition inheriting from building.
  public section.
      methods          : inspect_water_quality redefinition
                       , inspect_air_quality redefinition
                       , inspect_for_insect_infestation redefinition
                       , inspect_for_fire_safety redefinition
      methods          : accept redefinition
                       .
endclass.
class commercial_building implementation.
  method inspect_water_quality.
    assessment = perform three-hour water quality inspection
  endmethod.
  method inspect_air_quality.
    assessment = perform three-hour air quality inspection
  endmethod.
```

```
method inspect_for_insect_infestation.
  assessment = perform three-hour insect infestation inspection
endmethod.
method inspect_for_fire_safety.
  assessment = perform three-hour fire safety inspection
endmethod.
method accept.
  visitor->visit_commercial_building( me ).
endmethod.
endclass.

class manufacturing_building definition inheriting from building.
  public section.
    methods       : inspect_water_quality redefinition
                  , inspect_air_quality redefinition
                  , inspect_for_insect_infestation redefinition
                  , inspect_for_fire_safety redefinition
    methods       : accept redefinition
                  .
endclass.
class manufacturing_building implementation.
  method inspect_water_quality.
    assessment = perform eight-hour water quality inspection
  endmethod.
  method inspect_air_quality.
    assessment = perform eight-hour air quality inspection
  endmethod.
  method inspect_for_insect_infestation.
    assessment = perform eight-hour insect infestation inspection
  endmethod.
  method inspect_for_fire_safety.
    assessment = perform eight-hour fire safety inspection
  endmethod.
  method accept.
    visitor->visit_manufacturing_building( me ).
  endmethod.
endclass.
```

Notice that implementations for the abstract methods previously defined by class *building* have been eliminated, replaced with implementations for method *accept* that class *building* now acquires by implementing the *visitable* interface. As a consequence, the inspection activity previously performed by the building subclasses has been transferred to the new concrete visitor subclasses, shown in Listing 26-13, where each of the different types of inspections now becomes a class implementing the visitor interface, each playing the role of the *ConcreteVisitor* participant.

Listing 26-13. Classes Implementing the Visitor Interface

```
class water_quality_inspector definition.
  public section.
    interfaces   : visitor.
    aliases      : visit_residential_building
                     for visitor~visit_residential_building
                 , visit_commercial_building
                     for visitor~visit_commercial_building
                 , visit_manufacturing_building
                     for visitor~visit_manufacturing_building
                     .
  private section.
    constants    : inspection_specialization
                     type string value `water quality`.
endclass.
class water_quality_inspector implementation.
  method visit_residential_building.
    data assessment             type char10.
    assessment = perform one-hour water quality inspection
    if assessment = 'passed'.
      call method building->receive_inspection_certificate
        exporting inspection      = inspection_specialization
        date                      = sy-datum.
    endif.
  endmethod.
  method visit_commercial_building.
    data assessment             type char10.
    assessment = perform three-hour water quality inspection
    if assessment = 'passed'.
      call method building->receive_inspection_certificate
        exporting inspection      = inspection_specialization
        date                      = sy-datum.
    endif.
  endmethod.
  method visit_manufacturing_building.
    data assessment             type char10.
    assessment = perform eight-hour water quality inspection
    if assessment = 'passed'.
      call method building->receive_inspection_certificate
        exporting inspection      = inspection_specialization
        date                      = sy-datum.
    endif.
  endmethod.
endclass.
```

```
    class air_quality_inspector definition.
      public section.
        interfaces    : visitor.
        aliases       : visit_residential_building
                          for visitor~visit_residential_building
                      , visit_commercial_building
                          for visitor~visit_commercial_building
                      , visit_manufacturing_building
                          for visitor~visit_manufacturing_building
                          .
      private section.
        constants     : inspection_specialization
                          type string value `air quality`.
    endclass.
    class air_quality_inspector implementation.
      method visit_residential_building.
        data assessment            type char10.
        assessment = perform one-hour air quality inspection
        if assessment = 'passed'.
          call method building->receive_inspection_certificate
            exporting inspection    = inspection_specialization
            date                    = sy-datum.
        endif.
      endmethod.
      method visit_commercial_building.
        data assessment            type char10.
        assessment = perform three-hour air quality inspection
        if assessment = 'passed'.
          call method building->receive_inspection_certificate
            exporting inspection    = inspection_specialization
            date                    = sy-datum.
        endif.
      endmethod.
      method visit_manufacturing_building.
        data assessment            type char10.
        assessment = perform eight-hour air quality inspection
        if assessment = 'passed'.
          call method building->receive_inspection_certificate
            exporting inspection    = inspection_specialization
            date                    = sy-datum.
        endif.
      endmethod.
    endclass.
```

```
class insect_infestation_inspector definition.
  public section.
    interfaces    : visitor.
    aliases       : visit_residential_building
                      for visitor~visit_residential_building
                  , visit_commercial_building
                      for visitor~visit_commercial_building
                  , visit_manufacturing_building
                      for visitor~visit_manufacturing_building
                  .
  private section.
    constants     : inspection_specialization
                      type string value `insect infestation`.
endclass.
class insect_infestation_inspector implementation.
  method visit_residential_building.
    data assessment              type char10.
    assessment = perform one-hour insect infestation inspection
    if assessment = 'passed'.
      call method building->receive_inspection_certificate
        exporting inspection    = inspection_specialization
        date                    = sy-datum.
    endif.
  endmethod.
  method visit_commercial_building.
    data assessment              type char10.
    assessment = perform three-hour insect infestation inspection
    if assessment = 'passed'.
      call method building->receive_inspection_certificate
        exporting inspection    = inspection_specialization
        date                    = sy-datum.
    endif.
  endmethod.
  method visit_manufacturing_building.
    data assessment              type char10.
    assessment = perform eight-hour insect infestation inspection
    if assessment = 'passed'.
      call method building->receive_inspection_certificate
        exporting inspection    = inspection_specialization
        date                    = sy-datum.
    endif.
  endmethod.
endclass.
```

```
class fire_safety_inspector definition.
  public section.
    interfaces   : visitor.
    aliases      : visit_residential_building
                     for visitor~visit_residential_building
                 , visit_commercial_building
                     for visitor~visit_commercial_building
                 , visit_manufacturing_building
                     for visitor~visit_manufacturing_building
                 .
  private section.
    constants    : inspection_specialization
                     type string value `fire safety`.
endclass.
class fire_safety_inspector implementation.
  method visit_residential_building.
    data assessment              type char10.
    assessment = perform one-hour fire safety inspection
    if assessment = 'passed'.
      call method building->receive_inspection_certificate
        exporting inspection   = inspection_specialization
        date                   = sy-datum.
    endif.
  endmethod.
  method visit_commercial_building.
    data assessment              type char10.
    assessment = perform three-hour fire safety inspection
    if assessment = 'passed'.
      call method building->receive_inspection_certificate
        exporting inspection   = inspection_specialization
        date                   = sy-datum.
    endif.
  endmethod.
  method visit_manufacturing_building.
    data assessment              type char10.
    assessment = perform eight-hour fire safety inspection
    if assessment = 'passed'.
      call method building->receive_inspection_certificate
        exporting inspection   = inspection_specialization
        date                   = sy-datum.
    endif.
  endmethod.
endclass.
```

Notice the similarity between the classes implementing the visitor interface shown above. They are virtually identical except for the value specified for the inspection specialization each one handles and the way each one resolves a value for the assessment of an inspection.

The invoking snippet of code, shown in Listing 26-14, is changed to facilitate the Visitor design pattern, with differences from Listing 26-9 highlighted. It plays the role of both the *Client* participant, since it creates the inspector, an instance of a class implementing the visitor interface, and the *ObjectStructure* participant, for containing the definition of the table of references to building instances over which the inspector will visit.

Listing 26-14. Code for a Component Invoking the Objects Described in Preceding Listings, with Differences from Listing 26-9 Highlighted

```
o
o
data street                    type string.
data inspection_type           type string.
data last_inspection_date      type sydatum.
data assessment                type char10.
data inspector                 type ref to visitor.
data buildings                 type table of ref to building.
data building                  type          ref to building.
o
o
get inspection_type from selection screen
get street          from selection screen
create inspector type (inspection_type).
create into buildings instances of all buildings on street
loop at buildings into building.
  call method building->get_last_inspection
    exporting inspection       = inspection_type
    importing date             = last_inspection_date.
  if last_inspection_date older than 5 years ago.
    case inspection_type.
      when 'water_quality'.
        assessment = building->inspect_water_quality( ).
      when 'air_quality'.
        assessment = building->inspect_air_quality( ).
      when 'insect_infestation'.
        assessment = building->inspect_for_insect_infestation( ).
      when 'fire_safety'.
        assessment = building->inspect_for_fire_safety( ).
    endcase.
    if assessment = 'passed'.
      call method building->receive_inspection_certificate
        exporting inspection       = inspection_type
        date                       = sy-datum.
    endif.
    building->accept( inspector ).
  endif.
endloop.
```

Notice how much simpler the snippet of invoking code has become. We no longer have the case statement determining the type of inspection to be performed, nor does the inspection_program handle granting a new certificate when a building passes an inspection assessment. Both of these changes have eliminated virtually all of the conditional logic that once appeared in this component.

Adhering to the Open/Closed Principle

After refactoring the inspection program to use the Visitor design pattern, Ace Business Services recently became aware that the town council of Galveston, New York is considering implementing a new type of inspection for grounds safety. Ace decided to get ahead of the change and to determine what it would take to implement this new type of inspection. After a few discussions, it was determined that there would be a need for one new class, grounds_safety_inspector, implementing the visitor interface *and no changes to any existing components!* One of the programmers produced the pseudocode for the new class, shown in Listing 26-15.

Listing 26-15. Class grounds_safety_inspector

```
class grounds_safety_inspector definition.
  public section.
    interfaces   : visitor.
    aliases      : visit_residential_building
                     for visitor~visit_residential_building
                 , visit_commercial_building
                     for visitor~visit_commercial_building
                 , visit_manufacturing_building
                     for visitor~visit_manufacturing_building
                 .
  private section.
    constants    : inspection_specialization
                     type string value `grounds safety`.
endclass.
class water_quality_inspector implementation.
  method visit_residential_building.
    data assessment              type char10.
    assessment = perform one-hour grounds safety inspection
    if assessment = 'passed'.
      call method building->receive_inspection_certificate
        exporting inspection    = inspection_specialization
        date                    = sy-datum.
    endif.
  endmethod.
  method visit_commercial_building.
    data assessment              type char10.
    assessment = perform three-hour grounds safety inspection
    if assessment = 'passed'.
      call method building->receive_inspection_certificate
        exporting inspection    = inspection_specialization
        date                    = sy-datum.
    endif.
```

```
    endmethod.
  method visit_manufacturing_building.
    data assessment                type char10.
    assessment = perform eight-hour grounds safety inspection
    if assessment = 'passed'.
      call method building->receive_inspection_certificate
        exporting inspection    = inspection_specialization
        date                    = sy-datum.
    endif.
  endmethod.
endclass.
```

That's it! Only one new class. No changes to any existing components. Accordingly, the new Visitor design pattern enables maintenance of the inspection program to adhere to the Open/Closed Principle.

Visitation Pros and Cons

As impressive as it is to rely on the Visitor design pattern to be able to add new visitors to the mix without the need to change existing components, there is a downside to using this design pattern. Notice that our inspection program example limited additional processing only to new types of inspections, which the Visitor design pattern accommodates as independent classes implementing the *visitor* interface. As long as the changes to the program are restricted to new types of inspections, then Visitor will handle this nicely.

However, Visitor also relies on a stable set of *visitable* components; stable in the sense that the set of objects implementing the *visitable* interface does not change. In the example, the visitable components are the three different types of buildings for which inspections are performed. If we were to change the inspection program to include a new type of building, such as public_building (post office, library, school, etc.), then we would need to change the *visitor* interface to include new method *visit_public_building*, which now would require us to change every class implementing the visitor interface to include an implementation for this new method.

Accordingly, some thought needs to go into the design when using the Visitor design pattern. Whichever set of objects is more likely to change over the course of the maintenance cycle should be considered the visitors (inspectors), leaving the set of objects less likely to change as the visitable entities (buildings).

Revisiting Static Polymorphism

Many textbook and website explanations about the Visitor design pattern assume that the language used to implement the pattern supports static polymorphism. Recall that static polymorphism is characterized by a class or interface having multiple declarations for the same method name, with each method differentiated from all the other same-named methods in the class by a unique method signature. The caller of the method implicitly designates which of these multiple implementations is to be invoked by providing parameters matching a specific signature. Recall also that static polymorphism is *not supported in ABAP*. Without support for static polymorphism, a method name may appear only once for a class or interface. Accordingly, with the Visitor pattern there are subtle differences between those languages that do support static polymorphism and those that do not.

Using our new collection of interfaces and classes provided by Ace Business Services, let's consider the implications when static polymorphism is and is not supported.

Our interfaces are

visitable

visitor

Our classes are

building	Abstract; implements visitable
residentialBuilding	Inherits from building
commercialBuilding	Inherits from building
manufacturingBuilding	Inherits from building

Table 26-1 shows how the availability of static polymorphism affects the Visitor design pattern, specifically the interfaces and implementations to be contained in the accept method of the various building classes noted above.

Table 26-1. *How Availability of Static Polymorphism Affects the Visitor Design Pattern*

Participant	With static polymorphism	Without static polymorphism
Visitable interface	accept(Visitor visitor)	accept(Visitor visitor)
Visitor interface	visit (ResidentialBuilding visitable) visit (CommercialBuilding visitable) visit (ManufacturingBuilding visitable)	visitResidentialBuilding (Visitable visitable) visitCommercialBuilding (Visitable visitable) visitManufacturingBuilding (Visitable visitable)
ResidentialBuilding.accept	visitor.visit(me)	visitor.visitResidentialBuilding(me)
CommercialBuilding.accept	visitor.visit(me)	visitor.visitCommercialBuilding(me)
ManufacturingBuilding.accept	visitor.visit(me)	visitor.visitManufacturingBuilding(me)

Visitable interface

The signature of the accept method provided by the visitable interface is the same regardless whether static polymorphism is supported.

Visitor interface

With static polymorphism, the visitor interface indicates the specific dynamic type of visitable in the signature for each of the multiple *visit* methods. Notice that the signature of each *visit* method is unique, each indicating a different type of concrete *visitable* object.

Without static polymorphism, the visitor interface indicates the specific dynamic type of visitable in the unique name for each of the multiple *visit* methods.

Concrete visitable object implementation for *accept* method

With static polymorphism, the accept method is implemented the same way among all concrete visitable objects. This simply reflects the presence of multiple *visit* methods that can be provided by the visitor interface.

Without static polymorphism, the accept method is implemented to invoke a different visitor method name with each concrete visitable object. This simply reflects the lack of multiple *visit* methods that can be provided by the visitor interface.

Summary

In this chapter, we learned how to implement a design through which our subsequent maintenance efforts can minimize the number of classes requiring change, so a new operation can be applied across the elements of an object structure without the need to change the classes representing those elements. We learned that the Visitor design pattern is based on the concept of double dynamic dispatch, where the dynamic types of two different reference variables will determine the implementation of the method to be used. It also facilitates adherence to the Open/Closed Principle, which states that once components have been moved to production they subsequently should be open for extension but closed for modification.

Visitor Exercises

Refer to Chapter 23 of the functional and technical requirements documentation (see Appendix B) for the accompanying ABAP exercise programs associated with this chapter. Take a break from reading the book at this point to reinforce what you have read by changing and executing the corresponding exercise programs. The exercise programs associated with this chapter are those in the 316 series: ZOOT316A through ZOOT316L.

CHAPTER 27

■ ■ ■

Design Anti-Patterns

The next stop on our galaxy quest through Design Patterns takes us to the alternative universe known as Design Anti-Patterns. Nothing from this region is registered in the GoF catalog.

When I first began experimenting with object-oriented ABAP, I approached the challenge by taking one of my reasonably well-designed report programs written using the procedural style and converting it into a program using as much object-orientation as possible. My goal was to become familiar with the object-oriented paradigm using a familiar program, so I could compare its execution with a proven procedural counterpart. Having no experience at the time with any of the object-oriented design principles presented in this book, I simply created the same procedural program using methods in place of forms and using a single static class containing public attributes in place of a main driving subroutine with its collection of global variables. In the end, I was satisfied that I was able to get it to work using the new ABAP Objects statements that I had recently made an effort to learn, and began using this as a foundation upon which to build subsequent programs I was asked to design.

Now, years later, I cringe when I reflect upon the rookie mistakes I made with those simplistic designs and my naïve approach to writing object-oriented code. I merely succeeded in applying the use of object-oriented statements with a procedural design. Lacking any concept of instances and of classes offering a specialization of data management, I simply created one static class, named *this_program*, into which I placed all the processing previously contained in procedural subroutines.

However, it is exactly this path that many programmers have already taken and that many will continue to take as they struggle with the transition from thinking only procedurally to being able to think *objectively*. A static class offers a stepping stone from procedural thinking to becoming fluent with using the statements, before one eventually grasps the concepts of encapsulation, abstraction, inheritance, and polymorphism that typically are absent in their early attempts at designing programs with object-oriented ABAP statements. None of us suddenly become experts with object-oriented concepts simply because we have read the books or have been taught by a competent instructor. It takes time before we can regard ourselves as capable object-oriented programmers. Meanwhile, we will make mistakes along the way, which could come back to haunt us during maintenance cycles, but by then perhaps we will have gained enough experience and have learned how we should have designed the program the first time and thus can refactor the program accordingly.

My early object-oriented designs, where I defined a single static class and merely dumped all the processing logic into it without regard for whether or not the processing was applicable to the class, are examples of what are known derisively in the industry as *God objects*.

- God object: An object that has too many capabilities and responsibilities

© James E. McDonough 2017
J. E. McDonough, *Object-Oriented Design with ABAP*, DOI 10.1007/978-1-4842-2838-8_27

A God object is just one of the many types of software techniques known as *design anti-patterns*, techniques regarded by scholars in the industry as undesirable elements in software design. These design anti-patterns have been used over the years frequently enough to have become identified by names and reasons for avoiding their use. Perhaps you might recognize some of them:

Big ball of mud	A system lacking any recognizable structure
Boat anchor	A component serving no useful purpose
Gold plating	Expending effort that contributes no additional value
Magic numbers	The use in algorithms of numbers having no explanation
Object orgy	Exposing object internals to unrestricted access due to lack of proper encapsulation
Spaghetti code	Components having a structure or flow difficult to comprehend

Indeed, in our exercise programs we are using the following technique, which is regarded as a design anti-pattern:

Constant interface	An interface composed solely of constants

We are using a constant interface to define those constants associated with the program-generated initial selection screen, an entity that in ABAP necessarily must exist externally to object-oriented components. A constant interface is considered a design anti-pattern because it often results in a component exhibiting low cohesion.

Since our constant interface contains only constants related to the initial selection screen, it does not suffer from the low cohesion it might reflect were it also to contain constants having no relevance to the initial selection screen.

Although the subject of design anti-patterns is not the focus of this book, it is useful to know that such patterns exist and that they may lurk in our subconscious until we become more experienced with how to avoid succumbing to these design pitfalls.

CHAPTER 28

Solidifying Robust Design Habits

Much has been learned over the years about what constitutes good object-oriented design, some of which has been gained at the expense of object-oriented pioneers, who, through trial and error, have discovered cases of poor design and have shared their knowledge with those of us who otherwise would find out the hard way why some designs are not viable.

The Gang of Four offer these nuggets of wisdom:

1. Program to an interface, not an implementation.[1]

2. Favor composition over class inheritance.[2]

3. Encapsulate the concept that varies.[3]

The first of these statements is exemplified by, among others, the Strategy design pattern; the second by, among others, the Decorator design pattern; and the third by, among others, the Adapter, State, and Template Method design patterns.

Robert C. Martin, one of the foremost authorities on the subject of object-oriented design and affectionately known within the software industry as Uncle Bob, compiled the following five principles of class design as part of his Principles of Object-Oriented Design:[4]

Single Responsibility Principle

> A class should have only a single responsibility (i.e. only one potential change in the software's specification should be able to affect the specification of the class).

Open Closed Principle

> Software entities should be open for extension, but closed for modification.

Liskov Substitution Principle

> Objects in a program should be replaceable with instances of their subtypes without altering the correctness of that program.

---

[1]GoF, p. 18.
[2]GoF, p. 20.
[3]GoF, p. 29.
[4]See http://butunclebob.com/ArticleS.UncleBob.PrinciplesOfOod

Interface Segregation Principle

Many client-specific interfaces are better than one general-purpose interface.

Dependency Inversion Principle

Depend upon abstractions. Do not depend upon concretions.

The first letter of the first word of each principle produces the acronym SOLID. These principles advise object-oriented designers of software design considerations found to be beneficial toward simplifying subsequent maintenance. In the preceding chapters, we encountered both the Single Responsibility Principle (in Chapter 3's "Considerations for Using Encapsulation Effectively" section) and the Open/Closed Principle (in Chapter 26's "Sorry, We're Closed" section) and the beneficial effect each one contributes to maintenance cycles.

Although each of these principles had their origin in previous papers, articles, books, and blogs published by him in the late 1990s, Martin compiled them all into a document written in 2000 with the title "Design Principles and Design Patterns."[5] These principles and the concepts they embody have subsequently been embraced by many in the software industry as an essential foundation for designing maintainable software and promoting excellence in programming.

Indeed, Martin, one of the original signatories of the Agile Manifesto and a guiding force in the software industry for nearly 50 years, in recent years has authored books and given lectures on the topic of *clean code*, dedicated to the prospect of leaving code in a state that easily can be understood and maintained by the next programmer. His books *Clean Code*[6] and *The Clean Coder*[7] address the ways in which programmers can improve their craftsmanship in pursuit of this goal.

---

[5]https://web.archive.org/web/20150906155800/http://www.objectmentor.com/resources/articles/Principles_and_Patterns.pdf.
[6]Robert C. Martin, *Clean Code: A Handbook of Agile Software Craftsmanship*, Pearson Education, 2008.
[7]Robert C. Martin, *The Clean Coder: A Code of Conduct for Professional Programmers*, Prentice Hall, 2011.

CHAPTER 29

■ ■ ■

Where No One Has Gone Before

Congratulations! You have reached the end of this book. If you have also been diligent in keeping current with the exercises, then perhaps you are able to reflect upon all your hard work and recognize all the new concepts you have not only learned but also reinforced through the exercises. Perhaps you have even experienced some of your own *Aha!* moments when an elusive object-oriented concept finally became clear for you.

In the 1960s, Gene Roddenberry brought *Star Trek* to a nation of American television viewers. Each episode began with the following prologue:

> Space. The final frontier. These are the voyages of the starship *Enterprise*. Its five-year mission: to explore strange new worlds; to seek out new life and new civilizations; to boldly go where no one has gone before.

With the help of our knowledge of the basic principles of object-oriented programming, we now have explored some new worlds in the form of design patterns. However, we have only scratched the surface of this topic. There are many more design patterns that remain unexplored and still others undiscovered.

Meanwhile, now we are much more prepared to navigate throughout the galaxy of software design to explore and discover new design patterns; to seek out new ways to simplify our development and maintenance efforts; to raise the development discipline of our colleagues to a higher standard, perhaps elevating the art of software development in our entire organization to a bold new level *where no one has gone before.*

© James E. McDonough 2017
J. E. McDonough, *Object-Oriented Design with ABAP*, DOI 10.1007/978-1-4842-2838-8_29

APPENDIX A

███

Comparison of Capabilities Between Function Groups and Classes

Table A-1 shows the comparison of capabilities offered by ABAP function groups and ABAP object-oriented classes. The √ symbol denotes support for the capability, while the Ø symbol denotes no support.

Table A-1. *Comparison of Capabilities Offered by ABAP Function Groups and ABAP Object-Oriented Classes*

#	Capability	Function group	Classes	Comments
1	Encapsulation	√	√	Offers at least some rudimentary aspect of encapsulation
2	Encapsulation unit	√	√	
3	Public attributes	Ø	√	
4	Public behaviors	√	√	
5	Protected attributes	Ø	√	
6	Protected behaviors	Ø	√	
7	Package attributes	Ø	√	
8	Package behaviors	Ø	√	
9	Private attributes	√	√	
10	Private behaviors	√	√	
11	Abstraction	√	√	Offers at least some rudimentary aspect of abstraction
12	Levels of abstraction	√	√	
13	Static	√	√	

(continued)

© James E. McDonough 2017
J. E. McDonough, *Object-Oriented Design with ABAP*, DOI 10.1007/978-1-4842-2838-8_30

Table A-1. (*continued*)

#	Capability	Function group	Classes	Comments
14	Instantiation	Ø	√	
15	Inheritance	Ø	√	Offers at least some rudimentary aspect of inheritance
16	Polymorphism	Ø	√	Offers at least some rudimentary aspect of polymorphism
17	Independent interfaces	Ø	√	Offers at least some rudimentary aspect of independent interfaces
18	Signature with behavior	√	√	
19	Functional behavior	Ø	√	If <functional behavior goes here> eq true …
20	Screen handling	√	Ø	Classes have no standard screen processing capability; with classes, this is facilitated through the use of function modules or by WebDynpro and its successors (UI5, etc.)
21	Remote procedure calls	√	Ø	Function module needs to be marked "remote enabled" call function … destination (synch RFC) call function … starting new task (asynch RFC) call function … in background task (transactional RFC)
22	Execute in update task	√	Ø	call function … in update task

■ ■ ■

Requirements Documentation and ABAP Exercise Programs

A zip file available for download at

www.apress.com/us/book/9781484228371

contains the following:

- The file containing the functional and technical requirements document describing the associated ABAP exercise programs (.pdf)
- The files containing the source code for each of the ABAP exercise programs (.txt)
- The files containing the diagrams describing the ABAP exercise programs (.pdf)

© James E. McDonough 2017
J. E. McDonough, *Object-Oriented Design with ABAP*, DOI 10.1007/978-1-4842-2838-8_31

Index

Get the eBook for only $5!

Why limit yourself?

With most of our titles available in both PDF and ePUB format, you can access your content wherever and however you wish—on your PC, phone, tablet, or reader.

Since you've purchased this print book, we are happy to offer you the eBook for just $5.

To learn more, go to http://www.apress.com/companion or contact support@apress.com.

Apress®

Printed in the United States
By Bookmasters